Ngā Uruora

The Groves of Life

To my children, and those who will find the generosity of spirit that nature in the 21st century will need from us.

Ngā Uruora

The Groves of Life

Ecology and History in a New Zealand Landscape

Geoff Park

Victoria University Press

VICTORIA UNIVERSITY PRESS

Victoria University of Wellington
PO Box 600, Wellington, New Zealand

© GEOFF PARK 1995

ISBN 0 86473 291 0

FIRST PUBLISHED 1995
REPRINTED 1996

DESIGNED BY:
Turi Park, *Wellington Media Collective*

PRINTED BY:
GP Print, *Wellington*

DAVID INFANGER

CHAPTER 1

The author talks about the destruction of New Zealand's forests as it turned into a dairy industry. Interestingly enough, the Europeans considered the land wasted if it wasn't converted to manufacture. Within a short time, the Kahikatea populations were decimated, and viewed as "progress." The Europeans attempted to convert New Zealand into a first world nation; the massacre almost succeeded b/c the Europeans didn't realize what they'd found. They only saw what they wanted ~~to see~~ the land to become. The author concludes his account by proposing the only way to salvage what's left: conservation and restoration ecology. These methods have been aggressively & pursued over the twentieth century, but they are small

N.Z. ~ 1001 ~ Z.N

29.JAN.98

N.Z. ~ 1001 ~ Zb.

CH S.

Missionaries w/in N.Z.
↳ Schmackenberg

CONTENTS

ACKNOWLEDGEMENTS

THE ENDEAVOUR that became this book has never been easy, but nor has it lacked support at the crucial times when it could have fallen over; whether Lindsay patiently ignoring its impact on family life, Ronda Cooper's first critical read, Daphne Brasell's, Walter Cook's and Ian Wedde's interest, or responses to bits I was worried about from David Young, Bob Kerr, Barrie Cook, Jan Heine, Andrew Mason, Craig Potton, Richard Sadleir, Kaye Green, Te Oriwa Stephenson, Di Lucas, Rangipo Mete Kingi, Rosie Little, Eru Manuera, Maui John Mitchell and Tony Dreaver.

Jock Phillips, I thank especially, for opening the Stout Research Centre door that enabled an ecologist to look at New Zealand history, culture and society through the lens of 'the landscape'; the Stout Trustees for making it possible in the first place and providing that wonderful space and camaraderie in 1986-87 to gain energy, read history and think; Richard Sadleir for recognising the connections between history and conservation ecology and allowing time and resources when they were needed; my parents when their quiet insight was needed.

The good fortune to be able to talk with the late Sir Charles Fleming and Monte Holcroft in the dusk of their lives gave the project a foundation in ideas for which I will be forever grateful. George Seddon and Ross Gibson in Australia don't know the influence they have had, at beginning and end respectively. Nor Eric Rolls, his way with land just across the water.

From my initial, tentative searches with Moira Long in 1985 when the Alexander Turnbull Library and its images of 19th-century New Zealand were still on Wellington's Terrace, the project grew to demands on staff of many other collections and institutions: National Archives; Museum of New Zealand: Te Papa Tongarewa; General Assembly Library; Victoria University Library, notably the Beaglehole Collection; Canterbury University Library; Auckland University Library; Massey University Library; Mitchell Library, Sydney; National Library of Australia, Canberra; The British Library, London; Petone Settlers Museum; Wellington Public Library; Auckland Public Library; Auckland Museum; Waikato Museum of Art and

History; Nelson Provincial Museum; Greymouth Public Library; Colling-wood Museum; Taranaki Museum; Palmerston North Public Library; the former Department of Lands and Survey and NZ Forest Service; and the Department of Conservation. Ross Galbreath helped me into the Buller archives. Ian Wedde made me think about European impact in the wider Pacific. Peter Horsley led me to consider the influence of men who lived in Europe three centuries ago on our landscape here today, Di Lucas kept me seeing it as a garden, and Ronda Cooper never let an idea on enclosure and the picturesque get away.

Craig Potton took most of his wonderful photos in 1986 when the project began. Their existence kept me thinking that a book would emerge eventually. Fergus Barrowman's and Rachel Lawson's editing made it read like one. Chris Edkins I thank for converting my sketches to maps, and Turi, of course, for the creativity of his design.

The Department of Conservation, through its Science and Research Division, has assisted in the publication of this book, and at periods during 1987-92 resourced some of the research. Some of it has already filtered through into the care of the places the book is about. However, this is a very personal work. The views and interpretations of history expressed here are mine and not necessarily those of the Department of Conservation.

Many people—some I can no longer thank personally—in the places where the search led me lent their memories and opinions. At Mōkau: Te Oriwa Stephenson, Steve White, Fred Black, Aunty Eileen Taimanu, Aunty Mary Turner, June Opie in St Ives, and Graeme Gummer. At Papaitonga: Joseph Tukupua, Josephine Paki, Urorangi Paki, Ngāwini Kuiti, Charles Royal, Whatarangi Winiata, Tony Dreaver, Bert Richards. At Te Tai Tapu and Whanganui Inlet: Joyce Parkinson, Jack Nicholls, Rosie Little and Bruce Hamlin, Gilbert Richards, Ralph Irons, Ron and Ivy Walker (née Rhodes), Sue Livingston (née Gooding), Don Mackay, Ken McKenzie, Phil Skilton, Fred Cowin, Simon Walls, John Mitchell, Paul Morgan, Tina Marsh. At Punakaiki and Pakiroa: Sandy Bartle, Bruce McFadgen, Derek Onley, Maika Mason, Trevor Worthy and Richard Holdaway, Hemi Te Rakau, Alan McKenzie, Graeme Champness, Arthur Sheldon, Mrs Langridge, Fred Stewart and Lindsay Matthias. At Hauraki: Warner Hunter, Dorothy Bagnall, Hugh Hayward. At Petone: Pauline Harper, Hera Hill and Pam Tam and the children of Wilford School for finding a way of bringing something at least of ngā uruora back.

GEOFF PARK, OCTOBER, 1995

Landscapes are collections of stories, only fragments of which are visible at any one time. In linking the fragments, unearthing the connections between them, we create the landscape anew. A landscape whose story is known is harder to dismiss . . . At its best, telling the landscape's story can still feel like a sacred task.

FRANK GOHLKE, 1995

E UROPEANS FIRST imagined New Zealand as 'a garden and a pasture in which the best elements of British society might grow into an ideal nation'—just as they thought of Australia as a 'prison-scape for the incarceration of the British criminal class'. When the smoke of their colonists' fires cleared at the end of the 19th century, New Zealand had become a different country. Māori had lost their most precious life-support system. Only in the hilliest places did the forest still come down to the sea. Huge slices of the ancient ecosystem were missing, evicted and extinguished. Our histories, however, have had neither the sense of place nor ecological consciousness to explain what has happened. There is, as the novelist Janet Frame says, much to expose in New Zealand that 'for some reason wasn't there before'.

We cannot get very far without stories, without history. New Zealanders who want to know their landscape need to know about 19th-century Britain and the behaviour of its explorers abroad, about their preconceptions of land and native people. We need to know what the land they saw was like, and how its own people lived in it; what was behind the New Zealand Company's plans for a fortified rivermouth city and why its ships of surveyors and settlers left England without even verifying a site for it.

The full consequence of what the Australian Phillip Adams called nature's total, deliberate extermination from New Zealand's plains has never been grasped. With no evidence of the forest's trees, ferns and birds, there can be none of the signals from the wild that might one day predispose their inhabitants to walk more lightly on this part of the planet.

As the New Zealand ecosystem was constituted before the arrival of Europeans, the plains forests were like key pieces in a jigsaw puzzle, a pattern of life available nowhere else on earth. Aotearoa's 70 million years of isolation from other land masses had preserved some of the world's oldest and oddest life, plants and animals from the ancient tropics of the continent of Gondwana. When these pieces were removed and the ecosystem's birds no longer had access to its rich floodplain forests and coastal swamps, the hill and mountain forests went silent.

I began writing this book when I realised how vital the coastal lowlands had once been as a piece in this jigsaw. I wanted to find out what might have survived. And why, if the rout was so comprehensive, *anything* had survived.

In 1869, exactly 100 years after that spring morning when a group of Europeans first set off to explore a riverplain of tall trees, the politician and naturalist William Travers compared New Zealand's ecosystem to a decrepit house, having reached a point at which 'a blow struck anywhere shakes and damages the whole fabric'.

Almost everything I saw as a young ecologist 100 years on confirmed what Travers had written. Almost. Then one summer's morning I slid a canoe into Whanganui Inlet, the remotest harbour on New Zealand's western coast. I was well out across the water when, into view from behind a headland, came a flat shoreline of forest. In the warm silence, its big trees seemed to float above the emerald water. I felt I was looking at something elemental to the history of this country, glimpsing the land in its original order. There was not much of it, a forgotten corner of ancient trees overlooked by the timber-getters who dragged out every tree they could find, but a connection was made and that led to this book.

That place became the subject of one of the book's chapters, one of a series of journeys as much through time as through the land. Each journey centres around a place that reveals what V.S. Naipaul calls 'the wiped-out, complete past below one's feet'; the truths, often unpleasant, about ourselves and our attitudes and perceptions that the landscape divulges along with its native ecology.

The opening chapters consider the beginnings of European encounter with the plains and their people. The first begins in 1769, when Europeans first ventured inland, up a river, out of sight of their ship and, in the magic combination of tall timber, fertile soil, useful plants and hospitable natives, found a site for a colony. It depicts how, as news of the discovery spread, New Zealand entered the European imagination as a land where they could freely expand their preferred way in the world. Next, we go to the beachhead where English land speculators, bent on turning a profit from such antipodean waste, took the idea to its inevitable consequence. Promoting New Zealand as a flat land 'perfectly adapted' to agriculture, they promised its plains to thousands of immigrants. Led by beliefs as ancient as the Roman

Cicero's—We are the absolute masters of what the earth produces . . . The rivers are ours. We sow the seed and plant the trees . . . We stop, direct and turn the rivers . . . to make it, as it were, another nature—they rushed up the grid settlements whose rigid geometry shapes so much of the life of New Zealand today.

The following four chapters, the main part of the book, journey through four survivors of ngā uruora and reveal the remarkable facts of their survival. The survivors are more precious to us now than they, or their ravaged ecosystems, used to be. The final chapter addresses itself to some of the principles that emerge from all this.

In the years this book has been evolving, I have found the landscape a fertile site for contemplating fundamental if elusive truths. Some landscapes can tell us more about ourselves than others, but our histories are remarkably silent on such things. Focusing on people, they pay little attention to the original land, just as our environmental literature tends to marginalise people as wreckers of a mythical, ancient world that had no need of them.

We need more than that. Slowly, as the land works on us and, generation after generation, shapes a new culture, there is gathering awareness in settler societies like Australia and New Zealand of the increasing necessity of what the Australian Ross Gibson calls *ways of knowing with country*. When he asks what it means 'to know a stretch of country in the twentieth century, in a nation formed out of the second wave of European military imperialism' he means more than some lazy appeal to instinct. He means looking intently at a landscape we live in or value to see what it reveals of systems of wisdom and warning. He calls it political ecology.

Mention of ngā uruora today is like raising something from the dead. Go into a lowland kahikatea forest in autumn when its koroī are ripening, lie under the towering trees listening to the cacophony of birds and the constant patter of the inedible bits hitting the leaves around you, and you'll know what 'the groves of life' mean. These are the ecosystems that are now, like huia and kākāpō, vanished or down to a few survivors in need of intensive care, their wildness something to wonder at. What did it mean for Māori to lose them and their soils, their best soils, to Europe's settlers?

I was a scientist when my own looking intently began, as I tried to put a rational and measured face on a forgotten New Zealand. I saw history as vague and subjective. Soon though I saw that, like every fenceline and drained paddock, every remnant of the forest is the result of some human decision. In faded colonial documents I saw how the coastal plains frustrated the very people they attracted. I read the words of those who hated their wet forests, who, unable to imagine living with them, felled them the moment they took possession. But I also met people to whom they were places of ancestors and spirits and others who remembered when their air shrieked with birds.

As I found what still lay hidden in the ground, tracked my way into archives and had Māori memories revealed to me, I came to know the lost forests of the plains. I found that the ecology of a stretch of country and its history are far from unrelated. They work on one another. They shape one another. If you go in search of one, you are led to the other.

The best landscapes, says the writer Paul Theroux, hold surprises if they are studied patiently. Reading the landscape is like collage, interweaving the patterns of ecology and the fragments of history with footprints of the personal journey. The journey, in time as well as space, plays no small part. It is like the artist David Hockney has described Chinese landscape painting: a walk through the landscape in which the static viewpoint is avoided. It is the history of ngā uruora's survivors that has excited me with its surprises. It has waited, hidden under the skin of the land, from the days when this kind of country was at the centre of things. It has changed the way I see New Zealand.

When you become involved with the landscape in this way it becomes much more than a view. Even to draw a carp, Chinese masters warn, it is not enough to know what the animal *looks* like, and to understand its anatomy and physiology. It is also necessary to consider the reed which the carp brushes up against each morning, the oblong stone behind which it conceals itself, and the rippling of water when it comes to the surface. These elements should in no way be constituted as the carp's environment. They belong to the carp itself. In other words, the brush should sketch a life, since a life—like the landscape—is constituted by the traces left behind and imprints silently borne.

THE IMMENSE TREES OF OOAHAOURAGEE

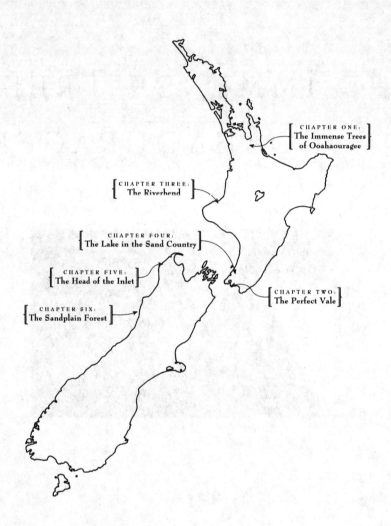

NOW HE COULD SEE what they were yelling about; a long, low stain between sky and sea. A familiar estuarine reek filled him with disquiet. It was no strait between the lines of hills. It was a vast, wooded plain—and, unless the haze and distance were deceiving him, its trees must be an extraordinary height.

The tranquility of the shore this evening was reassuring. Yesterday's threats from canoes, the cries of death from the unknown natives of the wild shore, had unsettled him. And the canoe holed by his musket ball. It could have been yet another native death. But then, today's visitors from the beach, coming on board with their stinking fish, had seemed friendly enough.

As surely as violence was shaping everyone's view of New Zealand, he was becoming certain that the news of his ship was moving along the coast in front of them. This land was not going to be easy to possess. And was it worth it anyway? He had seen few meadows or fertile plains, and from the outset, dead or wounded natives had been the prevailing consequence of landing, or even approaching the shore.

But maybe this would be different. The soundings, shallower and shallower as *Endeavour* inched toward the distant trees, were something they had not encountered since England. He would anchor then, and in the morning, take the boats ashore. He didn't want to leave this place without a closer look.

'All history,' said the philosopher of nature Aldo Leopold, 'consists of successive journeys from a single point, to which we return again and again to organise yet another search for a durable scale of values.'

HIKUTAIA CREEK, HAURAKI PLAINS,

18 DECEMBER 1987

Unloading the canoe from the roof-rack, I wonder what the day will bring. I know it will be no ambitious adventure in the wilderness. Where James Cook, 218 years before, looked incredulously at what nature had created here and dreamt of a colony, I'm limiting my expectations to willows and stopbanks. A milk tanker starting up breaks my thoughts. Lumbering off the gravel onto the tarseal, just as it did yesterday, and will tomorrow, it slows as it passes, the face at the window implying that what I am doing, launching a canoe into what is more of a drain than a stream, is not done every day. In its petrochemical wake I feel like some sort of trespasser, tolerated and harmless.

Down from the road, I lift the canoe over rusty, weed-shrouded barbed wire and slide it through the mud under the willows. It is just on high tide and I feel good at the prospect. Cook had hoped to ride the ebb right down to the sea and the waiting *Endeavour*. Night beat him. But maybe, with fewer distractions in the landscape, I'll make it.

Nothing signals that there is anything special here. Yet a culture's most precious places are not necessarily visible to the eye. Where English willows now hang in the mud, giant trees once governed the flatness, their dead leaves staining its rivers and streams dark, the air organic with their smells and the conversations of birds. This was the country that mid-19th-century 'New Zealand' was all about. South Westland's cold, wet plains hint at it, but elsewhere it has become an extinct experience sensed from little else but a few words and images stranded in history.

This is an auspicious place to begin my search. Not just because we are a society to whom James Cook is almost the Almighty. Nor that in its vanished trees and fertile silt he saw spars for his navy and a country that would supply an 'Industrus people . . . not only with the necessarys but many of the luxuries of life'. This is where you see most clearly the tremendous violence and waste that attended the furious, meticulous work of Britain's mission in New Zealand. Whatever your views of empire—that it is the forest's greatest enemy, or that nations grow from huts in the forest to villages then cities—this is a place for pilgrimage. It is a place too that rebukes the notion that, where New Zealand was forest before the summer of 1769, it was vacant space. As its soil is more than an accumulator of fertility for pre-destined farms, its forests have a human past that, as we uncover evidence of the experiences it extinguished, is becoming part of our young society's dark quarrel with its soul.

Our society, for the most part, remains embedded in the Western isolation from nature. But more people nowadays are aware of 'ecology' and the great possibilities of nature. They speak out when they sense a threat to a piece of native land. They don't all, of course, link 'conservation' and 'sustainability' to country like this. Powerful idealised images of wild New Zealand lead them elsewhere. Yet environmentalism, in the deepest sense, is about more than wild, indigenous things defended. It is about the elemental union of self and other species and the land itself. The circumstance of being a New Zealander ties every one of us, economically if not instinctively, to country like this plain. It is why my journey must begin here.

How we inhabit a place can be the most telling expression of how we sense its worth, our intention for it and our connection with it. This place is as close as you might get to the site of New Zealand's true beginnings as a modern society—an antipodean outpost of a way of life further from home than it had ever been. The first people to test their metal against its trees, to sense in its soil the promise of cities fed by acres of grass and cows, did so here.

James Cook was as much an agent of industrialised agriculture as a great navigator. It was his *Endeavour* that first brought ashore Europe's intent for plains country like this, his men who implanted the seeds of ecological change in this soil the moment they saw the giant trees it grew, laying the groundwork for the food trade that has joined together the earth's extremes. We take for granted the replicated European food-producing ecosystems that have become our ordinary landscapes, as we do the global paths of their produce and the semen-straws that jet genes across oceans so the plains' farmers can maintain the inventiveness constantly demanded of them. Much has been made of Europeans' fear of nature and their separation from it—wherever they spread in the wake of Columbus, it would seem, they had pledged to nature they would free the world from it. But seldom did they take things to the degree that the succession of explorers, missionaries, governors and governments, settlers and drainage engineers took this wet plain.

Privatised, ordered into rectangles and given over to uniformity, the production of milk and the control of wild water, this ground is saturated with that conquest. Stopbanked and straightened to keep its water and silt from its plain, Cook's River Thames is still there, but of the great trees he said 'adorne its banks', nothing survives. Foreign plants imported in the campaign to fulfil his dream have taken their place. However, as surely as the dairy farms continue to change hands, and new owners, new ways, come and go, the past insists on its presence. Hidden in the ground and in documents from the century before are clues to the previous country—the stranger we never talk about.

Most plains people plead ignorance of such things, yet local history has not overlooked the great navigator's brief moment here. Down the river at Te Kopu, between the Peninsula Cafe, the bowling club and the abandoned 'Thames Home of Country Music', a bleak plaque has it that 'near this spot James Cook with the naturalists Joseph Banks and Daniel Solander landed while exploring the River Thames'. Nearby—where it stood beside the highway bridge until decreed a traffic hazard—you can see the shell heaps of long-ago Māori settlement in a drain by the Skyline Garages factory. 'Memorials like this one at Kopu are of great value to all of us,' said the Honourable James Thorn MP when he unveiled it on 2 November 1941. A 'disheartening' and 'dreadful thing', Cook's famous biographer called it. James Thorn said it reminded everyone of the fundamental place this 'exact spot' played in their 'rich heritage'. But it is not where the English navigator landed. Contending that it would be 'impossible' to fix the location of Cook's landings, the campaigners for monuments determined it should be at Te Kopu.

'Try to imagine the colourful scene here 172 years ago today,' James Thorn sweet-talked them. 'From the swamp and the mud of the river banks mighty trees soar to the sky. From the untidy Māori pā on the mudflats, the curious brown men of New Zealand watch the strange craft bearing strange men with white skins.' Further upriver, duckshooters' V8s wheelspin in the loose gravel of Captain Cook Road and more signposted history points to a stopbank plaque where the *Endeavour*'s shore party craned their necks at trees taller than any of them had seen.

From the minute I am down in the creek and out of sight of cows and paddocks, I sense my plastic vessel's connection to the generations of craft that have known this stretch of water. The long kahikatea waka of Ngāti Maru and their predecessors, for centuries pushing upstream, laden with fish and pipi from the far-off estuary, for whom this was a common, familiar road, the last effort before home. Long-boats nosing their uncertain way up on the tide, 200 years ago, the eyes of the sea-weary men from the confines of Sydney Cove scanning the strange wet forest that had closed around them. And then the smells of bush and peat burning, hanging over the place for weeks, the noise of the saw-mill and the flax stampers. The depressing floods and silt through the little cottages, the smell of diesel drifting across from the river ferry and the dredges. Pasture slowly but surely replacing the battered, beaten forest. The calls of men from a distant war, arriving to balloted blocks of wilderness and mud, fencing and laying roads, moving cattle and cursing the tall fescue they couldn't eat.

I push off through the rampant fescue, out into the muddy water. Duck footprints baked into the mud by yesterday's afternoon sun slide past beneath like some sprawling submerged ceramic. Further out the ubiquitous redshank leaves disappear down into the gloom. Two dawson-flies hover over the water, then dash sideways and alight on the yellow heads of St John's Wort. The distant Coromandel foothills go out of sight. A breeze slips the arms of the willows.

If it was just a matter of plants, I could be in a stream in the English countryside. I could round the first bend without noticing the white seashells sliding down its collapsing bank, the only clue to what once was the crème of the Hauraki Plain's river pā. Not until the flow is about to take me out of the Hikutaia into the Waihou do I pull into flooded cow tracks and pick my way ashore. I climb up onto a grassy flat fast vanishing under a yellow tide of ragwort and spreading islands of blackberry. An abandoned milking shed flaps its rusted iron roof in the wind. A harrier arcs up and away grasping for currents of air. There is not a native plant to be seen. Once, before the hooves of the dairy economy, you could have plunged your hand into loose, rich, pliant humus. Now my feet are quickly clogged with the gouged, clayed ground of a meaner soil.

The men of milking sheds and butterfat like to think that their 'dairy nation' has lead the world. As its products have shaped our diet, land of this kind has had an influence on New Zealand's economy and society so great that the centennial survey of farming in 1940 called the average New

Zealand dairy farm more of 'a factory for producing milk rather than a farm in the full sense of the world'. The economic success of supplying a faraway 'Mother Land' with dairy products coloured the belief of generations of New Zealanders that nature's eradication and its replacement by grids of paddocks, drains and hedges was the hallmark of New Zealand as a nation. We have never thought of the farms as the emblems of an *extractive* economy. Nor of the vanished forests as the source of New Zealand's 20th-century wealth, their ancient, stored soil carbon exported out of the ecosystem with the butter, milk and meat. Nothing in these paddocks carries any sense of the 'immence woods' that James Cook saw here—that were destroyed to produce them—nor is anything likely to be as enduring. The urge of our lives is to leave some mark on the world. But what is scary here—if you have some scent of what it was like a century ago—is the flash of time it has taken to reduce this ecosystem's amassed, natural capital to this worn, meagre residue.

New Zealand's colonial history carries the reason why. It in turn is tied inevitably to *Homo sapiens'* spread out of the Africa in which we evolved, and where most of our genetic diversity is still, into every corner we could inhabit. It fell to a European branch to inherit the suite of wild animals and plants most suitable for domestication and thus to develop the agricultural base prerequisite to the rise of technology and cities. This propensity to expand nurtured, not only the political situations that fired dreams of empire, but the evolution of infectious diseases and immunity to them that made it so easy for Europeans to overwhelm the distant lands that attracted them. It was this portmanteau of the ecology of invasion, as it has been called, that determined who was coloniser or colonised between the 15th and 19th centuries.

Every revolution, said Emerson in his essay *History*, was at first a thought in one person's mind: 'And when the same thought occurs to another man, it is the key to that era. Every reform was once a private opinion . . .' New Zealanders' ordinary landscape has been created by what is, in ecological terms, nothing less than a revolution. The 'inexhaustible' plains country—'full two-thirds rich alluvial'—which the New Zealand Company pledged its settlers in 1839 was not derived from its own explorations. The company was in too much of a hurry for that. At the root of its dream, and the myth and gross exaggeration it founded, were James Cook's alluring words about 'the banks of "the Thames"' as the best place for a colony'. These words, the first of the *Opinions as to the Settlement of an English Colony* that Edward Gibbon Wakefield quoted in *The British Colonisation of New Zealand*, which led to British settlers pouring ashore in the 1840s, may have never been written had Cook not seen *this* plain. Reinforcing them are others' words about 'space so ample . . . soil so fertile', 'immense surplus of native productions', 'level ground . . . deep and navigable rivers', 'one of the fittest places in the world for an industrious and enterprising colony . . . of greater importance to Europeans than any other'. Wakefield's plan 'for colonizing waste lands' ends in biblical Māori: the Spirit of God bringing light to an alluring land of darkness.

Sir Apirana Ngata compared words to powerful charged particles. Language lies at the centre of James Cook's influence on us and our landscape. In naming this place 'Thames' he not only transformed it into an object for European understanding; he made it a symbol, invested with intent. 'Home' to the men who looked out upon New Zealand in 1769 was the organisational centre of the world, the Georgian England of fens being drained and woods and commons being enclosed. Nature by itself was believed wild and barren. From its sailors to Joseph Banks and his aristocratic greyhound, the *Endeavour* was a microcosm of a culture that aspired to order and improvement, to a time when the entire inhabitable world would be tilled like a garden.

Cook, said Banks, was impressed with the 'very fine river', as 'broad as the Thames at Greenwich' they had found; 'so much pleased with it that he resolved to call it the Thames'. Un-English the Waihou's woods may have been, but much of what was seen from the boats was, as Cook said, 'Marchey such as we find about the Thames in England'. He was struck too by how even '12 or 14 Miles within the entrance . . . the tide of flood run as strong as it doth in the River Thams below bridge'. They didn't leave, he said, 'before we had named this river the Thames on account of its bearing some resemblance to that river in England'. And maybe, in the back of his mind, was an even more distant Thames, the same river Joseph Conrad imagined a conquering Roman commander seeing at 'the very end of the world' almost eighteen hundred years earlier, or 'the other day', as Conrad says: 'Sand-banks, marshes, forests, savages—precious little to eat fit for a civilised man, nothing but Thames water to drink.'

As Cook extolled his 'New Thames', its faraway namesake was being pumped dry and converted to farms. The metamorphosis of the low country sprawling seaward from London had begun a century earlier when King James I saw the productive order of Holland's polder landscape—the surroundings, for a while, of René Descartes, the French philosopher with whom we associate the philosophy of men as nature's masters. James was so impressed he commissioned Cornelius Vermuyden, the Dutch engineer, to rebuild the Thames Wall and drain the fens. Vermuyden made so little allow-ance for peat shrinkage that the result was an ecological disaster. Cook's vision, though, was with the agricultural revolution—the liming, marling and manuring, selective livestock breeding, nitrogen-fixing legumes, water meadows and new fodder crops—in which the Thames had pride of place, changes as far-reaching as the social revolution of enclosure sweeping England.

THE WAIHOU AND THE HAURAKI
PLAINS, 1983.

Fly over the country where the European culture staked its claim to New Zealand's best land: the coastal plains of the Hutt, Nelson, Canterbury and Kaipara, Manawatu and Rangitikei, the Waikato and Hauraki. Look down on the grid towns preserving forever their origin on drawing boards in England, and beyond them, the geometric checkerboards of greens and browns stretching away. Miles and miles of straight fences, barberry hedges, roads and drains, intersecting at right angles. These manifest the goal of British colonisation—but it is also the kind of country in which New Zealanders founded their breed of freedom in the brief frontier of its cheap, flat, fertile acres. Until it ran out.

The colonial surveyors' grid reshaped New Zealand's best land with all the features that had enclosed Britain's open fields and commons and pauperised millions of its rural people. Fenced and hedged 'so that not for a moment would the ownership of a single square inch . . . be open to doubt or dispute', the plains became symbols of order and per-manence. From its plains victories, the theodolite has instilled an obses-sion with land boundaries in New Zealand society, and made individual rights and private land—such hard-won and tenuous achievements of Western history—central to our way of life. It is ironic, though, how the original agent of New Zealanders' freedom has created a landscape from which they are more prohibited than is the case in the Britain their ancestors escaped.

By 1900, when the pleas of men like Harry Ell to 'make small reserves of native forest every 3 or 4 miles' began having an effect on politicians,

New Zealand's best land had all been privatised. In our distant hindsight from the events it *is* tempting to blame someone. But the man who began it all was as inevitable as those who read about the empty antipodean plains and set off to grasp them. If James Cook hadn't come, someone like him would have, with a similar baggage of visions, with the same plants and animals—before the 18th century was out. Cook was simply the able and intelligent agent of an appealing idea at a pivotal point in his culture's spreading.

With luck there is going to be enough tide in the Waihou to drift, as the *Endeavour's* boats did, up to the site of Cook's revelation, and then catch the 'first of the Ebb' he had hoped would return them to the sea. I head back to the canoe in the hoof-pocked shallows wondering what another two centuries will bring to this place. Will our descendants still be treating the river as beaten and conquered adversary? Will they still be sealing its floodplain from it?

At 2PM the Boats returned from sounding not haveing found above 3 feet more water than where we now lay; upon this I resolved to go no further with the Ship, but to examine the head of the Bay in the boats, for as it appeared to run a good way inland I thought this a good opportunity to see a little of the Interior parts of the Country and its produce.
. . . at Day light in the morning I set out with the Pinnace and Long boat acompanied by Mr Banks, Dr Solander and Tupia.

In the six week passage of the *Endeavour* between Nicholas Young's sighting of the mudstone cliffs of Poverty Bay on 9 October 1769, and Cape Colville at the tip of the Coromandel Peninsula, an inhospitable, hilly land prevailed. Its people looked and spoke like the friendly Tahitians, but their fierce territoriality led to death after death from the *Endeavour's* muskets. Cook's decision to more closely examine the flat land at the head of the Hauraki Gulf may have seemed trivial at the time. Rain or low cloud could have obscured his view. He could have dismissed the break in the hills as a strait and sailed on across the gulf, as unaware of the vast floodplain as he was of virtually all the harbours that would become New Zealand's principal ports. Had that been the case, New Zealand might have entered the British imagination with few colonial virtues. As it was Cook sensed a kind of country New Zealand had not yet delivered, and given the shallow soundings all around the *Endeavour* and the low-lying land at the head of the bay, his instincts led him on.

Cook's three voyages between 1768 and 1779 took him further into the unknown than anyone before him. He was the one who, as a contemporary said, 'fixed the bounds of the habitable earth, as well as those of the navigable ocean'. Of all his landings or attempted landings that fateful summer of 1769, the day, and the unplanned night he spent on the Waihou, was the longest, and the furthest he penetrated inland. Although he never returned to 'The New Thames', it was always, to him, where New Zealand's greatest trees grew.

The men on the *Endeavour* saw no more country like the Hauraki Plains. Four months later they headed away from New Zealand out into the Tasman. Cramped in their tiny cabin, Cook and Banks recorded the 'Convenient Situations' of the country they had just circumnavigated and, as the Admiralty had commanded, 'observed with accuracy'. Their depictions of the wet plain into which they'd floated as their antipodean summer began are so alike that powerful cultural presumptions must have been at work. We can imagine them striving for words to ensure others would follow them. While the great trees asserted themselves almost irresistibly, what not to say also had to be decided. They had 'rowd for the ship as fast as' they could, but overtaken by the tide, were forced to overnight on the riverbank. Sydney Parkinson, the artist left on board, blamed a strong nor'westerly driving up the river. Strangely, neither Cook nor Banks mention their only night out of reach of the *Endeavour*. Whatever they saw of the nocturnal aspects of the new country or its people's manners and habits—if indeed they spent it in Māori company—we are not to know. Of the plains' significance to the empire however, they have plenty to say. Here is how Cook said it:

> *Should it ever become an object of settleing this Country the best place for the first fixing of a Colony would be either in the River Thames or the Bay of Islands, for at either of these places they would have the advantage of a good harbour and by means of the former an easy communication would be had and any settlements might be extended into the inland parts of the Country, for at a very little trouble and expense small vessels*

might be built in the River proper for the navigating thereof . . .
So far as I have been able to judge of the genius of these people it
doth not appear to me to be at all difficult for Strangers to form a
settlement in this Country.

Joseph Banks proclaimed the River Thames

. . . indeed in every respect the properest place we have yet seen
for establishing a Colony; a ship as large as Ours might be carried
several miles up the river, where she would be moored to the trees
as safe as alongside a wharf in London river, a safe and sure retreat
in case of an attack from the natives . . . The Noble timber, of
which there is such an abundance, would furnish plenty of
materials either for the building defences, houses or Vessels. The
River would furnish plenty of Fish, and the Soil make ample
returns of any European Vegetables sown in it.

He accented the

. . . Swamps which might doubtless Easily be drained, and
sufficiently evinced the richness of their soils by the great size of
the plants that grew upon them, and more particularly of the
timber trees which were the streightest, cleanest, and I may say
the largest I have ever seen . . . we were never but once ashore
among them, and that but for a short time on the banks of the
River Thames; where we rowd for many miles between woods of
these trees, to which we could see no bounds.

Imperialism has never, as a rule, hid its worldly intentions. Joseph
Banks' purpose was with transforming the new-found plain. The moment
he saw it he was deciding who would plan its future, who had the right to
settle and work it. Through his design for its drainage, he turned its
strangeness into 'home'. But as with Cook, the might of mythology deflects
our minds from what was really going on. Banks was native to flat, watery
country like this, his youth one of shooting and fishing the wilds of
England's Fens. His passion for swamp drainage, inherited from his father
along with the wet acres of the 200 farms of his Lincolnshire estate, had
more impact than the botanising and scientific describing of new lands for
which history—and his name latinised, immortalised on a host of antipodean

plants and pieces of land—wishes us to know him.

Banks' journals, like Cook's, were not readily available, in the actual words of the author, until they were edited by John Beaglehole in the 1960s. The 18th- and 19th-century public read accounts edited by others who had plenty of zeal for the task, but had never seen the Pacific. John Hawkesworth knew an eager public was waiting to learn of the new southern world. Almost immediately the *Endeavour* had returned to England, he was altering and dramatising Banks' and Cook's observations into a popular book. Repeatedly reprinted, it was soon an essential item in the library of anyone with notions of creating colonies or missions in the new-found hemisphere, and indispensible to any sailing master with thought of 'the South Seas'. In enticing his readers to regard the banks of the Thames as 'the best place for establishing a colony', Hawkesworth drew on both Banks' and Cook's words.

About the entrance of the narrow part of the River the land is mostly cover'd with Mangroves and other Shrubs, but further inland are imence woods

. . . we landed on the West side in order to take a View of the lofty Trees which adorn its banks . . . in many places the woods grow close upon the very banks of the River

. . . we had not gone a hundred yards into the Woods before we found a tree that girted 19 feet 8 Inches 6 feet above the Ground, and having a quadrant with me I found its length from the root to the first branch to be 89 feet, it was as streight as an arrow and taper'd but very little in proportion to its length, so that I judged that there was 356 solid feet of timber in this tree clear of the branches. We saw many others of the same sort several of which were taller than the one we measured and all of them very stout; there were likewise many other sorts of very stout timber-trees all of them wholly unknown to any of us. We brought away a few specimens and at 3 oClock we embarqued in order to return on board with the first of the Ebb

. . . the finest timber my eyes ever beheld of a tree we had before seen but only at a distance in Poverty bay and Hawks bay; thick woods of it were every where upon the Banks, every tree as streight as a pine and of immense size; still the higher we came the more numerous they were. About 2 leagues from the mouth

we stopped and went ashore. Our first business was to measure one of those trees; the woods were swampy so we could not range far, we found one . . . We cut down a young one of these trees; the wood proved heavy and solid, too much so for mast but would make the finest Plank in the world.

From a boat standing where the *Endeavour* anchored off the Coromandel coast, the pine and macrocarpa shelter belts of the Hauraki Plains' countless dairy farms appear, in the warm salty air, to be a levitating forest. The kahikatea forests Cook saw would have been at least twice as high. Witnessing them just before they vanished, Thomas Kirk declared 'there could be no more striking sight . . . than a virgin kahikatea forest':

Straight unbranched trunks rise one after the other in endless series, and in such close proximity that at a short distance no trace of foliage is visible except overhead, or in the immediate vicinity of the observer; the naked symmetrical shafts tapering almost imperceptibly, appear to form dense walls which completely shut out every glimpse of the outer world.

If my journey in Cook's wake has a particular intent it is to find the spot where, with an axe and a quadrant and some carefully chosen words, his shore-party enshrined such trees in New Zealand history. Today a highway sweeps past it but I want to arrive, as they did, by river. At the mouth of the Hikutaia I float into a swollen nexus of tide and flood. The rain and a prospect of shelter from a grove of karaka trees persuade me to cross to the Waihou's far bank. Another mess of trampled mud. Generations of cows have huddled under the karaka for the same reason I'm here, compacting the river silt to expose fire-blackened, rounded stones. Shiny black flakes of obsidian gleam among them, brought to the kainga by even further-travelled canoes— emblems of a different, native, time. Months later, in a missionary's journal, I discover the karaka mark Te Kari, the same 'town with but few inhabitants' perhaps, that Joseph Banks described downstream

THE KARAKA GROVE OF TE KARI ON THE WAIHOU.

from their landing. Then I find it again in old treaty papers; here, one night late in 1840, the tapu was taken off the plain, opening it to settlers and soldiers.

Back in the canoe I paddle along a bleak riverbank beside Captain Cook Road. For twenty minutes I wonder when the push of the sea will give way to the floodflow of days of inland rain and calm will become contest. Then far off in the rain I see the concrete obelisk surrounded by its fence. Sliding towards it past out-of-season duckshooters' hides I run the canoe ashore where plaqued history says the *Endeavour* shore-party stepped stiffly out of their yawl and long-boat. I cast about in the vain hope a fragment of native life may have hung on from the day, that a clump of fern or flax may have escaped the rout. A few young kahikatea stand alone in the paddocks across the river.

The vanishing of the great forest is recent enough for one of the settler children who saw it to be responsible later in life for having a monument constructed in 1969 to commemorate Cook's visit. The timber-milling crowd of Gordon Fisher's father, five uncles and all their families landed in the 1890s from the paddle steamer *Patiki*, pitching their tents somewhere near here beside 'the vast forest dominated by the great kahikatea stretching before them'. Fisher never forgot the delicious tawari, the fruit of the dense kie kie vine thickets, nor the fires that soon consumed them 'as the milling moved back from the river's edge' and the sequence of tramlines, grass seed, bullocks and cows penetrated deep into the forest. His landscape quickly became one of drains and stumps, some massive enough to prove Cook's measurements no exaggeration.

Approached by road six months later the landing site seems a different place. The crash of a shotgun as I turn off the highway into the side road named for Gordon Fisher's family tells me it is also someone else's. I stop outside the nearest house, curious to see if anyone with some link to the big trees still lives here. A face peers out from under a car in the dark of the garage as I tap on the ranchslider. Inside, a row of plains women sit under hair dryers. The young woman who comes to the door knows Cook's monument but she has no idea how her road got its name.

At the river, silhouetted against the dull, heavy sky, three men in swannies with guns and dogs are standing on the stopbank, watching me. Off in the drizzle I can see their big cars on the crest of the man-made bank between the willows' cold winter skeletons. The wet, still air is heavy with the reek of silage. I go through a gate, along a gravel track covered in plantain and dock and up on to the stopbank. Bank to bank, even more swollen than when I was on it, the Waihou pours past.

Scanning the land really is, as Barry Lopez calls it, old human business—making sense of what is immediate to the senses, subjecting what you see to what your culture leads you to know, as Cook and Banks did to those huge trees that were here. Below me a holed dinghy is dying in a patch of raupō, the only native plant in sight. Willow logs, four-by-twos, sheets of iron and plastic containers litter the river's flood space. But the overwhelming impression is of chemical green flatness stretching away between the willows and the macrocarpa shelter belts, a flatness reinforced by the mechanical lines of the stopbanks keeping the river and its silt from the plain, which Cook, were he to see it today, might not recognise as his River Thames.

Almost certainly he would not have mourned its vanished trees or the beauty that Thomas Kirk saw. Cook's and Banks' interest in the Waihou's kahikatea was in their timber and the soil fertility manifest in their sheer size. Sydney Parkinson—who a few weeks earlier had written of Tolaga Bay as a place of beautiful shrubs, which was 'agreeable beyond description, and, with proper cultivation might be rendered a second Paradise'—had different preoccupations. Parkinson was not taken up the river, but among the plant specimens the shore-party brought aboard the *Endeavour* for him to draw, he recognised the same tall and stately 'palms' 'which fill the air with a most fragrant perfume'. He noted the 'pandanus-like' appearance of the sample of kie kie and the pine-smelling foliage to be of the 'large tree of which we had seen so many groves formed in different parts of the coast'—the one the spar traders would, in 30 short years, be calling 'a stick of first rate quality'.

James Cook's boundless plain of giant trees and tidal river would wait 60 years for a European to see it as beautiful. Seduced like everyone else by the great navigator's words, the Rev Samuel Marsden's London Missionary Society saw it as a place where the obligation 'to bring into service, the resources of the country' was obvious. Early in the 1830s, they dispatched William Yate to the Puriri Stream to establish a mission station. 'The extensive flat . . . upon which the kahikatea and the mangrove flourish undisturbed' struck him 'very forcibly', but not as his employers had expected. At first glance it reminded him of his arrival in the low-lying landscape of Tonga:

But the scenery is most lovely on the fresh-water banks of this river: the only drawback to its enjoyment is the difficulty of landing, except at high water, on account of the depth of mud deposited on its banks. It is true, that, for fifty or sixty miles, there is a great sameness in the views, being confined by hills on one side, and an immense flat forest on the other; yet the whole is so peaceful, so well suited for meditation, and fitted to calm the ruffled passions of the soul, that hearts, even the most insensible to the beauties of nature, must feel its influence . . . The copse-wood and flax, with reeds and rushes of every description, flourish most luxuriantly on the banks of this noble river; ducks, and other water-fowl, sail proudly and undisturbedly on its placid bosom, and are so remarkably tame, as to come fearlessly within reach of the paddles, with which our boats are rowed. Nor does the fragrance exhaled from the flowers and shrubs fail to increase the pleasure derived from an excursion on this stream. Indeed, the whole atmosphere seems impregnated with perfumes; sweets are borne upon the wings of every gale; and every breath inhaled stimulates the system, and strengthens man for the labour which may lie before him.

William Yate's words, as far as I know the first stirring of recognition that New Zealand's seemingly primeval purity offered Europeans respite from the grime and industry of civilisation, were soon to influence European settlement. But no one in his century came to the Hauraki Plains and talked about guardianship of a national heritage, significant natural values and such matters. 'Different now, 1887,' someone wrote 45 years later, in the margin of the copy I read of William Yate's book.

Cook measured and detailed the Waihou's kahikatea because, as a naval man, he had a duty to do so. His employers, the Admiralty, needed to know such things existed, especially tall, strong mast timber—even if they were on the far side of the world. Britain had been in a quandary over shipbuilding supplies for over a century, ever since the Civil War routed the royal forests and the Industrial Revolution began its relentless demand for wood. 'God knows where materials can be had,' the diarist Samuel Pepys, who worked in the Admiralty, had scrawled when he learned the extent of it. By the time of the *Endeavour*'s voyage, over 600,000 trees a year were being imported from Russia alone to maintain and expand the navy. The immense spars needed for the topmasts of the larger ships had become so scarce and expensive to obtain in Europe, it was necessary to look for them elsewhere.

Cook was undoubtedly convinced he had found an answer; vast forests of a hard-wooded, towering tree, waiting beside a navigable river. However, the tree they felled and whose foliage Parkinson drew was not the soft-wooded kahikatea that prevailed on the Waihou's banks, but matai, a related, but significantly different and far less common, species. Unaccustomed to the subtleties of antipodean plant life, the English eyes failed to detect the difference between the foliage of the two species. That afternoon of field botany was to have far-reaching impacts on New Zealand's landscape and history.

In another season, the highlight of Parkinson's drawing might not have been the strangeness of such an obviously pine-like tree having such tiny leaves, but kahikatea's fruit. Had it not been spring, Joseph Banks, and even Cook, might have added a line or two about pigeons and parrots flocking into the great trees—or meeting canoes laden with fruit. In the autumn of 1841, the botanist John Bidwill saw the plain's 'enormous' kahikatea 'loaded with their beautiful scarlet and black fruit', or koroī. 'In those places where the trees are abundant . . . they formed a great part of the food of the natives during the season', the river people bringing 'large baskets full of the berries of the kaikatora' for sale. At a hui further up the river at Matamata the following year, he counted 60 baskets of them.

Gathering koroī is almost unimaginable to us today. The famous whakatauākī *He toa piki rākau kahikatea, he kai na te pakiaka*—'the champion kahikatea climber is food for the roots'— fuses the mana of fruit-gathering with the risks of climbing 100 feet or more off the ground, then scrambling out among the thin branches of the canopy where the koroī are most abundant.

Kahikatea's ancient name has roots older than the first Polynesian colonisers who saw it. Named after a Southeast Asian fruit tree their distant ancestors brought into the Pacific thousands of years before, it evokes the prodigious Aotearoa the first people saw and the fruit-eating birds that must have flocked to the tall trees in those days.

A native climbing the kahikatea to gather its fruit, J.J.MERRETT, EARLY 1840S.

Through Polynesian names like kafika, ka'ika, 'ahi'a, oohi'a to kapika, the proto-Oceanic name of the Malay apple (*Syzgium malaccense*), linguists have been able to reconstruct kahikatea's name back 5000 years.

White pine, the early Europeans' name for kahikatea, reflects *their* colonial interest in it. Its scientific label—*Dacrycarpus dacrydioides*—reveals none of this. Younger than most of the botanists who use it, it is a legacy nonetheless of the 18th-century era when science was out beyond Europe discovering new lands like this plain, and a warehouse clerk in Uppsala, Sweden was laying his system of binomial nomenclature over the life of the world. 'The bitter fruit of the tree of Uppsalan knowledge,' the novelist John Fowles has called it.

Kahikatea is the supreme survivor. The fruit basket of the forest, revered by Māori hunters and modern conservationists for its attractiveness to birds, connects us to a birdless, flowerless world in which huge ammonites stalked the sea-floor and pterodactyls the air. The most remarkable thing about a kahikatea landscape, looking through tall trees across a river mouth to faraway ranges, is that the *trees* are the oldest things your eye encounters, not the mountains. Kahikatea persists from an old, swampy, worn-down, tropical archipelago, utterly different from the cool, young, mountainous New Zealand of today. You can find it in the hills, but it only prospers in the swamps. It would vanish without them.

Geologists believe they have found traces of kahikatea's pollen and leaves in Jurassic rocks, some 160-180 million years old. It belongs with such ancient animals as tuatara, weta and the landsnails *Powelliphanta* and *Wainuia*, the survivors of the great extinctions at the end of the Cretaceous when the earth's species suddenly declined by half. When the latest great revolution in the history of the earth's life began and the flowering plants— the vines, lianes, epiphytic lilies and orchids and broadleaved trees with which it coexists—evolved and spread into all corners of the planet where life is possible, kahikatea was already ancient.

New Zealand is a special place to biologists because of the birds that belong to families now found nowhere else on earth. Yet when their ancestors arrived, probably as wind-blown immigrants about 60 million years ago, kahikatea had been in place for at least 100 million years. By then, the other species in the forest for which it evolved had become extinct. It is not too incredible to imagine the pterosaur, or flying reptile, whose remains have been found in New Zealand recently, perched in the branches of kahikatea overhanging a tidal river, drying its clumsy wings.

The ecosystem in which kahikatea came into being is unverifiable, but it nonetheless stretches the human imagination. Each species in the maze of interaction and obligation slowly shaped by geographic isolation and geological upheaval has its own history. No more organised than it is understood, the maze subverts the appealing notion of the primeval rainforest as a perfected system of species evolved in symphony. By the time the first birds evolved, kahikatea had already long outstayed the ecological niche of the animal, whatever it was, for which its tasty koroī evolved. The kererū that flock noisily into its branches as soon as they ripen had nothing to do with it.

The rainforests of New Zealand in early Tertiary times—some 50 million years ago—were much richer in plants than they are today. Nīkau, now New Zealand's solitary palm species and the world's southernmost, was not alone then. Other palms, including *Cocos*, the coconut, left traces in New Zealand rocks of this time. As new species arrived and spread through the pattern of islands, the seams of Gondwana were widening, progressively isolating the archipelago from its tropical origins. It was a low-lying land of forested plains, coastal swamps and estuaries. Hill and mountain country contracted and, with them, their diversity of plants. What wasn't flooded by rising Eocene seas persisted for the next 30 million years or so as a worn-down land of leached and impoverished soils.

Northwest, about 20-25 million years ago, a southward rotating continental plate containing the Malaysian-Indonesian rainforests and a host of newly evolved tropical plant genera began arcing out into the Pacific. From it, currents brought palms, mangrove swamps and coral reefs which established around the New Zealand coast. But by late Miocene times, the ecological character of New Zealand had changed dramatically. The Antarctic icesheets began to grow and influence ocean currents. The westerly winds that resulted, and that still dominate New Zealand weather today, began bringing plants into New Zealand from Australia and more distant southern lands. By 5-15 million years ago, many of the tropical environments had disappeared from New Zealand, and all but the most robust of their plants perished.

Kahikatea survived it all, and presumably will survive the era of human effort against nature that has brought me to this plain looking for its last sign. There is a biological truth in the whakatauākī, *He iti hoki te mokoroa, nāua i kakati te kahikatea*, that a tiny grub can fell a great tree, but perhaps the greater truth is that kahikatea's ecosystem is one in which a sudden, brief, catastrophic event like a flood can take away everything on which people have depended for centuries.

A kahikatea forest requires us to look at the landscape with the sense of time of geologists and mystics, as well as the urgency of conservationists. It resonates with paradox. This oldest of trees loves the youngest of soils. The flip side to the vastness of its history and the long life of its individual trees is that the land on which it prefers to live is among the most ephemeral on offer. Several times a year this plain was under water. Its first kahikatea inhabited the edge of an estuary that had previously been an arm of the sea into which the Waikato flowed before the Taupo eruption forced it west to another, wilder coast. This, essentially, was the ecosystem into which Polynesians stepped and with which, as they became Māori, they found a way of life; that the *Endeavour* shore-party entered centuries later.

How are we so certain this is where Cook and his men were—that this is the piece of ground on which we end up if we wind back the tape of New Zealand's colonial history to the germinal moment of European intent? There is nothing so specific in either Cook's journal or Banks'. If there had been, Beaglehole would have used it, but he had another source altogether: 'Mr Leslie G. Kelly tells me that their activities were watched by Maoris close by, and the tree remembered in tradition which in due course was passed on to Europeans. It was felled for milling a little before 1900, but abandoned as the trunk was hollow.' Keeping every oar stroke under surveillance, but out of sight and unknown to the Englishmen, Ngāti Maru on the riverbank had followed them up the river.

In the same footnote to Banks' journal, one of many on virtually every page, amplifying and explaining, decoding and naming, Beaglehole allows a rare emotional note: '. . . Cook and Banks were in the great forest of kahikatea or *Podocarpus dacrydioides* that then covered the valley of the Waihou or Thames river for about 25 miles—now alas! completely vanished.' His gaze upon the river, heavy with silt from the chain reaction of forest loss, ill-tended farms and erosion, Beaglehole sensed a deteriorating landscape beneath the plains' prosperity and economic significance. Merely 200 years in the *Endeavour's* wake Cook's proposition that 'a ship of a moderate draught of water may go a long way up this River with a flowing tide' already seemed nonsense.

One of Beaglehole's most rewarding moments was when near the end of his life he stepped ashore in a cold, wet Dusky Sound forest and touched the axemarks on the tree stumps cut by Cook's 1773 expedition.

He cherished places in which, in the 1960s, he could discern continuity with the past, especially where James Cook had stood—a sense of New Zealand nurtured by the primordial places he passionately sought in his youth.

But Beaglehole says little about what was perhaps the most far-reaching notion of 20 November 1769: how the Englishmen on their closely observed passage up the Waihou decided they were in an empty landscape— that this great, fertile plain, its woods so swampy its discoverers couldn't 'range far', was to all intents and purposes useless to its inhabitants.

⁓⁓⁓⁓⁓

> . . . *proceeded up the River untill near Noon, when finding the face of the Country to continue pretty much the same and no alteration in the Course or stream of the River or the least probillity of seeing the end of it . . .*
>
> *. . . from this place it still continues the same SBE Course thro' a low flat country, on broad Valley that lies parallel with the Sea Coast, the end of which we could not see. The land on the East side of the broad part of this River is tolerably high and hilly, that on the west side is rather low, but the whole is Cover'd with Woods and Verdure and looks to be pretty fertile but we saw only a few small places that were cultivated.*
>
> *Above this [Indian town] the banks of the river were completely cloathed with the finest timber . . .*

What was a tapu, food-rich labyrinth of waterways, forest and swamp to the river people was a vacant wilderness to the men in the *Endeavour*'s boats. In Cook's reckoning, it did not seem that seizing its untouched, empty acres for a colony was going to be 'attall difficult'. For centuries, Europeans had rehearsed their encounter with 'Indians' with a mixture of longing and loathing. Land as patently fertile as this was pre-destined to be cultivated—or forfeited. Ancient belief, authenticated by their culture's philosophers, told them that land that is 'left wholly to nature, that hath no improvement of Pasturage, Tillage, or Planting, is called, as indeed it is, *waste*'. No one could claim dominion over land whose soil did not bear the marks of their labour in it.

Cook sailed away. But when European settlement began in earnest 70 years later, his culture's assumptions festered into frustration that quickly

ran to war. To settlers promised flat, unencumbered acres, a treaty with the
natives that on the face of it conserved natives' rights to any land they chose
not to sell—regardless of how wild it looked to English eyes—was a
ridiculous hindrance. 'All this chaffer about the rights of the natives to land
which they had let idle and unused for so many centuries,' one wrote in
1843, in an early New Zealand Company's newspaper, 'cannot do away
with the fact that, according to God's law they have established their right
to a very small portion of these islands.'

Indeed it was as though God was on the company's side, the country
divinely presented to them—the very 'impulse which prompts the colonisers
of New Zealand'. 'Is it not the will of God,' ventured Edward Gibbon
Wakefield, 'that the earth should be replenished and subdued, that the desert
should give rise to the fruitful field, the frantic war-cry to the hymn of
praise, and the frightful depository of the unburied dead to the country
steeple and the village school?'

It was not quite that straightforward. To others on the first boats
ashore at the few sites with navigable river mouths and fertile flats, it was
obvious that Māori claims to their land extended *well* beyond their gardens.
'Land, apparently waste is highly valued by them,' William Swainson said
years later in 1859. 'They claim and exercise ownership over the whole
surface of the country, and there is no part of it, however lonely, of which
they do not know the owners. Forests in the wildest part of the country
have their claimants . . . Forests are preserved for birds; swamps and streams
for eel-weirs and fisheries. Trees, rocks and stones are used to define the
well-known boundaries.'

By 1844 the surveyor's grid was sweeping over the coastal plains like a
mechanical tide. Few of the settlers in its wake conceded Māori any rights to
these environments. They laid siege to the British government and Governor
Grey, urging abandonment of the Treaty of Waitangi. Many influential colonial
voices agreed with them. The pact with the natives of New Zealand, declared a
House of Commons committee, was counter to an 'ancient and acknowledged
principle of colonial law': 'If native rights to the ownership of land had only
been admitted when arising from occupation, there would have been no
difficulty in giving at once to the settlers secure and quiet possession of the
land they required, and they would have thus been able to begin without delay
and in earnest the work of reclaiming and cultivating the unoccupied soil.'

By 1846 discontent was creeping towards war. With a package of
Royal Instructions, the British Colonial Secretary, Earl Grey, sent his

besieged namesake a letter that he hoped would solve things once and for all. He acknowledged that 'a large class of writers' considered the indigenous inhabitants of any country to be the proprietors of every part of its soil 'they were accustomed to make any use':

> This claim is represented as sacred, however ignorant such native may be of the arts or of the habits of civilized life, however small the number of their tribe, however unsettled their abodes, and however imperfect or occasional the uses they make of the land. Whether they are nomadic tribes depasturing cattle, or hunters living by the chase, or fishermen frequenting the sea-coasts or the banks of rivers, the proprietary title in question is alike ascribed to them all.

But Earl Grey could only 'entirely dissent' from its application to New Zealand's troublesome natives and their claim to its 'vast extent of fertile, but unoccupied land'. He referred for authority to *The Englishman's Register*, the 1831 version. 'Men were to subdue the earth,' he quoted. 'When our fathers went to America and took possession of the mere hunting grounds of the Indians—of lands on which man had bestowed no labour— they only exercised a right which God has inseparably united with industry and knowledge.' Then he delivered his verdict. New Zealand's natives, he said, were not 'a people of hunters'. But in their dependence on cultivation,

> . . . the extent of land so occupied by them was absolutely insignificant, when compared with that of the country they inhabited; the most trustworthy accounts agree in representing the cultivated grounds as forming far less than one-hundredth part of the available land, and in stating that millions of acres were to be found where the naturally fertile soil was covered with primeval forests or wastes of fern, in the midst of which a few patches planted with potatoes were the only signs of human habitation and industry.

On the plain of James Cook's vision the same imperative had been at work from almost the moment the treaty was signed. Before 1840 was out, the Governor of New South Wales, Sir George Gipps, was expressing concern that 'the minds of the Natives in these Districts have been worked upon by some designing and dissatisfied Europeans, so as to induce in them a distrust of the intentions of Her Majesties Government'. 'To counteract the ill feelings of the natives towards the Government, arising from their natural jealousy,' he sent George Clarke, Protector of Aborigines in New Zealand, from Sydney to the Hauraki Plains. Clarke's trip, however, had another objective, best explained by Gipps' description of the Thames as 'by far the largest block of land in New Zealand that is, in its whole extent, fit for cultivation'. Clarke's instructions were 'to treat with the natives for such portions of their land as they may be disposed to part with and can conveniently spare'.

Clarke spent Christmas Day of 1840 singing hymns at the Church Mission Station at the mouth of the Waihou, waiting for a boat. Then he and the principal chief, Hou, headed upriver to the 'native fort' Te Kari, whose karaka grove sheltered me from the rain 147 years later. Perhaps it was Hou, pointing out the signs of flood, who told Clarke what he would have seen in another season, how 'every winter the swamps from the entrance of Piako to the interior for about thirty miles is an inland sea in which nothing but water and the tops of a few kahikatea trees are to be seen with canoes sailing in all directions over the expanse of water. The only place secure from these inundations . . . becomes an island, and if a small town was built thereon it would remind you of those on the Nile at the time it overflows its banks.'

Clarke was in no doubt about the fertility of the place, but its wetness overwhelmed him. He could see 'no probability of redeeming a country lying so low and receiving such an immense body of water from the interior'. Water wasn't the only drawback: the plain was only 'part clean'. 'Heavily timbered with kahikatea: it will require great labour to clear it, but being on the banks of a river the timber might be available either sawn on the spot or floated down to any market in the Thames.' His instructions kept caution at bay. Late in the afternoon they landed at Te Kari to talk with the chief, Taraia, who was expecting them. The evening's events reveal much about the way the inhabitants of a landscape they considered sacred were so speedily relieved of what George Clarke said they 'might feel free to give up':

> The old man arose and vociferated to an hour to his people and
> visitors, not very sparingly on the rank his family held, and told
> his people to be very careful how they parted with their land, and
> the necessity of demanding a large payment, not omitting to assure

them that the whole of the Thames was 'Tapu' or sacred land.

The conversation lasted until midnight, when the old Chief consented for us to proceed up the river to look at the land, assuring us that the Waihou River (the Thames) had always been held sacred and that no one had dared profane it by passing his residence to sell land, although attempts had been made by some of the Thames Chiefs to introduce Europeans, but all feared the notice of his musket and the keen edge of his hatchet.

Again we had to labour against disadvantageous reports carefully circulated, and to assure the natives that his Excellency had the interests of the New Zealanders very much at heart. After these assurances Taraia arose and said—such a Governor as described was welcome: his land was waiting to receive him, and his river which had hitherto been held sacred, was now open to receive him or any person he might like to send, but he urged that the Europeans should be immediately sent to take possession. He did not (he said) want Missionaries nor Native Europeans, but he wanted gentlemen and soldiers.

A native standing by asked the old man if he would not be afraid to see so many Europeans settled about him. He replied 'If I was a thief or a murderer I might but as I am neither why should I fear? Tell (the Governor) . . . Go up my sacred rivers: go where you like . . .

Its tapu lifted, the plain that George Clarke said was 'adapted for immediate culture' was ready for Europeans. 'I have scarcely seen a piece of land today,' he wrote after the next morning's tour upriver, 'on which pretty farms might not be laid out to great advantage.'

As settlers poured into New Zealand, the expectation grew that Clarke's coup would be emulated on every other plain. By the time Governor Grey received the decree from London that Māori could claim no more than their gardens, it effectively had. In his reply Grey told the Colonial Secretary how one Ngāpuhi chief saw the consequences of his decision: 'Those who have sold their land are obliged to cultivate on the tops of the hills, and the clefts of the rocks.' In losing their plains, Māori had lost their best country.

Two years later, and a third of a century before he came back to remind the settlers of Thames of the great city that James Cook believed 'must ultimately stand here', Grey canoed up the Waihou with George

Cooper. No more than a few settlers and their English roses inhabited its plain. 'When you turn a bend in the river and open up a fresh reach . . . banks thickly wooded with trees of different shades of foliage and the water calm as glass and reflecting the clear blue sky,' Cooper wrote, ' the effect is extremely picturesque and pleasing.' But he saw nothing picturesque and pleasing about the riverbank kāinga like Opita: '. . . a wretched place . . . a dozen miserable raupo houses all tumbling to pieces. We found the natives in a very poor condition, not a living animal had they, save four geese, a hen with a brood of young chickens and a few skeleton-looking dogs; they had neither potatoes nor kumeras, but were living on fern root and a few eels which they catch now and then.'

Hauraki's plains were not, like the Hutt's, the Waikato's and Taranaki's, a place of war. But there were other Opitas and flashpoints like 'The Hikutaia Outrage' when Ngāti Maru resentment boiled over. In 1885, the Minister of Native Affairs, John Ballance, visited 'the Hauraki Natives because the settlers were having trouble with disrupted land and stock'. To the Ngāti Maru, the issue was more a matter of broken promises. Pineaha te Wharekohai spoke bitterly about the speed with which—with the government's help—settlers had so totally changed a sacred river whose tapu had been lifted to allow Europeans and Māori to live together. Now they were taking even the snags in the river:

> . . . that is where they get the eels from. He held on and would not give them up until Mr Bryce came and took them away by force. The Government, through Mr Bryce, took these things away and gave no consideration for them. He [Wharekohai] will have to fell a kahikatea and let it fall into the river so as to make a place for the eels. Te Wharekohai said that this was causing him a great deal of darkness, and if something was not done he would have to fill that river up again with trees. Now the steamers that get up the river are continually carrying away the banks, and some Europeans cut down a tree that had some dead bodies in the branches, and they drifted away in the river.

Māori, in their brief habitation of Aotearoa, had not acquired as profound an alliance of spirit and ecology as has evolved over the great expanses of time for which, say, Australia's aboriginal peoples have known their country. Nonetheless, between their arrival sometime around 1100 AD and the 1700s, with rituals like placing exhumed, ancestral bones high in trees to fuse their lives with nature, they had developed an elaborate, spiritualised connection with country such as the Waihou.

The old river culture of the Waihou welcomed the first Europeans 'in the most friendly manner immagineable', but their very hospitality helped sow the seeds of destruction of their way of life. The legacy of the history that prised Māori from their best land persists, not least in conflict over whether traditional Māori society intuitively cared for nature—living, as William Swainson believed, in mindful connection with nature, or relentlessly despoiling it. The truth, as it often does, lies somewhere between.

Among the sceptics are many of New Zealand's natural scientists and archaeologists, who, having seen the bones of extinct birds and correlated the charcoal they have found in swamps with Polynesian fires, tend to the conclusion that early Māori mounted a continuous 'assault on the forests', burnt 'whole river catchments' and caused 'widespread . . . destruction of the swamp forests'. The result was the transformation of the rich, fertile coastal lowlands where, prior to the arrival of Europeans, most Māori lived: 'all . . . the areas which are today valued for intensive agriculture'. 'They were doomed,' they say, 'from the moment of first human settlement.'

The earliest European settlers, to whom Arcadia was pastoral country with 'fine domestic grasses, clumps of graceful trees and lack of underbrush', would have been thrilled to have found the coastal lowlands unencumbered with forest—or 'clean' as they said in those days. Yet that is not how they portrayed them. In Tasman Bay, for example, while Māori had virtually deforested the coastal hills, they had kept ancient groves of kahikatea— 'enormous trees with the upward thrust of dark green foliage'—on the flats. Cook saw similar forests, close to kāinga, at Turanga, or Gisborne, and off the Manawatu and Horowhenua coast, where Charles Heaphy depicted them 70 years later in his famous coastal profile. Aidan Challis' study, *Motueka*, reveals a long, sustained relationship between kāinga and forest, along with the nearby river mouths and estuarine reaches, swamps and hill country. Immediately European land law arrived in the 1840s, confining Māori to native reserve sections, curtailing seasonal movements and access to resources, the relationship ended.

The relationship between Māori and these forests, ngā uruora, was an important, sustaining one; one still alive in Māori art. Patterns that to the uninitiated may seem hieroglyphics are, as the carver John Bevan Ford has explained, much more: 'I can remember Pine Taiapa telling me of a kōwhaiwhai pattern called ngutukura, that is the beak of the kura. If this group of people had this pattern, it more or less recorded that not far away they had the type of bush that attracted this parrot to it, this kura which they could capture and kill, and feed people with.' The whakatauākī, *Tungu te ururua kia tupu whakaritorito te tupu ō te harakeke*—'set the overgrown bush alight and the flax shoots will spring up'—also derives from this kind of country. From the very beginning of Polynesian life in these wet, floodplain environments, *fire* has been integral to it. Any floodplain forest could have been incinerated at any time. A kahikatea swamp forest is particularly combustible. As countless 19th-century settlers discovered, a fire touching such a forest sweeps from floor to tree-tops in no time, explosions of flame bursting from one inflammable species to another. That the ground is waterlogged counts for nothing.

The few archaeological studies that have examined the nature-culture relationship in these environments suggest an intimate and highly deliberate connection had evolved by the 19th century. One, set in the Waikato when it was a landscape of forest, swamp and waterways, like the Waihou flood-plain, was recorded in 1972 by Richard Cassells in the international journal *Mankind*. Cassells assumed that humans visited the Waikato swamplands, if not inhabited them, soon after they first occupied Aotearoa. However, his concern was less with the 'mistakes' of the Polynesian pioneers in the throes of adaptation than with how their subsequent ecosystem functioned. He depicted it as comprising nine 'resource zones'—poorly drained soils in semi-swamp kahikatea forest, peat swamp, raised bog, steepland broadleaf-podocarp forest, river, stream, lake and clearable land either in forest and fern or in kumara. Comparison between the food resources available in each with the ethnography of 19th-century scholars revealed 68 plant species traditionally eaten by Māori. Settlement sites were nearly all beside forest or fernland rather than clearable, croppable soils. All were close to water, half beside navigable streams and a third by rivers.

The picture that emerges is of a developing give-and-take relationship between people and nature. The artificially created preferred environments were not very different from those that were naturally present anyway—such as the 'forest edge communities created wherever a stream ran through the forest'.

Such landscape manipulation, Cassells suggested, was a consequence of affinity with the land and its life, its resilience and fragility. It grew as much from the observation that this means different ecological communities varied widely in the richness of resources—and that the richest were the *edges* between them—as from the common human practice of living as close as possible to key resources to conserve energy. Because Māori traditionally placed themselves at the centre of their environment, as long as this country of edges was their central food source it was cared for as a garden might be.

Against this, of course, is a wealth of evidence that these islands' first Polynesians predated unsustainably on the easy resources they encount-ered—docile seals that lay back on rocks and birds that did not take off when people approached. It is not uncommon to hear Māori blame the dramatic depletion of shellfish that has occurred around urban centres on Pacific Island immigrants. Neither is it difficult to imagine the colonising predecessors of Māori, accustomed to tropical growth rates and to thinking of nature as perpetually renewable, dealing to the new environment in precisely the same way.

As the pioneering phase passed, means of conserving crucial resources were developed. The people who met the *Endeavour*'s shore-party 'with open arms' still cultivated the few domestic plants that had survived their ancestors' journeys from the tropical Pacific. But indigenous plants were their mainstay. Some were gathered from the wild, others cropped and intensively researched. In the 1870s, from a few North Island districts alone, the botanist James Hector recorded some 70 Māori names for different flaxes, where the Linnaean system recognised two species. Each of the 70 was known for its special use.

The early Māori were capable of burning forests, and certainly did. Centuries of hunting led to the extinction of many bird species. But the natural forest cover of plains country, with slow-growing, fruit-bearing trees like kahikatea, matai and hinau, was kept intact because these rainforests were often a better source of food than cultivated land or second-growth vegetation. Before the arrival of European crops and domesticated grazing animals, nature's diversity and richness—in fertile, coastal environments like these plains—could hardly be improved upon. Wild land of this kind was as valuable as cultivations.

It has taken over a century for wildlife ecologists to establish how vital the lowland plains were to the native Aotearoa ecosystem in pre-settlement times; and as long to appreciate the huge areas of forest which the larger and most endangered native birds need to survive and multiply, and recognise the need of many species to move daily or seasonally between the inland hills and the richer, warmer coastal lowlands. Māori hunters, their sense of bird behaviour evolved from not-too-dissimilar Pacific forests, would not have been blind to what an observant European explorer like Dumont D'Urville noticed immediately he stepped inland. The forests of the coastal flats, 'more rich in birds . . . so full of life' contrasted dramatically 'with the funeral silence which I had observed on the ridge nearby'. It is not surprising that by Cook's arrival, Māori knowledge of the forest, and their connection to it, was rivalled only by their ability to move through it unnoticed.

Cook saw none of this. No human sign meant no human interest, and that is the message his readers received. The rural England of his upbringing was not the domain of land wasters. This had its ancient roots in the origins of his culture in the Fertile Crescent, the once prodigious, and now exhausted, alluvial plains of the Middle East, where the European version of settled agriculture began some 10,000 years ago. Not coincidentally, the domesticated plants and animals that Cook's culture would bring to this plain had similar origins. Cook had firm ideas on how a fertile plain should look if people were living well with it, and 10,000 miles from home, his Pacific encounter suggested a similar handling of ground which 'benevolent nature hath supplied . . . with abundance of superfluities'.

By the time he saw Hauraki Plains, entered their forests, peered across their swamps and met their people, Cook himself had experienced country with which comparison was obvious. As Beaglehole has said, there was very little that was aesthetic or emotional about him. Nevertheless, there were landscapes that could move him. The presence on the *Endeavour* of the Tahitian Tupaia, and the obvious closeness of the river peoples' language to his, would have sharpened the contrast with what Louis de Bougainville a few years earlier had called the 'charms of the plains' of Tahiti. 'One would think himself in the Elysian fields,' he acclaimed. 'All the flat country from the sea-shore to the foot of the mountains is destined for the fruit-trees, under which . . . the houses of the people of Taiti are built.' Cook wrote of 'flats fruitful and populous' with 'people dispersed everywhere' among the verdance, and would later describe Tongatapu in similar terms. It was, he said, like being 'transported into one of the most fertile plains in Europe, here was not an inch of waste ground . . . Nature assisted by a little art, no were [sic] appears to in a more flourishing state than at this isle.' Imagining what might lie beyond Tahiti, Joseph Banks lost all objectivity : 'the truest picture of an arcadia of which we were going to be kings that the imagination can form.' As far as an 18th-century gentleman of his ilk had been from the England of landscaped estates, here he was in a world that fitted perfectly the ideal his culture's art and literature craved. A world, of course, the English were expecting. Only a year or so before, Richard Walter had enthralled England's landscape designers with his tale of an island 'most beautifully diversified by the mutual encroachments of woods and lawns'. Tinian in the Marianas became another name for Paradise; 'Nature improved' on a faraway Pacific island verifying the muses of the poet Milton and the painter Claude Lorrain. This was the Pacific of European fantasy, with which the New Zealand the *Endeavour* came across a few weeks later had to compete.

The river country was only deceptively empty. Far from being waste land, the floodplain was cherished and intimately known, its places and rhythms named and valued from centuries of lives tied elaborately to it. The Ngāti Maru were known as uruhoa ō nui—skilled forest men—for their ability to travel fast and unnoticed across their swampy plain, as Cook himself discovered when news of the *Endeavour* and the metal nails it carried crossed the Coromandel Peninsula from Whitianga faster than he sailed around. Kahikatea, the tree-child of Tane and Hine-wao-riki which they saw the white men gaze at incredulously, was special to them too. Its white sap-wood lacked durability, but its hard, resinous heart-wood, or mapara, was eagerly sought for implements and weapons and for torches for night fishing and travelling. Burned, it made the finest tattooing pigment.

As invisible to James Cook as the Waihou's people were the dozens of kāinga up its myriad, hidden watercourses. Archaeologists estimate that drainage and flood control works have destroyed 70 per cent of them. A 1980s survey of the vicinity of Cook's visit located almost 100 sites, on the Waihou's eastern flank alone. Some are in the foothills, but most are close to its banks and tributaries like the Hikutaia. Ten sites are the remains of major pā that stood on the banks of the river or former watercourses before agriculture drained the land. All except one had been built up by shell transported by canoe from the sea coast. Upriver, the sites progressively thin out inland from Te Kopu. Correlating them with the early timber traders' maps and a hydrographic survey made during the milling era, the congruence between Māori, river and forest is obvious.

The Admiralty instructed Cook to observe the way of life of the local people. All around the coast, this was prevented by ritual challenge from the beach. Here the problem was sheer flatness and the thick vegetation. Of the network of settlements and cultivations up the side channels, and the food storage sites on the higher ground, Cook's party in their long-boat could see nothing. The impression given in the *Endeavour* journals was of a fertile land left wild and barely entered, of settlements as ephemeral as their way of life was marginal, tied to the edge of a vast wilderness of swamp and forest—a few meagre cultivations, fishing nets and canoes in the muddy river, and beyond, an emptiness never used, where all had yet to be created.

We found the inlet end in a River about 9 Miles above the Ship, into which we enterd with the first of the flood and before we had gone 3 miles up it found the water quite fresh. We saw a number of the natives and landed at one of their Villages the Inhabitats of which received us with open arms; we made but a short stay with them.

In our return down the River the inhabitants of the Village where we landed in going, seeing that we returned by another Channell put off in their Canoes and met us and trafficked with us in the most friendly manner imaginable untill they had disposed of the few trifles they had.

We saw poles stuck up in many places in this River to set nets for catching of fish, from this we imagined that there must be plenty of fish, but of what sort we know not for we saw none.

About a mile up this was an Indian town built upon a small bank of Dry sand but totally surrounded by Deep mud, so much so that I believe they meant it as a defence. The people came out in flocks upon the banks inviting us in, they had heard of us from our good friend Torava; we landed and while we stayed they were most perfectly civil, as indeed they have always been where we were known but never where we were not. After this visit we proceeded and soon met with another . . .

Before my river journey began, it was clear that there was one momentous place I would not reach. The drainage schemes by which the 20th century dealt to the Māori landscape of the Hauraki Plains would disorient anyone who expected to paddle up to the site where, after days of musket shots and death, a relieved James Cook met a 'town' of hospitable people.

The site was not located precisely until the late 1970s. An archaeologist, Simon Best, who was shrewd enough to look at aerial photographs of the Waihou in flood, realised that 'the Indian town' that Cook and Banks described approaching by one river channel and passing again when returning down another, could mean only one place, a 'laboriously constructed' swamp pā called Oruarangi. Conceivably a pioneer settlement, but certainly a cardinal river bank pā throughout pre-European times, Oruarangi is now inaccessible from its river, unless you canoe down a drainage board canal, climb the stopbank walls and the electric fences that keep cows in. To see Oruarangi today, you drive there.

If there wasn't a milking shed, a roundabout drive for the tanker and a potholed road outside it, Warner Hunter's house and garden could be in any neat New Zealand suburb, just as the rectangle of bright green pasture behind it could be any dairy farm. There is a pattern and organisation here. But Warner's farm is one of the longest continually inhabited places known in New Zealand. As far as I'm concerned it belongs on the first page of the history of the European in New Zealand.

As we came along the race in the tractor, Oruarangi straight in front of us as we threw hay to cows, Warner gesticulating as he told of an old local, Charlie Murdoch, coming back here after every flood and every ploughing, following the blades with a rake for what they brought up, I saw no sign of that history. Then, at the edge of a flat mound, Warner stopped and slid off: 'This is where old Charlie said the Maoris used to beach their canoes.'

Here on 20 November 1769, at the bottom corner of Warner's farm, two boats from the *Endeavour*, a yawl and a long-boat, pulled up in the mud. Watching Warner's neighbour's son rev his noisy farmbike across the low sweep of ground that used to be river, I try to imagine people standing here watching two strange boats full of even stranger people come silently up the river. The Ngāti Maru gather around the boats in excited chatter, eyes on the ornamented firearms and the buckles and buttons of James Cook's and his companions' exotic, musty clothing. The observant English eyes take in everything, watching the surprise as Tupaia breaks the ice with his Tahitian. The Waihou's fine grey mud on their shoes hints at the productivity of this place, and the familiar, clinging smell reminds them straight away of their own country's flat estuaries.

Islanders met islanders; two divergent pathways of the Neolithic Revolution suddenly coming together. The people of the river considered themselves part of their landscape, had learnt how to survive in it by allowing its natural rhythms to shape their lives. The ship people on the other hand had turned their faraway island into a tightly organised, densely populated and increasingly industrialised garden with only scraps of wilderness left. In ecology's terms, they were learning to broaden their niche by reorganising other people's lands to the rules they had learnt on their own island.

The English met a culture that had also perfected sophisticated gardening techniques but did not rely solely on cultivation for its food; a culture that understood trade and the technology of sail, but lacked the tools and domesticated biota necessary to transform new country, and that in adapting its tropical island ways to temperate ecosystems had become intimate with the diverse natural life of the river country. The new-comers, too, were intimate with other species—those their ancestors had domesticated thousands of years before. They played as central a role in European culture as the metals and firearms the islanders on the river so admired.

The poignancy of Oruarangi is heightened by its very ordinariness, by the absence of the monuments and plaques we like to erect wherever there is a whiff of conquest. Without Warner, distinguishing the low flat rises of Oruarangi and its neighbour Paterangi from the rest of his farm would have been difficult. Without the privileged knowledge that brought me down his road, I would have no reason to be here. Even if I had happened here by chance, there is nothing to catch the eye.

Yet the moment we step on to Oruarangi's mound, I see scattered all over it dozens of huge, wave-worn—canoe-delivered—Coromandel Peninsula boulders. Pipi shells glint everywhere the cows have broken the ground. I begin to see this is a *built* place and to fathom the generations of human effort that have gone into keeping Oruarangi from the chance of flood.

Conversation with a person who has lived for many years in a place like this keeps leaking fragments of information that shape a picture. The rain starts coming down so hard we head for the hay shed. Warner keeps chatting about the patches of fire-blackened soil with stones and shell he knows all over the farm, on the edge of every little watercourse. The green blades of raupō sprouting as soon as he cleaned out an old drain: 'The bloody seed must have been lying there for a hundred years or more.' The terraces of a pā he knew as a boy, where he points up into the rain to the faraway Coromandel foothills, where the pines are today. He's sure it had something to do with this pā on the river.

Back in Warner's house he gets his photographs of the big flood in 1981 and spreads them out on the kitchen table. The children clamber round grinning at how they have changed in the few years, and remembering how they had to go and stay with their cousins. There is Oruarangi all right, and Paterangi, the only bits of land above a sea of water. The blue house in the old channel on Phil's place was well under. 'The water was in the sink of the blue house,' says Warner. He brings out a Catchment Board photo of another flood. There, bound by the Waihou and another channel of water, is the island in the river which the boats from the *Endeavour* went up one side of and down the other.

There is something else Warner wants to show me. His neighbour across the road has decided he is too old to run dairy stock any more, and as soon as I see his paddock of thistles I know it is quite a while since it felt a plough. The sheep have slowly compacted the soft soil in a way that has probably never happened before. Warner strides away from the fence toward that invisible river, then, just as I am distinguishing Oruarangi from the rest of the flatness, he stops. Lying at his feet is a kahikatea as big as I have ever seen. Had it been standing it would have been almost three metres wide at the forester's measurement of breast height. As the sheep have trampled around it year by year, its old shape has slowly reappeared. A nor'westerly gale must have felled it.

Warner kicks at a patch of fire-burnt soil, scattering seashells into the old channel. Striding across the paddock, he kicks other similar patches apart, looking back at me with an expression that says he knows I know that we are on yet another piece of once-inhabited ground. I look up the old channel trying to imagine water between me and the slight rise 200 metres away which I now know is Oruarangi.

The channel ceased to exist when the Hauraki Catchment Board, in one of their endeavours to control the Waihou, constructed the Matatoki Canal and its stopbank through the southern end of Oruarangi. By the 1980s canal and bank needed upgrading. The care of historic sites had also become enough of an issue in the New Zealand landscape that, before the new works could start, an archaeological survey was necessary. The first test holes revealed the tiny amount of sediment deposited on the site when it was inhabited, compared to the huge quantity from each flood since the Waihou's deforestation for agriculture. No less apparent was the massive human effort that had gone into keeping Oruarangi from a river that frequently became a vast inland sea. Throughout the shell and clay fill were the remains of rows of huge posts, many over 300mm diameter. Some, like kahikatea, pukatea, rātā, matai and maire tawake obviously came from nearby river forests. Others like hard beech and kanuka would have been retrieved from the river. But most—kauri, totara, tanekaha, pohutukawa and puriri—would have been canoed to the site from distant forests.

Whatever caused this activity probably took place about 500 years ago when Oruarangi was one of the earliest pā constructed in Aotearoa. Archaeologists are still uncertain whether the building of these coastal swamp pā reflected the movement of people into a 'difficult new environment', or a decision to strengthen and defend a resource-rich landscape that had already been occupied for centuries. What there can be no doubt about is that Oruarangi was a very *organised* place; a nexus of chiefly authority.

Ecologically diverse and rich in resources, estuaries and river mouths have always been prime sites for human habitation. Precisely when or where the first people from tropical Polynesia came ashore may never be known, but it is apparent that by 1200 AD their descendants had thoroughly explored the whole country and were fully conversant with its natural resources. Life in the estuary of a major floodplain would have had its hazards, but of the environments Aotearoa offered a thousand years ago, the Waihou would have been one of the best.

Oruarangi's natural height above flood level would have attracted small seasonal bands of hunters and gatherers, and perhaps also gardeners. Then, from about 1550 AD, canoe-loads of sand and shell were brought in—some, tradition says, from shellbanks as far away as Miranda, 20km across the Firth of Thames—and layer after layer, some with flakes from tool making, dumped over the old ground surface and tramped down.

Anthropologist Jack Golson says there is no comparable site in New Zealand. He means much more than that his discipline regards it as a type site for 'Classic Māori' culture—some of them call it the 'classic Classic'. Oruarangi is revered because it is one of only a handful of places where occupation has been long and continuous enough to see evolution in the material culture of Māori society, from its East Polynesian beginnings right through to the pottery, musket balls and pig tusk pendants of early European settlement. For over 100 years, though, fossickers like Charlie Murdoch have plundered Oruarangi, damaging the historical sequence of the material that generation after generation of inhabitants have left here over the centuries. 'It is a pity,' Jack Golson wrote (with some understatement), 'that the rich finds from a site which on traditional and archaeological grounds does not seem to have had a short or simple history should have been recovered with no regard to their aerial or stratigraphic distribution.'

Traditional history names the Ngāti Huarere as the original owners of Oruarangi and its landscape, and records how, about 1650 AD, they were dispossessed by Ngāti Maru, the people who met the *Endeavour* party and still have mana whenua over Hauraki today. Another account says a people called Uri ō Pou, later overwhelmed by Tainui, were its original inhabitants At the root of the Tainui invasion, only a couple of generations after their arrival in Aotearoa from Ra'itea, it is said, was an ecological quest for resources similar to what happened here after Cook told Europeans about it:

> . . . at that time a new garment was brought into the district, which is called a tatara (loose), . . . which is made of the flax called wharariki. When seen by the people of Maru-tuahu they were much pleased with the flax of which it was made and asked 'Where does the flax grow of which this mat is made?' The owners of the mat said, 'It grows in the Hau-raki district'. This caused the women of the Maru-tuahu's tribe to wish for some, and to go and procure it . . . Five women . . . therefore left their home to obtain the flax . . . and landed at Wara-hoe, a little to the south of the Totara pa (in the Waihou estuary) . . . and there procured the coveted flax.

Waenganui, the wife of Tauru-kapakapa, was captured by the Uri ō Pou and taken to Oruarangi pā. To rescue her, the avenging Ngāti Maru assembled a war-party. Oruarangi was attacked on a flood tide, razed and all its cultivations seized. When Tauru-kapakapa was killed in revenge by the people of another river pā, Matangi-rahi, the Ngāti Maru overran every Hauraki settlement, virtually emptying what tradition says was a thickly populated district.

By the time of European arrival, the plain and its resources were controlled and defended by a couple of river pā only. Unimpressed by the mud-surrounded bank of sand with its fishing poles in the river, Cook's party didn't even bother to record its name—but merely by stopping, they acknowledged Oruarangi's importance.

Cook came within cooee of the other power nexus, but he didn't see it. Nor on my downriver journey did I. So overwhelmed is the landscape by the green pastures and flapping, orange electric fences of the dairy industry that I had no idea of Kakaramea, like Oruarangi, until I had seen its name on old charts and read about its significance.

After many years another ship of goblins came to Hauraki, and the goblins of this ship worked the kahikatea of Wai-hou, and took them away. And some time after this another ship came . . .

After rowing about 4 or 5 miles came to a large town, containing better houses than any we had seen before, finding the Captain to be here, we went ashore surrounded by the Chief (whose name is Hupa) his brother, and about 300 natives . . .

The natives call this town Kokremare, it is the residence of Hupa, and the second in magnitude to the towns, or villages about the river Thames. In the morning . . . the Captain went with the men, to make beginning of cutting down the timber, and gave a present to the chief who promised that the natives should assist in getting the timber to the water.

Had I known about Kakaramea I would have had some regard for the subtle, flat-topped rise above the main plain so plainly visible from the bridge over the Hikutaia where my journey began. It is nearly winter before I return to the creek. The willows whose soft leaves I pushed through in December are brown and leafless and the paddocks are becoming quagmires. And from the moment I turn out of the traffic into Ferry Road I approach the place differently.

The place that more permanent locals know as Pa Hill, its current owners in the house across the paddock know as nothing more than an elevated bit of their new farm. Kakaramea, that once stood pallisaded, high above anywhere else on the Waihou floodplain, confronting anyone who came up the river, has been incorporated into a catchment board stopbank and is surmounted by the concrete remains of a water tank.

But once you are standing on Kakaramea, its uniqueness is apparent straight away. Almost encircled by water, like Oruarangi, Kakaramea is effectively a river island, an island of anticipation whose inhabitants knew attack was as inevitable as flood. The current offensive suggests Kakaramea will not be here for much longer—the curving bank undercut by the muddy Hikutaia below me is spilling pipi shells from faraway beaches, firestones, charcoal and, when I look closer, bits of bottle glass that looks far too old to have something like *Dominion Breweries* or *ABC Bottlers* etched on it. Were I to hazard a guess at its origin, I would reach beyond the time in which the word 'dominion' has gathered its New Zealand meaning. The bottles have lain here since they did the job for which they—or what they contained in the 1790s—were brought up the river.

Only two pā—the 'hippah' of Oruarangi and Kakaramea—feature on William Wilson's 1801 *Chart of the River Thames in New Zealand*. Captain Wilson was as matter-of-fact about the purpose of his map as he was about the little village symbols surrounded by forest, swamp and water:

> As the object of ships going to the River Thames is to procure Spars, the best Season is from the beginning of November to the latter part of April, during the rest of the Year there are frequent gales from the Northward, when the anchorage is dangerous, and Spars taken on board with difficulty and fatigue . . . Short timber may be got from the Hehe a cheif [sic] on the Eastern, but the best Spars are at Kakramare and other parts of the small River.

The Europeanisation of a country, says Alfred Crosby in his book *Ecological Imperialism*, had three prerequisites. Firstly, the land had to have the qualities to attract Europeans and their organisms, which, secondly, had to arrive in suffi-cient quantities to disrupt the indigenous ecosystem and its dependent human society. And something

WILLIAM WILSON'S 1801
Chart of the River Thames

beyond mere desire for new things had to motivate the indigenous people to provide what the Europeans were used to wanting. Mutual advantage typified the early meetings of Europeans and Māori. Māori demand for the new domesticated food plants, clothes, metal and ideas was as aggressive—and avaricious—as the European interest in their timber and flax.

The South Pacific of the last years of the 18th century was not exactly a free market. Rules of empire embodied in monopolistic enterprises like the East India Company forbade private British vessels from trading, or even sailing, between the Horn and the Cape of Good Hope, unless their cargo was convicts or missionaries.

The first sight those on the *Royal Admiral* had of New Zealand after their arrival one night in 1801 was of laden canoes heading straight to the ship. Among the fish and kumara were turnips and the kind of potato that anyone from Britain would recognise: 'The potatoes and turnips are excellent, and superior to those of New South Wales, and are very plentiful over the Island we are informed.' It was clear immediately what the market-gardeners were after: 'Several canoes came alongside with fish to barter for iron tools . . . One of the hatchway bars and some odd iron tools were stolen by the native to day . . . On the 24th we were informed that two axes were stolen by the natives from the men at work. The Captain detained . . . some of the chiefs . . . however . . . they found means to escape. Three muskets were fired after them, but without effect . . . they . . . got clear away through to the wood.'

Ngāti Maru already knew what the white men really wanted. As one of the missionaries on the *Royal Admiral* said repeatedly during the weeks they stood in its stream, the river people seemed eager to dispose of their kahikatea. 'Since they had been here the natives behaved in a peaceful and friendly manner, and were cheerfully assisting them to get their timber . . . they had several trees cut down in the wood opposite the ship and in another place up the river . . . the natives . . . persuaded the captain to go to the easternmost shore to see the wood. Several canoes visited us today, and brought several things to barter, also a spar as a specimen of the wood on the shore opposite the ship.'

The reason the *Royal Admiral,* a convict ship by trade, was on the Waihou lay directly with William Wilson's London Missionary Society passengers. Cook's journals had scandalised England with accounts of the lewd Tahitians of Matavai Bay, but the River Thames in New Zealand was the only place where the great navigator had mentioned timber trees.

Well up the Waihou, another ship, the *Plumier,* was also loading spars, and indeed there had been many like it in the previous decade, ever since the celebrated arrival in Sydney on 15 April 1795 of the cutter *Fancy* with 'upwards of two hundred very fine trees, from sixty to one hundred and forty feet in length, fit for any use that the East India Company ships might require'.

Much of the interest in the *Fancy*'s cargo was because of the conjecture in Sydney the previous September when, armed to the hilt with Indian sepoys and 'a commission from the Bombay marine', she had so mysteriously slipped away. Her commander Mr Dell 'affected a secrecy with respect to his subsequent destination . . . but purported to be running to Norfolk Island'. However, from the number of cross-cut saws rumoured to be on board, the general surmise was that he 'was bound to some island whereas timber fit for naval purposes was to be procured'. His target was obviously New Zealand where 'force, or at least the appearance of it was there absolutely requisite'.

Smarting from the loss of several of the *Fancy*'s crew to territorial New Guineans earlier in the year, and undoubtedly aware of like news coming out of New Zealand since Cook had been in the River Thames, Dell was taking no risks. We may recoil at the image of Indian sepoys, armed to the teeth, stealthfully creeping through Hauraki harakeke, but most cultures go well armed to exploit a new land. In the event, in the three months the *Fancy* lay in the Waihou, although some seamen claimed 'in their usual enlarged style, that they had driven off and pursued upwards of three thousand of "these cannibals"', just two Ngāti Maru men and a woman were killed. Their only hindrance to the timber-getters had been their relentless thieving of axes, or any other iron they could get their hands on.

No one was more excited about the *Fancy*'s voyage than a lonely, driven man out in mid-Tasman who, forever looking out in the direction of New Zealand, saw the cutter arrive a few weeks earlier. Whenever Phillip Gidley King heard the ceaseless rustle of the flax blowing in the salty wind, he became frustrated at the very point of his isolation. Here he was, Lieutenant-Governor of the 'Pore Mersable Place' that was the convict colony of Norfolk Island, surrounded by what its discoverers had championed as tall pines and the flax said to be one of the most useful plants in the world, but with one proven useless and no chance of making the other useful. 'The flogging Govner' had tried to no avail, even kidnapping two Ngāpuhi from the Bay of Islands to teach the Norfolk convicts the ways with flax. To Phillip King, the *Fancy*'s news of the River Thames, like her new running rigging of flax, was proof a mistake had been made and vindication too of his campaign for a colony on New Zealand's 'Northern Island'. There, rather than the parched, infertile coast of New South Wales, was the sort of the place his kind of people should be. Finally he had the evidence.

When the *Fancy* landed in Sydney Cove, she carried in Dell's cabin, en route to the Governor of New South Wales and his superiors in London,

King's rave review of 1790s New Zealand. Fresh from Cook's River Thames
was a very different view of the land whose natives' savagery had cast shadow
on its prospects for British settlement. Within months, the masters of
Britain's colonies were reading about a River Thames of masting timber
and flax in which any ship may lay 'in perfect safety', whose natives 'on
many occasions assisted them very much', how on the *Fancy*'s departure:

> . . . the Natives regretted their separation, and promised very
> faithfully to take care of the spars they had cut . . . the timber
> grows in the greatest abundance in many places close to the banks
> of the river; which abounds in salmon, flounders, bream, soles
> and many other fish; also great quantities of crabs, clams &c Close
> to the place where the Fancy lay, some thousand acres of the flax
> plant were growing in a very luxurient manner.

And, as certainly was not ignored on the *Fancy*'s arrival in Sydney, the
New Zealanders had, contrary to their reputation, made no attempt 'to
become the masters'—something to consider should the Governor ever think
this extraordinary river 'an object worthy of his attention'.

The voyage of the *Fancy* had broken the seal on the plain of Cook's
promise. As her men stepped ashore at Sydney Cove, autumn rain fell on
quagmires of stumps and flooded over chips of ancient white wood their
feet had ground into river mud. In raupō huts at Oruarangi, Te Kari and
Kakaramea, Ngāti Maru admired the blades of the axes their river's wealth
had brought and looked at the new gaps in its banks.

Even with the big trees gone there are long, lonely stretches of the Waihou
downstream from Te Kari where, on misty, wet days with the hills invisible
and the river's low banks forming the horizon, it is so flat it doesn't seem
like New Zealand at all. Sitting low on its broad sheet of water as James
Cook and William Wilson must have, you can imagine, believe even, that it
really does continue 'pretty much the same' for hundreds of miles.

William Wilson's faith in his *Chart of the River Thames in New
Zealand* came from more than his own observations. Unlike the great
navigator 30 years earlier, he and the missionaries who wandered around

the river banks had time on their side. They knew they were exactly where Cook had been: on one of their trips ashore, the missionaries met an old chief who brought out of hiding a firing piece with the words *Joseph Banks Esq* engraved into the brass.

Everything in their reports confirmed a far more populous landscape than the *Endeavour* journals conveyed. 'In going up the creek we saw a great number of huts, several canoes and a multitude of natives. We also saw several large tracts of land apparently good and in a state of cultivation, enclosed and divided into many small portions.' Unlike 'the careless Indians of New South Wales' Ngāti Maru seemed 'capable and eager to learn any thing from the European'. Their soils, moreover, 'would produce anything that is cultivated in Europe'.

Their bodies bore the telltale signs that they could too. Venereal disease told as plainly as potatoes and turnips that, by 1800, Europe had arrived. The blond-haired children that soon appeared along the Waihou's banks—and the complaints of the river's chiefs that 'their women had been inveighed on board . . . for such refreshments as the place afforded, and then carried off'—corroborated James Cook's and Joseph Banks' regard for its hospitality.

But any prosperity from Ngāti Maru's tree sales was as fleeting as a spring tide. It was simple human ecology: in the filthy blankets of barter worn wet or dry, night and day, the strange diseases the Europeans carried with them flourished in the low-lying ground. Tempting Māori away from their hilltop pā down into these more productive but less healthy riverbanks, this era between the visits of James Cook and 1840 is believed to have seen a plummeting of the Māori population of Aotearoa.

Floating just ahead of knowledge, the New Zealand of European imagination in 1801 was an image of unlimited possibility. William Wilson's *Chart of the River Thames in New Zealand* did nothing to dispel it. His low, flat valley 'said to extend to the Southward as far as Cook's Straits and having a navigable stream for canoes for most of the way' seems absurd to us, but it froze the dream in history. It took such firm hold that settlement plans as late as the 1830s described the average soil of the North Island as 'a rich alluvial'.

For those beginning to promote and market the dream this was not inconvenient. The dismayed masters of Australia's First Fleet might have proved James Cook's Botany Bay 'meadows' a mirage, but it was still possible to believe his great New Zealand river of timber and flax flowed serenely all the way to the strait that bore his name—especially if the natives said so. If the sealers and whalers now ranging round the wild shores knew otherwise, they weren't writing home about it. Few of those busy bartering muskets for women were in contact with the dreamers of settlement schemes, those in the educated circles likely to procure, say, John Savage's 1807 *Account of New Zealand*, and on its first page read that:

> Remote in Southern Seas an Island lies
> Of ample Space, and bless'd with genial Skies
> Where shelter'd still by never-fading groves,
> The friendly Native dwells, and fearless roves;
> Where the tall Forest and the Plains around,
> And Waters wide, with various Wealth abound.

For two hours I have been pushing against the wind. Even with the tide falling, and running with the flood, the nor'westerly coming up the Waihou has made it seem I'm dragging an anchor. Perhaps this is what upset James Cook's plan to drift back to *Endeavour* on the ebbing tide. Perhaps it was here where the river chop fills the canoe that the *Royal Admiral*'s crew, three decades after Cook, kept losing their rafts of kahikatea spars before they could be loaded.

Rounding the last big bend into the long reach down to Turua, I can see the dairy factory's high roof 5 km away. Above the wind, the noise of roaring water, strange in this flatness, is soon filling the landscape. Frothing cascades of water, muddy and full, pour out of floodgates and down the crumbling bank—a drain emptying its twice-daily load. The shore beyond is a soft scree of collapsing land and the debris of failed erosion control. Whoever has taken on the task is throwing everything they can at it: old tyres, bits of cars, four-by-twos, waratahs and nylon cloth have been brought in to save the pasture in what seems, from a canoe on the river, a hopeless business.

As the flow takes me away, I think of the abandoned river diversions, the concrete and ironwork of superseded floodgates and the stopbanks that have been in my landscape all day. Water will always find its way through the country, and the ground that is collapsing is, after all, simply river matter temporarily taking time out, before it is on the move again. How a great river like this works as maker of the landscape, sculptor, fertiliser, diminisher of human effort, will always remain unknown. Why did it make a turn there, and head out in that direction where the wind is coming from, instead of over here? Was it just the lie of the old land that causes where I am now to be river, or was it a weak point centuries ago in some flax on the bank that let a trickle through to cut a new path? I can't help thinking that these crumbling banks are caused by more than water, that what swept past when they had their flax, their toetoe and native trees, would have been cleaner.

The wind whistles through the arc of wire that reaches from pylon to pylon above the widening, muddy vastness. I have lost interest in the shoreline of erosion plantings and out-of-season maimai. Relief floods into my arms as the buildings of Turua begin to dominate the view where, a century ago, tall ships and stacks of timber would have. A photograph from those days, 1892, shows a three-masted barque, 'loading N.Z. White Pine at Turua for use by Australian butter box makers . . .', and a sprawling timber yard above the sloping muddy bank, rows and rows of tall stacks of kahikatea, cut thin for the export trade, stretching from the wharf and out of view.

Underwriting that scene was the discovery of refrigerated shipping in 1882, and the sudden demand for millions of butter-boxes and packing cases. Kahikatea's soft, pale, odourless wood was perfect. For the Bagnall brothers, lumbermen from Prince Edward Island in Canada's Gulf of St Lawrence, the fortuitous acquisition of a New Zealand riverbank mill in 1877 must have been like discovering gold.

Some people regard the sudden capability to send dairy products and meat to the other side of the world as the best thing that ever happened to New Zealand, the true foundation of the Britain of the South's Golden Age. Others like Roderick Finlayson believe 'no single act of modern sorcery has been so destructive of our soil, our health and our social structure':

> Now the settlers were able to ship abroad, frozen in a state of suspended decay . . . This industrialisation was again increased a hundredfold by the invention and use of machinery for the milking of huge herds of cows. Till soon practically all of the easily available land, especially in the North Island, became a grazing ground . . . It made impossible the harmony of man with Nature, and destroyed the hope of a social harmony founded upon that

harmony. All that was left undestroyed of whatever was indigenous and native, man or bird or vegetation, began to wither and die.

Much of that busy 1890s riverbank has been swept out to sea. Lines of stakes driven into the mud are all that survive of the vain attempts to hold it against tide and flood. My gravelly landing is watched by a pair of goats keeping their feet dry on a block of crumbling concrete, the only hint of the mill that was here. I step out and stretch legs that have spent the last four hours confined. Pulling the canoe out of the flow, I realise that, under the fennel and tall fescue keeping the riverbank on hold, are thousands of slowly rotting heaps of algae-covered slats of sawn kahikatea, collapsed just as you would imagine the neat stacks in a timber yard, were the ground beneath them suddenly to disappear. Irony indeed, these invisible remains of what Thomas Kirk called one of New Zealand's most striking sights shoring up the land against the river of their vanishing.

Gordon Fisher remembered the 1890s timber-getters as like men at a goldrush:

> *First the crosscutters would fell the trees and saw off the heads, then came the tramlayers and then the jackers who would jack the logs on to the trams for the journey to the river's edge. There they were made into large rafts . . . The bushmen also wore specially nailed boots for a foothold on the slippery logs. Only the best timber was taken out in the first cutting. Some years later a second cutting was made and steam haulers with winches and long wire ropes were used . . . As the boundaries of those who had cutting rights were often not identified disputes would arise between the cutting gangs and it would be dangerous and nerve-wracking to be standing in the path of a suddenly falling tree.*

Shirley Bagnall saw the slats being made, the muddy logs coming into the mill, some with ferns on, rolled onto skids, jacked up ready for the big breaking-down saw, severed, on through the circular saw, trimmed and measured and wheeled away to be stacked and dried ready for another ship from Australia. 'Such large stacks they were, at times, completely hiding our view of the river which ran so close by.'

The slats must have lain here 70 years. Some have rotted away completely, but others are still as hard as the day the Bagnalls' saws cut them. Plains settlers like Gordon Fisher's family learned the hard way about the 'two types of kahikatea; the white pine called "Cowrie" used largely for butter-boxes, and the yellow kahikatea durable for building purposes and equal to any timber'. But it was many years before kahikatea's first exporters realised that the towering spars in the swamps of James Cook's famous river had nothing of the durability of trees from dry sites.

The 213 kahikatea spars which the *Fancy* brought to Sydney Cove in April 1795—the longest and straightest spars that had ever been seen on an English ship—caused a sensation not quickly forgotten in a town reliant on gum trees for timber. Whether in masts, hulls or buildings though, kahikatea soon sullied its reputation. John Bigge's 1820 Inquiry into the State of New South Wales heard how most of the timber imported from New Zealand had been 'the inferior species called kaikatina, and it has been easily used either for naval or domestic purposes. The Americans, who have visited New Zealand, consider it well adapted for the China market, and have also used it in the repairs of their own vessels.' Robert Elwes, master of the *Coromandel* wrote from the River Thames how 'the Krycatera abounds most in swampy places', but that while Māori carved their canoes from it, they did not 'speak in favour of its durability'. Thomas Moore, Superintendent of the Sydney Cove Dockyard, 'put very little value upon it, I do not think it fit either for masts or any other kind of work from its liability to Decay . . . although it is tough when it is first cut Down, it becomes very brittle when Dry.'

Samuel Marsden displayed his foresight by asserting that Britain need not go to the expense of *colonising* New Zealand to 'derive all the advantages', spars and timber for example. His missionaries had read their Cook's Journals well enough to know where the Pacific's best wood stood. Faraway in Tahiti, the Thames' kahikatea which the *Royal Admiral* had delivered to build the Matavai Bay mission was rotten within five years. In the information network of the early 19th-century South Pacific, Joseph Banks' 'Noble timber' soon ensured the river trees of New Zealand's River Thames were being sailed past. When the launch from the naval store ship *Coromandel* returned from examining the river in 1814, it was to report friendly natives everywhere and 'immense forests of the wood called Cacitea close to the river, but no cowrie'.

Some of the friendly natives may still have been here at Turua living among the rotting palisading and earthworks of the old pā, where the

Hauraki Sawmilling Company, 50 years later, erected their mill and wharves. I'm aware of a face at a kitchen window watching me warily as I poke about in the shell heaps exposed in the old mill's drains where I guess Turua Pā's canoe-landing became Mill Creek. Briefly back in the canoe, I land finally at a concrete boat-ramp poking into the muddy torrent, not muddy enough though to disguise the fact that the Waihou at Turua Mill is no longer the 'deep water close to the bank' of a century ago.

Turua was 'to all intents and purposes' an island in 1892, 'an abode of desolation' dominated by a huge pile of sawdust stretching hundreds of yards along the river. To come and go, you went by boat. Inland was bush 'extending for miles across to the Piako, the trees standing in a great tidal swamp', a hunter's landscape unimaginable to those who stalk its stopbanks today.

> *Thurs 2nd July, 1891*
> *. . . At about 1 pm we get our boat off. A heavy fog comes on. We landed at shell bank or bar at mouth of Thames River in hopes of getting a shot at some curlew, continued pulling, and at about 5.30pm reached the telegraph tower on bank of Thames river. Hauled our boat up. Put provis. etc. in . . . shanty. Some tucker. Then go out on swamp. Build titree ambush alongside of pond and wait for ducks. Bang at hawk. No ducks, wait till 6.30pm. Short bagged a teal. Loses one, another 3 . . .*
> *Rose at 7am go out in hopes of getting a shot. Rise a pheasant., a bittern and turn out a weka. Not able to get a shot at either. Lough misses a pukeka and Short stayed in bunk . . . at about 4pm go into swamp up to the knees in black stinking mud at every step build ambushes alongside big pond. wait for ducks. down comes a passing rain. Ducks plentiful but settle in swamp grass, not in pond.*
>
> *Easter Monday 26 March, 1894*
> *Early in morning after. Got a few. After breakfast Natives down again for more boxing etc. playing cards with them. At 2 pm say good bye, strike camp, on boat and start for home. Do some shooting while coming down the river . . . See pukekas land. Take two guns and revolver. A couple of bullocks looked rather ferocious and one began to sail for us. My maroon guernsey and red scarf no doubt attracted his attention. I put a bullet into him*

*from the revolver. Not likeing that treatment he cleared. Seeing
a big boar about 3cwt all head and shoulders Mr Stevenson stalked
him and shot him in the head. He got into the scrub and we lost
him. I shot a smaller one however with revolver, Cleaned it.
Another start for home. Stuck on mud off Thames, out and push
boat. Get to Thames at 8 pm. 25 brace of birds, ducks and teal.*

Friday, 26th June, 1894
*In morning stroll through settlement Maoris busy thatching
whares, erecting others, making fences preparatory to planting
riwais. Give our bloke some fish. Go to outskirts of kahikatea
bush—no pigeons—hear a few kakas. Drift down river no ducks—
two fly . . . Leave Kerepehi and pull down the river . . . shot
pukeka. Two beautiful swans sail up river—too far for a shot.
Stop at stockyard, have yarn to Māoris give them the last bundle
of fish.*

Saturday, 27th June, 1894
*Pukeka shooting . . . Dick made a pukeka stew (a dab hand at
cooking) . . . bats flying around. Teal began to pour into the pond.
No light could not get a shot—missed some wounded others. Two
swans came over. One settled on my pond . . . flopped about. I
rushed out but he rose and flew . . .*

Back at the Thames goldfields school where he taught, his classroom
may have resounded with shrill voices singing of '. . . the glory of the South
where all the face of Nature smiles, where noble forest crown the hills, and
streamlets thread the vales', the song with which they welcomed Governor
Grey to their 'happy home in fair New Zealand's Isles', where they 'love to
stroll in summer's morn, and gather flow'rs and ferns and moss . . . shelter
'neath the trees and hear the tui's Song . . . on this British Southern soil'.

In reality, the Britain of the South was the 'thousands of cattle
browsing on the finest pasture in New Zealand' that enthralled a *Weekly
News* reporter in 1918: 'hundreds of people are living where ten years
ago the wild duck and the pukeko had their haunts'. The Hauraki Plains,
another said, depended more upon their fertility and production of
wealth than upon their 'picturesqueness'. Underlying this view of New
Zealand was what James Cook said he had seen and Britain's Home
Office had described as 'Formed of a Virgin Mould, undisturbed since

the Creation'—recognising its superiority to 'the exhausted Soil of Europe'.

Ironically, the changes on the Hauraki Plains began just as the government first responded to anxiety that New Zealand's native scenery was vanishing and commissioned a plan to preserve it. A levels survey was commissioned in 1902, and by 1908 the government had the legal machinery to compulsorily acquire Māori plains land. By 1911 the Hauraki Plains Act had 5200 acres drained and burnt ready for balloting to eager, waiting settlers: the 'splendid results' that newspaper columnists of the day loved writing about. Changing 'useless swamp into rich farm land', making 'a wilderness carry a prosperous population and produce ever increasing wealth', building stopbanks 'to prevent the tide backing up over the flats and . . . the rivers from spreading where they chose', straightening and deepening the rivers so that 'their surplus waters could quickly reach the sea', cutting great drains 'to free the land from surplus water' was, they said 'work of which any community may well be proud'.

By 1914 when the Hauraki Plains' first dairy factory opened for business—at Turua—Europe held an astonishing 85 per cent of the earth's land area as dominions like New Zealand, as colonies, protectorates, dependencies and commonwealths. Of empire's enterprises, converting an antipodean forest's soil into butter, freezing it in boxes from wood of a primordial tree from the same forest and sailing it to corner shops on the other side of the world without tainting, was merely one of the connections by which the world, as William McNeill says in *The Politics of Power*, was united 'into a single interacting whole as never before'.

But in the landscape of supply a crisis was looming. Anxious at the vast volume of kahikatea leaving for Australia from mills like Bagnall Bros. at Turua, William Cook of the Palmerston North Cooperage and Butter-box Factory told the Premier, Richard Seddon, that such a timber 'can never be replaced' and would be almost unprocurable in 20 years: 'Sawmillers have a good market for all they can supply, at good prices, and by conserving the timber Government will save the colony hundreds of thousands of pounds and give employment to hundreds of men . . . By placing a heavy export duty you will benefit both the sawmilling and also the working-men of this Island.'

The early 1900s were also the flax industry's boom years. Flax mills needed huge timber volumes to fuel their noisy stampers. And most flax swamps had easy, soft-wooded kahikatea right alongside. The National Dairy Association urged Seddon 'to preserve the white-pine bush, and prevent the wholesale destruction of this timber . . . now taking place'. Nothing happened. Between 1909 and 1916 the national remains of kahikatea more than halved from over 2,600 million superfeet to 1,117 million. By winter 1917 it was down to 985 million.

In 1913 the Bagnall Bros started winding things down, running their Turua mill only intermittently, sending fewer crosscutters out into the remains of the forest than they had 'cleaning up'—stumping and burning, and scattering grass seed. While Europe inched towards war, a Royal Commission was asked to decide in what manner the areas of New Zealand 'still under standing forest' should be dealt with. 'No forest land . . . which is suitable for farm land,' decided the two farmers, surveyor, builder, furniture manufacturer, and the botanist Leonard Cockayne, 'except it be required for the special purposes of a climatic or a scenic reserve . . . should be permitted to remain under forest if it can be occupied and resided upon.' On one kind of forest they were pleased to report complete unanimity:

> *As is well known the soil of the white-pine swamps, when drained and the trees removed, forms one of the richest of agricultural land, which when grassed, is extremely useful for dairy farms . . . Since no land is more suitable for occupation than that of the white-pine swamps, when drained . . . their value in this regard is a strong plea in favour of the removal of the trees forthwith.*

The government quickly adopted the idea. Kahikatea occupied country suitable for 'close settlement', and 'in view of the pressing demand for, and limited area of first-class land in New Zealand', it had to go.

Soon, however, the Forest Service was anxiously reporting that settlers acquiring kahikatea forests were not even waiting for a sawmiller to fell them. Within two decades, it was questioning the wisdom of the use of 'the Dominion's white-pine' being determined by the dairy industry's craving to supply the British market. By 1947 any reference to kahikatea was in the past tense: 'These forests stood in the main on swampy lowlands or good rich land which has now been converted into dairy-farms . . .'

I look downriver at the sprawling flatness. Somewhere out there Oruarangi lies low and invisible—and today, unreachable. I drag the canoe up the concrete ramp from the river through a strandline of mangrove seeds, left from the top surge of the last big tide, drying in the sun, a reminder that the sea is a factor here, even if out of sight. The noise disturbs a white-faced heron feeding along the tide line. It lifts off, arcs out over the river and turns landwards. I watch it disappear beyond Turua's houses and into the unmistakeable shapes of kahikatea trees. After a long day of canoeing past unceasing willows, pasture and stopbanks, I elect to follow.

I had heard that the Bagnall Bros had left a trace of the ancient plains forest for future generations to ponder. In 1937 one of the Bagnall children wrote a piece in *The New Zealand Herald* called 'Where the Village slew the Forest', about a 'grand and noble forest' and 'the beginning of the end for the feathered world that inhabited its depths'. Many years later another, Shirley Bagnall, began to feel deep sorrow at the death of 'trees that had taken such ages to grow. Trees that had sheltered the birds and had lived as the song says "intimately with rain", that had thrust their heads skywards seeking the light, and had clothed themselves in the beauty of their foliage.'

Any hope that Turua Domain may hold a sense of James Cook's 'imence woods' evaporates as soon as I see it. Swamp forest has become dry woodland. Beneath the trees, grass and sheep govern. Ferns and mosses have long yielded to nightshade, ink weed, dock and thistles. From the stumps it would seem someone comes and fells each tree as it dies. The heron I have followed from the river reveals itself one of a nesting pair, this the best roost they can find. But it decides I'm a nuisance and heads back to its supper.

Somewhere just near here, a settler's daughter remembered fantails coming to perch on her outstretched arms—as vivid a memory as her arrival on the plains in 1915, her younger brother in the pushchair her mother dragged along a track of mud and water from the wharf to their balloted block. And where we see Australian herons nesting, Hazel Kingsford loved to watch great flocks of shags encircling the kahikatea, 'the sky looking quite black for a while, and then lighter and lighter as more and more found their own favourite resting place, so often fighting in the flurried way to hold their position. In the morning we watched the same scene in reverse, as the first birds woke, took to the air and hovered over, round and round until all were awake and ready to take off back to the seas again.'

Aldo Leopold tuned his land ethic over the years, but he never gave up its key idea: we have duties to the ecosystems with which we share the world and that sustain us in it. They are more than just commodities for us. They contain life forces we have to learn to live *with*, to respect, to revere in fact.

Had Leopold seen the Hauraki Plains as they are today, it could only have confirmed his theory. In the patchwork squares of dairy farms, and rivers sealed from their floodplains, he would have recognised a parallel with his vanished American prairie in the obliteration of their natural ecosystems and production capacity. It was Leopold, with his poet's eye, who once perceived 'that only the mountain has lived long enough to listen objectively to the howl of the wolf'. To live sustainably with any country, he believed, we have to evolve an agriculture that fits within and works in concert with its native ecosystem.

The keys are conservation and restoration ecology. But where do we start learning about such things in a landscape like this? Where are the places that show us what nature intended for the plains? Over the years, settler families have given tiny bits and pieces of dried-out, weed-infested floodplain bush like Turua Domain to the County—one, Speedy's Bush, is even on the cover of its centennial history. Government conservation agencies have protected other scraps: two hectares of kanuka forest on a stream terrace near Morrinsville; two small remnant peat lakes with rush, raupō, manuka just as far inland near Patetonga; over 800 hectares of willow-infested flax, rush and raupō swamp on the banks of the Piako River. On the coast near Miranda, eight hectares of shell banks have been excluded from farming for migratory wading birds. Inland, the 7,000 hectares of natural wetland forming the huge Kopuatahi peat dome keep apart the catchments of the Waihou and the Piako Rivers, and still resist farm development. Most of the mangrove woodlands that Cook saw at the mouth of the Waihou are still there. But of the great floodplain and levee forests with silt high in their branches there is not a single stand.

Almost all the landscapes New Zealand's plains people now live in are like this. They were made so, by choice, by Cook's 'Industrus people' expressing their economic drive and aesthetic preferences in what was, in effect, a campaign against nature. But what might New Zealand have become if it *had* all been the low, flat country whose 'average soil was a rich alluvial' that the New Zealand Company told its settlers to expect?

Conservation has gained great support in New Zealand in the late 20th century. Nonetheless, many of our country's unique ecosystems are collapsing. The ecologists who contemplate the ecosystems' disrupted food chains and successions and their incapacity to maintain themselves in the aftermath of invasion by alien pests and predators, and look vainly for solutions, liken themselves to cancer biologists. Nowhere is the damage worse than in these lowland river plains.

The plains' fertility will ensure their land values will remain high and their soils will produce wealth long after the forest has returned to the clay hills. But agriculture's history doesn't promise permanence for any society that has so consumed the land's natural capital it has removed the process that created it. Still tapu and wild in 1840, the Waihou reminded George Clarke of 'the Nile at the time it overflows its banks'. A thousand years before the birth of Christ the Egyptians who depended on the Nile's life-giving silt, and whose taxes rose with the magnitude of flood, outlawed the practice of flood control. 'Do not hinder the waters of inundation,' ordered the Book of the Dead. At the end of the 20th century, however, the notion of the Waihou as anything but nuisance and adversary is unheard of.

Many times since the victories of the drainage engineers of the early 1900s the river has been trying to tell the plains people that it would prefer to be creeping and seeping over its floodplain as it did for thousands of years, rather than squeezing between high stopbank walls. When the Waihou behaves as the Mississippi did in 1993 and breaks its confinement, will we allow the river to retain some of what it reclaims—as the Mississippi has been allowed—or will we send bulldozers to push silt back up the failed stopbanks and make new ones?

Our answer depends on our tussle with a wider question: how, as inhabitants of a world that has realised there are no more fertile plains like this to discover, we decide to live and act in it long-term. Do we continue making the plains a product of people who believe the more physical power they can bring to bear on nature, the less spiritual power it will have over them? Or will that notion prove as ephemeral as the empire that brought it here? Will we in its wake decide survival depends on interdependence with nature?

I read many stories preparing for this journey, from genealogies and the presumptuous remarks of explorers to passages about the riverbank's 'strange, secret villages'. One had particular resonance:

It was manifest that a land which nourishes the stateliest forests and the densest underwood in the world, must be eminently fertile.

Throughout the lower part, the river is skirted by belts of wood, consisting chiefly of the Kaitkatea, interspersed with Puridi, rima and other hard woods of considerable value. These trees are of great size, and will, doubtless, in progress of time, constitute an important resource to the inhabitants. The belts of wood alternate with extensive fields of the flax plant, growing so closely that it is impossible to force a passage through them; and with spaces, overgrown with ferns, myrtles, grasses, and cabbage palms, constituting a mixed brushwood, which offers but very little impediment to the plough, and in dry weather can be burnt down with ease. In many parts of the plain, formerly under native cultivation, we observe grass in considerable abundance . . . my friend Ngata remarked that the soil was 'kapai mo te wheat,' meaning that it was very good for the production of that inestimable plant . . .

The year was 1840. The scene was witnessed by an English traveller and quoted in a pamphlet by one Theophilus Heale, a New Zealand Company settler whose image of arcadia had been upset by his company choosing the Hutt Valley for its first settlement. I think I know why the passage made an impression on me. He exaggerates, and he has not yet got his tree names right. But there is something else too, a fleeting prospect of coexistence with the pattern of nature that had created such fertility—a brief possibility of a way of life *with* Nature that learnt *from* it. Far from boundless, Cook's 'imence woods' were a mosaic of forest patches and flax swamp—what an ecologist might expect where changing climates and a rising land have lifted an estuary from the tide's ebb and flow across its mudflats, where water wandering at will for thousands of years has built a rich, nourishing ground of silt, sand and organic matter.

'I think it is plain,' Theophilus Heale ended his tract, 'Captain Cook saw, with a prophetic eye, when he declared the district of the Thames was the site for a capital of New Zealand.' John Bidwill, a botanist who saw it a year later, went even further. It was, he believed, 'one of the most splendid situations for a Colony that could be found in the whole world'.

Many people love the geometric tapestry of a broad, farmed plain. As an ecologist, forever on the lookout for signals from the wild state, I see history's invisible violence in the Hauraki Plains' monotonous geometry of long straights, stopbanks and shelterbelts bending in the wind. There is tragedy in nature's absence. It is only in the most recent phase in human history that we have had this consuming interest in fertile, temperate plains. Indeed, where in the world has agricultural *Homo sapiens* allowed such country to keep its forest? As the screws tighten on a world creating too many people for its natural capital to sustain, ecology's philosophers are pleading with us to think twice about our indifference to nature.

If there is such a notion as the Spirit of the Plains, it is likely to have more than a little to do with what Theophilus Heale and George Clarke said they saw. Yet life at Hauraki goes on as though the Spirit of the Plains is a drainage engineer. In human history's terms, we have, as John Mulgan says in *Report on Experience*, only just begun to live in this country, but already we've consumed its richest native ecosystems with our awesome capacity to remove every trace of nature that obstructs our plans or doesn't serve our immediate needs. We have led other ecosystems to within what Jonathon Porritt calls a footfall of extinction. One of the world's youngest and least populated societies, we are also one of its most demanding. We like others to imagine New Zealand as pristine and untarnished. Yet many New Zealanders remain blind to the enormity of their culture's destructiveness. For a culture faced with living sustainably in a finite world, these plains of our beginnings are a landscape of warning.

THE PERFECT VALE

CHAPTER TWO

I T WAS ONE of those clear Cook Strait summer mornings. The wind
from the south that seemed forever to flatten the forest against the
steep harbour edge had cleared away. The sea surged against the dark
rocks, its spray wedging the riders against the wall of wild antipodean
verdure. Then suddenly the high, steep land gave way to sand and gravel,
and what the lieutenant colonel called a delta. Scattering the screeching gulls,
he cantered away from the hill to the crest of the storm beach, from which
he could see far up the valley. 'It is certainly worth fighting for,' he would
write. 'Richly alluvial, and therefore by the natives vehemently disputed
. . . the vale itself seems perfectly flat, the soil very rich, the timber magnificent . . . not less than 30,000 acres of what will be first-rate meadow land,
when the bush shall have yielded to the axe and saw.'

A cursory glance at the pā in the sandhills, its fence 'still decorated
with the hideous symbols of the Heathen', and the horsemen were riding
along the great swathe the settlers had cut inland through the windswept
coastal scrub. Crossing the flat toward the gap in the bush beyond, they
could sense the trees getting taller and taller as the sea fell behind.

They were soon into flax country, a swamp that ran through to bush
of great vine-tangled trees. To a military mind, the land reeked with danger,
and it was with some relief they saw the new stockade walls of Fort Richmond through the foliage. Beyond the clearing was even taller forest. Here,
in the extraordinary, ambivalent language of his type and times, is what the
rider saw; one moment a luxurious kaleidoscope, the next as treacherous a
threat a colony could offer:

Leaving the little fort, we spurred along a fine wide road—as long and straight as a French chaussée. Right and left to a distance of fifty or sixty feet, the timber had been felled, and beyond this arose the tall, tangled and impervious forest. Many of the trees were of majestic growth, and several—among others, the Kaikatera—are very valuable as timber, for hard and durable qualities.

Some of the tree ferns must have been not less than forty or fifty feet high, shooting their slender stems through the dense underwood, and spreading their wide and delicate fronds to the upper air like so many Hindostanee umbrellas. A hundred feet above them tower the ruder giants of the forest, yielding them that shade and shelter which, both in New South Wales and New Zealand seems necessary to their existence. What would some of my fern-fancying friends have given for my opportunity!—for the arborescent fern was by no means the only kind here. Hundreds of beautiful specimens, infinite in variety, arrested one's attention at every step. Innumerable parasites and climbing plants, vegetable boa-constrictors in appearance, flung their huge coils from tree to tree, from branch to branch—dropping to the earth, taking root again, running for a space along the surface, swarming up and stifling in their strict embrace some young and tender sapling, anon, as if in pure ficklesness, grappling and adopting some withered and decayed stump, arraying and disguising its superannuated form in all the splendour of their own bright leaves, and blossoms, and fruits; and having reached the top, casting their light festoons to the wind, until they caught the next chance object. Grand broadleaved ferns, palmated like the horns of the elk, niched themselves grotesquely in the forks of the oldest trees; and another kind, long and wide as a double-handed sword, looked so unlike a fern, as not to be recognisable but by the mode of carrying its seed. Enormous mistletoes hung upon, and seemed, like vampires, to exhaust the life-blood of the plants on which they had fixed their fatal affections. The graceful clematis spangled the dark recesses of the groves with its silver stars. Below was a carpet of lichens, and mosses, and fungi, among which the kareau, or Supple-jack, matted the ground kneedeep with its tough network. I had not advanced fifty paces into the bush, with the intent of measuring one of the tree-ferns, ere I was completely made prisoner by its prehensile webs, and did not escape with a whole coat or skin. A plague on such country for campaigning! I willingly admit that, if pushed by superior orders into a bush of this nature (for no will of my own would take me into such a position) with a party of first-rate British light-infantry—aye, even my own old company of the gallant 43rd—and told that only an equal force of Maoris opposed me, I should consider my men, myself, and my credit, in a very critical predicament!

It is unquestionable that a road like the noble one we were now travelling on, running right through the heart of a new country inhabited by a savage and undisciplined people is as fatal to their continued resistance as the thrust of a rapier through that of an individual foe. Yet at present, even with this fine and level thoroughfare, passable for any kind of vehicle and ordnance, and with its quasi-cleared margin . . . an English force, however well composed, marching along it with aggressive purposes, would be exposed to great risk of discomfiture. The clearings are encumbered with gigantic felled trees, some of them six or eight feet in diameter, with spreading tops, affording excellent cover for an enemy clever at skirmishing, obstructing the operations of flanking parties . . . delaying the advance of the main body; while the bush itself, absolutely impervious to the belted, booted, chaco-ed and comparatively clumsy soldier, has paths along which the naked savage, with his double-barrelled piece, can—as he has proved—move on the flanks of the regulars as fast as the latter can march along a smooth road. This, therefore, will not be a military road, until both sides have been cleared to the distance of a musket shot, and that can only be done gradually by the axe and the settler.

The year was 1846—exactly a century before I was born—the rider Godfrey Mundy, a British army officer from India visiting the empire's latest colony. Some of my earliest memories are from the countless childhood journeys along Godfrey Mundy's 'noble road' to and from our new Hutt Valley house in the manuka and my aunties' old Wellington houses. It's still 'as long and straight as a French chaussée', if no longer as elegantly wide. But no one ever told me its origins were military.

It was in this stretch of country of constant mechanical noise and movement that I first became aware of the history that made me. Where Godfrey Mundy saw gigantic kahikatea and treeferns spreading their fronds to the upper air, I first felt the need to know why it was barely possible in New Zealand anymore to walk from a flat, sandy beach into its forest.

What must it have been like, I wondered, to sense the sea gradually disappear behind trees and vines.

Today, the landscape in which Godfrey Mundy turned his horse away from Pito-one Pā and pointed it off the beach toward the forest is filled with the roar of traffic on a highway interchange. In its midst, a tiny, surveyed-off rectangle of grass and graves is all that remains of Pito-one Pā. Cars and trucks pick their way through the surrounding grid of factories and warehouses. Not long ago, when the sea you occasionally glimpse between buildings was reddened daily with the blood of sheep and cattle, the same narrow streets were packed with freezing workers' houses. Now mirror glass and concrete have taken over.

Further along the track when Mundy met the flax and manuka of Te Mome Swamp, Door City advertises 'Automatics at $499' among countless other word-beacons—Welcome to Craig Lyne Motors, Compressed Air Equipment, Plastic Wholesalers, Takeaway, Discount. The Settlers' Motel hints at the past, but the only sign of it is the faded green Art Deco stucco of the Regent Flats.

From the railway overbridge you can trace the route of Godfrey Mundy's ride across Te Mome, between the repeating roof pattern of Victorian and Edwardian houses packed into tiny fenced rectangles, past the Ados glue factory and its stacks of red 40-gallon drums of chemicals, a wrecker's yard and a dairy. A phantom of the swamp lurks in a pumping station and street that bear its name.

Had Mundy made his ride 30 years later he would have seen the same railway. But of the great forest and swamp, so manifestly wild, he would have seen hardly a tree or a lingering flax bush. With the cottages and cart, horse and bullock teams that 'gave a dash of Home to the picture', the few settler clearings he saw in 1846—'more or less perfect, and, in peaceful contrast with the wild woodland'—had coalesced into a landscape of fields and fences spread right across the valley. So had the roadside English weeds: 'proof, if proof were wanting that . . . evil as well as good has crossed the seas and taken root on this land, with British occupation'. But the hundreds of parakeets 'of beauteous dyes, but odious accents' he saw feeding on the thistle-heads were gone.

Somewhere along the railway in the winter of 1882, before today's tight grid of streets was laid out, William Adkin, a young draper from Leicestershire, fresh off the ship, fancied he was on an English road. The chirping of sparrows and a lark 'high in the air singing with all his might, make one almost forget that it is on New Zealand soil that I stand . . . Stepped over a fence where some clearing was going on. Saw a huge tree (still standing) on fire, this being the way in which they are improved off the face of the earth.'

Godfrey Mundy's 'entangled and impervious forest' hasn't quite vanished. A few nīkau palms can still be seen in the centre of Lower Hutt. Countless 19th-century travellers said of the forests they saw in New Zealand the 'elegant nikau palms give them quite a tropical aspect'. Alfred Ludlam certainly thought so. Taking over Francis Molesworth's estate when he returned to England in 1845, Ludlam began a garden and kept the nīkau as centrepieces. When he died, in 1877, James McNab bought the land and turned Ludlam's venture into public gardens. By the 1890s 'the nikaus, ferns, palm trees, rata and other representatives of the New Zealand forest' were 'the most pleasing features' of 'a favourite resort'. Some of the nīkau that spread their fronds over Victorian rosebeds managed to survive the gardens' subdivision into house lots in the 1940s, when the campaign to have Ludlam's vision preserved for the nation failed.

With domestication, the native living memory of a place dies. There is something mythic, now, about Edward Jerningham Wakefield's first impression, in 1839, of this place being 'covered with high forest to within a mile and a half of the beach, when swamps full of flax, and a belt of sand-hummocks intervened'. There is no hint of it in the bronze and concrete that celebrate his settlement company's colonists' arrival, but it *was* the cultivable land by a river they had come for—wetter and more wooded than they'd have liked, yet flat and fertile as they'd been promised. As Ruth France's poem about the moment says, if you are one to whom history is only the constant struggle of human endeavour,

> There is no need to remember swamp-grass
> Or how the first women (let the rain pass,
> They had prayed) wept when the hills reared up
> Through the mist; and they were trapped
> Between sea and cliffed forest. No ship could be
> More prisoning than the grey beach at Petone.

There are many who still think there is no need to remember; for whom the only reality is the present for whom colonial beginnings, 'the 1840s timewarp', are irrelevant to contemporary New Zealand. Without the sense of nature that comes from regular encounter, what does identity with country mean? Once we have tamed land like we believe we have this floodplain, are we immune from the life forces that shaped the land and the plants and animals that inhabit it? For the history of the European in the Pacific, the grey beach at Petone and the broad flat behind it is one of the most telling places. Nothing quite like what happened here when the buyers of utility arrived in the first few weeks of 1840 had ever happened before.

In *The Fatal Shore*, Robert Hughes likens the moment the first Europeans entered Port Jackson and stepped ashore on Australia to the breaking open of a capsule. Nothing had prepared the Iora people for what was to come, nor the Europeans for what the place was like. The remarkable thing about Sydney is its instantaneous beginning. One summer morning the place was as it had been for tens of thousands of years, then within a few hours a thousand Europeans were felling trees and erecting tents where none of their kind had ever been before.

Every piece of New Zealand's urban ground can be similarly traced back to what James K. Baxter called 'that one moment in history as a primitive and sacred bride, unentered and unexploited'. The germinal event of European arrival at Petone was trifling and forgettable in itself—the crunch of wood on gravel and a wet burst through the waves—but, as with the arrival of the first canoe of settlers from tropical Polynesia, myth takes the moment well beyond that. To those straining their eyes on the *Aurora*'s deck, 'Petone did not look like the "new pastures" they had been promised':

> We were all full of hope and anxiety to see what had been represented to us as a sort of earthly paradise . . . But men seeth only as through a glass darkly. Within a few short months I was doomed to witness those very beings who were cheering and shouting as they left the land of their nativity, cast—as it were— upon a barren dreary and inhospitable shore.

'You couldn't move for the forest,' one later wrote. As the *Aurora* came up the harbour, Samuel Deighton and John Wallace, who claimed to have been the first official European colonists to land in New Zealand, watched the land ahead shape into a flat forested plain stretching back to mountains.

They listened to the murmurs of dismay as those crowded around them at the rail realised what the relentless line of heavy dark trees meant, then pushed to the front of the first dinghy.

We prepared for landing. Richard Samuel Deighton and myself were the first to land, opposite the native village or pa at Petone. We strolled a short distance to the edge of the bush. Observing perched on one of the trees, several wood pigeons. Each of us shot one . . .

These two young Englishmen had the key to the country, the power to live with it or ruin it. Hunger, curiosity, the primal instincts of the hunter and practical experience are what lead them up the beach. But how could they love so alien a place? With only one real passion in their hearts—possession of a piece of earth, enough to feel free—this empty, wet forest must have seemed up for grabs. They had no notion of what we know, that it was a finite resource. They had been brought here on a promise that land like this was limitless. It had nothing to teach them, was no use as it was, and was not to stay like that long. Out of the sea came guns knocking birds out of ancient trees which axes felled, cattle pushing through the wet ferns, surveyors cutting lines, private property, barbed wire, spades for drains and locks for gates.

The actual landing site is not marked—in 1940 it was so filthy with meatworks' waste that the centennial monument was erected further along the beach. My first memory, from the early 1950s, is of a criss-cross of railway lines sweeping between the Gear freezing works and the wharf; of bells clanging and cars banking up whenever a train of meat crept out of the dark halls of corrugated iron. In the midst of it, a cemetery with Māori names on the gravestones. Years later I learned it was where Te Puni Kōkopu, the Te Atiawa chief of Pito-one who had welcomed the New Zealand Company, was buried—the narrow street beside the urupā is named after him. Where it meets the broad expanse of The Esplanade, a little circle of brass, a survey mark, almost obliterated by layers of tarseal, and crushed beer cans and icecream wrapping, is set into the kerbing. In the first days of 1840, a plan for a grand, utopian town rolled under his arm, a surveyor stood here and peered through his theodolite along the sweep of sand-dunes.

A new generation of surveyors was busy the moment the freezing works was bulldozed away in the early 1980s. Where Pito-one Pā had sat in the dunes, a freshly cut hole appeared right in front of Te Puni's urupā, behind a sign declaring the investment merits of the six-storey office block SouthPac Property Developments was about to erect on it. Driving past one day, I saw it out of the corner of my eye, the sharp edge of the cut still marked by a line of string. Below, soldiers' buttons and bits and pieces of old, industrial Petone were slipping out of the loose beach gravel. Under them lay wedges of pipi shell and charcoal from the centuries before, briefly opened to the sky before being buried again, behind poured concrete. Blade ready for the next scoop, the digger operator watched me. I walked over and yelled up into the cab over the roar of the motor, asking him if he'd seen anything more interesting. It was, I added, historic ground he was loading into the truck beside him. 'What the hell are you on about?' he yelled back.

Soon after the office block went up, a seafood restaurant opened next door. Once, as Wellington emerged from a southerly that had wreathed it for days, childhood memories or just curiosity took me across the traffic to the beach. I found the beach buried in flood debris swept up into the marram grass by the high sea. Plastic bags and packaging straps, tampons and timber were intertwined with clumps of the big brown seaweed, *Lessonia*, which had been ripped off harbour-mouth rocks, and the estuary's slimy green *Ulva*. Closer inspection revealed much of the debris had little to do with either sea or people. Nature had been at work as though we weren't here. Most of the bits and pieces were from mountain plants—Tararua silver beech, kamahi and mountain toatoa. I even saw an ancient land snail—*Rhytida*, Gondwana survivor—delivered perfectly intact through the rapids and gorges.

At the head of the beach where the southerly had opened long-buried layers of road gravel and tarseal, shells from one of Pito-one Pā's rubbish heaps spewed out onto the beach. Nearby among the clumps of spinifex grass whose balls of seed the nor'westerlies hurl along the beach, the unforgettable greeny-yellow of pingao was holding out against the aggressive conquest of European marram. One of the most precious and endangered species on the New Zealand coast—the very same plants, perhaps, which the people of Pito-one used.

I first knew this ground as a ritual Sunday afternoon visitor with my grandfather in the early 1950s. One of his weekly habits was driving his old Austin to Petone Beach, parking it facing the sea-wall and sitting back to watch the harbour he'd lived most of his life around. Until I was 10, when he died, we travelled to the beach of Sam Deighton's and John Wallace's landing after the roast almost every Sunday. I never liked the place. From the wildness and smells of the manuka scrub where we lived, I was transported to a stinking grey shore of concrete and rust where the wind never stopped. I would wander around the big concrete monument with its bronze map of the world and the ship made from cement, centennialised, facing the land covered in old houses, and wonder what it had all been like in 1840. I learned that the streets were named after the ships that had brought the people from England, and having seen men laying new roads across paddocks I had played in, I asked myself what was there before them. Years after these expeditions ceased, when I first saw a reproduction of Charles Heaphy's drawing of the Petone foreshore from the western Hutt hills in

Port Nicholson from the Hills above Pitone in 1840 (DETAIL), CHARLES HEAPHY.

THE SAME VIEW IN 1990.

1840, I couldn't believe that his landscape of heavy forest, swamps and windswept scrub was the same place where I had spent those countless Sunday afternoons.

Nineteen-year-old Charles Heaphy was draughtsman on the New Zealand Company's advance ship *Tory*. Later in life, amazed at the vanishing of the Hutt Valley's birds, he liked to say he saw it 'before the settlers', when it was a fresh, new place, in his words, 'in a more primitive condition than any of the surrounding harbours'. Prior to the rush of settlers in 1840 the floodplain forest he painted was 'teeming with birds. Of twelve or fourteen species . . . then to be seen in every wood, only the tui, the fly-catcher, and the wren, with the sand-lark, in the open, are now (1878) common, while the robin, the bell-bird, the titmouse, the thrush, the popokatea, the tiraweke, and the ririroro, are rarely seen or have entirely passed away.'

It was the estuary, at the valley's eastern edge, that he thought 'most interesting and picturesque. A pa stood at the mouth of the river on the eastern side, with large war-canoes drawn up on the beach, while at the hill-foot were tall stages, from which hung great quantities of fish in the process of sun-drying.' However many Māori there were, and however long Māori had lived there, their visible imprint on the place by 1839 had been slight:

> The indigenous birds had been entirely unmolested, save when the Maori snared them in his furtive and noiseless manner. I remember, especially, the enormous number of waterfowl frequenting the mouth of the Hutt River. Cormorants, ducks, teal, oyster catchers, plovers, sand-pipers, curlew, and red-legged waders, were there in pairs, detachments, and masses, and so tame it was slaughter, rather than sport to shoot them.
>
> From the pa we pulled up the Waiwhetu River, which there had lofty pine trees [kahikatea] on its banks. The various bends were very beautiful and secluded, and seemed to be the home of the grey duck and teal, and numerous other wild fowl. Here and there, on the bank, was a patch of cultivation and the luxuriant growth of potatoes, taros, and kumeras indicated the richness of the soil. As seen from the ship, or the hills, a lofty pine wood appeared to occupy the whole breadth and length of the Hutt Valley, broken only by the stream and its stony margin. This wood commenced about a mile from the sea, the intervening space being a sandy flat and a flax marsh. Of the larger birds, the kokako, or crow, the rail, pukeko, pigeon, kaka and huia were numerous in their respective localities or feeding grounds. Of a night might be heard the booming, or 'drum' of the bittern . . .

Although estuaries were traditional centres of Māori life, many still had their forests and reed swamps largely intact when Europeans arrived. Their mosaic forest-edge zones were home to many poorly flighted birds like pateke, or brown teal, that were once incredibly abundant in estuaries like the Hutt but have since almost completely vanished.

Charles Heaphy was not the first to see the Hutt and its estuary before it became a European place, nor was his the first New Zealand Company. In 1826, while Edward Gibbon Wakefield's theory of colonisation was still just an idea, while he was still in Newgate prison serving out his abduction sentence, a shipload of colonists seeking the same 'fine level country' for which New Zealand was becoming famous had landed and looked around.

Where James Cook had noted a 'good Harbour' but sailed past at a safe distance, a coast that 'may be found to differ something from the truth', the brig *Rosanna* came straight in. If its 'excellent harbour . . . land fit for cultivation . . . excellent flax . . . and considerable quantity of timber' were any criteria, 'Whanga Nui Atra' was an obvious place to settle. Its river mouth was navigable and abounded with 'good fish, ducks, and a variety of other birds'. All this and only 'about forty or fifty natives'.

Thomas Shepherd, 'Surveyor of the New Zealand Company', an English landscape gardener and friend of Humphrey Repton (one of the designers of the great landscaped English estates) was trained to see the spirit of nature in a landscape. In his youth he had worked on estates designed by a pupil of the great Capability Brown, who created a new fashion by trading rigid linearity for more natural curvy lines, making formal ponds into lakes, allowing trees to be trees, and emphasising open, grassy space. But hard times for his trade in the 1820s drove Shepherd to try the antipodes.

The *Rosanna*'s visit was part of a reconnoitre of New Zealand and she soon put to sea again. Shepherd was so impressed with New Zealand's fertile harbours at Kaipara he even purchased land. But not construing their welcome by Hokianga Māori as a particularly favourable omen—or, as Shepherd put it, 'not finding the concern to come up to the views of the Directors'—they headed for 'less intimidating Sydney', where they were just another boatload. Thomas Shepherd found himself in charge of the colony's Nursery.

'When you, gentlemen, first got your estates,' he was soon castigating the Sydney settlers clearing trees from the harbour edge at Woolloomooloo, 'your ground was well furnished with beautiful shrubs. You ignorantly set the murderous hoe and grubbing axe to work to destroy them, and the ground that had been full of luxurient verdure, was laid bare and desolate, and the prospect ruined.' Compared with Britain, where 'pure nature is seldom seen', the colonies held the stuff of landscape designers' dreams. In Sydney's eucalypt woodlands Thomas Shepherd saw the perfect prospect: 'When trees are too thickly crowded in a forest, and the desired effect cannot be, then, large opening must be made through the valleys, to open the same, and the trees on the high ground may still be left for ornament; . . . cattle and sheep grazing upon the cleared land and upon the hills would add greatly to the beauty of the prospect. Our scenery would assume a cheerful picturesque character, full of luxurient verdure, and varied by hills, dales, valleys, plains, rivers and lakes.' But the ruination of the woods of New South Wales, by colonists eager to get at the antipodean soil, left Shepherd bitter and exhausted. He was dead in less than a decade. 'By their destruction,' he wrote, 'I have lost the idol of my soul.'

What if the *Rosanna* had stayed in Wellington Harbour, and in those crucial weeks of settling and shaping a new landscape, Thomas Shepherd had been at the helm? 'Struck with astonishment at the beautiful appearance' of the New Zealand he saw in 1826, a country 'ornamented with handsome trees and shrubs', his colony's landscape might have been very different from that which flowed from Edward Gibbon Wakefield's dreaming:

WHANGA NUI ATRA

At the head of the Harbour on the right side is a valley of large extent probably 10-20 miles in depth and about 2 miles in width. About half a mile of this valley next to the harbour is light sandy soil earth and marshy or boggy ground with many lakes of water and brooks and two Rivers which pass through it to the interior of the country, here are growing in the greatest perfection a large quantity of fine Flax from 8 to 10 feet in height a number of straggling shrubs, fern, grass and tufts of wood flax. After passing through this half mile which fronts the harbour in going up the left branch of river about two miles is a rich loamy soil of a great depth of staple chiefly thickly covered with beautiful trees and shrubs but no large timber. This river in most places is sufficiently deep for boats but the way is obstructed at some places by trees which have come down with floods.

We was informed by one of the natives that it would take us three days to go to the extremity of this river and that we could find very large trees . . . of the Towtarra . . . in the interior . . . the flood seems to rise very high at times as we could see its marks upon the banks, we are of the opinion that this river would be found very serviceable in conveying timber from the woods to the harbour. The mouth of this river is what may be called a bar as the water does not rise more than 6 to 7 feet over it . . . the ground on its banks is also covered with the most beautiful sorts of trees and shrubs many of which I have not seen before but time would not allow to take a description of them. At the entrance of this river the natives have a few tempory [sic] huts where they are building a small canoe. Here we were kindly received by the Chief who rubbed his nose upon ours and asked us to eat with him.

Where Shepherd sat down for kai, a long line of concrete blocks and slabs of demolished brick walls holds the riverbank from the big tides. Where he looked admiringly back up the estuary to the forest, the wilderness is now one of signs and red cranes and yellow dust from the gravel-crushing plant hanging over long grey factory roofs and petrol storage tanks. Looking down at it from the bridge, the only lingering clue to his 'beautiful trees and shrubs' is a tiny patch of taupata scrub making a stand against the tall fescue and fennel. A pensioner looks up quizzically, wondering what I am about. Three Tokelauans fishing from the walkway nod at me as I pass. Trucks drown the piercing call of a pair of oystercatchers defending their territory from the black-backed gulls swooping up and down along the edge of the flow. Seemingly oblivious to them, a white-faced heron steps tentatively across a polluted bed of green algae and then reaching the grey sand hurries across to the lagoon of old boatsheds and rotted jetties.

Somewhere on the edge of that lagoon William Mein Smith, the actual Surveyor of the New Zealand Company, sat down with his watercolours and painted the forested estuary in one of its last winters. Today where its long tidal arms of sea rushes once ran back into flax and manuka and the tall, dark crowns of kahikatea and pukatea, are Hutt Park Raceway and the brick and tile of hundreds of post-war state houses. William Mein Smith's *A Wet Day, July, 1853* (see colour illustrations) seems like South Westland. Indeed, the collection of paintings in which I discovered it had it listed as from another part of the country. On a hunch that its faraway blue hills were familiar, I had a copy made. Sure enough, when I lined up Mein Smith's horizon, it matched the eastern Hutt hills exactly.

Charles Heaphy's companion, the naturalist Ernst Dieffenbach, described the outlet of the river 'Eritonga' as a broad basin in 'the sandy downs of the coast . . . joined, not far from its mouth, by three tributaries, the Okatu, Emotu, and Waiwatu'. Two years after Mein Smith painted it, the 1855 earthquake lifted its mudflats and reed-beds out of the reach of the tide and changed the scene overnight. The Waiwhetu—'the water that sparkles like the stars'—still winds into the estuary, but just as it enters the field of the idyllic view of Thomas Shepherd and comes under the influence of the tide, it becomes the stream that, in the 1980s, made the name Waiwhetu synonymous with urban pollution.

Until the introduction of legislation in the 1970s, industrial waste flowed unchecked into streams and harbours. As recently as 1972, you could read newspaper headlines like *Stinking Mudflat Mess to be Transformed into Useful Area.* As the sea view became an industrial zone, the Waiwhetu and its estuary became its disposal unit. From sediments collected downstream from its battery and paint factories nearby, a West German laboratory measured lead levels that, at the time, were among the highest they had recorded in streams anywhere in the world. Lead and its companion heavy metals are still present in the deep, central basin of the harbour, as well as in the estuary.

Fennel, gorse and blackberry, piles of tyres and abandoned machinery crowd the oil-impregnated bank of the Waiwhetu's last run to the sea. What would Shepherd feel, what would Heaphy say, if they could visit their landfall now? Oily sludge. Toxic solvents. Pathogenic chemicals. 'Most interesting and picturesque'?

If you look carefully behind the factories, oil tanks and workshops, you can still see the shells from meals gathered long ago. The same pipi and cockles too are everywhere the sandy ground of the urupā has been turned over.

The people who shared their kai with Thomas Shepherd were Ngāti Mutunga, a Taranaki people who had recently banished the estuary's previous inhabitants and established their own series of settlements. Their slender presence around The Eye of the Fish was yet another of the reverberations of the musket through Aotearoa. Behind them lay a major battle of conquest on the shore of the estuary, when they took it from the latest of a succession of occupants going back centuries.

Just as the strait into which it opened was always more a highway than a tribal barrier, Whanganui-a-Tara was a place of passage more than a centre. With the arrival of the musket, tribes from the western coast, Waikato and Taranaki, replaced the long-established links with the Wairarapa. The 1830s were turbulent with tribal conflict and movement. In 1835, needing a safer haven, Ngāti Mutunga suddenly left Whanganui-a-Tara as part of the migration that sailed to the Chatham Islands in the brig *Rodney* and led to the near-annihilation of the Moriori of Rekohu. Into the vacuum, insecure in their inheritance, slipped more Taranaki people, Te Atiawa. By the time the New Zealand Company's *Tory* appeared at the harbour's entrance, Te Atiawa had had only four years to establish their authority as tangata whenua.

Before the musket, the head of the harbour was occupied by Ngāti Ira, the descendants of Ira-turoto. In the early 1800s, they had fortified pā on the islands in the harbour and at Waiwhetu at the head of the estuary, and fishing villages in the sand and gravel ridges near the river mouth. But by tradition the original people were Ngāi Tara, after whom the great harbour was named. They called the river Te Awa Kai Rangi because of the fruitfulness of its ecosystem, and lived around its changing mouth for about 11 generations before the Ngāti Ira arrived from the East Coast about 1650. Ngāi Tahu also lived here, fighting a major battle with Ngāti Ira on the banks of the Waiwhetu, near the present Hutt Park Raceway, before their migration south about 1600. Other longer term inhabitants during the late era of Ngāti Ira were Ngāti Mamoe, the people believed to be the planters of the Cook Strait coast's karaka groves. They called the river Wai ō Rotu.

Ngāi Tara's traditions tell of a landscape continually reshaped by the earth's forces. At the beginning of their time here almost all of present-day Petone and its long grey beach was under the water of a tidal inlet. At the time of Te Aohaeretahi the two plates of the earth's crust that meet only a few miles away in Cook Strait slid along one another, and Ngāi Tara experienced an event more dramatic than any other human inhabitants of the southern North Island have ever witnessed. When Te Hao Whenua struck about 1460, the landscape changed overnight: the buckling earth liquified the floor of the valley, collapsing forests and creating the sandy beach and new swamps behind it.

Ancient Māori attributed the life of the estuary to the dynamic tectonic forces that every now and then convulsed the estuary and left it different from the day before. According to traditions the harbour and the estuary are the work of two great taniwha. The estuary, once a great lake, was the home of the mild-mannered Whataitai; the wilder Ngāke lived at the more turbulent southern end. The estuary with its flat floodplain was formed when Ngāke surged toward the northern shore in a desperate attempt to escape into the open sea. Trapped in the shallows, he wound himself up 'into a great fury, his tail lashing backwards and forwards, scooping up sand and piling it in the corner, which is why it is so shallow now'.

Archaeology has revealed several Polynesian sites around Aotearoa's coast dating to at least the 11th and 12th centuries, in sheltered harbours, estuaries and rivermouths. None of these sites are in the Hutt Valley or thereabouts, but that does not mean some of those early people were not living here. The region is renowned for the names Kupe, the explorer from Rarotonga, gave it, and there is evidence in the ground that, not long after him, people were moving all over the country—and not just around the coast.

Sometime between 1200 and 1300, before Ngāi Tara's time, in a climate considerably warmer than present, a travelling party camped high in the Tararua's silver beech forest. Beside their umu, they left behind a water-worn greywacke boulder that had probably been pre-heated and slid inside a bird to slowly cook it as its carrier walked. Whoever they were, they also had access to the famous obsidian of Tuhua, or Mayor Island, in the Bay of Plenty, because they left a vast quantity of its flakes. Even if these people hadn't climbed up from the Hutt River, they would have seen its floodplain and estuary from where they camped. They would have known enough about their new land's ecosystems to know these environments to be some of the richest in fish, birds and food plants. It is as hard to imagine they didn't know the valley as it is to believe there was no one living there.

By the time Charles Heaphy, William Wakefield and the New Zealand Company stepped from the *Tory* into the estuary in 1839, it contained six Te Atiawa pā on the foreshore and the estuary—Pito-one, Te Tatau ō te Po, Paetutu, Hikoikoi, Owhiti and Waiwhetu. Of Hikoikoi and Waiwhetu, whose elders Thomas Shepherd met in 1826, the only trace now is the urupā opposite the furniture factory on Seaview Road. Even that is post-European, on the outskirts of what was Owhiti village; the original urupā is under a road junction in the middle of the industrial area. The land where Hikoikoi pā stood and commanded the river mouth was washed away by river erosion before 1930. Only the Pito-one urupā of Te Puni and his descendants still stands.

It was after visiting one of these kainga that William Wakefield returned to the *Tory* and wrote of how Te Puni Kōkopu and the other Te Atiawa chief Wharepouri had 'begged' him 'to look at the place' and 'tell them what I thought of it'. Offering a stranger a gift, said the behaviourist Konrad Lorenz, is a way of defining your territory—particularly, perhaps, if your hold on it is as tenous and besieged as Te Atiawa's was by late 1839, with Ngāti Toa coming over the hills from Porirua. Wakefield obliged next morning, rowing far enough up the river with them to establish that 'the valley in which it flows seems to be about forty miles in length, and is for three to four miles broad . . . At about three miles up . . . commences a grove of fine trees, of the best description for ship and house building, intermixed with large pine trees. One of these called the kaikatea, measured twenty-one feet in circumference, and was nearly the same size upwards for sixty feet without a branch.'

Finally, after more than a month in Cook Strait chasing level land, the New Zealand Company's Principal Agent was in the kind of place his directors meant him to be. Already he had not merely the possession but the total reshaping of the valley in mind: the draining of the inundated, the clearing away of encumbrances, the improving upon the neglected that was automatic to an Englishman with his sense of purpose: 'The land on both sides is a black soil, and in the patches the natives cultivate produces potatoes, Indian corn, and oats which are carelessly thrown amidst the stumps of the half-destroyed trees and the most beautiful shrubs.' Soon Wakefield had seen 'all that was necessary to confirm my opinion that the whole extent of the valley will be capable of cultivation, and will amply repay the labour of clearing, by its extreme fertility, when the river shall be confined and its streams united'. The Hutt's floodplain was the *kind* of place they wanted, for sure, but he was already beginning to wonder about its capacity for both farms *and* the directors' grand new 'commercial metropolis'. 'Large tracts of flat land . . . ready for ploughing' it may have had, but it was barely a third of the area the Company's schemers were seeking.

William Wakefield's finding of the Hutt Valley was no historical fluke. His directors' Instructions had told him 'that harbour in Cook's Straits is the most valuable, which combines with ample security and convenience as a resort for ships, the nearest vicinity to, or the best natural means of communication with, the greatest extent of fertile territory. So far as we are at present informed, Port Nicholson appears superior to any other.' They suggested he check the rumours with the whalers and traders in Queen Charlotte Sound or Cloudy Bay before going there.

The New Zealand Company's directors wanted a location from which they could control New Zealand. They were as aware as anyone of the 'advantages' of the place James Cook had called The New Thames. But if one navigable river watering a boundless fertile plain with magnificent timber and an endless supply of the flax existed, others must too. 'Of merely fertile land there exists so great an abundance,' they wrote in their Instructions to Wakefield's brother, William. Cook Strait had the additional attractions that, a decade earlier, had tempted Te Rauparaha and his muskets from the Waikato. Somewhere on the shores of this strategic passage of water, the Company believed, lay the place for their colony. 'In making this selection you will not forget that Cook's Strait forms part of the shortest route from the Australian Colonies to England, and that the best harbour in that channel must inevitably become the most frequented port in New Zealand.'

By the time they decided to act, the prospect of government control was threatening the venture. In a ship selected for its speed under sail, bought with other people's hopes and money, William Wakefield was hurried across the world to find 'the shores of safe and commodious harbours, the sheltered embouchures of extensive rivers communicating with a fertile country— these are the situations in which it is most desired that you make purchases of land.'

The idea that the target country had more than 'a sufficiency of level land for the wants of the colony' rested on the vegetation travellers had seen in the first few decades of the 19th century. But the pamphlets promoting colonisation in New Zealand did not describe the country in general. They concentrated on the forests near the coast, on the flat vales of the sheltered harbours—as of course, the explorer traffic itself did.

By 1839 though, fertility of the soil had become subservient to other factors. Learning from Britain's experience in America and the unsystematic landgrabbing that had been the sequel of the Australian penal colonies, Edward Gibbon Wakefield's theory of a settlement plan for New Zealand was promoted as an ideal alternative to an overcrowded Britain. In the effort that culminated in his brother's rush to Cook Strait, Wakefield's sponsors had made much of 'testimony' like William Wilson's 1801 *Chart of the River Thames in New Zealand*, of boundless acres of rich alluvium stretching all the way to Cook Strait.

After the *Tory*'s race across the world, the reality of Cook Strait must have been a crushing disappointment. One glance at its windswept cliffs and William Wakefield knew the pastoral idyll he'd held in his mind was a fantasy:

> *Friday August 16th 1839*
> *Fine weather. Saw LAND on the Southern Island Tavai Poenamoo at 12 o'clock noon, it being the 96th day from Plymouth only having seen it at forty miles off the Island of Palma . . . since the Lizard . . .*

Saturday August 17th
The first appearance of the coast on the Southern Island is
extremely unpromising . . . a succession of apparently barren
mountains stretching away till they reach those covered with snow
but as you approach you find wood in the interior . . .

William Wakefield had seen plenty of steep hill country during his
military service in Spain. And he was no aimless itinerant wandering the
oceans. He was in Captain Cook's wake, on a mission of empire, as both
his and his nephew Jerningham's journals reveal: 'Cook dwells on not having
seen land during a voyage towards the South Pole of 10988 miles. We have
run 14680 miles since Palma and 16000 from England.' Directing the *Tory*
straight to Cook's famous camp at Ship Cove, he watched dismayed as the
Sound's forested hills and tiny wafers of flat land slid past. To his nephew,
'the scenery became more and more majestic as we advance into this noble
estuary'. 'How well Cook has described the harmony of the birds at this
very spot!' the young Wakefield wrote at Ship Cove. 'The hills rise . . . on
three sides of the cove . . . covered from their tops to the water's edge with
an undulating carpet of forest . . . Every bough seemed to throng with
feathered musicians.'

Still wild and beautiful, its ancient forest sweeping down to a white
British obelisk on the beach, Ship Cove is instilled in our minds as a place
of European beginnings in Aotearoa. Yet it was more than a place for
careening ships' hulls and recording flora and fauna. It was here that the
invasive ecology of imperialism was first unleashed, and with it the
devastation Europe's technology has wreaked on New Zealand's birds. Near
Ship Cove, Cook's men blasted 30 birds out of their trees in one day,
including 12 kererū, four South Island kokako, two red-crowned parakeets,
four saddlebacks and one falcon. Virtually all are today close to extinction
or extremely rare. In nearby Cannibal Cove, the Englishmen put ashore 'a
Boar and a Breeding Sow so that we have reason to hope that in process of
time this Country will be stocked with Goats and Hoggs', as they did
elsewhere around the coast, only to find on their return that 'all our
endeavours for stocking this Country with usefull Animals are likely to be
frusterated by the very people who we meant to serve'. Seeing his English
pigs hadn't survived the interest of the local Māori, Cook got more on his
next trip to Tonga. So well did they survive that, if it weren't for hunters
and dogs, their descendants would have reduced the landscape 'so closely

cover'd with Wood' that Cook's men 'could not penetrate into the Country' to a ghostly shadow of itself.

It was 'hardly possible', Cook claimed, 'for all the methods I have taken to stock this country with these animals to fail'. His view that the Sounds were vacant waste—'as to Wood the land here is one intire forest'—and that its people had little stake in it—'they live desperse'd along the Shores in search of their daily bread which is fish and firn roots for they cultivate no part of the lands'— became determination to improve it. 'Making room for better plants', the Englishmen set fire to Long Island. Using his childhood farming skills, Cook soon had a host of European crop plants thriving in the ashes. Some of 'the several Gardens on the Islands and Coves where we transplanted several hundreds of Cabbages' were still recognisable when the Russian Bellingshausen and the Englishman Cruise visited Ship Cove in 1820. By the spring of 1839, wild cabbage was so common throughout the Sounds, that the *Tory*'s botanist Ernst Dieffenbach wrote of yellow carpets of it. On Kapiti, across the strait, Ngāti Toa were growing it in plantations.

Finding these manifestations of Cook's seeds of empire brought William Wakefield curiously close to his company's hero, but it couldn't keep his real purpose at bay. With each new day, it was dawning on the Englishmen that their company's planners might have got carried away. Heaphy captured the growing sense of disappointment on the *Tory*: while 'without exception the finest harbour in New Zealand', the hills of Queen Charlotte Sound seemed 'to leave no space for cultivable land'. For the best part of a month Wakefield coasted the Sounds and Cloudy Bay. A few cove bottoms had 'sufficient flat land for a considerable settlement', such as where Picton is today, which despite the concentration of people such a place attracted—'altogether . . . the most miserable specimen of inhabitations I ever saw'—was still 'like the rest, covered with evergreen trees and shrubs of the most convenient growth'.

Eventually Wakefield abandoned the search. The southern side of Cook Strait had some of the right ingredients: 'land, with excellent water communication, and of great fertility'. But, 'not adapted for colonization on a large scale', it 'would not suffice to carry out the plans of the Company'. It must have been a relief to be told by the whalers at Tory Channel that the other side might. Dicky Barrett's and Worser Heberley's Māori wives had relatives over there. So, on 20 September 1839, they piloted the *Tory* across the Strait and past the black rocks and the bay that would soon be named for them.

Immediately he was inside Wellington Harbour, Wakefield was writing about hills that presented no obstacles to cultivation and comparing them to the 'formidable height' of those they had left that morning. Even the foliage of Port Nicholson's trees was brighter. Again it is Charles Heaphy who captures the sense of relief on the *Tory* at such a 'noble expanse of water surrounded by a country of the most picturesque character, formed a scene of indescribable beauty; and as the valley of the Hutt opened to our view . . . we wondered that a place which seemed so much to invite settlement had not before been colonised'.

It is surprising that William Wakefield was so long in getting here. Apart from Cook's glancing 1773 reference to 'a new inlet' he couldn't enter, there was, by the time the *Tory* left England, plenty of intelligence on Port Nicholson. A son of a Kapiti chief, Ngā Iti, who lived in England for about two years in the 1830s, described a thickly wooded valley at the head of the harbour drained by a river comparable to the Thames. In 1837 Te Pahi was even quoted in Edward Gibbon Wakefield's New Zealand Association advertising pamphlets. 'Tupai Cupa', as he was called, spoke temptingly of 'two inlets leading from Cook's Straits into the heart of his territory, both deep and spacious enough for the largest vessels' and a river 80 miles long, at the head of an inland sea whose shores are 'covered with lofty trees of the cowdie [kauri] species to the water's edge'. In *The British Colonisation of New Zealand*, Edward Gibbon Wakefield devoted several pages to the harbour 'where the River Haritaoua falls into the sea . . . a safe anchorage and complete shelter for any number of ships'. It was probable, he wrote, that the 'valuable productions' Te Pahi described 'might be procured with more facility, or of better quality, from this than any other district of New Zealand'.

Tucked away in William Wakefield's cabin—and no doubt repeatedly taken out and read during the *Tory*'s month in the Sounds—were his Instructions to find an antipodean river with banks vast and flat enough for his Company to erect their speculative dream. But efficient administration was never the Company's forté, not least in connecting the critical practical matters like land survey and town design with the actual nature of their target country. Ironically, in 'imposing the greatest responsibility' on the man who would be on the spot, their Principal Agent, William Wakefield, they specifically cautioned him of the 'propriety of carefully avoiding any thing like exaggeration in describing the more favourable features of the country'. Sometime just before his sudden departure from England, however, they sought the services of a London draughtsman to design them

a 'commercial metropolis ... inhabited by Englishmen' set in 110,000 acres
of fertile, level land. The 1,100 acre grid plan Samuel Cobham drew from
their sketches, cornered by fortresses and with a President's Palace and
barracks as well as all the symbols of a sophisticated city, was never, apparently, published by the Company. Yet it shows what they dreamt of
transplanting to the Antipodes.

Instead of the parks and squares of a grand southern city, the New
Zealand Company directors had islands and headlands named after them.
Although the phantoms of Cobham's grid plan are still there amid Petone's
matter-of-fact suburbia, Britannia—as the first, brief 'habitations in the
wilderness' suggest it might have been called—certainly was not designed
with the hill-bound Hutt Valley in mind. Had William Wakefield found
Ship Cove a fertile plain and navigable river, it would have been laid out
there. Even at Petone there were many who watched with scorn and
incredulity as the surveyors lay its lines through Te Atiawa's gardens:
'Unfortunately, these spots have been reserved by the Company for public
purposes, for boulevardes or some such nonsense; the land immediately in
the rear being covered with timber of such extraordinary dimensions as to
require at least £40 per acre to clear it.'

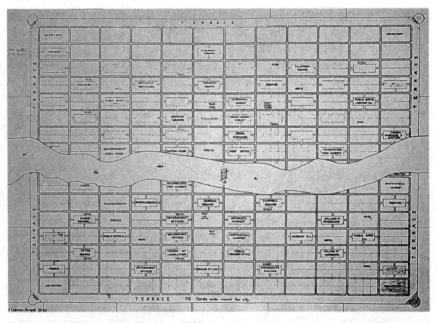

SAMUEL COBHAM'S PLAN OF BRITANNIA, 1839.

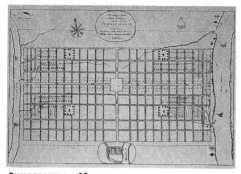

PHILADELPHIA, 1683.

MILITARY TOWN BY ROBERT BARRET, 1598.

Samuel Cobham's plan was no sketch of a small village in a forest clearing from which a city and a fertile plain might grow. It was from the beginning a search for order, an arrogant claim on land it neither knew nor owned, whose inhabitants fished the river mouth and hunted the forest edge while, on the other side of the world, some speculators' draughtsman was laying names like 'Covent Garden Market' and 'Hungerford Fish Market' over their domain.

Britannia survives as no more than an archival curiosity, yet its place in New Zealand's history is undeniable. Although its grip on ecological reality was slight, it was far from an original design. Cobham's precise division of new, unknown space is almost identical to the defended grid towns with which Europeans invaded North America. These were direct descendants of medieval military towns which, in turn, reach back through the Roman occupation of Britain to the ideal cities of the Old Testament. Britannia was an *aggressive* claim, ready for war. You can see almost exactly the same enclosed grid in the 1683 plan of Philadephia—right down to the public squares in each quadrant—and in Robert Barret's military town of 1598 and its Machiavellian precedent of 1521—right down to the forts in each corner.

Nothing, says the landscape historian J.B. Jackson, more clearly shows the cherished values of a group than the manner in which they organise space. William Wakefield and the *Tory* were sent to New Zealand with every intention of establishing Britannia. Their masters may have imagined a garden city, but they were ready for resistance. The prisons and Presidential Palace among the boulevardes and squares, docks and markets are graphic demonstration of what the New Zealand Company venture was expecting. But Cobham's was a placeless plan—designed for any riverine plain— and the swampy floodplain of the Hutt only partially qualified. Merely a

A Bird's Eye View of Port Nicholson (DETAIL), CHARLES HEAPHY AND THOMAS ALLOM, EARLY 1840s.

suggestion of Britannia was actually laid down, yet spreading like a virus from every surveyor's theodolite, imprinted in fence lines and land titles, it changed the feel of the country forever.

There is another image from the 1840 encounter, as graphic and unreal as Samuel Cobham's dream city—and as far-reaching. Along with Charles Heaphy's sketches, and his and others' words on the Hutt's 'extraordinary fertility', the charts of the *Tory*'s master, Edward Chaffers, with the magic words 'Rich, Alluvial Soil' laid across the head of Port Nicholson, were sped back to London. The New Zealand Company's directors took them to the lithographer Thomas Allom. What he created is a remarkable perspective to anyone who has looked down on Wellington Harbour from a Boeing. 'A Bird's Eye View of Port Nicholson' is propaganda. This country definitely *was* an arcadia. Obviously empty, a sweeping coastal plain awaited pastoralists in their thousands. Its river hints at the unlikelihood of floods. Wooded like the vast parklands of gentlemen's estates, meandering out of view through the low, vague hills where the Tararua mountains should be, the Hutt Valley seems boundless.

In 'the very highway between New Holland and the Western World,' William Wakefield wrote after seeing Te Atiawa's forest, he had found 'land exceeding in fertility any I have seen in these islands, and equalling that of an English garden'. And if his newfound valley was no more than a third the size of what he needed, the myth that New Zealand's Northern Island was largely fertile alluvium was still intact: 'What may be the termination of this valley I cannot surmise from the confused and varying accounts of the inhabitants, though it is not unlikely that it may communicate with the fertile plains between Mount Egmont and East Cape.'

Within four days of William Wakefield's entering their harbour, visiting every settlement, bargaining for every bit he could get, Te Atiawa had 'sold and parted with all right, title, and interest in all the said lands, tenements, woods, bays, harbours, rivers, streams and creeks . . . forever, and in consideration of having received as a full, and just payment for the same, one hundred red blankets, one hundred muskets . . .' That accomplished, William Wakefield posted the shoreline with 'New Zealand Land Company' signs, hoisted the Company's flag on the beach and added a few labels to their map of a blank landscape. Then he and the *Tory* sailed away from their antipodean plain to find more like it.

In the months and years to come the armaments and axes would play a role reshaping the landscape of 'impenetrable' forest. Te Atiawa's new umbrellas wouldn't get through the first southerly, but the clothes from the land sale would give them a status amongst Te Upoko Te Ika's iwi that their harbourside land hadn't. Yet, as the attentive Charles Heaphy would later write, the more influential Te Atiawa chiefs were not really all that concerned about the amount of the payment, or even their loss of land. What they wanted, some of them at any price, was Europeans in their midst, for security, 'and to bring cattle and grow corn'.

In England, the New Zealand Company was so confident of its new land it didn't even wait for its advance scouts to report back. A month or two before their first expedition sailed the directors began considering matters like a chief surveyor. Some believed the venture demanded a military man. They had one in mind in Colonel William Light, who had laid out the elegant urban spaces of South Australia's Adelaide, but he inconveniently died before the *Tory* sailed. By the time it arrived in Te Whanga-nui-a-Tara, they had appointed Captain William Mein Smith Surveyor-General and sent him on his way in a fast-sailing barque, followed a week or so later by the first ships of colonists. The *Cuba* left Gravesend with three assistant surveyors, a Land Commissioner and 22 workingmen. Smith's cabin, like Wakefield's on the *Tory*, contained the plan for a 'commercial metropolis'. With it, though, were Instructions that 'you should make ample reserves for all public purposes such as a cemetery, a market place, wharfage and probable public buildings, a botanical garden and extensive boulevards . . . the beautiful appearance of the future city to be secured—rather than the immediate profit of the Company'.

While the *Cuba* was speeding across the Indian Ocean, William Wakefield, knowing that he had to find more level land than the Hutt offered for the shiploads the company had recruited to their utopia, headed up the west coast of the North Island to find the alluvial expanses his brother Edward had praised in *The British Colonisation of New Zealand*. Two months later, having followed his Instructions into Kaipara Harbour, but scared by a grounding on its bar, he was warning his London directors off 'a shore that hinders every communication with it'. Taranaki was 'out and out the finest agricultural district in the island' but the more he saw 'the more satisfied I am with my purchases in Cook's Strait. Port Nicholson, though not possessing a large flat district is, with its site for a large town at Thorndon, and the valley of the Hutt for farms, infinitely more eligible than any place I have seen, for the first settlement. It must be the commercial capital.' By the time he could get back there, Smith and the *Cuba* had already arrived.

The only European to greet the surveyors was another Smith, a trader Wakefield had persuaded to establish vegetable gardens and shelter at the present city end of the harbour in time for for the settlers' arrival. All through the long weeks at sea, Mein Smith had had in his mind a riverine plain vast enough, once the 1,000-acre town had been laid out, for a further selection 'of the most valuable portion as respect fertility, river frontage and vicinity to the town'. One look convinced Smith that there was simply no way he could fit the Company's vision into Thorndon Flat.

But he knew that he had only a few weeks before the settlers would be demanding their pegged-out allotments—not enough time to wait on the beach for Wakefield and the *Tory* to return. Wakefield, before he left, had already 'fixed' a place for the town where the railway is today. But Smith had other ideas. As soon as he came ashore from the *Cuba* on 7 January 1840, he went to the river end of the beach and 'commenced reconnoitering the flat ground as I think it will do for the town'.

The next day Smith and his assistant surveyors took a canoe upriver. There was no doubting its obvious fertility: 'a most valuable acquisition to the Company'. But a site for Cobham's grand town plan was another matter: 'At a short distance from the beach the ground is swampy . . . I do not think it is subject to malaria, but it is low and sandy and will not afford a foundation for houses, at least not good ones I should think. I suspect too it would be subject to very great inconveniences from the spray of the sea in a S.Easter, further back the land is better in all aspects.'

The New Zealand Company directors prided themselves that theirs was a *planned* operation, that they had 'a guarantee that a knowledge of the country will in all cases precede settlement. The importance of this will be apparent to all who are cognisant of the history of civilisation'. But as David Millar said in his history *Once upon a Village,* things went wrong from the moment William Mein Smith first peered through his theodolite. Had the Company's plan been more in tune with the land, had they waited a mere six months more for Wakefield and the *Tory* to return, informed, to England, our ordinary landscape might have been very different. We who inhabit the cities that grew from their company towns would probably not see streets that, where the first surveyors ran out of space, leave the flats and go straight up the steep encircling hills.

Behind Petone's sandy beach ridges, in the tall impenetrable flax swamps, 'much interspersed with sluggish creeks', and forest so dense 'it impeded the rapid progress of the necessary measurements', it was soon obvious it would be months before the company could provide the settlers with their town acre. Even then, as Charles McGurk, a contract surveyor, said, 'a great many of the streets would run through swamps and marshes, in some places six and ten feet deep'.

When ten days had passed and Wakefield had still not turned up, the surveyors began laying out 'a more correct survey of our valley'. The *Tory* finally sailed in late the next day, and first thing in the morning Principal Agent Wakefield and Surveyor-General Smith went walking. Furious at his decision for a Thorndon town site being contravened, Wakefield demanded Smith cease surveying the swampy flats forthwith. Smith took the high ground, insisting the choice of a town site was his prerogative. Until nature spoke and autumn floods inundated Smith's survey lines, forcing Wakefield to relent, he continued to hint that vanity—'that his name would be coupled with the most regularly built city in the world'— drove his Surveyor-General's motives more than a concern for settlers. Within months Wakefield was asking London for a replacement Surveyor-General. Meanwhile, at Petone, they were busy with inspection and decision:

> *January 19. Captain Smith and myself examined a valley on the east side of the harbour. It is perfectly level, and of considerable extent, but from the marshy nature of the soil, and its liability to inundation, at present unfit for the settler. It produces large quantities of flax; and may, with draining become valuable. A walk through the swamp occupied us all day.*

January 23. I allotted today portions of land on the land near the sea, to be reserved for the park and public grounds, to the passengers of the Aurora.

January 27. The appearance of the beach has become most interesting. Landing of goods and passengers, house-building and preparations of shelter in every form, in vigorous progress, give sign that the wand of civilization has been stretched over the land.

January 28. Surveyors hard at work in cutting lines and laying down the course of the river.

The withering of the dreams of the first load of settlers was captured by Jerningham Wakefield:

The sand-hummocks at the back of the long beach were dotted with tents of all shapes and sizes, native-built huts in various stages . . . and heaps of goods . . . lay about anywhere between high-water mark and the houses . . . A rough path had been cleared by the surveying men along the bank; on either side . . . the colonists had been allowed to squat on allotted portions until the survey of the town should be completed . . . Captain Smith . . . had preferred the lower part of the valley of the Hutt to Thorndon . . . as the whole 1100 acres, with sufficient reserves for promenades and other public purposes, could be laid out on perfectly level ground . . . The dense forest and swampy nature . . . impeded the rapid progress of the necessary measurements; and these temporary allotments had therefore been made by Colonel Wakefield on the proposed boulevards and public park of the town . . . on the scrubby and sandy ground near the sea and a broad belt along either bank of the Hutt.

As the Company's first settlers were unpacking on Petone Beach, one of its directors, Sir William Molesworth, was persuading an audience in Leeds of the benefits of the fertility in which he assumed the settlers were revelling. 'As long as vast and fertile countries are uninhabited or uncultivated, it is our own fault if we suffer from an excess of population.' The fruits of colonial labour in New Zealand, he said to repeated cheers, brought more than employed colonists; their purchasing of the products of British industry 'furnishes employment for members at home, and enables a greater number of persons to live in comfort upon the British soil'.

Two participants in the experiment, John and Harriet Longford, wrote to their parents in Birmingham that they were still on board the *Aurora*, on 26 January 1840, because 'this being the first ship that has arrived, there is therefore no habitation for us; they are busy erecting some . . . The land is excellent, no danger of starvation, and the scenery is beautiful; and we have no doubt we shall do well.' John Lodge, another still on board, hadn't realised he was coming to a hunter's landscape. He told his mother she 'may guess what wilderness we had to go to—nothing but trees and a few native huts, and surrounded by the native savages . . . I very much regret not bringing out with me a gun with powder and shot . . . we are obliged to shoot our own birds.'

George Duppa was one who brought a temporary shelter. From 'Hollingbourne Tent', he told his father at Hollingbourne House in Kent, it was just good to be ashore in such a prodigious and beautiful place:

> *The soil is perfectly wonderful: the rapid growth of anything planted in it is something extraordinary. Every one appears to agree that it is capable of producing from five to seven quarters of wheat per acre as any of the most highly manured soils in England. A dense forest which has enriched the soil for ages, covers the country in this district . . . The native potato-grounds show what the land is; they grow enormous crops by merely scratching the surface with a sharpened stick . . . likewise the valley itself, most densely covered with timber, excepting on the banks of the river, which have, at one time or other, been cleared by the natives for potato-gardens . . .*
>
> *The scenery of these rivers as you go paddling up them in a canoe, is most enchanting. Picture a most enchanting serpentine river, overshadowed by trees of richest verdure, emblossomed by every colour, enlivened by the deep mellow and quaint notes of the tui, or mockingbird, besides those of hundreds of others equally rich and curious, and every now and then paroquets of the brightest greens and reds fluttering from bank to bank and adding their chattering to the general concert.*

The surveyor Charles McGurk's life was very different from what he had led in London—'rise at five, breakfast and out to the woods at six o'clock . . . home at six in the evening . . . very hard work . . . wet all day'— but he liked it 'amazingly'. It was a mistake though, he said, for the Company's pamphlets to say the river was navigable for eighty miles.

Not everyone was so easily satisfied. In July 1840 a subscriber to *The New Zealand Journal* wrote enclosing some 'Remarks from New Zealand' from a friend who had been to Port Nicholson, taken one look at 'the first tent the first immigrant pitched at that, their supposed garden of Eden', and left. 'They appeared to be very low-spirited, and wishful not to stay to cope with the hardships of forming a new settlement.' The weather was the problem. Those who kept alive thoughts of living in the sheltered northern harbours James Cook described were incredulous at the choice of this site for a town. A blunder, Theophilus Heale called it, 'worse than a crime':

> *Bitter was the disappointment of the first settlers when they looked upon the steep and barren hills which surrounded them . . . In the history of colonisation . . . the circumstances under which Port Nicholson was chosen . . . are, perhaps, unparalleled. The Hutt, though laid down in some of the recent maps as a large river, and talked of by the company as such, is but a streamlet—across which I have waded at its mouth, and have found it impossible to ascend it further than seven or eight miles in the lightest boat . . . its limited fertile lands . . . so densely covered with timber of valueless description . . . and enclosed in a continual storm.*

The Hutt River's windswept floodplain may have become one of the New Zealand Company's 'spots of natural advantage', but there was a warning in the landscape of which they yet knew nothing. William Mein Smith sensed it immediately. His surveying experiences in flood-plagued 19th-century London lead him to make 'many enquiries of the natives . . . whether these rivers ever overflowed their banks. They assured me they did not. I therefore proceeded with my plan of the town site cutting lines about six feet wide for the lines of the streets which tho' necessary was a very tedious operation on account of the extreme density of the forest.'

Upriver, settlers felling trees found silt high in their branches. If they were shaken, William Wakefield wasn't: 'Up the river today, the settlers had taken a sudden fright at the appearance of some of the trees indicating occasional floods on the land. This may be the case to a trifling extent in heavy freshes, but will be obviated by clearing the course of the river. The assistance of an experienced engineer accustomed to rivers and harbours is much wanted here.' A century on, that confidence was still alive and well:

> The Hutt Valley Development Scheme presents few difficulties from an engineering point of view . . . the river shall be swung to the west on a wide arc . . . shortening the run to the sea by many chains and leaving the present river mouth completely cut off from river flow and separated from the new mouth by a reclamation of some hundreds of acres . . . it could be carried out without interfering with private property . . . the industrial firms already established in the valley are unanimously of the opinion that berthage should be established for overseas vessels . . . there is, a potential increase of 500 per cent in the number of industrial workers in the valley.

When, inevitably, the floodplain did speak to the newcomers in 1840, it rewrote the New Zealand Company's plans. Within a month of the first clearing being cut in the riverbank forest, Edward Jermingham Wakefield was inspecting 'what damage the flood had really done'. The settlers had moved to the higher ground of an old beach ridge, but the river pouring through their huts had rattled them. With Smith's assurance that 'the nuisance' could be overcome by clearing the snags out of the river and cutting flood channels, Wakefield declared 'the swamps would be thrown out', the surveying proceed and the town stay at Britannia. Within days, however, the settlers had persuaded him to move the colony to Thorndon.

The river that left silt high in the trees kept Britannia almost deserted until well into the 1870s. Every winter the low-lying country became swamp. A huge flood inundated the valley in 1849, then again in 1855 when the entire floodplain was bank to bank with what is believed to be largest flood witnessed so far. Throughout the 1850s flax and toetoe grew over the New Zealand Company's clearings, and the river became choked with the trees its settlers had felled into it in the hope they would be washed away.

Two floods in 1878 caused the settlers to establish a river board. In March 1880 another wall of water swept a child to his death. Spring rains in

1887 brought more drowned fields. In 1893 Petone constructed its first stopbank. In nearby Alicetown, that simply worsened the problem. When the next big one came, three years later, 'Alicetown residents, armed with picks and shovels, attempted to break down the bank so that the water could take its old course through Petone. To combat this Petone organised a patrol, and when a flood was signalled by the ringing of a bell, the patrol took up its duties of doing sentry-go along the length of the bank. Sentry boxes were erected for their protection.'

Quirky local history? Or hints of something of greater magnitude? As recently as the 1930s, people could remember the whole lower floodplain under water. The mountains that delivered last century's massive floods are still there. Ravaged by alien animals, their forests have even less capacity to hold water than they did in the 1850s. We don't really know whether a flood today on the 1855 scale would stay within the stopbanks.

'The settlers on arrival will be relieved from all the usual difficulties which assail the process of civilization,' proclaimed the New Zealand Company's directors early in 1840. 'Everything will be prepared for them. Houses, even, are in the course of erection and the first colony will really go out to a home.'

It was midsummer when the first load arrived on the *Aurora*. A blustery, summer southerly blew onto the shore and whipped sand into the faces of the strangers. A surf was running, swamping some of the boats before they could make the beach. Rain soaked the piles of travellers' chests and household goods spread along the sand in front of the pā. The wind blew stronger, wrecking boats dragged high up for temporary shelters, blowing some over and over until they were completely smashed. Huddled beneath whatever they could find, the men looked out through the driving rain at the windshorn scrub. The women waited on board.

A few wealthy settlers like George Duppa had prefabricated houses, but most had to turn to Māori know-how—and nature. Close enough for Sam Deighton and John Wallace to wander into after pigeons, the forest was far enough away to make it 'rather tedious to build these huts on account of the distance of bringing wood and sedges'. But desperate for shelter the cold, wet settlers were soon watching Te Atiawa show them how to stick poles in the ground, thatch the sides with raupō, and fasten it all with flax and supplejack.

'We had to build our huts ourselves,' one settler wrote home, 'and, what is most strange, there is not a single nail in them—all flax. The flax grows to the enormous height of 12 feet and upwards.' By 4 February, a straggling line of huts appeared on the interim land grants that Wakefield had hurriedly allocated along Smith's first boulevarde. Things were looking up: 'They are all working away, in excellent spirits, at houses made of flax, bark and rushes, chiefly by native architects, and at small gardens for potato-gardens.'

Huts of the First Settlers, Petoni Beach.
WILLIAM SWAINSON

Wakefield wrote that his settlers were 'eyeing with satisfied looks the rich land, into which they are eager to thrust their spades'. Within a month, John Wallace had cleared his allotment of 'timber, brushwood, etc' and was beginning a garden. The excellent soil, he wrote home, 'will produce anything, but a great deal of labour is required to clear the land ready for cultivation . . . Go where you will . . . through the forest now, you will hear the ring of the axe, and the crash of falling timber.' All autumn the forest kept falling. 'People are grumbling about . . . the want of flat land,' one settler wrote in the middle of the 1840 winter, 'but I think the valley of the river bids fair to furnish as much as will be wanted for some time.' The speed with which the animals of the boats fattened on the fertile alluvium was no less spectacular than the first crops. The first phase of pastoralism does not depend on pasture. 'What the cattle and sheep fatten on,' said Lord Petre, from his clearing at Woburn, 'I am unable to say; they browse to a great extent on the young shoots of various trees and shrubs, and they find a great abundance of agreeable and nourishing food.'

Petone may have disappointed with its wet wildness, but it was in this immediate, total dependence on the forest and swamp of Petone that the European settlement of New Zealand truly began. Ninety-seven years after the *Aurora*'s arrival, a letter to Wellington's *Dominion* described how deforestation had ruined the Hutt River. 'For half a century sawmills operated in the valley, moving back and back as they worked out the bush. They produced the millions of feet of timber which built much of Wellington city. Timber for Parliament House and Government House, and the "biggest building" came from this forest . . .'

TE MOME STREAM, FEBRUARY 1840

When the *Oriental* arrived with the second load of settlers, William
Wakefield sent them around into the estuary and up the river where high
banks and trees would make it easier to erect the landing cranes for their
heavy equipment. They started on the forest immediately. 'Before dark,'
Wakefield wrote on February 3, 'a considerable space of ground was rendered available for the purposes of their intended settlement.'

While he praised the speed with which 'the energetic and combined
movements of the Orientals have quite changed the appearance of the banks
of the Hutt', others were dismayed 'not the least preparation had been made
by the Company's Chief Agent for the shelter of either our property or
persons'. Nor, said Edward Hopper, 'was even the site of the town yet fixed
upon . . . Seeing something must be done I prevailed on Colonel Wakefield
to allot me 40 of the emigrants to cut a good road through the bush to the
spot where he then considered it probable the town would be.' Slicing
through a mile of coastal scrub and low windshorn forest, Hopper's road
had to cross the stream by which Te Mome Swamp emptied into the river.
Hopper had few regrets about Britannia, as the 'rows of native houses, single
settlements, tents and rick-covers' beside the river were soon being called.
He and his partners had found themselves a beautiful spot shaded by a karaka
grove where 'our dwellings appear to be built in a shrubbery . . . trees of the
richest foliage . . . bearing a fruit the natives are very fond of'. Here, where the
vegetation was so thick it was hard to move without slashing a space with an
axe, rather than the barren sand of the foreshore, the promises of the New
Zealand Company would surely be fulfilled. Here in this place of 'enchanting
scenery' and no wild beasts, three- to six-pound fish landed every time a line
was thown in the river, and in the forest were parrots and pigeons 'twice the
size of English Pidgeons'.

TE MOME STREAM, FEBRUARY 1990

The drainage board is having trouble with the stream in which the settlers
from the *Oriental* laid bundles of scrub and waded up to their waists to get
to their riverbank allotments. It's a drain today, forgotten under the houses
and streets. The ground between the ditch-diggers and the steel pipes is
littered with beach gravels, pipi and cockles, as fresh as if the sea has just
left them there; the wild earth suppressed beneath the tarseal of its
temporary, suburban skin.

Where Edward Hopper and his friends landed their farming equipment from the *Oriental* and in Europe's first settlement attempt on New Zealand's famed fertile alluvium began clearing 'the dense forest which has enriched the soil for ages', a midweek match is on at the Central Croquet Club. In the muddy, tidal mess alongside, all that remains of the river, a white-faced heron tracks along the film of water which slowly creeps over the urban debris of car wheels and bottles. A magpie squawks at us from a macrocarpa and swoops down for a closer look. The lunchtime sounds of a primary school come over the fence. Between the elderberry and sycamore branches, Day-Glo graffitists have left 'Master Flash Rasta' on the corrugated iron, and other messages in a new language code I'm not privileged to know.

A few months later I watched the school's children run along their riverbank with their arms full of young native trees. That summer there had been a police-killing in the Housing Corporation flats where many of them live, and then botulism struck the stream, decimating its water birds—like a symbol of what had happened to the community. During the clean-up operation, the children found out that to reduce the risk of botulism you created shelter. They also learned what the riverbank had been six generations before:

> *the Fern tree which hangs its majestic leaves . . . over the still glossy waters of the River . . . nearly all the fine shrubs hang dropping their evergreen branches in the water undisturbed by the hand of man. They seem to have been indulged as nature's pets revelling in the fullest enjoyment of health and beauty . . . in full flower hanging over the Banks of the river nothing can excel their beauty.*

And imagined what it could be six generations on. Braiding their new knowledge of their place with theatre, some dressed as the forest's parakeets and kowhai to recreate the saga of its vanishing. Others began bringing it back to life. Their endeavour is tiny and fragile but a symbol that something is missing and needs to be put back. As karakia rang out, new kahikatea and harakeke were heeled into the ground.

Watching the rush of activity—some plants fondly peeled from their plastic planters and patiently introduced to the bulldozed landfill that was their new home, others hurriedly ripped out and left, roots exposed to the wind—I pondered the effort involved in recreating a forest. It's hard to imagine a forest that has gone without trace. What we do know today and what we have growing regard for, unlike the British settlers who came to this piece of ground, is that rainforests like the one that was here are prodigious and infinitely complex ecosystems. Once you have skinned and gutted them, it is very hard to get them back.

Most of us think of rainforests in terms of trees and birds, but some 93 per cent of their animal biomass is, in fact, invertebrates—insects, worms and so on. In the forest's delicately interdependent networks, these animals have an influence quite out of proportion to their visibility on how the rainforest lives and grows, and how it reacts to the continually changing environment. The persistent elimination of nature that followed Europe's arrival on this floodplain ran those networks to collapse. The great diversity of birds that Charles Heaphy saw vanished because, without the networks, life became impossible. They left land that sustained one of New Zealand's richest life support systems in the control of a tiny biotic band, the industrial world's ubiquitous scavengers and perpetual pioneers—rats and mice, flies, gorse, willow, broom, oxalis and blackberry, sparrows and seagulls, and humans.

All of a sudden, forests have become a focus of ecological activism around the world—powerful symbols, once again, in the cultural imagination. More and more New Zealanders would like to imagine their country as the children of Te Mome do: free, clean mornings, native bush nearby, no smell of industry in the air—as distant from the acid rain and polluted acquifers of industrial Europe as it is possible to get. Perhaps that is why the children at Te Mome decided to bring back their river's ancient forest—and with each year's ritual continue to do so.

CHAPTER THREE

THE RIVERBEND

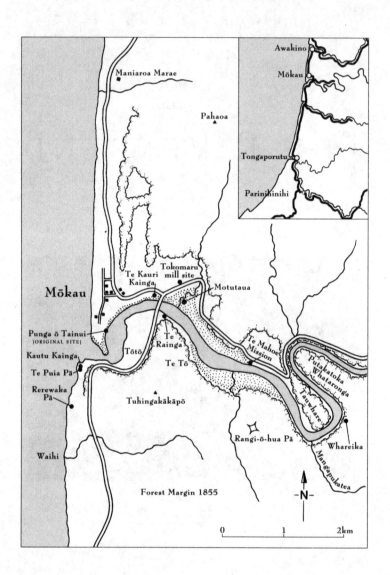

Awakino

Mōkau

Tongaporutu

Parinihinihi

Maniaroa Marae

Pahaoa

Tokomaru
mill site

Te Kauri
Kainga

Motutaua

Mōkau

Punga ō Tainui
[ORIGINAL SITE]

Te
Rainga

Te Mahoe
Mission

Putakatoka
Whataronga

Kautu Kainga

Tōtō

Te Tō

Te Puia Pā

Rerewaka
Pā

Tuhingakākāpō

Tawhare

Rangi-ō-hua Pā

Whareika

Waihi

Mangapukatea

Forest Margin 1855

-N-

0   1   2km

ORTH OF THE great volcano Taranaki, the coast of black sands and fertile, dairy-farmed terraces is defined by its sweeping ringplain, until it meets the towering white cliffs. Named Parininihi after an ancient taniwha, the cliffs force the state highway to find an easier route, inland over Mount Messenger. On the northern side of Parininihi, you are still in Taranaki, the locals say, but it is very different country.

The cliffs end in the spectacular earthworks of an ancient pā—facing north and the greatest prospect of invasion. Below it, a line of whitebaiters' baches hugs an estuary. Walk south beyond the dunes to where the burst of waves has eroded the cliffs into canyons and, high above the reach of the sea or anyone on the beach, you can see giant human feet chiselled into the sheer rock. They are strange images, six toes to a foot some of them— altogether different from what we expect Māori carving to be. Whoever made them did so a long time ago, before a changing climate or shoreline lifted them out harm's way. A little north, along the coast where the estuary of the Mōkau River once swept under bluffs, there are more giant feet, and beside them a beautiful impression of a stingray. These, still within reach of modern graffitists' knives, are as scarred as their landscape.

You don't have to be Māori to sense the human presence ingrained into this coast. It is connected to the terraces of defence pā that scuttle up ridge after ridge above the highway, and the blood in the ground they represent. But it is far older than them. Two anchor stones left in the estuaries by canoes that delivered Tainui and Taranaki people here from Polynesian tropics—that now lie in places less prone to plunder—take you closer. Even they, it is said, had others watching them land.

Yet the coast between Tongapōrutu and Mōkau is one of the very few in the North Island where old forest still reaches right down to the edge. Everywhere but on the riverflats and a thin strip of coastal terraces covered with the fertile ash blown north from the volcanoes, the burnt forests' nutrients supported a few decades of European pasture before they were washed away into streams, and the bush began its return over agriculture's vain endeavours. Inland, the sense of the sea quickly vanishes. Beech forests cling to the impoverished ridges. It is papa country—the steep, sliding mudstone of rural isolation and despair that Vincent Ward captured in his film *Vigil*.

Not long ago soldier settlers still filled this country with their optimism. A dairy factory was built on the ashes of a Māori kāinga, in readiness for the cows and grass which would replace the bush on their balloted riverflats. Well into the 1950s, their daughters had their debutante balls in the Mōkau Hall.

To the 19th-century Europeans of colonising schemes like the New Zealand Company, Mōkau was the portal to a rich hinterland of fertile plains, a place where one day a city would arise. Edward Gibbon Wakefield had heard of 'the river Mokou' not only as the Waikato and Taranaki tribal boundary but as a potential access to the famed fertility of the Waikato. He knew nothing of its source and extent, or for that matter whether any other west coast river 'forms a harbour or bay at its junction with the sea'. Yet 'from the native account of the plains and from what is already known of the extreme fertility of the rest of the Waikato country', he could see 'no reason to question its fertility, and it becomes a matter of great importance to explore it'.

When William Wakefield negotiated the much-disputed deed of purchase giving the New Zealand Company 'valuable superiority over the owners of ordinary lands' around Cook Strait, he made sure it extended north to Mōkau. He did not go there, however: the New Zealand of his imagination was still a country of plains, and for the brief time through 1839 into 1840 that the myth prevailed, there were more than enough opportunists ready to cash in on the growing confusion over ownership. One who had been with Wakefield on the *Tory*, a Dr Dorset, took his money straight to Taranaki and was soon able to tell his brother in England that he had 'in my possession two deeds conveying a property of immense extent, and comprising the most valuable land by far in New Zealand;—it is conceded by the natives of all parts that it is the garden of New Zealand.' He hadn't forgotten the river just to the north: 'Having trade enough left, I intend to go to Mokou and buy that.'

Whatever he did there was no sign of him the next summer when another young New Zealand Company colonist, Frederick George Moore, came across the Mōkau bar into the quiet estuary. What led Moore there is not known, but it was his second attempt to reach Mōkau since arriving at Port Nicholson. By the time he had sailed along its steep, broken coast however, he'd abandoned any dream of fertile plains. Soon after mooring the *Jewess*, he 'made visits of inspection of the surroundings. A party of leading men . . . invited me to take a trip up the Mokau River in a large and well-equipped canoe . . . The banks of the river were well timbered . . . what will become some fine day very valuable to our ever-consuming race.' If Wakefield's dream of a riverplain city was clearly a fantasy, the welcoming piles of food spread along the riverbank —'baskets of water-melons, pumpkins and calabashes and kekia [kiekie] . . . mounds of steamed and baked potatoes and fish; pyramids of pigeons and the kakas; pork, roasted and steamed; wood hens, pipis, mussels and various kinds of vegetables such as kumaras, taro, Indian corn, cooked in the leaf'—suggested he was right about its fertility.

Moore's 1880s description of Mōkau was in hindsight:

> In all my travels I never met with kinder or more hospitable natives than those at Mokau . . . there seemed to be great unity amongst themselves . . . the matter and manner and motions closely indicated an unselfish and earnest . . . welcome for myself, my crew and all Pakeha friends to visit Mokau . . . nor shall I easily forget how I contrasted this native abundance with the . . . piteous picture of more civilised savages in Europe . . . from selfishness born to want and all its attendant sorrows and evils . . . no opening, and no hope beyond the long grinding days work . . . barely bread enough to keep life and soul together.

Moore's Mōkau experience made him more aware than most of the brutal crunch of white settlement. Within little more than a generation, Māori hospitality had been overrun by their dispossession and abandonment: 'God spare the Maoris from such fates and Colonists from the iniquity of grasping all the land, the unjust seizure of which, by the few privileged, is the source beginning and end of all human poverty and misery over the surface of the Garden of Eden, the Almighty Landlord Earth was never intended for monopoly by legalised robbers, but for a natural and free as air heritage to all present and coming people . . .' By the 1880s, Mōkau's Māori landscape had been appropriated and enclosed by surveyors and settlers, forest and gardens alike relegated to the realm of collective memory. Missionaries had intervened in its ecology and weaned its inhabitants away from their cosmology. For a decade it had been the frontline of the Rohepōtae, the post-war zone of exclusion we still call the King Country. The first surveyor allowed up the river saw 'the evidence everywhere' of a 'once large Māori population', of cultivations going to ruin 'everywhere that the land was suitable'. 'One feels surprised,' he said, 'what food is grown even for the few who remain now.'

The Mōkau of boarded-up shops and weekend baches that most people sweep past on the highway seems another country from the 'very prosperous circumstances' in which Ernst Dieffenbach said the 'natives . . . called Nga-te-Meniopoto' lived. On the Waikato side of the estuary a road leaves the highway and heads inland across riverflats. Shedding its seal at the foot of the hills, it winds past the riverbank middens of Te Māhoe, a karaka grove signposted Historic Place and, staying alongside the river, climbs up past the traces of the biggest midden of them all—the recently-buried county tip; the agricultural chemicals that soaked it leaking out of sight into the river. Just as it seems you've seen the last of the river, the road slices through a papa cutting and the river sprawls across your view again. But no longer is it an estuary.

Only from a plane or way above the paddocks on the other riverbank, can you see why some people call the lump of land enclosed by the river's sudden twisting around to greet the sea 'The Island'. Many more have known it as Tauwhare (or 'Tawari', the spelling that has prevailed ever since the 1890s when the name was first recorded in government documents), one of the best naturally defended sites on the entire west coast. Cutting through from one side to another, the car culture completely ignores what, to an ecologist, makes Tauwhare such an auspicious place.

It is early morning, wet with dew, as I stand under Te Māhoe's karaka and look up the estuary. Around the end of Tauwhare, a row of huge kahikatea trees is disappearing out of sight. In front of them a film of water is sliding in across the mudflats. A good sign: I won't have tide as well as river against me. My feet crunching shells that have slipped out of old pipi heaps, I lower the canoe down a whitebaiter's cliff track and into the water. Pointing the bow upriver to the big trees, I hold it against the bank while I get myself seated. Then the flow takes me out into the stream.

From low on the water, the big kahikatea seem to guard the head of the estuary. Their forest is the last of its kind in the North Island, but there was a time when trees like them stood on the tidal flats of almost every river. Other than the ravaged hills and the fact that most of the bleached, stranded logs littering the river are willows, the scene is as close as you are going to get today to what was seen by the first canoe-load of people to come out of the waves and up an estuary.

As I close on the kahikatea, a marsh of rushes and ribbonwood appears between them and the river, behind it a tight thicket of manuka—to the ecologist, a sure sign of disturbance. The same marsh is marked on an 1870s surveyor's map, but it is some time before I discover the extraordinary reason for the manuka thicket. At this distance, the kahikatea forest is a kaleidoscope of colours and textures. Each huge native pine teems with kahakaha and kōwharawhara, the 'bird-nest-like masses . . . perched high up in the forest roof in the forks of the trees' that so fascinated the first Europeans to encounter a New Zealand estuary. Cook's botanists mistook them for parasites, but they were right in suspecting they were lilies. With less time for botany, early European settlers called them 'tree flax'. Science has given them a succession of names, but now settles for *Collospermum haastatum*, after the 19th-century German explorer Julius Von Haast, and *Astelia banksii*, after the *Endeavour*'s naturalist. That their Māori names, like harakeke, share their linguistic roots with useful and similar looking plants in the Polynesian tropics, suggests they may not have been quite as strange to the migrating ancestors of today's Māori.

Funnelling rain and nutrients into aerial ponds, kahakaha's and kōwharawhara's leaves sustain them through the dry spells that are surprisingly common in the high, windy canopies of a New Zealand rainforest. The dead leaves, twigs and micro-organisms they funnel as well also render them perfect sites for a host of other plants. Many Māori, like the older people at Mōkau, consider them the home of patupaiarehe, the forest fairies.

Over centuries, humus accumulates so deep that even small trees can establish. Eventually, though, the inevitable happens. Sodden with rain, top-heavy in a storm, the mass of ferns, orchids and epiphytic shrubs crashes down into the swamp below.

A solitary young mangrove plant was recently seen in the Awakino estuary just to the north, and sometimes mangrove seeds wash up in the Mōkau. Were it a few hundred kilometres further north, a mangrove forest would guard the kahikatea from the tide. Instead it is a non-wooded zone of wiwi, the orange and black jointed rush, and the green sea rush. In the river's fertile silt, wiwi's tubular leaves reach in excess of two metres. A different plant altogether from its knee-high cousins on exposed, rocky coasts: one day it can be swirling around you in the wind, hiding you from sight the moment you step ashore; the next day a storm or spring tide can mow it down into great flattened swathes. Wiwi's tensile strength is enough to suspend piles of forest flotsam above the ground for months at a time, but it is also so brittle that one human step can snap off dozens of stems at a single step. The evidence of one walk from river to trees persists until next spring's new growth.

Spring brings other things—like the whitebait the far-reaching tides deliver to the maze of riverbank rushes where they can spawn unmolested. Exactly a month later, the Mōkau suddenly becomes noisy with jet boats and human voices. For the forests' birds, it is the season of real scarcity, when the last of the fruit crop has gone. The insects are quiet, in the hidden, immobile part of their annual cycle. Then the riverbank kōwhai start swelling.

In the days before muskets and farms, he ua kōwhai was an event in the landscape which demanded response. As pīpīwharauroa's call that it was back from the tropics signalled time to plant root crops, kōwhai's dilating flower buds meant kererū would soon start gathering and that snapper should be left alone to breed. But if anything signals spring, it is the sudden appearance of the bright green triangular shoots of the riverbank rushes emerging from the mud among last year's collapsed, straw-coloured remains. Within weeks, they are hiding the whitebaiters' plastic juice bottles and dirty lumps of polystyrene.

Circling the riverbank, a young kāhu monitors my landing. Wary of the tide, I push the canoe ashore beside a collapsing whitebaiter's hut, as far up into the jointed rushes as I can get it. A few steps toward the big trees and my legs are saturated. Damp, milky-green lichens trail from each tiny-leaved ribbonwood and coprosma; from everything, in fact, on which it can hang. A screen of cutty grass and harakeke marks where spring tides nudge up against the front-line of trees. Back turned, face shielded, I slip from salty mud into deep, soft forest floor; my eyes adjust to an interior light, deep greens and large leaves.

A forest like this one, barely changed since dinosaurs knew it, makes human time seem like dust on a rock. Unable to find a way through the myriad profusion of plants, I clamber instead high above the ground and black water pools, over a slippery maze of stems and aerial roots, until eventually my feet touch a drier forest floor. In this rare world of parataniwha, young palms and ferns, one fern, the spectacular parātawhiti, is a thrill to see. Now one of lowland New Zealand's rarest plants, surviving only where people and their predatory grazers can't reach, modern botanists believe it and its close relatives elsewhere in Polynesia to have ancient tropical origins. To the 1870s surveyor Edwin Brooks, parātawhiti was evidence of a place being 'long inhabited by the natives'. The Taranaki Māori who he watched 'first boil it then pound it with a pestle in the same manner as they made the fern root ready for the palate' told him their ancestors brought it to New Zealand in the Aotea canoe.

Parātawhiti's origin, whether it's been a New Zealander for millions of years or a mere thousand, no longer makes much difference to its place in the forest. All around the Pacific, in forests little different from this, its close relatives live with the same kinds of ferns and flowering plants it does here. Nearly all of them have an ancient tropical Gondwana ancestry evolving long before the evolution of mammals began. Over the time they have been stranded in a temperate climate, they have adjusted to the fact that there is not going to be an afternoon shower every day in the wet season. Yet some tropical forest features, like the drip-tips on many broad-leaved species, and the liverworts growing on them, they have obviously had reason to retain.

On a wet day, when the water pouring out of the countless leaves drenches you in minutes, you can be in no doubt you are in a rainforest, a pattern of plants with daily water needs far above what flows off the surrounding high land. Some species feed direct from the fertile river silt, but much of the profusion of foliage—the epiphytes, climbers, ferns and mosses—lives, like tropical rainforests, off organic material that the forest itself has produced over centuries. In contrast to the dramatic seasonal changes in the riverbank rush communities, the riverflat forest barely changes. While early settlers hoped that with winter's arrival 'the gloomy forest and repulsive waste' would drop its layers of leaves and open up a little, rainforests did not evolve to suit European sensibilities. Standing in the sunless interior, I can begin to understand why my ancestors were in such a rush to cut them down.

From deep inside the kahikatea forest, the huge trees that so dominate it from the outside seem few and far between. One of the world's most ancient trees, its leaves found in Jurassic sediments contemporaneous with dinosaur remains, kahikatea's evolutionary strategies must make it one of the most successful trees on earth. The enduring paradox though is that the land on which it grows most successfully, is the youngest and most ephemeral. Any day, the river whose water creates the floodplains and brings the life-giving silt on which it thrives could wipe the tree away.

Any New Zealand forest is locked into a cycle of unpredictable natural destruction, but it is especially so in kahikatea's forests. Within days of a flood taking the forest's trees away to sea, there will be a flush of new growth. Herbs, and shrubs like manuka, will soon cover the new surface. The traffic of birds will drop millions of seeds among them, many of them kahikatea. In a few decades kahikatea's pointed conical crowns, packed tight, will be poking through the scrub, shaping a new riverflat forest. Competition will squeeze the weaker ones out, and if another torrent does not sweep them all away, the survivors will grow into the kind of trees that Captain Cook believed would make the perfect naval spar.

Eventually, after a few centuries, rātā seeds will germinate in the kahikatea's forks, take root, send their aerial roots down to the ground and begin taking over. Some kahikatea will topple, top-heavy, in storms. Younger ones, and other trees like pukatea, will appear in the gaps. As the forest opens up, a more complex forest—the kind clothing the riverbend today—will develop. Eventually, after about 800 years, if a flood or a tsunami hasn't scoured the little flat clean again, all the old kahikatea will be gone.

When virtually all lowland New Zealand was clothed in forest and before any people inhabited it, every rivermouth and coastal creek contained this mix of primordial conifers, palms, laurels, lianes and vines, perching lilies, ferns and rushes tied into the seasonal flood of silt and the daily surge of tide. Those that have forest today are still biologically rich places compared with the hill country that envelops them. But in the days of the birds that neither experienced nor feared humans—the eagles, moa, pelicans, geese, rails and waders—a place like this would have teemed with them.

Leaving the riverflat forest can be as dramatic as entering it. One minute I am under towering trees, in the primordial dark and wet, anything more than a few metres away invisible in the press of life, then suddenly I emerge through cutty grass into bright light beside a mudbank and a backwater of rushes curling away to the now tide-swollen river.

The top of the mudbank is obligingly dry. I sit in its sward of native grass for a couple of hours, the sun on my face. Kererū and tui criss-cross the river. Kingfishers dart into the backwater and out again when I move. Tree shadows inch over the rushes as the sun drops toward Tauwhare's bluffs, then vanishes completely. Chilled by the sudden change, I begin picking my way back to the river. The tide is sliding out again, but still high enough to confine me to the mudbank—close enough to catch a glimpse of the white glint of hundreds of sea shells, spilling out of a water-cut face packed tight with charcoal and fired soil. Humans have lived in this place, which, had I not seen the shells, I'd have gone on thinking of as wild and primeval. The odd dryness is now explained—it would seem the entire mound is shells, someone's rubbish heap wedged between forest and river. Now little more than a lump in the bush, it must have been imposing in its time.

Just when I was trying to connect with a peopleless world, millions of years in the making, the shell mound made it satisfyingly human. Who would inhabit such a place? Long ago pihāro fishers watching their weirs? Kākā and kererū hunters? Was it an outpost for the big pā that once stood high above on Tauwhare? Or a more permanent, homely place? Countless early Victorian travellers have left paintings showing whare clustered at the foot of great riverbank trees, just as the shell mound would suggest was the case here. Yet the persistent imperialism of the natural science on which I was brought up prefers to see such evidence as romantically distorted rather than prosaically factual. To those who need a culprit for the disappearance of New Zealand's amazing, unknowable animals, it has never been a convenient image, ill fitting the notion of big beach barbecues of primeval birds and Māori torching forests, forcing them off the plains.

When 17-year-old Percy Smith ventured up the river in a hired canoe en route to Taupo in 1858, Mōkau was still a large riverbank settlement. Smith was so struck by the picturesque scene of thatched whare set in front of the forest that he drew a map of the line across the landscape where the narrow, cleared coastal strip met the wild. Tauwhare's old kahikatea forest and the shell mound were well on the wild side. So too was Whareika, a settlement on the river's opposite, Taranaki, bank whose huge shell mound is being eroded away faster than the scrub can reclaim the paddocks around it. High above Whareika are the remains of the hill pā that confronted Tauwhare. Farm work has exposed pipi shells, black soil and umu all along the adjoining riverflat.

Childhood ventures to North Taranaki, saturated with Methodism, had engendered in me a feeling for Mōkau as a dark place, dense with history, long before a surviving forest of rivermouth kahikatea drew me to it. A history neither brief nor sparse, if the marks in the land said anything. Almost every road cutting and riverbank carried shell heaps of old settlements. Every prominent hill with an outlook, a flight of terraces cut to build palisades and repel attack.

Not the sort of environment conducive to the survival of wild forest. Yet in the centre of one of the west coast's densest concentrations of pā and riverbank kāinga was one of its oldest, most precious lowland forests. A superficial glance might explain it as an accident—a remote riverflat whose white pine somehow eluded bushmens' saws and settlers' fires. A closer look shows otherwise. In a similar estuary in northwest Nelson, I once measured identical-looking kahikatea to be 800 years old. Were these great trees rising up from the Mōkau's silt as ancient, they had to have spanned almost the entirety of Māori settlement.

Mōkau ke runga
Tāmaki ki raro

Originally a warning to the bordering tribes, Ngāti Tama of Taranaki and Ngāti Whatua, these are words all Tainui know. As they allude to the deep roots between people and river back to Hoturoa and the great journey from Ra'iatea, they chart Tainui's domain from Mōkau to Tāmaki. A waiata composed at the death of Tawhaio carries a similar passage:

Ka ngau Mōkau, ke ngau Tāmaki,
Ka ru te whenua, ka mate te mārama
Ka taka te whetu ō te rangi
I te unuhanga ō te taniwha i te rua!
Aue, aue, aue, te mamae e!

Recent events keep alive the notion of the river as the edge of one tribal domain and the beginning of another. Christianity has been in residence for more than a century and a half, yet the river and its estuary are still invested with tapu and taniwha. River tapu is scrupulously observed—as much as Maniapoto fear death when lightning strikes the high hills above Te Kauri, the old kāinga at the rivermouth, so are Ngāti Tama apprehensive of any flash up in Rakeiura, the high land south of the Mōkau named for Rakei, the navigator of Tokomaru waka.

The simplicity of such traditional vignettes belies their fallibility. What seems instantly persuasive—Mōkau, the river, the boundary—is in reality far from so. There is evidence in old urupā maps of Ngāti Tama flourishing right to the rivermouth, even on the northern, Waikato bank. But the 19th century's succession of musket raids, heke, war and confiscation has confined Ngāti Tama almost landless, to the south of Parininihi's cliffs—greatly confusing the land claim researchers who a century and a half later have been trying to unravel it.

Tainui's precise and confident whakapapa runs their presence at Mōkau back to about the year 1350. Archaeology has found no evidence of it. While archaeologists dispute just where and when the first people came ashore and settled Aotearoa, Tainui's traditions insist that this coast had people long before Tainui themselves arrived. When they came we may never know. The rivermouths and estuaries that attract people to coasts like this are constantly changing—if not eroded by the tide, the land heads back to forest as soon as humans leave, masking everything but the most recent signs.

Barely had the surveyor William Skinner arrived at Mōkau in 1883, than the Maniapoto kaumatua at the rivermouth were acquainting him with their turangawaewae. Their ancestors' first act on coming ashore, they said, had been to attack Mōkau's original people in their pā, Rangi-ō-hua. Apart from one woman, he was told, Tainui drove all the original inhabitants inland—by a subterranean passage—to the open country of Taupo. From there they moved to the East Coast, then the southern North Island and across Cook Strait—becoming Kai Tahu.

Percy Smith had a different interpretation, based in part on the number of Mōkau families in the early 1900s who were, he said, descended from intermarriage of the only Kai Tahu who remained, a man, Rokiroki, and a woman, Kaea, with Ngāti Tama. Smith's *History and Traditions of the Taranaki Coast* records 'stories current on this coast of a people called

Maero . . . wild men of the woods . . . the remains of some of the original people driven to the forests and mountains'. Ngāti Tama, he believed, routed them before Tainui came. Recognising Rangi-ō-hua and the same tradition in the genealogy of Taiaroa of Kai Tahu in the far south, Smith attributed Rangi-ō-hua's early occupants to distant ancestors of the southern Kai Tahu of Takitimu descent.

Towering over Tauwhare and its kahikatea on the bank opposite, Rangi-ō-hua is a superb defence site. No one could move unobserved on the Mōkau. Fascinated by what he had heard, Skinner climbed up and found 'undisturbed forest growth' over the whole site. A rātā tree, three feet thick, growing out of one of the pits, suggesting it had been many centuries since the pā had been abandoned, was enough to convince him. Proof enough, he thought, that 'the pa had been deserted soon after the coming of the Tainui migrants'.

Mōkau's coast may be riddled with 300–400-year-old pā, but the earliest Māori did not fortify themselves in defended settlements. Pā like Rangi-ō-hua began to be built only about 1500 AD, a response it is believed to competition for the land with the best resources that persisted as the focal point of Māori polity until the arrival, 300 years later, of European ways of resolving the problem. The prevalence of pā on a once-populated coast like this, with a major tribal junction plumb in the middle, is as good evidence as any perhaps of resource depletion.

Tribal traditions are no less absolute about Tainui waka's anchor-stone. Until Punga-ō-Tainui was shifted to the ancestral pā, Maniaroa—the consequence of a Waitara trader stealing it, and suddenly dying—this huge dumb-bell of volcanic rock is believed to have lain in the mud near the Mōkau's mouth since it was offloaded from Tainui waka in the 14th century. There are at least two explanations. In one, Tainui travelled down the west coast after portaging across the Tāmaki isthmus, staying out to sea from Aotea and Kawhia and not making a landfall until Taranaki. Finding Tokomaru people in possession, Hoturoa turned Tainui around and, after a brief stop at Mimi, beached it at Mōkau. It stayed there while the inland country was reconnoitred, before being taken up the coast to its final resting place at Kawhia. Another version has one of the Tainui crew, who had married into the tangata whenua and renamed himself, relaunching it from Kawhia and sailing south. One of the party allegedly desecrated the great canoe. When the news reached Hoturoa, he had Tainui brought back to Kawhia forever, leaving Punga-ō-Tainui behind.

Over generations of continual attentiveness to its powers, Punga-ō-Tainui gathered a powerful tapu. But by the 1890s, the influence it exerted over Mōkau people had become a distant memory—as the kaumatua Tanirau Wharauroa told James Cowan:

> . . . when I was a youth we never failed to take the first mullet or kahawai we caught when we were out fishing in our canoes and offer it with a prayer to the atua, the god who sent us the fish. We laid these offerings on a sandbank there, between the Stone of Power [Punga-ō-Tainui] and the Heads, the holy place Te Naunau. But these days no one bothers about offerings and first-fruits. We are like the Pakeha; we don't trouble about the tapu now. He aha te tapu?

The Mōkau landscape the young Percy Smith mapped in 1852 was an ecological mosaic. Supporting cultivations and community forests, both rich in useful species, it contrasted dramatically with the European idea of conservation which was to set aside large wildernesses free of human interference, or keep remnant patches in a monocultural expanse of crops and plantations. Little of the Mōkau was left unexploited. Its people didn't act with any particular ecological nobility: they did whatever they had to do to feed themselves and their families. The first brought Polynesian concepts like rahui and tapu ashore. Over time their way with the new land acquired a regularity that revealed nature's rhythms and showed how yields could be increased if fishing and hunting were kept in line with them. From that knowledge came rituals that kept life within ecological limitations. And as the river landscape filled with history, it filled with emotion.

———————

The riverbend, Tauwhare, is known primarily as the place where Tahu Tahu Ahi, Te Rauparaha's great heke into the southern North Island, finally departed the Waikato homelands in 1822. Tahu Tahu Ahi's prominence in traditions is a consequence of the dramatic transformation it effected in New Zealand's balance of tribal power just before the Treaty of Waitangi fixed tribal boundaries like a historical cement. When the heke came down the coast from Maro-kōpa, Te Rauparaha, apprehensive of an attack from Maniapoto, learnt the Mōkau was in flood.

Karanga pa mai?
Tena ka mene kei waho,
Kei tai e kokoti kino ana, i te ngāru tua manomano,
Tai ki Karewa,
Ko to paenga ia,
Waho ō Maketu,
Ko te one tiatia, ki te tao matārua,
Te tonga puaroa,
Ka rimua ō iwi ki runga ō Tauwhara, [Tauwhare]
Taka mai Rawhiti;

Tauwhare was no mere crossing point. Te tonga puaroa, it is tūāhu; sacred, ancestral, a place of ritual.

I knew none of this the first time I drove up the river road and glimpsed the riverbend's big kahikatea. Many times before I stumbled across the shell mound, I had canoed past the big trees and pondered how it was they had eluded the settlers' razing of the rest of the Mōkau landscape. In the way Tauwhare stood out in aerial photographs and lay among the hill pā, pasture and second-growth like an untouched, ancient island, I could sense it was an auspicious place. Yet not a word in the reports of scientists who had surveyed the riverbank reserves and found rare plants still surviving in Tauwhare's dark riverflat forest had intimated it.

Unable to grasp what caused people to inhabit a damp riverbank in the shadows of towering trees, I knew the time had come to sound out local knowledge. Enquiries quickly led me to the person who looks after such things. I knew the preservation of Tauwhare's kahikatea was no accident the moment I alluded to them.

'You be careful,' she warned. 'You're talking about a very powerful place, you know. A special place.' She murmured about its healing qualities, but with no explanation, and didn't mention Tauwhare's name. By the time I walked out into the night, however, I was well aware of the strangely serene bitterness its very mention engendered. I knew her family had a history of kaitiakitanga, guardianship, and that those who transgressed the Mōkau's tapu had suffered hair-raising consequences—a mild example being the first land-grabbing settler who one ancestor in the 1870s threw into the Mōkau with his load of stolen coal.

The government's signs and survey maps have called Tauwhare 'Mokau River Scenic Reserves' for almost a century now. But the riverbend's kaitiaki doesn't rank beautiful scenery especially high in her understanding of it. The place I know as the last of this sort of riverine forest anywhere in New Zealand, surviving here because a late Victorian urge to protect river scenery kept it out of reach of settlers, is to her taken land—taken, what's more, from people who had already paid a high price for securing it.

Ever since Mōkau had called her back from half a lifetime in Auckland's suburbs, the river had become her responsibility. Suddenly she found herself full of knowledge about it, more than she had imagined existed, and with no idea how it entered her. And when she did return, Te Rainga, the only childhood place where she could even begin to explain it, where 'you learned things without even knowing you were learning them', was gone. A big riverbank settlement of raupō whare in an 1870s photo, by the 1970s it was nothing but bits of concrete and iron strewn over a cattle-cropped paddock.

Tribal memory. Gap-filling the official record, it reminds Pākehā that the symbiosis between imperialism, dispossession and deforestation hasn't been forgotten. Months later, miles away, I began to grasp the reasons for her reticence. While looking through colonial archives, a dusty, forgotten box of far-reaching edicts of 1890s' officials was brought to me. Out of dead leaves of deeds and proclamations, voices began to confide in me. Tauwhare's kahikatea, they revealed, were no accident.

TE RAINGA, 1870S.

In July 1897 Pepene Eketone appeared before the New Zealand Native Land Court at Otorohanga. He was giving evidence on behalf of Pahiri Wiari about Section 12, Block 1, Awakino Survey District. He knew it as Tauwhare, or Tawari, as it was written in the Land Court Minutes: 'It was Takerei te Kaka who kept this piece of land out of the sale as his tapu—and the land belongs to his descendants who did not sell their interests here.'

By the 1890s the Native Land Court was completely reshaping the Māori landscape. Taking the power of sale from tribal elders and giving it to individuals, it was making decisions which will reverberate forever. As land-hungry settlers poured into post-war New Zealand, and Māori wellbeing reached its nadir, the Native Land Court was less a retainer of manawhenua than an agent of deprivation and inequity. As James Edward Fitzgerald, 'so sad about the Natives', wrote in 1883, 'We have time to introduce them to Civilized law, and what is the result? That they are being . . . fleeced in the vilest manner by lawyers until the whole value of their land is eaten up . . . in putting it through the Land Court.'

In the case of Tauwhare, Māori authority prevailed. One of four Mōkau Native Reserves brought under the Land Court's jurisdiction, 'Te Mahoe or Tawari Reserve . . . containing 76 acres' was formally notified in the *New Zealand Gazette* on 6 September 1897. In February 1899 the Native Land Court, at Te Kuiti, ordered as Pepene Eketone had pleaded; in favour of 16 of Takerei's descendants as its owners. A clear-cut decision it would seem. William Skinner had surveyed Tauwhare off as 'Native Reserve' in 1883. When the question of Mōkau reserves was being debated years later, at the time my father delivered mail to him, in 1937, Skinner vividly recalled the wariness with which his survey party was sent to the wild river at the edge of the King Country. They were given firm instructions 'to use care and discretion in following boundaries as desired by the Natives', and he remembered the relief that 'no trouble was experienced' from the old chiefs Takerei and Wetere Te Rerenga other than claiming more land for their kāinga. Taking him to each of the reserves, the chiefs pointed out the boundaries they'd insisted on 30 years earlier, before Taranaki erupted in war.

By 1849 the prospect of a settler town and port had taken the government's land purchase officer, Donald McLean, to Mōkau many times. He had come to know the chiefs who controlled the 'several flats of rich land well adapted for agriculture' by the river, and admired the commitment of the river's missionary to preparing the Mōkau people for the prospect of the land's sale. Under his tuition, McLean reported, the Mōkau natives were making 'considerable improvement'. But while Ngāti Maniapoto's willingness to sell was apparent, there was some land they were clearly reluctant to let go. 'As yet,' wrote McLean, 'no offers have been made to dispose of the land on the banks of the Mokau which would be most valuable.'

While the pressure to sell mounted and Donald McLean went on to greater things, Maniapoto hung on to what they knew sustained them. Then, in October 1852, the Ngātipehi hapu, headed by the chiefs Ngātaua, or Takerei, and Te Waru, conceded to a new land purchase agent, George Cooper, to part with a block 'about two miles square extending along the banks of the river to a stream called Mana-uira'. The sale, however, was dependent on Ngātipehi being able to continue living at the river, cultivating its fertile flats and maintaining their ties to it. So they offered the block subject to several 'reserves'. Ngātaua, reported Cooper, wanted to retain 'a piece of land called Te Kauri, consisting of about 30 acres, with a frontage of nearly a quarter of a mile to the river, and including almost the only available spot for commercial purposes'. Te Waru wanted a reserve of '300 acres of the best cultivable land in the block'. In addition, Ngātipehi sought three other small reserves, 'one of them comprising the greater part of the land now occupied as a mission station'. Another was Tauwhare:

> *A large tongue formed by a bend of the river is also excepted on account of being an ancient burial ground.*

At this rate, Cooper realised, the government would get little more than 500 acres of the kind of land its settlers wanted. He told the chiefs he would not listen to such a small offer. Late in November 1852 the Colonial Secretary, Alfred Domett, told him not to purchase a thing at Mōkau 'until the Natives are all agreed to dispose of the extent of country required by the Government'. Without it, he said, the land they were offering was almost valueless. Go back to them, Domett suggested, this time mention Sir George Grey the Governor. Let them know 'His Excellencie's approval of Ta Kerei's exertion to obtain land for Government'. Meanwhile, Cooper was told, the Resident Magistrate had been instructed to make Takerei a small present.

The Governor himself, said Cooper's letter to 'My Friend Ta Kerei', was very pleased to obtain 'a piece of land for his children', but 'Europeans would never think of going upon so small a piece of land':

*You had better therefore agree, the whole of you, men, women
and children from the North, the South and the interior—all the
people—to extend the boundary . . . Both sides of Mokau must be
given up at one time, and then I will go down . . . and conclude
the arrangements . . . that a town may be built at that place, that
it may be cultivated by Europeans, so that the land may be
improved, and that we will all and our children may dwell
together . . . grow and increase in wealth and strength as one
people, and that our children may climb together to the summit
of worldly prosperity.*

Land purchase under Grey's governorship was pursued with at least
some circumspection. Once he'd gone, McLean, Chief Land Purchase
Commissioner by 1853, went at it without restraint. Part of a policy that
soon led to war along the Taranaki and Waikato coast, McLean's all-or-
nothing requirement of Mōkau Māori shapes their landscape to this day.

*There is no Reserve whatever in this land now entirely given up
by us to Victoria the Queen of England under the shining sun of
the present day for ever and ever with all its lakes, rivers and
waters as well as all its trees all its stone and everything either
above or under the land and every thing connected with it now
surrendered by us for ever.*

Mōkau in 1854 had few Europeans who could explain to Ngātipehi,
at that crucial moment, what sale meant in McLean's terms; that the
unambiguous language of the deed being read to them, in Māori, meant
exactly what it said. One who did and undoubtedly tried was a trader,
Hopkins. At the time of the sale, he was buying up Ngātipehi's new wheat
and maize crops, and strenuously advising them against selling the riverflats.
Under the Native Land Purchase Ordinance his advice was illegal. Cooper
reported the trader to Auckland, even raised the possibility of a case against
him. 'Although the mischief he is doing is very great,' Cooper was resigned
to the reality that no Māori would give evidence against the trader.

McLean's first land-buying trip to Mōkau was 'at the request', as he
said, 'of Ta Kerei and other chiefs who are anxious to dispose of a tract of
land north of the Mōkau River'. If it's safe to assume anything from his
1849 observation of the chiefs' 'desire for the settlement of Europeans among
them', it's that Ngātipehi knew of the Europeans' notion of native reserves.

As Dieffenbach noticed earlier in the 1840s, 'the sale of lands and the colonization of the country by Europeans engrossed their whole attention'. Reserves were the way that Māori could keep the choice bits of Mōkau for themselves.

Native reserves were derived from the failure of the American colonies to safeguard the wellbeing of the indigenes. They were as much a part of the chain reaction of European colonisation as traders, missionaries and surveyors. The idea is said to have come from the celebrated Benjamin Franklin. Published in the immediate wake of Cook's first voyage, his *Plan for Benefiting Distant Unprovided Countries* was specifically to ensure that contact with 'the civilised world' would *improve* New Zealand's native people. Native reserves may have derived from people who considered themselves a master race conquering a fertile land, poorly and ephemerally used by uncivilised people, but Ngātipehi, for one, were attracted to it.

McLean, however, would not tolerate the idea. For £200, he wanted every one of the Mōkau block's 2,500 acres, other than Ngātipehi's kāinga at Te Kauri. For what they had already agreed to sell, he would pay no more than £100. The other £100 was 'withheld for the . . . three places' which on the title deed signed at Mōkau on 1 May 1854 had 'not yet . . . been given up'. By the time the deal was struck 18 months later, worldly prosperity for Takerei and the 67 who signed was £100 and a few tiny, disputed reserves. The sale deed makes no mention of the riverbend, Tauwhare, but we know from subsequent title maps and documents it was one of them. And following McLean's name on the deed is the signature of a Wesleyan missionary.

Ten years earlier, in 1844, a young German, Cort Schnackenberg, and his wife Amy arrived at Mōkau to open one of the Wesleyans' west coast mission stations. He already knew the coast as a trader, an experience that had implanted in him the same idea underlying the behaviour of the New Zealand Company: 'Wilderness land . . . is worth nothing to its native owners . . . Absolutely they would suffer little or nothing from having parted with land which they do not use . . .' His task became to effect this philosophy—or at least create the conditions that would pave its way.

It looked at the outset that it would be straightforward. The Mōkau people's desire for European things to complement their native prosperity hadn't gone unnoticed. They seemed keen to share their country with settlers, and like other ritualised hunter-gatherers, they believed its forest was there to serve them. They cleared land in the forest and in its ashes cultivated the crops that Ernst Dieffenbach and Frederick Moore admired. But the forest, like the sea, also contained the gods that connected them to their environment.

Before contact with the missionaries of the 19th century, Māori believed their physical health and wellbeing were achieved in two principal ways. One was by maintaining the mauri of their places—the life force by which their natural elements cohere. The other was by lifelong observance of the laws of tapu. Rites and rituals broke down the barriers between people and other species, allowed people to flow spiritually into nature and for nature's rhythms to permeate their own being. A host of daily tasks depended on conscious connection, both to benefit nature and limit human excesses. What gave the people of Mōkau life also gave them obligations.

European visitors 'beholding a plain . . . surrounded by a beautiful river, and inclosed by beautiful bush and hills on every side', told Schnackenberg he and Amy were living in the finest place in New Zealand. Yet the representative of a religion committed to getting away from nature could only see what he called 'The Tapu of Mokau' cruelly infusing the lives of the river people. They were intelligent enough, even 'touched occasionally by nobility', but their primitive union with nature had empowered 'the works of the devil'—pagan spirits, cruelty and superstition—to operate unchecked.

From Schnackenberg's arrival at the rivermouth, he wrote regularly to his superior, the Rev John Whiteley who led the Wesleyans in New Plymouth. Perhaps because Whiteley wanted to keep an eye on him, the young missionary's early reports contained passages from his first sermons:

> . . . apply the same rule to the cultivation of your hearts—the light from Heaven is shining upon you—look at yourself in that light and if you find your mind, your heart to be a wilderness, cultivate it in the same manner as you do your fields, cut down the bush, great and small—spare no sin.
> . . . dig your hearts by deep repentance that it may become soft and fit to receive the seed of God's word—if it strikes root

*within you. Watch it carefully and weed your hearts ever
afterwards until the harvest—in times past the preaching of God's
work produced no fruit in this place, because it fell on strong
ground, or was choked in the bush.*

'The people listened with deep attention,' he added, 'and I believe resolved
to comply with my requisitions, viz, to clear their hearts from the shrubs of
sin.'

Schnackenberg's campaign for hearts and minds presumed success
right from the beginning. 'The natives here are peaceable and improving,'
he was soon reporting. 'Nearly every one has this year a patch in with wheat,
and they have just purchased two mills at some ponds each besides sieves
and reaping hooks. They also bought a vessel for 200 pigs . . .' But many
Ngāti Maniapoto who planted wheat and came to sing Schnackenberg's
hymns continued to explain everything that happened in the Mōkau
landscape via the community of gods and spirits. Even a simple phenomenon
like wind funnelling around riverbends was a sign. The missionary became
consumed with sweeping the landscape clear of such intensities.

As Mōkau became familiar and his number of Christian converts
grew, he discerned localities where the tapu particularly affected people,
malevolent places which Ngāti Maniapoto 'attended with great respect'. By
the end of 1846, after an incident when a woman's illness was blamed on
her eating food cooked on tapu firewood from Tauwhare, 'war was declared
against remaining heathen customs':

*An occurrence took place in the beginning of December which
made many ashamed of their heathenish superstition . . . as a
consequence of which I may mention, that the tapu, which perhaps
exercised a greater influence over the Mokau natives than any
other on the coast, has in a great measure been destroyed.*

*About this time many were employed in making fishing
nets and as there were several tapued places in the river where
hitherto it had been thought death would follow the fish, it was
resolved that the Christians should destroy Te Tapu by holding
prayer at each of the places. This was done on the 24th Dec. On
the morning of that day, the priest Tawha visited the tapued
places, but no other kanoes were seen on the river till towards
evening when a large kanoe with Christian natives called on me
to accompany them as they were then going to wakamatea*

[whakamate] nga wahi tapu o Mokau [put the sacred places of Mōkau to death]. The spots said to be the residence of the kikokiko, were at the turnings of the river, where I suppose Kanoes may have been obstructed by the rushing of the waters in time of floods or by the wind causing in such places a great tide ripple.

Tauwhare was just up the estuary from his mission station; so close that some old documents include them under the same name—Te Mahoe:

When we got to the place, we landed, forced our way through the long grass up to a large tree which we surrounded; in this singular position and place we sang the 71 hymn, E Ihu e te Kingi nui etc. Hemi then prayed that Jehovah the only true God would destroy the native's tapu, all the works of the devil at Mokau and in their hearts etc.

But more than prayer was needed to ensure obligation and loyalty to the new god:

The religious ceremony being over they set fire to the tree and place, after which we left that spot to serve others in the same manner. On that interesting occasion their countenances beamed with joy and they caused the Kanoe to glide through the water like a steamer . . . Since that time all the sacred places on the Station and many other places, have been made common.

Only with a symbol of purification as abiding and pagan as fire could the church deal to the tapu and the fear it engendered. Piled up around the great kahikatea, the riverflat's dry rushes, cuttygrass and sun-dried logs would have made an excellent blaze. Quickly gathering heat, the flames would have ignited the tree's cloaks of kiekie and raced spectacularly up into their crowns. Everything alive between ground and tree-tops would have been incinerated. Within decades, the soft-wooded kahikatea would have collapsed onto the riverflat and vanished. Today only the observant ecologist notices the band of old manuka trees that grew up in their place.

One day in the middle of winter, the Mōkau almost stationary as the flow from its damaged hills met the surge of the tide, I was drifting around Tauwhare in my canoe, contemplating the very same trees in which Cort Schnackenberg had imagined his enemy. I could see as well as hear the big

Kenworth semi-trailers lumbering across the highway bridge three kilometres away. For a moment, I imagined the Ngāti Maniapoto pulling their canoe ashore, Schnackenberg with his prayer book wading through the mud and rushes to the big kahikatea. Two cultures glancing uncertainly at one another, and then up at the flaming trees that diminished them both. Suddenly, with no warning a rush of air hit the canoe, flipped the paddle out of my hand and away into the current while I struggled to keep upright.

In years of kayaking, I'd experienced nothing like it. Was it, as part of me wanted to believe, no more than the wind 'causing in such places a great tide ripple', as Cort Schnackenberg said? Or something not so easily explained? Every riverbend, Tainui believe, has its taniwha: 'They don't need to be talked about. Locals know about them—what more is there to say.' As the surface of the water gathered its calm, and I my paddle, the edifices of science and reason trembled a little. Something had cautioned me; something out of their reach.

Today, a Methodist minister singing hymns at the foot of an 800-year-old tree before setting it alight to exemplify the power of his God would be outlandish. Cort and Amy Schnackenberg knew the symbolism of trees. They swiftly responded to the Māori craving for peaches and pears to supplant their karaka and kahikatea. Some of them endure today. What was it though that made the riverbank kahikatea the locus of the river's evil atmosphere and drew Schnackenberg to do what he did? Kahikatea is one / of the most revered trees in the Māori landscape, not just for its timber and its fruits' attraction to birds, but as a symbol of conception. While the placenta, te whenua, of the newborn is as the land, the umbilical cord, iho, is as the strength of a tree trunk. When an auspicious child's iho was buried in a sacred place, or placed at a land boundary to strengthen tribal influence, it was commonly beneath or on a kahikatea.

What did Schnackenberg's new Christians tell him about these kahikatea? That the epiphytic clumps of kahakaha and kōwharawhara, suspended high in their forks like nests in the sky, were where patupaiarehe, the forest fairies, lived? Or did he suspect that there was something else up there? There are some clues in the auspicious term 'te tonga puaroa' in the waiata of Te Tahu Tahu Ahi. And in the allusions in Schnackenberg's letters to his new Christians' readiness to abandon their old beliefs. 'E wehi ana mātou ki ngā tangata, kāhore a mātau wehi ki te kikokiko,' they boasted. 'We might be afraid of people, but we are not afraid of the places with the ghosts of the dead.' Māori not only sensed that trees have souls themselves;

like many other peoples before the spread of Christianity, they believed the souls of ghosts, gods and demons inhabited them. Blinded by the new faith into a moment of indiscretion, the missionary's new adherents revealed that way up there in the kahikateas' branches, among the thick masses of epiphytes, were ancestors' bones.

The strongest bonds of the Māori community, said the historian Keith Sinclair, were untied on the insistence of the missions. Immediate and continuing harm was done to the practice of tapu, and as its vital role in the Māori sense of identity and place declined, so did Māori themselves. Yet, while belief about tapu and the dangers manifest by the dead has changed, burial places—urupā, wāhi takotoranga tupāpaku, wāhi horoi tupāpaku— and tūāhu—places where sacred rites were performed—still instil fear and awe. Many Māori still avoid trespassing on wāhi tapu in case, as the ethnologist Elsdon Best was told in the early 1900s, 'those bones of the dead will turn upon the intruder and slay him or affect him grievously'.

The first immigrants from the tropical Pacific brought with them the traditional Polynesian closeness between the living and the dead. Until the advent of pā warfare and the secreting away of the dead to avoid desecration by enemies, most people were buried near their living families. In the vanished days before Europeans brought their god to displace those of forest and sky, when forests and people were in closer proximity than we ever see today, bones were commonly laid to rest in trees. Some hapu of Tuhoe, for example, never used anything else: 'A tree is selected which has masses of . . . kowharawhara growing in its branches. Among these thick masses are concealed the remains.'

The burial kahikatea of Ngāti Maru, Ngāti Maniapoto's relatives, lined the tidal banks of the Waihou James Cook visited in 1769. Yet his shore-party was no more aware of the fact than it was of the people who stealthily trailed the visitors upriver. Neither were the settlers who followed Cook, and felled them just like any other kahikatea. You could say that Ngāti Maru buried their dead in trees simply because their landscape lacked other possibilities, but its occurrence at a place abounding with other suitable sites, like Mōkau with its cavernous limestone bluffs and the rivermouth sandspit Te Nau Nau, suggests tree burial was more than a habit of plains people.

When Tauwhare was made a native reserve in 1897, Pepene Eketone claimed it had been kept out of sale as Takerei te Kākā's 'tapu'. Among 19th-century Taranaki settlers, the word was as feared as the wet forest that

surrounded them. Much more than an 'idle objection to the sale of land', tapu ✓
was the clearest evidence that Māori were simply savages. Like Schnackenberg,
most settlers believed that order would only come to the land when its Māori ✗
were removed from it. Yet even Schnackenberg learned that in some instances,
it was not quite the simple matter he imagined. Years after the riverbend tree-
burning he was still admitting 'some places and customs, it is true, are still
much respected, even by our Christian natives'. To many Mōkau people, despite
his assurances that his god now held sway and that the tapu riverbends had
been made common, the ancient fear remained. If they ever had cause to pass
Tauwhare's kahikatea, it was with eyes averted.

A clump of white lilies, the certain sign of domesticity capitulating
to the wild, marks the Schnackenbergs' mission station at the Te Mahoe
end of the riverbend. A closer look reveals a few persistent survivors of
their orchard. A Historic Places sign peppered with shotgun pellets records
their years here. Of the people whose rubbish heap of white shells glints in
the sun nearby, and who, centuries before the missionaries' orchard, planted
the other, more vigorous grove of karaka trees still dropping their orange
fruit each autumn, there is no mention. Cliff Black, who farms the land
today, frequently plows up piles of shell and patches of black soil, some of
it from the Schnackenbergs' efforts against the wilderness, but most from
the people before them. One afternoon, not long after I'd found the original
Mōkau land sale deed, I called in to see him.

I arrived in the middle of an important midweek Taranaki rugby
match. No sooner had fulltime sounded, than Cliff got up, switched the
television off and turned his attention to the copy of the old plan of Tawari
Native Reserve I'd brought with me. I could tell by the way his finger crept
along the line between his land and the reserve that, although he'd grown
up beside Tauwhare, inherited the block from his father, he hadn't seen the
plan before. Tauwhare itself, no more than a ridge of second-growth bush
from here, kept vanishing in clouds of smoke blowing downriver from the
county tip. Cliff joined me at the window: 'That reserve of yours was all in
manuka when I was a kid. It was a pā.'

> My father was told the burial place was below it. In those white
> pines. Bodies were placed way up in their forks for the flesh to rot
> off.

The Schnackenbergs left more than fruit trees and the start of a farm. From their renaming of the young chief Te Rerenga 'Hoani Wetere' after their faith's founder John Wesley, a profusion of biblical names has spread through Tainui, testimony perhaps to the early regard in which the Wesleyans and this new god were held. But with the mission station still enveloped by forest as verdant as when the missionaries had arrived, it was, whatever Cort Schnackenberg's measure of success, 'too small to cheer us much'. 'On the other hand,' he said, 'our discouragements are very great.'

Watching the missionary with the government's land agents, the people of Mōkau didn't take long to see their intentions were one and the same. From the way Schackenberg's converts continued to come to his sermons and language classes, he may have thought no one noticed, or minded. On the contrary, Ngātipehi felt betrayed, and determined to keep his hands off their land. Even clearing a patch for his own garden was resisted: 'If I cut down a Manuka tree that may be in my way or any other of no value whatever to the natives, I am often reminded that I ought to have got the consent of the owner of the land or in other words ought to pay for it.'

Schnackenberg was tiring too of 'the covetousness and ingratitude of New Zealanders' and the inevitable reply, 'We are in our own place', whenever he asked a recumbent Māori visitor to the mission house to move. Exasperated that, although 'Messrs McLean and Cooper had told me that a reserve would be made for a M. Station, and they told the Natives so likewise', nothing had eventuated, he pleaded with his superiors to apply for a Crown Grant instead: 'from the bottom of my garden eastward to the bend of the River Mokau'. Schnackenberg's copious letters rarely resorted to underlining, but he was beginning to despair at Ngātipehi's contradictory ways: 'The party who refused to sell own part of my Station which they said should remain tapu for themselves and me, but at Mr McLean's request and my own *they consented to give up their claim to that part of their land which is included in the Mission Station.*'

But he was beginning to believe that 'the Natives' idolatrous attachments to land' were not as great as he had once supposed. His earlier observation that 'they would sell a tract of land, but they never dream that in such an event they would lose their chieftainship in the river' was, by the 1850s, overrun by bitterness at Ngātipehi's refusal to allow him to 'proceed with my improvements and operations on the station'. 'Our grand folks,' he complained cynically, '"tikarohia" the most valuable parts even of this for themselves.'

Unable to establish anything more permanent than a reed-roofed house, while the Mōkau chiefs had allowed the 'evil adviser' Hopkins, the trader, a house and a place for his vessel, as well as their confidence, the Schnackenbergs decided it was futile to remain. But not without Cort declaring where his loyalties lay. 'The sooner the Natives part with their land,' he wrote to Rev Turton, 'the better it will be for themselves and the general prosperity of the Colony. I have rendered Mr Commissioner McLean and the other Government officers all the help I could, to further the purchase of Land in this neighbourhood, and shall think it my duty to do the same in future.' He would do 'all I can to hasten it'.

Barely had Schnackenberg left than Donald McLean's land policies plunged Taranaki and the Waikato into war and confiscation. There was no Titokowaru or von Tempsky among Mōkau's trees, but from the beginning of the wars to their bitter end, the rivermouth played its ancient strategic role. The precipitating act, Wiremu Kingi's declaration in 1859 of the Taranaki tribes' refusal to sell land, was with the authority of a rūnanga of the tribes from the Mōkau to the Waitaha Stream south of Waitara. Only a few miles from the abandoned mission, the alliance implicit in Schnackenberg's testimony saw his superior, Rev Whiteley, slaughtered by a taua from Mōkau led by the same chief the Wesleyans had named after their founder. Convinced Whiteley was a spy for the military, and that what had happened to Ngāti Tama's land was about to happen to Maniapoto's, Wetere te Rerenga's taua lay in wait high above the seacliffs of Parininihi and killed him the moment he entered Ngāti Maniapoto territory.

A government steamer cruised up the Mōkau and subjected Ngātipehi's kāinga, Te Kauri, to the last artillery bombardment of the New Zealand wars. Six hundred warriors waited ready. But the taua had gone upriver. Tauwhare acquired another sense of sanctuary—and the settler name 'Black Mick's Point'—for concealing the warrior who is said to have killed Whiteley. Safe in the closest place to Te Kauri where he could ensure the military wouldn't find him, Taianui lived off the snapper which leapt out of the water by the riverbend, until the military's desire to track him down faded.

Well into the late 1870s, Mōkau remained a totally Māori place. The mission house Schnackenberg left in the care of the 'native teacher' Hone Eketone collapsed and vanished. By 1883 'the only indication of European occupation was a smothering growth of sweet briar, doubtless from the hips of a single plant brought to this wild spot from a far distant garden, and tended with loving care by the missionary's wife as a reminder of her distant homeland'. Still tapu enough for Ngātipehi to have had the government formally reserve it, it was as a 'wild spot' that Tauwhare next entered the European imagination. As Hone Eketone's son gave his evidence to the Native Land Court and Tauwhare Native Reserve was gazetted tapu, another kind of reserve altogether was taking shape. It would keep Tauwhare safely out of settlers' hands, as Ngātipehi had intended, if not as they had pictured.

On 4 October 1769, as the *Endeavour* approached New Zealand from Tahiti, the poet Thomas Gray was high above the Vale of Derwentwater in England's Lake District. Angling his Claude glass to ensphere the view across meadows and wooded slopes to the water, he told Thomas Wharton it was 'the sweetest scene I can yet discover in point of pastoral beauty'. Soon after, not far away at the Milnthorpe ironworks, he was marvelling at 'the demons at work by the light of their own fires' and 'the thumping of huge hammers'.

'Picturesque' beauty and heavy industry were born together, as the 'natural' became hemmed in by the 'artificial'—nature's variety, intricacy and irregularity framed by rural enclosure and urban sprawl, and threatened by human activity. Gray's response to landscape over two centuries ago is strikingly similar to our own. In this brief period of the mid 18th century, our culture's way of looking at the non-human world turned a corner. Painters like Claude Lorraine and Salvator Rosa created a style that rapidly found its way, in England especially, into the design of parks and gardens, and into the very definition of beauty itself. By the mid 19th century, 'the Picturesque' had spread beyond England to the newly possessed edges of its empire, to become a term on nearly every traveller's lips for describing strange beauty.

No small part of the English legacy in Africa, says the Kenyan historian Ali Mazrui, was in the notions of scenery and beauty that the colonisers brought with them as they fled, like refugees, the industrial ugliness of their homeland. When New Zealand's colonising century ended, scenery was more than something in which exhausted settlers took a break from bush-burning and jaded townsfolk picnicked. There was money to earn from the tourists who were crossing the world for the picturesque sights of other lands—but it needed wild waterfalls, gorges and cool, wooded riverbanks.

The government handed the task of acquiring them to a Scenery Preservation Commission it established for the purpose in 1903. To lead it, they called out of retirement a Surveyor-General, Percy Smith, whose obituarists 20 years later highlighted his 'eye for the picturesque', and who by the time Tauwhare was gazetted Native Reserve in 1897, had become renowned for his efforts to keep the country's scenic corners at least secure from the ravages of land clearance. Smith was uncommonly conversant with Māori language and custom and complemented his surveying profession with a private passion for Polynesian ethnology, particularly of Māori origins and canoe traditions. His *History and Traditions of the Maori of the West Coast of the North Island* and *Lore of the Whare Wananga* are still widely consulted by Māori and Pākehā alike. But the 'scenic reserve' he created was not interested in the Māori spiritual landscape; it was a late-colonial afterthought from men on whose survey maps country like Mōkau was labelled: *Land in the Hands of the Natives over which the Native Title has not been Extinguished.* A pleasure of imperialism, set aside 'only when . . . the needs of settlement . . . have been amply met and provided for'.

Percy Smith believed preserving scenery was a Crown responsibility and advocated it years before legislation made it possible. 'In future,' said his memoranda, 'attention must be given in dealing with Crown lands to the reservation of all places of natural beauty of whatsoever nature, which are likely to become resorts for the people of the country hereafter.' He had a special concern for riverbanks, particularly 'along the larger rivers, more especially those which are navigable, not alone in the interests of the conservation of their banks, but in the interests of tourists and other travellers'.

Smith's Scenery Preservation Commission was created at a crucial time. Without its efforts, hundreds of places that are now protected would have been cleared for farms along with everything else. Each one, the Commission decided at its first meeting, was to have a clearing for bush picnics. At the top of its second agenda, in August 1904, were the banks of the Mōkau River. A deputation awaited them of 'representative gentlemen' from New Plymouth envious of the revenue being generated by the droves of tourists attracted to the scenery of the Wanganui River. They wanted action to preserve 'the beauties of the Mōkau and its great importance to their Province'. Their Member of Parliament, Mr Jennings, told Smith's commission he was all in favour of preserving large areas of the Mōkau's 'valuable flatlands' along with the riverbanks 'in the interest of the district and the colony as a whole'. However, it need not exclude settlers as 'their homes along the riverbanks greatly improved the scenic effort of the country'. They were all, said Smith, unanimous on that point.

As a 17-year-old survey cadet, just before war thrust him into military frontiers and land confiscation, Percy Smith had known Mōkau as a 'certainly very picturesque' and almost exclusively Māori place. For much of his adult life spent taming Taranaki, 'this most beautiful river' at the edge of the Rohepōtae, the forbidden forest and wild rivers of the 'King Country', had symbolised Māori resistance and reclusiveness. But this was a job for a younger man. James Cowan, son of King Country settlers and soon to become a famous writer and historian, was sent to report. He was captivated.

> There are some parts of our land that ought to be inviolate and wild, tapu to the Maoris and the trees and the birds. The Urewera country is one; the Mokau river is another. They should be kept so primitive that only the real nature-lover and camper-out would venture in. When they become too comfortable the charm of exploring will be gone. I don't believe in making things too easy for the trippist . . .

Cowan's fluency in Māori enabled him to get to know the few old kaumatua like Taniora Wharauroa surviving from the days before the Pākehā, and to learn of the sad fate, at Mōkau at least, of the idea of 'reserves for the natives': '. . . on the Little Tokomaru flat, we see the remains of the old water-mill where the Maoris ground their corn in the golden days before the war . . . But the wheel lies there broken and the old flint sandstones lie half-buried in the grass, melancholy symbols of the decay of native industry. Isabella grape-vines grown wild, trail along the ground and festoon the titoki trees.' Inland, the fires of land-clearing were burning apace. Cowan pressed for the urgent gazettal of a continuous, protected strip of forest along the river, imagining it the perfect site for a convergence of two cultures that had been in such conflict.

Cowan was struck, as the young Percy Smith had been in the 1850s, by the way the cleared coastal land at Mōkau suddenly gave way to forest.

On one side of the river, he wrote in the *New Zealand Weekly Graphic*, rose Rangi-ō-Hua:

> . . . *the river banks close in, the southern side lifts up into the towering cliff, wooded from high water to skyline, a foretaste of the forest glories of the Mokau. High above the clinging woods and the hanging gardens of ferns are the remains of the ancient fortified Rangiahua.*

and on the other, Tauwhare:

> *The timber grows tall. Rata and rimu and kahikatea . . . crowd to the river bank, their forks are hung with bunchy astelias and the long, drooping leaves of the kiekie. Bush vines hang down over the stream, and the feathery fern-trees rise in soft tiers of frondage . . . and often lean their heads over us as we paddle close to the bank . . . Everything finds perfect reflex in the brown watery mirror.*

A local newspaper reporter attracted by the excited talk of New Plymouth's businessmen was similarly effusive: 'The beauties of the river were introduced immediately. Barely had we gone one hundred yards before we came upon scenery far surpassing anything we had anticipated and which increased in luxuriance and picturesqueness the further we went. There were no bare patches, it was just one unbroken mass of foliage from the hill tops to the water's edge.'

Yet both Rangi-ō-Hua and Tauwhare were Māori land, and no matter how beautiful they were to the tourist gaze, the new Scenery Preservation Act as it was in 1904 had no power to acquire them. Wherever Percy Smith and his commission looked, what had escaped 60 years of settlers' fires and was still wild and beautiful tended to be Māori land. Pressing for changes to what seemed a ridiculous situation, he asked the Prime Minister, Sir Joseph Ward, for amendments to make the Act 'more satisfactory'. 'There are,' he explained, 'in the hands of the Natives at the present time, many forest clad ranges etc., which have been from time immemorial preserved by them for the purpose of snaring birds, such lands being called Pua-tahere; . . . just such places as the Commission would wish to see reserved in order to preserve the forests and the scenic features of the country.' Were honorary Māori rangers appointed and a season prescribed for bird-snaring, he intimated, 'the Maoris will hand over some of their Pua-tahere without cost'.

To the Polynesian scholar in Percy Smith, the Māori connection to the forest would never again be what it had been prior to European settlement. The ethnologist Elsdon Best spoke for many like him when he wrote in 1906 that, now the young colony was a settler country, that was a past that would never return: 'The forest is conservative, repressive, making not for culture or advancement. None of the higher types of civilisation of antiquity originated in forest lands. Primitive man remains primitive in sylvan solitudes. Some day a civilised tribe, from open lands, happens along, and hews down the forest. Then the Children of Tane, human and arboreal, alike disappear, and the place knows them never again.' In every field men like Percy Smith operated were Social Darwinists whose every act assumed Māori were a vanishing race.

By the 1900s the wave of land clearance, certainly in Taranaki, had left precious little river flat country in bush. Keeping what did survive out of the hands of settlers and timber-getters—for scenery—met vociferous opposition. Remote in its beauty, the Mōkau was a last chance. But it was still a settlers' landscape and the scenery preservationists had directions from the Prime Minister to be 'the least nuisance possible'. Their caution is evident from an annotation on a map of their proposals: 'Even where the land is flat enough for settlement, it is distinctly advisable to preserve the bush . . . otherwise the banks will cave in and the river will widen and shallow.' Their imperative became confined to hill country, 'leaving the culturable flats on the river bank between the Reserve and the river to be available for settlement . . . should it turn out parts of the reserve contain flats suitable for cultivation, they should be cut out'. It was strictly for viewers from the water, to protect the very minimum ' . . . bounding the line of vision from the river . . . the object . . . to preserve the forest as seen from the river'.

SS *Mokau* AND KELLY'S MILL, C.1908.

Even that protection was far from guaranteed. Within months of their trip, Smith's commission learned the Mokau Timber Company had acquired rights over a large part of the land they were recommending for protection and was 'hard at work cutting and selling the timber thereon'. The Taranaki Scenery Preservation Society wrote anxiously to the Minister of Lands that 'a great asset for the Colony' was threatened. The following summer the Scenery Preservation

Commission sent its secretary, W.R. Jourdain, and the Inspector of Scenic Reserves, E. Phillips Turner, back to the river to see just how far their recommendations could be modified and what areas were 'specially attractive'.

By the time the newspaper readers of Taranaki learned of Jourdain's and Phillips Turner's fear that saw-milling would decimate the Mōkau's 'unique scenery', any possibility of James Cowan's continuous strip of protected riverbank forest had evaporated. 'There are,' the two were forced to concede, 'portions of the land abutting onto the river which it is not necessary to reserve, rich flat land where smiling homesteads will presently add diversity to the scenery.' In all classes where it seemed advisable, they explained, 'land that is better suited for settlement than scenery preservation has been excluded. Only that class of land that cannot be utilised . . . has been recommended for reservation.' In the event, they were too late for even that.

Mōkau's Māori, if they ever knew of the scenery preservationists' grand plan, were silent. It was not until 1910 that Percy Smith succeeded with his amendment to the Scenery Preservation Act and had the power to take Māori places like Tauwhare under the Public Works Act. By July 1911, when the Scenery Preservation Commission got around to applying their new powers to their Mōkau problem, the Minister of Lands' under-secretary already had surveyors up at Mōkau cutting lines around the sacred riverbend. The Commission's field inspector, Phillips Turner, went to check up on them in the middle of August and, by early September, the under-secretary was able to send a certified schedule and plan of the native land to his counterpart in the Public Works Department for 'the necessary action to secure the land under the 1908 Public Works Act'.

So central had Tauwhare become to scenery preservation at Mōkau that no one bothered with the fact that it was already reserved for Māori purposes. The Lands and Deeds Registry Office, however, had no record of Tauwhare; nor did the registrar of the Native Land Court. Percy Smith's commission must have known from the 1883 survey map that it was native reserve. It wasn't 'pua-tahere'. A Notice of Intention to take Land appeared in the *New Zealand Gazette* on 16 November advising that the details, and a Māori translation, were pinned up in the Awakino Post Office along the coast. Anyone 'affected by the taking of the said land'—a place called *Tekiona 12 Rahui Maori (16244 puruu)*, Section 12, Māori Reserve—had 40 days in which to send any 'well-grounded objections' in writing. Of

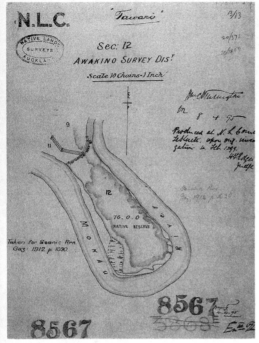

**SURVEY PLAN FOR THE
TAKING OF TAUWHARE, 1912.**

Tauwhare or Te Mahoe, though, or even the Mōkau itself, the notice made no mention.

Two months later, the under-secretary of Public Works had the Proclamation and Order in Council taking the land ready for signature, but was still asking how it became a native reserve and who administered it. It is 'patupatu land', replied his counterpart in the Lands ministry, 'not a gazetted reserve and it is not administered by any person or body'. So on 14 March, a Proclamation appeared in the *New Zealand Gazette* taking Tauwhare, by Order in Council, 'for scenic purposes' and vesting it in His Majesty the King from 12 April 1912.

The Native Land Court, meanwhile, was meant to be finding out who should be compensated and what they were owed. A telegram from the valuer-general did arrive the day after its sitting at the end of April, advising of valuations that eventually came in the middle of winter. Tauwhare had two prices on it. The district valuer in Te Kuiti, H.A. Allison's, was typed out, matter-of-fact:

> (Native Reserve)—Awakino S.D.—76 acres: Capital Val. £190— Unimpd. Val. £190: Owner—Natives: Occupier—nil

He had looked over 'the 76 acres known as N. Reserve, commonly termed The Island . . . almost surrounded by the waters of the river', seen 'a good deal of rough feed and some old cultivations which are in a neglected state' and considered that 'practically the whole of it can be cultivated'. The valuer Jas Rattenbury's scrawled note from the White Hart Hotel in New Plymouth raised Tauwhare's market value to £228. Much of what he'd seen was a steep and narrow sandstone ridge, but it was more than compensated by 'about 10 or 12 acres of flat land of good river silt soil'. Should it be taken to court, he added, 'I would recommend Mr Walter Jones of Mokau should be asked to give evidence as he is a local man and has a good practical knowledge of the country'. The under-secretary of Public Works felt the valuations somewhat high. Asked to explain, Rattenbury said he was thinking of the dairy industry which had not yet started at Mōkau, and the riverflats in question were, after all, 'very nice land'. In 1990s terms, his estimate would be about $15,000.

When the Native Land Court finally heard the case late in October, the owners' representative was there, but Anaru Eketone was no more interested in reminding them Tauwhare was wāhi tapu than in big money. A good living could not be got off it. 'For grazing land,' he said, it 'is not worth 40/-.'

It was 1914 before the Public Trustee advised the the Native Land Court that money had been paid into the Court's account for compensation. Again he asked if the native owners had been determined. No, they hadn't, the Court's registrar replied, but later that year, the Minister of Lands received a letter from Mōkau bearing Te Ainui Mika's mark and wanting his share of the money. He came to the point bluntly. 'If the Government dont wish this reserved, Kindly notify me as I would like to fell it, this season, an early reply will oblige.' Ngātoki Rimene, one of those named in Pepene Eketone's original list back in 1897, also wanted his share. There was, he was told, a proper way to claim it. 'If the interests of the owners have been defined by the Court and your name appears,' he was told, 'you should make your application . . . for payment due to you.' He did, repeatedly and unsuccessfully. Five years later, no one had been paid. The Court registrar, despite letter after letter from the Public Trustee, blamed it on the natives 'taking no steps to bring the matter on'.

Meanwhile, the preservation of Mōkau River Scenic Reserves was creating more urgent matters. With the end of the First World War, soldier settlers were balloted blocks of the poor sandstone hill country to clear. Disappointment turned to anger when they discovered that, while the government had seen fit to turn them out onto such unproductive acres, it had kept fertile riverflats for scenery. In February 1921 a furious delegation confronted the Minister of Lands demanding the government revoke any reserve on land they could bring into production. One settler had already had the reserve designation on his flats lifted, and the others wanted the same. Despite the Scenery Preservation Commission's assurances a decade earlier, Randell's block, for example, had 'a beautiful flat which had been cut out for a reserve', but 'of little value for scenic purposes. It couldn't even be seen from the river.'

Reserves, the soldier settlers complained, monopolised the riverbanks. Even the thin line of trees that had been reserved acted as a windbreak, preventing a decent burn, and making it difficult for stock to reach the river. And as long as timber stood on the banks (said the same men who, in but a decade, would be desperately thrusting willow wands into the same, sliding ground in their vain attempts to halt erosion and silting) they'd have trouble with snags in the river.

The Commissioner of Crown Lands sympathised but held firm. 'I do not know,' he wrote, 'of any flatpoint on the southern side that is now reserved.' Today, were you able to catch a glimpse of the flats through the settlers' willows, you would see no forest. Most would have been solid with immense kahikatea, as hard to budge as Don Sutton discovered when he began stumping his in the 1930s: 'blasting, winching and with monkey grubbers, then later with tractors, the only way of getting across, they were so wet'.

By the time the soldier settlers arrived, the scenery preservationists had taken more riverbank Māori land, at Mangapapa, in the same way as Tauwhare. Discovering 'there are about 60 owners', the District Land Registrar complained to the under-secretary of Public Works at the amount of searching necessary to unravel each succession order: '. . . the addresses of the native owners are not stated in the titles. They are simply referred to as aboriginal natives of New Zealand. Under these circumstances is it worth advising you of the names?' Even with a tiny piece of river-bank like Tauwhare, the Native Trustee's search for owners was still going on in 1924—unaware that four years previously, frustrated at Tauwhare's appearance in every pānui of the Te Kuiti Native Land Court since it was first prosecuted ten years before, Judge Jones of the Native Land Court had ended the whole business of compensation by dismissing it.

Once the defenders of the Rohepōtae allowed surveyors into Mōkau in 1883 to make good Donald McLean's 1854 purchase, virtually all arable land had slid into European hands. Abandoning their river and pā, most Māori had gone to the four winds. Many on Pepene Eketone's 1897 list of Tauwhare's owners, like Ngāhoki Te Ianui, had no idea that the scenery preservationists had been and gone and that now even the tapu riverbend had been taken from them. Then, late in 1930, the Great Depression took

Ngāhoki Te Ianui's daughter, Ngāhoki Rikihana, back to her Mōkau roots and the piece of riverbank she'd always been told was partly hers—if she ever needed it. With her was her Pākehā husband, Newton Taylor.

Ngāhoki, a direct descendant of Takerei, hoped to buy the other owners out. Taylor, in anticipation, went along to Tawhare and began clearing bush and cutting fence battens. Hearing his axe, the neighbouring Pākehā farmer, Cliff Black's father—busy felling trees for posts himself—came over to tell him he was in the government's scenic reserve. Taylor, infuriated, told him to get off and stop cutting timber; it was Māori land, his mother-in-law's in fact, and they needed it. But he was even angrier when a Lands and Survey field inspector arrived and confirmed what the farmer had said. Taylor wrote straightaway to the Native Land Court, and learned what no Mōkau Māori had been told in 30 years. The riverbend had been taken from them without its actual identity being known: 'It has only now been discovered that Tawari and Sec. 12 Block I Awakino are the names of the same piece of land.'

Misspelt by government clerks, the riverbend's old, traditional name was in the public record for the first time since Pepene Eketone had plead for its sanctuary in 1897. 'The question of payment,' the Court registrar told the Public Trustee, 'has just recently been resuscitated and it has been discovered that the title to the 76 acre portion was investigated by the Court in February 1899 under the name "Tawari".'

Ambushed by the Depression, Ngāhoki Rikihana and Newton Taylor had not been able to borrow money from the Native Trustee to start a dairy herd on the tiny Hingaringa Te Kauri reserve flat where Ngāhoki also had a share. If the prospect of compensation money was an opportunity, getting it was another matter. First of all they had to prove Ngāhoki's entitlement. Although the Native Trustee was 'holding moneys due' and he and the Registrar of the Native Land Court acknowledged Ngāhoki Te Ianui was owed some £200, Ngāhoki Rikihana had no proof of identity and there was 'insufficient evidence on the Court's records' to enable payment. So the Court began the daunting task of tracking descendants of the owners in the original 1897 list. The fact that some like Tanirau Hariata, Hariata te Akau and Ie Ianui Mihi had migrated to the Horowhenua, and died there in the 1920s, didn't make it any easier.

By the time Newton Taylor returned from the Horowhenua with the evidence he knew he needed to prove his mother-in-law's succession, he had, as he told the Land Court's registrar, authority to act for all the owners in Tauwhare. Some, meanwhile, were taking things into their own hands. Reporting 'Toheroa Marohau, Rangiauru Marohau, Ngakoti Rimene, Matutu Aterea, Ngataua Marohau threatening to cut down Government bush', the police constable at Mōkau said he informed 'the above-named natives . . . that they would eventually be paid for the land' and that they would be prosecuted 'if they destroyed any of the Bush on any of the land they sold to the Government'. He was, he said, 'of the opinion that these natives made this threat with intentions that they would get their money quicker out of government'.

It was a year before Ngātaua Marohau and his friends were called to a Native Land Court hearing in Te Kuiti to hear applications for Orders of Succession from the 1897 list. The Court's registrar copied the orders to the Native Trustee to enable transfer to descendants. Yet if anyone was ever compensated, there is no record. Reduced to a commodity by Māori desperate for money and government officials loath to pay, the Tauwhare the old kaitiaki had insisted must never be sold had become just another ordinary piece of taken land.

This was replicated across the river at Rangi-ō-hua pā, Percy Smith's and James Cowan's other scenic centrepiece. When the Native Land Court met in Waitara in 1878 both Ngāti Maniapoto and a Taranaki tribe, Ngāti Tama, claimed it. Tawhana Kaharoa's evidence was that, although it was on the southern, Taranaki, side of the river, a Ngāti Maniopoto hapu claimed it: 'Te Awa Tuwhenua belongs to Ngāti Hineuru as regard this land. All the part called Haumapu belonged to that hapu. They had cultivations there in older times, there are cultivations near there at the present time— cultivations now belong to his brothers.' Another claimant, Tatana Te Awaroa, spoke later in the day of the many hapu that clustered around the estuary: 'My hapus in regard to this land is N'[Ngāti] Parekarau. N'Waimaku, N'Hinerua, N'Hineuru. I can give my hapus under which I have a right at Tauwhare and Haumapu.'

Tribal bonds notwithstanding, Rangi-ō-hua and its cultivations went to a settler, Joshua Jones. Not until he had incinerated most of its forest, was bankrupt and had weathered a Royal Commission into his land-dealing were the steep slopes above the Mōkau estuary proposed for scenery preservation. In 1920 they were taken by proclamation. After her failed quest for ancestral land at Tauwhare, Ngāhoki Rikihana turned to the riverbank cultivations below Rangi-ō-hua. But her plea to the Commissioner of Crown Lands for their return met with complete resistance. 'The mere fact that these small areas were cultivated in the past by the ancestors of Rikihana,' he wrote, 'should not affect the position . . . The recognised descendants of the Maori cultivators sold the land to the Crown for Scenic reservation and its sanctity may well be preserved under the provisions of the Scenery Preservation Act.'

The Mōkau never got to compete with the Whanganui for the tourist gaze. The signs, Mōkau River Scenic Reserves, repeated at every riverbank bit of bush regardless of its Māori name, hint sadly at what might have been. Three years after Tauwhare was gazetted scenic reserve, after the timber-getters had dragged every money-making log they could take into the river, and the lower Mōkau was on its way to a farmed landscape, a huge flood in 1915 filled it with so much debris and silt it became unnavigable. Too costly to clear, the flood brought about the decline and the eventual insolvency of Mōkau Coal and Estates, the company established to take over the land Joshua Jones abandoned after his bankruptcy.

Soldier settlers home from Gallipoli and Paschendale, clearing their balloted river frontages and driving stock through reserves, soon had the Mōkau running yellow-grey with silt again. They were threatened with legal action, but it was easier for the government to revoke reserves than prosecute returned men scratching a living. Percy Smith might have believed that farms and bush together greatly improved the scenery, but scarcely any of those trying to make a living from it agreed. 'As long as we have settlements mixed up with scenery,' wrote one Commissioner of Crown Lands, 'so long will we have to combat the desire of the settlers to get rid of it where it interferes with the working of their farms; and the greatest care and discrimination will have to be exercised.'

The soldier settlers' children later spoke of virgin bush burning for weeks and wet flats full of stumps years after the kahikatea had gone, and of the years when their butterfat levels set records and the cream boat chugged up and down between the walls of forest along the river that was their highway. Then the erosion started. Floods flung logs across the flats. Willows, the funerary trees of ancient Celtic tradition, planted to hold the eroding banks, soon met in mid-river, making it impossible for the steamers which managed to keep their keel above the silt to turn around.

FLOOD DEBRIS OVER THE FLATS, MOHAKATINO, 1990s.

From the 1930s through to the 1960s, the Mōkau River reserves were all but forgotten in the government's preoccupation with land settlement. Every year or so a ranger might be sent upriver to check out a dispute about boundaries and survey, or illegal stock or beehives. For gravelling the coast road in the late 1920s, the Public Works Department simply quarried in the first scenic reserve they came to; no more concerned with scenery than they were prepared for the ancient bodies their blasting hurled out of the river bluffs. 'In no instance is there a reserve fit for a small farm,' said the farm valuer who looked them over in 1921. 'Suitable as a Scenic Reserve only', and not worth the very heavy expenditure to keep out straying stock, said his counterpart in 1929.

Then in the early 1970s the government's scenic reserve files explode in volume. As more and more New Zealanders began to sense that the land was where their identity and heritage lay, nature's remains took on new meaning. The agencies who governed the last of the wilderness became hungry for information. Ecologists able to tell them what it contained became as necessary as the bush surveyors with theodolites a century before. As a corner of the North Island with some remaining lowland forest, Mōkau's river reserves and their range of ecosystems from the estuary inland took on a significance the scenery preservationists could never have imagined. A bird survey found some of the North Island west coast's last bittern among Tauwhare's tidal rushes and across the river below Rangi-ō-hua. Botanists surveying the reserves on the Waikato side in 1984 noted the unusually good condition of Tauwhare's kahikatea-pukatea forest and some rare plants within it. That it was the last forest of its kind was not mentioned.

From Tauwhare's gazettal in 1912, through to the scientifically enlightened years of botanical surveys and wildlife reports, there is only one brief hint that the riverbend might be something out of the ordinary. Passing this 'extremely attractive and unusual sector of Mōkau Reserve' on a fleeting winter visit in 1971, a young government ranger, surprised that such a forest had survived in a place so ravaged, compared it to the forests fringing South Westland's Okarito Lagoon.

More than scenery links Mōkau and Okarito. Before their banks were cleared for farms, choked with willows and trampled by cattle, river after river along New Zealand's west coast would have provided the circumstances vital to the whitebait cycle of inanga. Now Mōkau's estuary is one of the last in the North Island with marshy flats and beds of low-lying rushes and sedges for fish to wriggle into on spring tides and spawn.

Eileen Taimanu remembers the 'big days' of catching and drying whitebait at Mōkau, when half or three-quarters of a kerosene tin in one scoop was common. All around the estuary, pā of supplejack and muslin were built to trap them, the catch poured onto sheets of corrugated iron, dried in the sun and stored for months. Ever since childhood, Aunty Eileen has carried the notion that the sudden, celebrated arrival of the first white-bait each spring—the event of the year to her whanau—underwrote the Mōkau's enormous importance to the old people. No longer though does she jostle among the holidaying Pākehā for a place on its banks—'too much trouble up there these days'. She has her own quiet, rushy spot on the Awakino.

Mōkau whitebaiting is now a way of life, the reason for most of the baches down at the rivermouth, and to many, the river's only value. The most productive fishery in the region, it is possibly its last remaining suitable spawning habitat. Catches have been made 35 km inland along its enormous tidal reach. Some 90 per cent of the whitebaiters sell all or part of their catch, supplementing pensions and seasonal work, or just making a bit of extra money. They return every spring like migratory birds to defend their little piece of riverbank. Sometimes tempers flare and someone ends up in the river.

Ignoring reserve boundaries and rangers' warnings, whitebaiters' huts lined the riverbank around Tauwhare until the early 1990s when the government had each whitebaiter's stand licensed and all huts demolished. I missed the silent solitaries sitting in front of their dilapidated humpies of re-used timber and corrugated iron, surrounded by the wild primeval forest. A new, up-market style had taken over; some new stands are now merely a post with a licence number marking precious territory, others are a major investment of jetties, steps and platforms—a new determination to stake a claim that officialdom recognises but struggles to control.

Two whitebaiters alongside Tauwhare are watching me, wondering what on earth I am doing on the Mōkau in the middle of the week in a wreck of a canoe—but without a net. I point to Tauwhare's kahikatea and say the reason lies with them.

'Go on. In that bloody bush? It's as wet as Hell in there.'

I say its Māori history would amaze them if they knew it. The less authoritative-looking one in the aluminium dinghy smiles, turns and leans back to his friend who is behind me on the bank with their net's boom. 'Anyone tell you it was a Māori place?'

They roar with laughter at the very idea, but with a nervous edge, so I tell them Tauwhare is one of the most tapu places on their coast.

'It's not bloody tapu! It's a reserve, mate.'

The one with the boom raises his chin toward Tauwhare. 'No tarsealed Māori road out there, eh?'

'There are pā all around you,' I say, extending his sweep across the river to Rangi-ō-hua's ridge of gorse and slips.

'Bullshit. There's no bloody pā up there. The buggers kept to the beach where the easy tucker was. You should get your facts right.'

'Go and look at that pā down at Tonga,' echoed the one in the boat as I slide away. 'Above the baches. You can't miss it. That's a pā for you. The men dug it out and watched the women do all the carrying. You bet, eh?'

'It's only history,' his companion calls after me.

On the other side of the riverbend, I see another whitebaiter without stand or shed among the bright green sedges in the mud at the foot of the great kahikatea. He looks up as I come into view.

'Working hard?' he calls out. 'Getting sunburn money?'

He has guessed what I'm about from my looking up at the big trees. 'It's a pity I'm not a nature-lover myself. I'd have tracks all through the bush here,' he says, lifting his head around to the green wall behind him. The absence of any construction, not even a wire tied to support his net, is unusual. I tell him he might be.

'In some ways, yes, but not scientific like. Imagine going from this to a freezing works in a couple of days' time. Three hundred men moaning and grizzling.'

The freezing works are at Waitara—blood and concrete on another revered, tidal river. But his heart is with this river. He has a photo at home of his kids, years ago, right there in the rushes. Lying back in their gumboots laughing. 'It's got all the bush in the back. One of my favourite things at home. Whitebaiting was different then. It's the same as everything else today. Too many people and too many nets. The Māoris know. They're not here.

'I was born at Mōkau, you know. My family were the first to whitebait on the river. That was in 1944-45. The end of the war, anyway. Up here is like coming home for me. A bit of fish and quiet. I have five weeks holiday now, and I spend it all up here.'

I decide against mentioning the old stories I've heard of pounds and pounds of whitebait drying on sheets of corrugated iron down at the rivermouth years before he knew the Mōkau. They dried on mats of harakeke for generations before that.

He wades out to help me pull the canoe up into the rushes. 'I don't know what I'll be doing next year. The industry's is a bad way. We've been told to make two million or that's it.'

I point to the tui and kererū dipping in and out of the kōwhai across the river. 'You should have been here 20 years ago,' he says as I go in under the trees.

He's gone by the time I come back to the river and the stranded canoe. The tide has turned. I stand under the riverbank trees, unseen by the blank faces as the boatloads of whitebaiters roar past, churning up the yellow water on their way back to the motor camp and lunch. I wait till they are out of earshot and Tauwhare's silence has returned.

⸻⸻

'The idea of a sacred place,' wrote the mythologist Joseph Campbell, 'is as old as life itself.' Modern science may not yet be particularly comfortable with such an idea, no more than with the notion of a life force energy, for it has no replicable data validating either's existence. But many of us believe, nevertheless, that the land itself is endowed with life forces and secret places of power. Tauwhare, I think, is one.

Just as the people of Mōkau stopped offering karakia and the first fish of their catch to the anchor-stone, Punga-ō-Tainui as te tino rangatiratanga weakened and each generation became further distanced from the authority of tapu, fewer and fewer approached the big riverbank trees with their ancestors' reverence.

By the time Percy Smith and his scenery preservationists saw Tauwhare, any knowledge it was wāhi tapu was so eroded that, had it not became scenic reserve, the burial trees on its flats would have been felled for pasture. Every other forest like it was lowered for its soil to be farmed. Cliff Black can remember when Whataronga, the big flat where the whitebaiters now congregate across the river, with signs of old kāinga abounding below the ridge pā, was logged in 1945. The kahikatea were huge, he says. Felled for timber and rolled into the river on an outgoing tide, some of them sunk out of sight in the silty water, causing great consternation until they were retrieved at the rivermouth.

Scenery preservationists like Percy Smith wanted nothing to do with tapu. Their task was romantic but not metaphysical, and no one in those days reminded them of the Treaty of Waitangi. Their recommendations were sometimes influenced by the curiosities of Māori history, but never by the Māori spiritual landscape. For Tauwhare or elsewhere, the complicated record of the government's Mōkau River Reserves contains only a single circumstance of anyone talking to the kaitiaki who knew the river's sacred places.

In 1904 James Cowan found much support for the preservation of the tapu estuary island Motu Taua. Had others involved in the quest for natural scenery talked with the kaumatua as he did with Taniora Wharauroa and Rangituataka, Pākehā might not now have the mortgage on conservation that they have. The two chiefs, he reported, 'expressed their interest to hand over the island to the Government without compensation, as a reserve in order that it may be preserved as a sacred spot and as a memorial of their tribe's achievements in the past.' Rangituataka obviously did not have long to live, and Cowan made the point that, should he and Taniora die before the island was handed over, their people would probably demand compensation. Eventually, despite Cowan's insistence, the idea was dropped when the chairman of the Mokau River Trust, Samuel Nicholls, identified disagreement: 'most of the people are willing to hand over the island for preservation purposes . . . there are some that dissent . . . the island is the burial place of his ancestors and the island is tapu'.

Many who know Mōkau believe the whole river is tapu. A Pākehā schoolteacher who taught for many years at the upriver settlement depicted in Maurice Shadbolt's novel *The Lovelock Version* told me, 'You know, in the whole time I was on the river, I never saw one Māori except for the cook at Mangatoi Station. It was almost as though it was tapu. The Māoris have a saying "Nothing Pākehā will prosper on the Mōkau." And look at it. Nothing has. Everything has gone back.'

Other Mōkau Pākehā sensed a different sacredness. In the 1920s Taranaki's settlers tried vainly to keep rabbits out of their province with a gate at their end of the Mōkau bridge. The rabbit-gatekeeper's daughter still brings smiles to the faces of kuia with whom she shared a rivermouth childhood. June Opie's victory over the agonies of polio depicted in her best-seller *Over my Dead Body* might not have been possible without Tauwhare's forest forever vivid in the country of her mind:

> *Safely moored, there were further struggles against cutty grass, bush lawyer and the knotted lianes of supple-jack, but then we stood on the very edge of the great forest. For a child the excitment of going in was often impossible to contain. Inside a new and mysterious world opened up—or it did for me. There was a complete change of light, changes of colour, the birds called more vibrantly, the smells and forms were different and the feel of things—a world of difference to the senses, and of limitless adventure. Adventure lay in the trees, their trunks often smothered in lianes and their branches supporting little living communities in the huge flax-like growths in their forks; in the gardens of ferns; the shaded undergrowth; climbers that tangled upwards across space making bridges for birds; and far, far above the canopy where no man could go, only high-flying insects that ate and pollinated the clematis flowers that opened there in the sun . . . the sanctified flower the Maoris called it.*
>
> *The forest offered a strange kind of sanctuary . . . my second world which, as I grew older and came to know other things, I recognised as the first world. Damp fungi, sphagnum and lichens formed a pattern of primal life . . . individual things died individually but even after death went on giving to life, making fertile points and new patterns for new growth . . . It was all in that green bush world, all of it open to discovery.*
>
> *Having envied those other children, who lived in Europe and had first hand knowledge of what I could only read in books, I determined to go. On arrival I became ill . . . It was a long illness and, during it, I held on to the trees I knew so well, my mind focussing on . . . a huge-girthed puriri, stately rimus, nikaus and the upright kahikateas rising to a height of over sixty metres. I tried to remember every detail, tried to sink some roots of my being into a remembered earth and stand as steadfastly as the trees. There was nothing comparable to our forest where I was; no one could bring me a green spray of aromatic kawakawa leaves, or a few golden karaka berries.*
>
> *Many years later, when I was able to travel to Europe, to*

go into those places where is said to exist the finest examples of all that epitomises man's culture and civilisation and, while appreciating what I found, grateful to the Greeks, to the builders of Chartres, the painters and sculptors, I still thought that there was nothing comparable to the native forest of my childhood in its creation and splendour.

By six o'clock the riverbend is in shadow. Overhead, the distant sound of motors, and then high above, the clearing cloud that has kept the air cool all day, a glint of light as the low sun reflects off yet another jet tracking from Wellington to Auckland. The sun slides down into a cloud bank way out over the Tasman then reappears. For a brief, unobstructed moment it illuminates Tauwhare's big trees and projects them across the river.

Until I came to the river and learned what I now know, nothing in my culture had prepared me for the insight into my country that these trees have given.

Looking at Tauwhare is like encountering the last kākāpō. Imagine the New Zealand when every estuary had towering trees like this, when they were flush with birds, the morning air shrieking with them. Eagles, the white of their underplumage reflecting off the water, launching themselves from their roosts in the clumps of epiphytes high in the kahikatea down to the river surface, talons tearing mullet from the shallows, then flapping with slow, terrific strokes across to the lower trees on the river cliffs. And after the moon of the equinox, the air awash with the sounds of the pulsing wings of geese on the move, beating over the pelicans, ducks and waders, and the rails in the reed beds.

The relentless overwhelming of a natural landscape cannot be reversed. New Zealand has kept few places where intimate human connection with nature is as palpable as here. Their preciousness extends beyond the survival of wild species and ecosystems—it touches the survival of our own sense of the life of the world.

Certain landscapes demand an emotional response, a deeper, even moral reaction to the land. Therein lies the spirit of place. Suspended still in its ancient protection, remote now from the imperial quests that removed anything like it elsewhere, Tauwhare is a last chance to acknowledge that

The Kaikaterre . . . growing to an immense height is found in swampy ground . . . on the banks of rivers, and is . . . easy to procure. Between the villages and their small spots of cultivation . . . the ground appeared never to have been disturbed.

RICHARD CRUISE, 1820

As we proceeded, the banks of the river became more and more
lovely, being in many places clothed with the richest profusion of
vegetation to the water's edge. Among the trees, the Kahikatea
was ever predominant ... Groves and clumps of that elegant pine
were intersected with small placid lakes and level plains, appearing
like a work of art.

ON THE WAIKATO, WILLIAM COLENSO, DECEMBER 1842

Billie McCord and Jack Anderson have been falling timber on main line that was burned by the fire . . . We have about 300 logs on new tramway going towards Duck Creek. James McInnis plowing No 7 down. Ernest Wyatt and Farmer Hardman looking after cows . . . Lees and Tully finished their contract clearing out drains . . . No 8 down is all ploughed up . . .

SETTLER DIARY, 1894
AS THE LAST OF THE IMMENSE TREES OF OOAHAOURAGEE GAVE WAY TO DAIRY FARMS

. . . *indeed in every respect the properest place we have yet seen for establishing a Colony; a ship as large as Ours might be carried several miles up the river, where she would be moored to the trees as safe as alongside a wharf in London river, a safe and sure retreat in case of an attack from the natives . . . The Noble timber, of which there is such an abundance, would furnish plenty of materials either for the building defences, houses or Vessels. The River would furnish plenty of Fish, and the Soil make ample returns of any European Vegetables sown in it.*

Joseph Banks, *Endeavour* Journal, 1769

THE LOWER WAIHOU AT TURUA, LOOKING DOWNRIVER TO ORUARANGI

. . . a lofty pine wood appeared to occupy the whole breadth and length . . . I remember, especially, the enormous number of waterfowl frequenting the mouth of the Hutt River . . . so tame it was slaughter rather than sport to shoot them.

CHARLES HEAPHY, 1878, REMEMBERING 1839

In the river's fertile silt, wiwi's tubular leaves reach in excess of two metres. A different plant altogether from its knee-high cousins on exposed, rocky coasts. One day it can be swirling around you in the wind, hiding you from sight the moment you step ashore; the next day, a storm or spring tide can mow it down into great flattened swathes.

Now one of lowland New Zealand's rarest plants, surviving only where people and their predatory grazers can't reach, modern botanists believe parātawhiti and its close relatives elsewhere in Polynesia to have ancient tropical origins. To the 1870s surveyor Edwin Brooks, parātawhiti was evidence of a place being 'long inhabited by the natives'.

Any New Zealand forest is locked into a cycle of unpredictable natural destruction, but it is especially so in kahikatea's forests . . . Eventually, after about 800 years, if a flood or a tsunami hasn't scoured the little flat clean again, all the old kahikatea will be gone.

WHITEBAITER'S POST AND BURIAL KAHIKATEA TREES

. . . 'no one "owns" this landscape in the sense of having clear, unquestionable title to it' . . . Invaders and invaded encounter one another in an unresolved, imaginary landscape, revealing that 'everyone "owns" (or ought to own) this landscape in the sense that everyone must acknowledge or own up to some responsibility to it'.

It is only at these uneasy, artificial edges between agriculture and forest that we can comprehend what happens ecologically when humans decide to channel a whole ecosystem's productive energy into themselves.

The ethnologist Elsdon Best blamed the way Māori were so 'persistent' in endowing nature's plants with sex on them having been 'a barbaric folk dwelling in a land of forests'. Nowhere is sexual purpose greater than in this intertwining of forest and swamp in Mua-upoko's sand country . . . Tane, manifest in the tall trees of the dry sand ridges, is locked in a reciprocal embrace with the swampy arms of the lake, feminine in its flows . . .

There has been a flood through the kahikatea forest. A film of fine, brown silt covers every seedling, leaf and frond near the forest floor. Yet only where rotting logs have banked up against the aerial roots of pukatea is any flow perceptible.

Looking upward . . . the struggle for space to exist still goes on. Colonies of flax-like parasites establish themselves high up in forks and rifts of the tall boles . . . 'Is there no way to save the finest of these trees?' But here was no way. New Zealand, teeming with resources and just feeling out for the markets of the world, was too desperately poor to deny the present for the benefit of the future.

HELEN WILSON, *Land of my Children,* **1955**

I was well out across the water when, into view from behind a headland, came a flat shoreline of forest. In the warm silence, its big trees seemed to float above the emerald water. I felt I was looking at something elemental to the history of this country, glimpsing the land in its original order.

Once, before we brought our farms and towns to this kind of ground, there must have been countless places like it, all around the coast. Had Europeans settled New Zealand in less of a rush— and with less anticipation of a low country spread waiting them— a few more forests of big trees might still stand on its tidal flats.

The last spring tide has left its calling cards among them: salty, white encrustations like hand-painted bands on every cylindrical rush leaf. Seen from a distance, the bands curve around the head of the inlet like a Plimsoll line . . . In behind the front line of rushes, twigs and logs, feathers, bones shells, and crab carapaces . . . held up by the rushes.

The damp floor is a sprawling jumble of aerial roots, which rise
every now and then in great buttresses. The impression of tropical
rainforest is no delusion: 30 million years ago, before the days of
birds—when reptiles did the flying and seed dispersal—before the
land that has become New Zealand broke away from the rest of
the ancient Gondwana continent, it was mainly lowlying like this,
forested and tropical.

RIMU TREE ON STORM RIDGE OF FORMER BEACH

. . . the intimidating press of the wind on the beach and the roar
of the sea drowning out every sound. And then, only a hundred
metres away, the lagoon cold, clear and calm in the pale winter's
morning, only the big trees stirring.

The first time I saw the tapu creek, before it succumbed—like most creeks of its kind on the Coast—to the drainage engineers, every surface below eye-level, every twig and leaf, right across the sandflat, carried a film of life-sustaining silt. Now only in floods does it look like a stream and then it is never out of its channel.

A Trans-Am from California and a surviving nikau from The Great Wood of Nelson, 1987

A FLOODPLAIN KAHIKATEA FOREST STILL INTACT, OHINETAMATEA RIVER, SOUTH WESTLAND

the brief human time in these islands has included a greater sense of nature than is common today.

Only in places that have this effect do you realise what Henry Thoreau really meant when he said that the preservation of the world lay in wilderness. Why his friend Ralph Waldo Emerson considered nature a temple. Places like Tauwhare challenge the secularity of modern conservation, its denigration of people and its preoccupation with species as entities in themselves. The riverbend is no outdoor, primeval museum piece; no place for tracks and boardwalks. It is a place to respect by keeping your distance.

As a window onto the ordinary landscape that vanished when Europe took over New Zealand's rivermouths and estuaries, Tauwhare is far from ordinary. Those who know it as te tonga puaroa keep the knowledge hidden from today's cynicism. 'It still has its mana, that place,' they say.

The Lovelock Version's improbable saga of settler endeavour against a wild intractable land, ends with the forest returning in the clearings and the valley left to its primeval sounds of wind and water, 'to legend . . . and the itinerant ecologist'. It was as such, I suppose, that I first saw the big kahikatea. I misread the remoteness of their muddy, abused river and judged their survival in such a ravaged place to be one of history's accidents. Now I cannot look up at them without pondering that old wisdom that left them here, the people in the long quietness of death high in the mossy reliquaries of their branches. In any itinerant ecologist's terms, the people have become part of the forest, feeding the kahikatea, kahakaha and kōwharawhara that feed the kererū which glide across the river.

Tauwhare's kahikatea were standing long before their people insisted they were kept out of Pax Britannica's seductive grasp. They were neighbourhood. People lived in their shadow, passing them and their abundant birds every day they canoed to and from the coast.

A gust of wind. The kahikatea shudder. I point the canoe toward the sea and let the tide take me through their ancient shade.

> *E Tauwhare!*
> *Morehu ō te Wao Nui ō Tane,*
> *Manākitia e te Kaihanganui a Te Ao,*
> *Tu ake ou rakau kaumatua i runga i ngā oneone momona ō*
>   *Papatuanuku,*
> *Tupu ana i raro i te maru ō Ranginui,*

Tohungia e te mahana e tiaho mai ana i te Ra,
Whakakākāriki e ngā wai ora e heke iho i ngā kapua i runga,
    hei irīringa,
Whakahangia e ngā marangai ō Tawhiri Matea,
He tirohanga ki te moana nui ō Tangaroa.
E Tauwhare!
Kei kona e rere ana Mōkau tata mai. No reira:
Tu mai tonu, noho mai tonu.

THE LAKE IN THE SAND COUNTRY

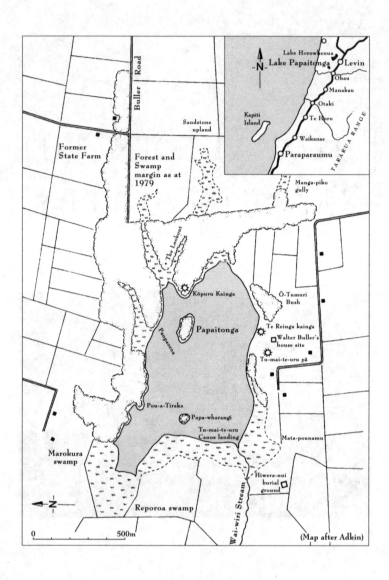

Buller Road

Sandstone
upland

Former
State Farm

Forest and
Swamp
margin as at
1979

Manga-piko
gully

The Lookout

Kōpuru Kainga

Ō-Tumuri
Bush

Papaitonga

Te Reinga kainga

Walter Buller's
house site

Tu-mai-te-uru pā

Pou-a-Tiraka

Papa-wharangi

Tu-mai-te-uru
Canoe landing

Mata-pounamu

Marokura
swamp

Hiwera-nui
burial
ground

Reporoa swamp

Wai-wiri Stream

(Map after Adkin)

0   500m

Lake Horowhenua
Lake Papaitonga   Levin

Ohau
Manakau

Otaki

Te Horo

Kapiti
Island

Waikanae

Paraparaumu

TARARUA RANGE

G EOMETRY, SAID the great architect Le Corbusier, is man's language. Surveyors have ensured the low, flat country that sprawls north from the seacliffs at Paekakariki is not where you lose yourself in the wild. The Horowhenua Plain has been said, though, to contain 'the finest soil in the world', and if anywhere does, expresses that 19th-century dream of 'a garden and pasture in which the best elements of British society could grow into an ideal nation, bringing the savage inhabitants into a state of harmony with this ideal nature'. The landscape is too airy and prolific to be oppressive, but as one with an eye for nature, I find it lonely and full of melancholy.

The uncompromising straightness with which Highway 1 and the railway beside it cross the flatness suggests that the people who laid them out believed nothing was in the way, or that what was here prior to their moment was useless, the land a blank slate. Yet, unlike the vegetable stalls with their signs—*Grannies $2 a kilo*—neither highway nor railway is a consequence of speed and traffic flow. Their unyielding course through the market gardens and orchards is only possible because, before them, a forest was here.

Four generations now have sustained the forest unseen in tribal memory. Place names still reflect its birds and swamps, its waterways and trees and the human lives to which they gave reason and ritual. The first European to capture an image of it, Charles Heaphy, painted it from a shipdeck in 1839: a green, unbroken seam between sea and mountains. Covering everything but the sand dunes and the wetter swamps, it survived

Europeanisation longer than any other forest of its kind. My grandmother would have known it had she had a Horowhenua childhood. Right into the 1870s, keen eyes like Percy Smith's saw 'one solid forest' from the Manawatu River until its low-lying flats met the steep, rocky Wellington coast. Palmerston North was a mere clearing in it.

European travellers—'distinguished men, foreign as well as English, scientists, artists, explorers, traders, pedlars, entertainers in great variety, vagabonds, runaway sailors and convicts as well as official parties'—kept to the open beach and gave the great forest a wide berth. Resisting land wars and confiscation, Māori held off surrendering their plain and riverflats to paddocks and fences. By the 1880s, when they were finally prised away, the Horowhenua had become an anomaly in the colonial landscape. In 1885 the Wellington–Manawatu Railway Company's surveyors began cutting the 'huge trench' through which William Adkin travelled to see his balloted block of bush. Excited by Stanley the African explorer and the imperialist rhetoric of empire, the young Lambton Quay draper saw the forested plain as *his* frontier. 'The bush scenery was grand', but it would not be an unworthy life 'to clear a portion of this fertile country and make a home'. A settler's daughter, Helen Wilson, thrilled at the 'sea of standing bush . . . through which the tram line cut a symmetrical tunnel'. Later in life she said its 'solemn rapturous beauty' had impressed her more than anything else in New Zealand. Watching the successful ballotees like Adkin clear their blocks as quickly as possible to avoid penal rates on still-standing bush, she knew no one would ever experience its like again. Such a sudden end to something so splendid would have far-reaching consequences: 'Few New Zealanders,' she wrote, 'have ever seen their own "bush" as it was in the beginning. The surviving patches of it . . . on hillsides or on poor stoney soil, or where stock has been through it . . . bear but slight resemblance to the virgin rain-forest grown on fertile flats.'

Nowhere in New Zealand is there still such a forest. South Westland still has plains clothed with a sprawl of forest and swamps, but they are cold plains swept by air flowing off high snow country. Leached by three times the rainfall, their soils hold little prospect for the subtropical lushness that cloaked Horowhenua's low country. Geology too, plays a part. Not long ago, the plain was a part of a more expansive Cook Strait. Rich alluvial deposits poured into it from the ancestors of today's rivers. Then the land rose. The sea receded. The windswept sand and gravel flats became plains, the brackish lagoons freshwater lakes. Matai, totara and rimu wooded the drier flats and sand dunes, kahikatea and pukatea the swamp and lake margins. 'Shaded with a lofty forest . . . banks clothed with beautiful evergreens to the water's edge, studded with lovely wooded islets . . . fringes of raupo alternating with overhanging bush', the Horowhenua lake country which the first Europeans saw was the 'most picturesque' in the North Island. It had its own life: 'a pair of papango, having emerged from a bed of reeds, are floating on the placid waters, a small black shag . . . settling itself in for the night in a kowhai bough . . . a solitary pekapeka flitting silently overhead, chasing in zigzag lines the minute insect life upon which this bat subsists'.

Never before or since has a New Zealand landscape been so quickly and ruthlessly 'cleared'. Within 20 years of the forest tunnel being cut, only nature's geological lineaments were still there. From a plane, it is evident the ground whose towns and market gardens seem so confident and permanent is in perpetual change. Every surface is one of water's myriad, temporary paths from mountains to sea. It is also apparent that the highway and the railway are far from the only straight lines: the entire plain is rectangularised. Reshaping nature is fundamental to being human, but we also have warnings in our history for those who have sacrificed forested country, unrestrictedly, to agriculture. 'Woe to those,' says Isaiah, 'who . . . join field to field until everything belongs to them and they are the sole inhabitants of the land'.

'A long, relentless war between man and the wild things,' Helen Wilson called it. Hopeful settlers reading the prospectus for the Horowhenua Village Settlement were told which bird, fern and tree species flourished on each section, and what that meant about the soil they might soon be turning over. But for most successful bidders the vast forest through which they picked their way along the grid of surveyors' cut-lines was 'no more than a place in which to shoot pigeons, and in what cattle went wild and were lost'.

Grid settlement divides landscapes, ideally level ones, into equal and tradeable segments. As suitable as it is to creating a society of small landholders—'the most precious part of a state . . . as few as possible will be without a little portion of land'—it is, by design, the death of nature. The promoters of the Levin Village Settlement fancied the same ordered utopia as Thomas Jefferson's American dream. The 1877 Land Act embodied it. 'As far as the features of the country will admit,' it commanded, 'all sections shall be of a rectangular form.' Some of the plain's towering forest was milled

TIMBER-GETTERS AND
KAHIKATEA,
HOROWHENUA, 1890s.

for cash, to reappear in the late-Victorian houses of Wellington city. But with Britain wanting all the sheep meat and dairy fat we could produce and saw-millers complaining how the government 'determined that the bush must be destroyed', thousands and thousands of acres were simply incinerated in the rush.

A century on from the advent of refrigerated shipping, New Zealand is becoming Aotearoa. The collapse of imperialism's old ways has revealed the extent of our loss of contact with natural life forces and what they offer. When ecologists talk about 'ecological bottom lines' and whether the basic life systems of New Zealand will live or die, it's the vanishing of things like Helen Wilson's green cathedral they have in mind.

In a tiny fraction of the landscape's history, we have got into a way of thinking in which the scraps of forest and the sudden flood are the anomalies, not us. Attitudes toward the past revolve around a catalogue of what was *absent* when colonialism finally came—roads and fences, farms and gardens, towns and shops. *Ecological* capital isn't visible in the market, so the balance sheets of rural economics don't include it. Yet had a moist, ancient forest not been here, its myriad plant and animal species constantly crumbling leaves, accumulating nutrients and keeping decay in pace with growth, the market gardens and orchards certainly wouldn't be either.

Catching my eye as I turn out of the highway traffic, the signs Buller Road and Papaitonga Reserve are reminders that a landscape's history is as much a matter of people as places. Buller Road meets the state highway with the bush surveyor's mandatory 90°. Within a kilometre dusty gravel replaces tarseal and your gaze is turned away from rows of cabbages and *Fresh Eggs and Frozen Chicken* signs, by a streak of wildness. Silhouettes of nīkau palms and kahikatea emerge above the barberry hedges—and between them, a dark stretch of water. It's another country—as the man whose name is on the road sign knew the moment in 1864 when he was 'struck by its singular loveliness':

Sixty miles from Wellington by the Manawatu Railway, and less than two miles to the westward of that line, there is one of the prettiest bits of scenery in New Zealand. This is Papaitonga, so called from time immemorial, the name signifying the 'Beauty of the South' . . . a freshwater lake of 135 acres in extent, with two exquisite islands covered with bright vegetation . . . it is enclosed by a beautiful native forest, which presents a thick fringe of tree-ferns and underwood along the water's edge; on the southern side there is open rising ground with clearings in the forest beyond, showing the snow-capped ranges . . .

Subsequent Governors, and others, . . . have negotiated in vain till, in 1891, I was fortunate enough to become the purchaser of the property which constitutes my country home in New Zealand.

Huddling out of the sea wind that sculpts the tops of the trees overhead, cows crowd the cropped green wall that strikes across the flatness. Generations of them patrolling the wire have repelled any advance of the foliage. Papaitonga always seems beseiged, despite the seeming indifference of the paddocks to this remnant of the forest that preceded them. Were the lines of wire not here separating pastoral from primeval, we can be certain the forest and the ferns overhanging the lake would no longer exist.

It is only at these uneasy, artificial edges between agriculture and forest that we can comprehend what happens ecologically when humans decide to channel a whole ecosystem's productive energy into themselves. Today most of us in Western societies use this energy in ways that keep us personally removed from the green plants that pick up what comes from the sun to build and power their cells and tissues, from the herbivores, and then the carnivores, and the scavengers and decomposers that use them in turn. Some 10,000 years we have been doing it, ever since our ancestors on the floodplains of the Middle East's 'Fertile Crescent' learned to herd mammals and crop grasses, leaving a succession of ruined, exhausted landscapes in our wake.

Smear a handful of forest soil between your fingers and feel how much of it is organic and how little is clay or silt and sand. Magnify it 10,000 times and you see the seething mass of living creatures you step on walking across a forest floor. You begin to understand the people who talk of a rainforest not so much as the trees, birds and ferns, but as an eco-*system* in which over 90 per cent of the animal biomass is present as invertebrates.

Imagine the myriad networks of links between those species and their environments, and the changes that would occur in the soil if the great bulk of that life ceased to exist. Then cross back over the fence and feel the pasture's soil. Straightaway you notice how difficult it is to pick up and how compact it is between your fingers. Magnification reveals only a tiny fraction of the life in the forest soil—merely the remains.

Not long ago, the two soils were one and the same. Above them, leaves fell, died and decayed and crumbled silently into a community of life of which we know virtually nothing. Then one day in the 1890s a surveyor set up his theodolite and chose the fence's arbitrary course across the sandplain: bush on one side to stay, on the other to vanish forever.

What happened that day at the end of Buller Road is central to the history of the New Zealand landscape. It was here a government first responded to the popular and political doctrine we call 'conservation' and kept a piece of lowland forest from being farmed—not to protect timber, watersheds or hold erosion, but simply in deference to the kind of forest it was. The government had taken its cue from a missionary's son intrigued with Darwinism and New Zealand's birds and the notion of the beautiful. Entwining nature conservation with imperialism, Walter Buller elegantly subverted his settler culture's agenda for the land whose every acre it was desperate to cultivate, keeping alive a forest his neighbours would have felled and swamps they would have drained.

SIR WALTER BULLER, C.1900.

Buller was an enigma. His natural history brought him fame but at its root was fascination at the ancient life of a primeval paradise failing to adapt to the empire. In a crude form of Darwinism, he drew parallels between 'the pathos of a great departing race' and native birds; that Māori were doomed, he had 'no doubt whatsover'. Those affected by his land-dealing or repelled at his trading in huia and kiwi corpses loathe mention of his name. Yet had he not been here in the vital years at the end of the 19th century, this place—the last trace of its kind of ecosystem, and one of New Zealand's most precious wild places—certainly wouldn't still be 'covered to the water's edge with dense bush'.

Buller's sense of the wild was certainly not 'if you look after nature it will look after you'. Epitomising that curious Victorian mix of extravagance and endeavour, he thought it fitting that 'nearly all this country is covered with smiling farms, supporting contented homes, and old Jenkins sleeps with his race in the picturesque churchyard at Otaki', even if his neighbours' ways with nature sometimes moved him to call them 'Goths and Vandals'. 'One is glad, of course,' he wrote once, 'to see the country thus reclaimed.' Papaitonga, he liked to say, was where he and his birds 'took refuge'—but, enthralled by publicity, he promoted his 'country seat' as a wealthy man's scenic folly. 'The perfect place for picnics,' said W.G. Adkin who took his family there regularly as a break from the fires, bumping the gig along the 'miserable winding track' through the sandhills. The new Horowhenua settler society was full of curiosity about what others were up to, especially if they weren't levelling the forest as vigorously as everyone else. 'We saw the spot,' Adkin told his 1893 diary the same week as Horowhenua's first stock sale, 'where we suppose Sir W. Buller will build. It commands the finest view of the lake, with a splendid slope to the water's edge.'

Buller's perception of New Zealand bird behaviour in response to Europeanisation and his lobbying for island sanctuaries are at the beginning of what today we take for granted as 'conservation'. Birds are the litmus of the landscape, quickly reflecting changes in ecology's balance. Buller was one of the first Pākehā to show how everything in the native New Zealand landscape is linked to everything else. From the forested landscape awash with birds in which he was born at a Kaipara riverbank mission station in 1839, his life paralleled the arrival and spread of European settlement—and the birds' vanishing. The hand-coloured lithographs in his *History of the Birds of New Zealand* are New Zealand icons even today. He was still a young man when it was published in 1873. His observations of flightless parrots and other strange antipodean birds attracted worldwide attention and lifted him to the eminence of a European knighthood and nomination for the auspicious Royal Society—by his revered Charles Darwin among others.

Three years before Buller was born, and on another mission farm not far away, Darwin had seen something that struck him deeply and became, years later, one of his theory of evolution's most potent examples of biological invasion and the survival of the fittest:

The endemic productions of New Zealand are perfect one compared with another; but they are now rapidly yielding before

*the advancing legions of plants and animals introduced from
Europe . . . From the extraordinary manner in which European
productions have recently spread over New Zealand, and have
seized on places which have been previously occupied by the
indigenes, we must believe, that if all the animals and plants of
Great Britain were set free in New Zealand, a multitude of British
forms would in the course of time become thoroughly naturalised
there, and would exterminate many of the natives.*

The simplistic version of Darwin's theory of evolution that has
become a major world view of our time holds that species fail according to
their lack of fitness to survive in a changing world. In Buller's time, it was
used to defend the spread of settler culture. For many like me who grew up
in its wake, Darwin's theory backed the thrill of witnessing technology's
endlessly new superior models invading the world of their instantly 'inferior'
predecessors. It had me believing that this relentless preoccupation with
improvement was some universal life principle; as it had Walter Buller
believing in the 'material advancement' and superiority of his own British
culture, and that the birds vanishing around him were, like Māori, doomed
by inferior genes—dying out because they were being subjected to stresses
for which their prior evolution had not prepared them.

As a lawyer, Buller liked to say he had 'the leading Native practice in
New Zealand'. He also considered himself a 'thorough disciple of Darwinism'.
Everything the young ornithologist saw seemed to prove Darwin's forecast
for the primitive life of the antipodes: 'the productions of Great Britain stand
much higher in the scale than those of New Zealand'. And with Buller's new
European admirers regarding the avifauna of New Zealand as 'one of the most
interesting and instructive in the world . . . exciting a lively regret in the minds
of all ornithologists', there was also good money to be made.

Buller was in his early twenties when he first saw the Horowhenua
Plain in 1864, a young magistrate 'selected' by Sir George Grey, as he liked
to say, to purchase the beautiful lake Papaitonga from Ngāti Raukawa for a
governor's estate. When his *History of the Birds of New Zealand* was first
published the plain and its precious lakes were still as Māori wanted them
to be. Combining the new European laws with traditional threats, its
centuries-old inhabitants, the Mua-upoko, had just reclaimed a strip of it
back from Ngāti Raukawa. Merely a handful of Europeans lived along the
great forest's margins. One of them wrote:

The lake lay clasped in the emerald arms of the bush which surrounded it on every side save immediately about where we stood. Mile after mile the bush stretched across the flat on which the town of Levin now stands, and swept up the mountain-side to the relief of the white snow-cap. Straight and tall the timber grew to the water's edge, fringed with flax and nodding manuka and over the bush, flashing their white breasts as they circled and wheeled in the sunshine, pigeons flew literally in thousands, drifting from tree to tree, rising in flocks of half a hundred or so, with a whirring of wings plainly to be heard across the calm waters; circling round in a wide sweep with characteristic rise and dip of flight, skimming the lake . . . to rise and sweep back over the bush and settle on some other tree . . . No other sound was in the air, nor sight of life was visible, save where the smoke curled slowly upwards from the stockaded pa of Raia te Karaka. Across at Te Hou and Kouturoa some Maoris called musically one to another; in front of us was only the lake, the unspoiled bush and the mountains beyond.

THE HOROWHENUA IN THE 1860S, WILLIAM SWAINSON.

No wonder Buller was drawn to the Horowhenua. Right into the late 1880s it was noisy with bird song. Then it fell silent. With each winter's plummeting temperatures, the search for food brought kākā down from the mountain forests to the coastal swamps and forest edges. Then one winter, their orangey-pink underwings didn't appear. Summer didn't bring them back. Sparrows and starlings replaced them. To Māori whose view of nature still depended on phenomena repeated and tested, the plain was like another country. Buller could not believe 'how changed everything was now from what it was a few years ago!' It was as though every native bird had taken wing and left: 'For a short time certainly there was a Tui singing gaily in a lofty tree-top; and then, moved by some sudden impulse, he darted downwards, passing through a sunlit glade in the forest, his white epaulettes shimmering in the light. Then all was silent again, save for the lively twittering of the sparrow and his foreign friends.'

THE HOROWHENUA, C.1887.

Something in him aroused the urge to save a piece of the great forest that was becoming a landscape of charred stumps and muddy roads:

> It is inevitable, of course, that with the progress of active colonisation, much of our lovely forest scenery must disappear. Even in this provincial district during the last few years, bush scenery of exquisite beauty—not to be equalled perhaps, in any part of the world—has to yield to the woodman's axe, and it would be only false sentiment to deplore the fact in view of the necessities of practical settlement. But I take it to be the duty of every colonist who has the means and the opportunity, to do what he can to protect and conserve some, at any rate, of the natural features of this beautiful land of ours.

Buller has been called 'the reluctant conservationist'. For most of his life, he had little interest in the idea of saving forest to keep New Zealand's birds from extinction. In his ornithology, he had long argued that widespread extinction was inevitable; that in the face of European immigrants, birds like huia would 'erelong . . . exist only in museums and collections'. But by the time he died he knew that his landscaped lake in the Horowhenua sand country had hugely influenced the embryonic scenery preservation movement. Old and ill in England, he realised he would never see his 'dear old Papaitonga' again, but he knew that what he had there was unprecedented. What he called 'conservation' was something in which he boasted New Zealand 'led the world'. He took 'extreme satisfaction' in the 'gradual awakening to the fact that we have animal and vegetable forms of life indigenous to the country which ought to be protected and cherished'.

Buller knew that, if left to its own devices, his settler culture would do what it had done on every other plain and let its 'reckless destruction' of nature run its course until every last wild tree was gone. But he didn't deny the vision of a new Eden: still standing beside his lake is the olive tree he planted to symbolise it. Yet something made him swim against the tide, prise Papaitonga from its Māori, suffer his neighbours' fires and weather their scorn, to save its swamps and forest. It was still Victorian symbolism, but concerned less with beautiful views than vanishing birds.

Like all great abiding ideas, it was bold and simple. 'My object,' he said, 'being to bring together, on my own property, as many as possible of these endemic forms.'

Buller knew that with 100,000 acres of forest 'swept clean in a single season' time was short. Had he known what we do about 'wildlife corridors', about island biogeography theory and its implications for the size of nature reserves, his 'means and opportunity' might have ensured that a forested strip of the plain from the sand dunes to the Tararuas might still remain.

Habitat fragmentation has been called the greatest worldwide threat to forest wildlife and the primary cause of species extinction. It has been mainly observed in temperate forests with a concentration of birds, like the Horowhenua Plain Buller knew. Birds flock here from miles around in autumn when Papaitonga's kahikateas' tiny, nutritious koroī ripen. Some stay here, flying across to the mountains whenever the urge takes them. Others breed here. 'On the slightest alarm,' he wrote of kererū in *History of the Birds of New Zealand*, 'it stretches up its lustrous neck, and gently sways its head to and fro, uttering a scarcely audible *coo*, slowly repeated.' He noted too the 'peculiar soaring habit which this bird indulges in during the breeding season. Mounting high in the air, in a direct upward course, it suddenly opens its wings and tail to their full extent, and glides downwards in an oblique direction, and without any apparent movement of those members.'

The ecosystem of birds like kererū, as seasonal bird counts by ornithologists in the 1970s inferred and radio-tracking has proved, can span lowlands to uplands and many different forests. Recognition of this has profoundly influenced the design of forest reserves in New Zealand, resulting in the protection of areas that would, by now, have been logged.

Never one to stake his reputation on a hunch, Buller went no further than noting how European settlement was 'obliterating the old boundary lines and changing the local habitat'. He left it to later ornithologists like Sir Robert Falla to declare that 'birds deprived of lowland forest into which they were accustomed to descend in winter have become extinct or very scarce'. Yet, watching bird numbers plummet as their ecosystem collapsed, and fluent enough to pick up Māori reaction to it, Buller must have sensed that Papaitonga's wellbeing depended on a life support system that works at the scale of kilometres, between coast and mountains.

An intricate green kaleidoscope encloses you the moment you go under Papaitonga's trees. It's the same plain but the view suddenly drops from kilometres to metres. Instead of scanning far horizons, my eyes are led to mosses clinging to a supplejack vine. My senses adjust to quiet cool and closeness. Sunlight shafts through kohekohe, titoki and tawa, time-travellers from the ancient Gondwana tropics. Some sun ends on their highlighted leaves, some reaches the spread of nīkau fronds or even the forest floor.

NOR'WESTER SHORN PUKATEA,
THE LOOKOUT.

It is not so much in the open space of paddocks as inside the forest, nearing the edge of the plain, that I sense the ocean. Suddenly agriculture vanishes and I'm in the down-flow of the land. The beach is still some three or four kilometres away beyond dunes, but curiously this never diminishes my awareness that this is a *coastal* place. There are days when the roar of surf would have you believing the sea is right here, days when you can taste the salt spray and see why the nor'-westerly so effectively shears the seam between forest and sky.

The sea *was* here. The sandplain is young land, changed entirely since the waves left, but its sudden edge in the forest still preserves the seacliff they cut thousands of years ago, before the tide retreated and sand build-up formed a lagoon that became the lake we see today. Between it and the ice- and water-cut mountains, a forest formed on myriad abandoned watercourses. Then the land rose, the dunes built out as the sea withdrew, stranding the old seacliff miles inland, enveloped in forest.

At its foot, where the waves lapped, everything changes. A wet edge-community of pukatea, maire tawake and kahikatea replaces the dry, open forest of kohekohe and tawa. Longer-lived shadows, persisting dampness, different plants. Slippery entanglements of kie kie and thickets of tall cutty grass. Water underfoot, and a deep black mud, paru, that only undisturbed millenia of rotted-down forest can produce. It's at this point, where a boardwalk winds out into the flax swamp, where the familiar landscape of pasture and hedges suddenly vanishes behind towering flax and kahikatea, that many people start talking. Talk, in the main, of not wanting to be here if the boardwalk wasn't.

Despite all the conservationist passion about 'wetlands', we are a culture with a persistent fear of being lost in swamps, up to our armpits in black water. Perhaps it is instinctive—some coded, memorial nucleic acid.

The colonial mind has been tormented by land just like this ever since the New Zealand Company's first wet week on Petone Beach. 'Wetland' might be a rallying call for those with thoughts of rare water birds and ecological balance. But to most people, it's as *swamps* that these places have any meaning, the way they appeal to something deep in the reptilian parts of our brains, find their way into movies like *King Kong*, and feed the imagination and language. Who's ever heard of 'getting wetlanded' or 'wetland fever'?

Isn't there a moral here? Once divorced from nature the modern plains landscape gave its inhabitants the security of always knowing just where they were. Land clearance quickly annihilated the settler generation's worst fear—getting lost, taken alive, out in a flax swamp. Mightn't 'swamps' be a better word than 'wetlands' to use when arguing care for places like this? Bits of country kept to remind us what the land we take for granted was before us.

The year after W.G. Adkin came through a tunnel in the forest to muse on prosperity, the Horowhenua's first flax-milling boom began. Papaitonga and this harakeke swamp were still Mua-upoko land, although Walter Buller was pressuring to procure them. Just up the coast at Foxton, James Cox, a young farm labourer fresh from Wiltshire, stepped off a steamer. He had heard 'a good deal of Flax is cut and dressed in the neighbourhood and I hope to get work at some of the Mills'. But he was nervous of the new, wild country, apprehensive at his chances: 'I am very downhearted and do not know how to get a job. I do not ask in the right way somehow and scarcely have the pluck to ask at all.' Someone told him to try Jones and Lyon's flax-mill eight miles away, but 'Going from the Shanty to the Mill I went wrong and got lost in the bush and was about five hours struggling through a dense and wet bush in water up to my knees often, I got in a mess, mud all over, and my hands cut and torn to pieces. I was fagged out when I got back to the shanty and did not reach the mill.' Cox started flax-cutting the next day, but the swamp had so poisoned his hands that he could not even earn enough for 'tucker'. It was another week before they began to heal, and he could collect fern to sleep on, and become a flaxie.

There must have been hundreds like James Cox who went out into the swamps after breakfast but were not back for tea. He, cousin of the English nature writer Richard Jefferies, was one who wrote it down and whose bleak diary has survived the century. If any never came back, they wouldn't have been the first in New Zealand history to die for flax. Along with seals and timber, flax was, to the first Europeans, what New Zealand was all about. When a ton of muka bought a musket from the Pākehā, the trade in flax fibre began the transformation of the Māori landscape. While it lasted, the Horowhenua's vast swamps of harakeke and eels were the mainstay of mana, and the central attractions to the Waikato people who overran them in the 1820s. Led by a vision of its flax becoming a money-spinner, the New Zealand Company tried to buy the Horowhenua Plain in 1839. But it was not until the 1880s, when establishment of an American market coincided with a new flax-stripping method, that men like James Cox began pouring onto the plain.

Well into the 20th century, when the stamper's heavy thump was part of the landscape, land in flax was valued second only to dairy farms. Farmers bought up swamps to leave in their natural state for fibre and royalties. From right here on a calm day, across the lake, you could have heard one of the last stampers. Harvey's mill, cutting flax from the big Reporoa Swamp between Papaitonga and the sandhills, closed only in the 1940s—the stamper's concrete platform is still there beside the last of the grove of karaka trees of the Mua-upoko kāinga that was there long before it. Yet as sure as its sounds have gone, flax country has vanished from sight. A 'flax museum' has opened over at Foxton, but half a century of neat, drained farms has made most of us ignorant of swamps.

———————

'Harakeke must be buried properly if it is not used. Sovereignty is wrapped up in it. It has done a lot of things for people over the years.' Joseph Tukupua is not happy at my mention of the piles of flax thrown into the swamp by whoever had been cutting a passage across the boardwalk. And the same undisguised disapproval is in the eyes of Josephine Paki beside him. 'It is part of the mana of the place. Tane cannot do without the harakeke. You must have the male and female together in everything.'

The ethnologist Elsdon Best blamed the way Māori were so 'persistent' in endowing nature's plants with sex on them having been 'a barbaric folk dwelling in a land of forests'. Nowhere is sexual purpose greater than in this intertwining of forest and swamp in Mua-upoko's sand country. Papaitonga retains for Māori the living impressions of the great creative acts in the beginning of life. It has a profound underlying order. Tane, manifest in the tall trees of the dry sand ridges, is locked in a reciprocal embrace with the swampy arms of the lake, feminine in its flows. Imbued with the female mauri, or life force, Niwareka, daughter of the union between Papatuanuku and Ranginui, made possible the plants like harakeke, nīkau and kie kie that bind people to the land—and gave people the skills to weave them. These opposing elements and their intimate consummation made the sand country lakes rich environments.

Joe Tukupua is a tohunga of substantial reputation, as staunch a guardian of Mua-upoko's knowledge of their ravaged sand country as they have ever had. I'd called on him because I'd seen some Māori leaving Papaitonga in a truck filled to the brim with kie kie, one of the best weaving plants. They were from up north. Joe knew about it, but someone else had given the word to harvest. Joe and I had had several meetings, exchanging bits and pieces of information about Papaitonga's fragility. He could sense my anxiety and wanted to reassure me. 'From the beginnings, that place has had great mana. It has its own protection.' The next time I came, he'd explain what he meant. 'The names are what's important,' he said. 'The names. Don't forget them.'

Mua-upoko construe themselves and the landscape of forest, swamp and lake as coming from the same beginnings. 'It is a celestial name, Pa-pae-tonga, a very powerful name from the gods. The mauri of that place and its name are ancient to us. Tonga-tapu. Southern and sacred.' Not only do old people lie here. Lake and forest, transmuted into ancestors' lives, are literally their ancestors too. To violate such a bond is to violate your own sense of life. If Papaitonga deteriorates—and you don't need to be an ecologist to see it is deteriorating—Mua-upoko themselves are diminished.

As they look at the lake, then out at the rest of the plain and see the growing number of artesian bores sucking water from it, they see its life-support system being dissipated like blood drawn off before it reaches the human heart. Water, nature's most generous gift, is what made places like Papaitonga sacred. In water's terms, the whole Horowhenua—from mountains to sea—is one ecosystem. There is only so much water circulating in it, and every artesian bore means less reaches the sand lakes.

To Mua-upoko, Papaitonga's mauri is not in the sand country; it is hidden high in the Tararua's mists—a mythologised, spiritual lake accessible only to tohunga, Hāpua Kō-rari. 'From the mauri Hāpua Kō-rari gives those awa, those lakes,' says Joe, 'has come the food of our people.'

When European settlement began puncturing Horowhenua's Māori landscape, Hāpua Kō-rari was excluded from the sale of the Tararuas to the Crown as a 1, 000-acre native reserve. But Hāpua Kō-rari proved elusive to the 1880s surveyors, so a reward was offered to whoever could locate it. In 1898 a small lake was found on the Wairarapa side of the range. However, it wasn't until the 1920s and the beginning of the era of Tararua trampers that an old track was found leading to a damp, flaxy hollow—and for some at least the 'mystery' was solved.

Yet Hāpua Kō-rari doesn't have to be an actual lake to serve its purpose. What sounds barely rational at first should be very familiar. The water cycle has served humans throughout history as a model of the natural world. Some early civilisations saw in it the basic pattern of life: birth, death and return to the source of being. Science, more recently, has shown the reality of that ancient religious metaphor: the unceasing circle going through all soils, the plants and animals of earth which Aldo Leopold called 'a round river'.

Mua-upoko's sense of Papaitonga as ancestor is handy for them these days. Invisible to most, contestation is nonetheless inscribed indelibly on the Horowhenua Plain. The government's decision to examine land claims back to 1840 is generating cross-claims between tribes and reopening old wounds. Now when Mua-upoko elders speak of places like Papaitonga and Rau-matangi, it is to remind the descendants of last century's tribal invaders that their landscape's names are deep in Mua-upoko genealogy, back in that country of the mind where people and land are one.

As has been said of Palestine, 'no one "owns" this landscape in the sense of having clear, unquestionable title to it'. Laden with Mua-upoko's sense of place, Papaitonga makes everyone else seem a cultural aggressor. The 19th century's arrivals from the Waikato, and then Europe, and their powerful myth-making, have reshaped its contours with their stories. Invaders and invaded encounter one another in an unresolved, imaginary landscape, revealing that 'everyone "owns" (or ought to own) this landscape in the sense that everyone must acknowledge or own up to some responsibility to it'.

But once a landscape stops being ordinary and is made 'special', everybody else claims it as part of their heritage, which is perhaps why Urorangi Paki calls Papaitonga 'the government's reserve'. As though it makes her ritual of taking Mua-upoko mokopuna all the way from their marae Pariri, beside Lake Horowhenua, to make their first kete there somehow illicit. As she says has always been the way, she makes sure they throw the kete back into the harakeke swamp. You could call it emotional tenure. Her Mua-upoko may have lost their title to Papaitonga last century, but in her mind she is visiting her ancestors, her spirit landscape, the stretch of country that made her, and where Mua-upoko wellbeing so speedily vanished.

Each of us brings to a landscape more than our emotional and animal instincts—the desire for shelter and security. What we imagine about the land and how we are disposed toward it is also shaped by the bits of knowledge that accumulate in our stories. Unless you know the Papaitonga in Urorangi Paki's mind it would be easy to believe, as the young scientists who compiled the first biological survey of the reserve did, that the forest down to the water's edge has always been there.

Most of Papaitonga's casual callers let the boardwalk lead them across the flax swamp, through a band of kahikatea, pukatea and entangling kie kie and then up to The Lookout, another headland of the old seacliff. A rare experience in lowland New Zealand today, it always has me imagining what Helen Wilson saw in the 1880s. Lifting their ankle-length skirts to avoid the slashed undergrowth, she and her mother picked their way along surveyors' cut-lines toward Lake Horowhenua. Eventually, emerging '. . . from the dim bush shadows, we came out into blazing sunshine . . . overlooking the lake'. It was dark by the time they turned to go back, daylight before they found a farmed clearing and got their bearings again.

From The Lookout, Papaitonga seems a wild, utterly natural place. The young scientists described and mapped it as a unique 'intact sequence' from lakeshore wetland to forest for which it is renowned to ecologists. They didn't see what I saw one morning climbing out of the dark damp of a kahikatea forest up onto one of the dry sand headlands. A heap of old kakahi, freshwater mussel, shells slipping out of the edge of a bank just above the big trees. And despite their interest in maps, it would seem they didn't see the one of Papaitonga in Leslie Adkin's remarkable book *Horowhenua*. The headland with the shell heap has a name. Pao-pao-roa. So does every other headland—Māoro-kura, Pou-a-Tiriaki and Kōpuru. On each there were kāinga, and around the lakeshore Adkin had captured the slender thread of the old people's knowledge of canoe-landings and eel weirs. The other big sand lake, Horowhenua or Te Moana-ō-Punahau, was the same; names packed in so tight that his map can barely contain them. Some were Ngāti Raukawa; the great majority though were Mua-upoko.

On each headland, and the islands, I discovered more shell heaps—virtually all of the bland, slimy kakahi from the lake, hardly a shell from the sea, some heaps so old and large they formed small cliffs in the forest. Where the young scientists saw karaka and ti kouka, cabbage tree, as just part of Papaitonga's rich lowland forest, I had learned to recognise that they were planted groves. In some places these were deliberate circles of huge old trees. And testimony, if I needed it, could be found in history's fragments—'Do you see that bare promontory on the island yonder? At that time there was a large house standing on that point belonging to Takare . . . The Muaupoko pa was on the Island of Papaitonga. At that time there was no bush on the island, only some karaka trees which had been planted by the inhabitants close to the water's edge.'

On any evening from The Lookout you can see the harriers, kāhu, out hunting over the lake, gliding above the harakeke and the raupō, beyond the headland of forest and out of sight. Then they come winging back, provoking a flurry of movement on the water and a beating of wings as kererū change trees.

Centuries ago, Papaitonga's eel-fishers would have kept their eyes on the sky for the gliding pinions of another bird of prey. Te hōkioi, the long-gone eagle, hunted the sand country, but if Mua-upoko's faint memories of it are to be believed, 'its resting place was on the top of the mountains . . . not on the plains. On the days on which it was on the wing our ancestors say . . . it was a large bird, as large as the moa.'

Te rau ō te Huia e noa te tinana tera to piki te Hōkioi i runga,
Ngā manu hunahuna, kāore i kitea
E te tini e te mano
Kia takaro ko nga taku tae i waho ō Waiwiri[Papaitonga] i roto ō
    Waikawa;
Ka eke koe ki runga ō Pukehou,
Ka whakamau e tama ki waho ō Raukawa,
Ko ngā moana ra e whakahana noa rā ō Tupuna i te kakau ō te
    hoe, Ngāro rawa ki Hawaiiki.

Memories of other birds aren't so faint. Like the 'never ending supply of fine specimens'—for overseas sales—of *Botaurus poeciloptilus*, the black-backed bittern which Walter Buller could obtain a century ago. And his successful attempt, with barely a season to spare, to save a piece at least of their habitat: 'what bitterns are left have retired to the great Makererua swamp further up the coast; but this too, is rapidly yielding to a great system of drainage. A few . . . have taken refuge with me at Papaitonga, and these will receive all the protection they need. Through inadvertence one was shot on the wing when crossing an arm of the lake, but this is not likely to happen again.'

Leslie Adkin's patient chronicling of the plain's place names through the 1920s, '30s and '40s revealed that what his pioneering father knew to be some of New Zealand's most fertile soils held stories of another life altogether: memory traces of countless cherished swamps, streams and bits of bush, every one vanished under settlers' fires and drains:

Mauri bush: . . . *principally kahikatea or white pine. The name is from the term* mauri *which indicates that a talisman or lodging place of an* atua *had been set up in this piece of bush to ensure the fruitfulness of the bird-life and other forest products.*

Whitiki bush: *A once magnificent piece . . . on the dune-belt. As a motu, or isolated area of trees or bush, Whitiki was unique; its form was that of one of the most attractive and romantic kinds of island—an atoll. Actually the name means 'a girdle' . . . a pure stand of white pine or kahikatea—lofty trees rising in close-set parallel columns to a continuous dense canopy; elsewhere pukatea . . . with a dense undergrowth of karaeo and kiekie . . . The primitive Maori during an occupation of centuries spared Whitiki, but his example has not been followed by the 'cultured' Pakeha, who in the course of a few decades has swept away from an out-of-the-way corner of little commercial value one of the choicest of Nature's works in Horo-whenua.*

Whare-o-tauira bush and flat: . . . *kahikatea, rimu, tawa and hohere; the twining kiekie grew abundantly there producing the edible fruit and flower so highly prized by the Mua-upoko . . . that the bush was long preserved for the sake of the supply of sweet food it provided.*

Prudently obeying customs that sustained valued species, people had shaped the sandplain. The Māori did not avidly preserve their habitat unchanged until the advent of the Europeans, they did what all colonising peoples did: to make a living they actively manipulated the ecosystem they lived in.

Mua-upoko or their predecessors could have incinerated the whole plain at any time, but what it is now fashionable to call 'biodiversity' was crucial to their quality of life, and they treasured it. Once they understand what sustains them, people usually honour rather than destroy it. As one settler explained before Mua-upoko's landscape vanished, they knew 'berries grow mostly on the outskirts, rarely in the centre of the forest'. Over centuries, they left patches of old-growth forest intact, and opened up and cultivated others. A consciousness of limits, creating, so to speak, a country of edges—lake against harakeke, swamp forest beside dune forest, open areas for moving through from one fruitful forest to another.

Some of the landscape's memories, though, are too old for people to know. For historians of the landscape, dunelakes like Papaitonga are like time machines. Beneath their still waters lie the accumulated evidence of thousands of years of land changes. Because they are undecayable, the pollen of any plants that have lived nearby can be identified. Any organic carbon, whether bits of plants or charcoal blown in from ancient fires, can be dated. Whatever has caused the ecology of the land to change, whether it's El Nino type climates thousands of years back or Māori fires seven centuries ago, the lake sediments will say. I suspected Papaitonga, now miles inland, had once been the lagoon where today's Ohau River met the sea, and that whoever had lived here before Europeans had kept the land in forest. But I wasn't sure. So in 1987 I persuaded a scientist friend with a reputation for great skill in these circumstances to wade out to the edge of the flax and lower a coring tube.

The first thing it revealed was that what looks like a shallow lake, is actually a very deep affair. If you flailed through the swamp like the flax-cutting gangs used to do every day, and stepped out into the lake, beyond plants, you would find yourself struggling in the consistency of the sort of pea soup in which spoons stay upright. Anything sinking into it would slowly descend 15 metres until coming to rest on a hard, sandy bottom— from the days when river or tide would have regularly kept it as free of forest debris as are South Westland's lagoons. Then, about 9,000 years ago, the lagoon became dammed by sand dunes. Waterflow was confined to small sluggish streams and groundwater. From that point on, virtually everything that entered the lake, like the fresh-looking harakeke leaves that came up with the sand from the bottom of our core-sample, stayed. Victims of tribal misadventure, or anything else that has slipped out of a canoe into the 'treacherously-fluid' mud, will still be there, perfectly preserved by the fine forest detritus with which Papaitonga has slowly been filling.

Two bands of volcanic ash, the finest white silica, from central North Island eruptions, one about 8,000 and the other 5,900 years ago, are suspended in the gel. This far south, the ash particles fell cold on the forested plain. Unlike many coastal lakes elsewhere in New Zealand, there is no ash from the other common type of fire—the sort lit to flush out birds or create new sites for aruhe, or bracken. Usually, lowland swamps like this contain clear evidence that the first wave of people through Aotearoa was accompanied by widespread forest firing. The evidence might be the sudden appearance of aruhe spores, or raupō pollen signalling nutrient enrichment as hill country catchments were burnt. Or tiny windblown charcoal shards from the fires themselves. It is as indisputable as the change from a diverse mixture of bird bones and shellfish to bleak piles of pure shellfish that archaeologists have detected in the early inhabitants' rubbish heaps. The pollen in Papaitonga's sediments suggest that its sand country was far wetter than it is now, with more tree ferns and rimu in the forest, and that after the second eruption it became seasonally drier, more like today. Yet while other Māori may have been firing forests and running down the ecological stock of their new land, Papaitonga shows no evidence of it.

There is evidence though of early people. A patu dragged up in nearby Lake Horowhenua, which is more 'Eastern Polynesian' in design than any other found in New Zealand, suggests some of Aotearoa's earliest people knew these lakes in the forest. By the 13th century, they were crossing the Tararuas. One of their earliest known middens reveals a strikingly rich environment: forest seeds and fruits like kie kie, marine and freshwater fish and *thousands* of forest birds like kererū, kākā, tui and kākāriki. One interpretation is of two settlement patterns: an early occupation of the coastal sand country, including the so-called 'moa-hunter' sites, and a subsequent move to around the inland lakes, in response to a shifting forest edge. But whatever the nor'westerlies blew in over the lake from the sand country, it wasn't charcoal. However these early people, and those who succeeded them, used fire, the evidence in Papaitonga is of continuous forest from beginning to end.

The way Māori found to live in the sand country—altering it, but without exhausting or trashing it—may seem a triumph. Yet it has a simple explanation. As Rod McDonald, an early settler, observed:

> In all these patches of bush, the kiekie grew thickly, and in the summer and autumn season, the Muaupoko fed full on the succulent tawhara therein produced. They were their orchards, and they preserved them accordingly. The tawhara was a toothsome sweet in a land where sweets were few; these pieces of bush were a regular, even though inconsiderable, source of food supply; the Maori was not lazy, although he never hurried, and he cheerfully paddles his canoe-load of firewood a mile or more across the lake rather than destroy this source of a much-prized delicacy.
>
> . . . where the kiekie grew high on the trees the ripening tawhara was watched carefully. As the time drew near when it would be at its most luscious stage, a flag was hung out in a conspicuous place . . . a warning that for the time being that bush was tapu, and no one might enter to pick tawhara until the prohibition was removed.

I know people who come here regularly just to keep that sense of country alive. Once, I disturbed a descendant of Te Rauparaha contemplating the lake, the two wooded islands and the hundreds of birds that sit with them on the shining water. I was horrified by the story he told me. But not long after, in Buller's papers, I found that it had been part of the 'scenery' for over a century:

> It is said that virtue has its own reward, but those ladies and gentlemen who came so far . . . must have felt more than rewarded at the scenery they beheld when they went out picnicking. Under the charge of Mr McHardie they were driven to the paradise of the district . . . and its surrounding forest near Ohau . . . The day was a lovely one and the lake shone like a crystal sea in the heart of a dark bush and the only ripple was caused by some waterfall. Mr Buller had kindly placed his canoe at the service of the holiday makers and their merry laughter, echoing under the pretty ISLAND OF PAPAITONGA gave rise to the thought of the hideous scenes and the dying shrieks and groans of the Maori

captives on this spot. It was here that 600 of the Muaupoko were slaughtered to appease the wrath of Te Rauparaha.

The mass-murder at Papaitonga was one of the most bloody and one-sided events in 19th-century New Zealand. Only the musket made it possible for so few people to kill so many others so quickly. And soon after, 300 more were killed in identical circumstances just a few miles away at Lake Horowhenua. Were something like that to happen anywhere in the world today, it would be an event of major significance. Were it to happen in modern New Zealand, it would be shattering. Nothing at Papaitonga prepares you, however, for the fact that the Europeanisation of New Zealand had such consequences right here.

The few lawn-mowered pā and battle sites, the 'historic places' marked with plaques in paddocks, tell us nothing of how dramatically the musket shifted the balance of power before 1840. To see why someone like Te Rauparaha is so significant in this country's history, how 'the power of his war-parties . . . his own ability and ruthlessness, and the weakness of the original inhabitants, all tended in one direction, the complete subjugation of the old residents', we need to be able to experience the rainforests and swamps in which 'his rifles' were so fatally effective.

Only the few whose lives are lived in the shadow of that day in 1823 can reach under Papaitonga's mantle of scenic beauty and nature conservation and feel the other landscape. Had the dead been white, or Papaitonga been an 1860s land wars battle site, a concrete monument would have stood in a clearing.

Every Māori in the Horowhenua knows how the Mua-upoko killing of Te Rauparaha's children led to the killing fields of the sand lakes and 'lent the war . . . a ruthlessness exceeding the ordinary tribal conflicts'. Like they know how his regard for Papaitonga's eels—*ki Papaitonga nei, ki te tiki mai i te kai mana, i te hākari tuna; he wai tuna hoki a Horowhenua, a Waiwiri*—lured him into the Mua-upoko trap at Te Wi; and Te Rauparaha's bitter vow on escaping the rout with the wounded Te Rakaherea that the sun would soon rise on a day when no Mua-upoko would survive to see it set.

Te Tipi at once swam out from Paopaororo . . . then, as now covered with low bush, tawa, hinau, mapou and other trees . . . Te Tipi reached the island, and he kept firing his gun as he swam . . . the enemy had already fled and were making for the shore in

*their canoes . . . the various sections of the war-party in the bush
combined to attack them . . . Here and there a man who was swift
of foot escaped, but the bulk were shot. All the chiefs were killed
. . . The dead numbered three hundred twice told, perhaps more,
and included the women and children.*

By 1820 Mua-upoko were well-used to defending their resource-rich
environment of eel stream, lakes and forest edges. Their island pā might
have been the perfect expression of their intimacy with it. But the musket's
range and fire power made fighting hand-to-hand from canoes and through
the forest with taiaha and tewhatewha instantly redundant.

Totara was one of the main trees on the Horowhenua Plain until
almost 1900. Much of the forest inland of Papaitonga was felled by Peter
Bartholomew in the early 1890s and cut up at his saw-mill. Tearing through
a big totara one day, the spinning blade struck a lead musket ball some
25cm below the surface, its scream sending men diving for cover. Aimed at
someone running away from the lake through the forest some 70 years
earlier, it had missed and embedded itself in the tree.

Survival in a landscape comes down to making the best of the
resources of the moment. Making better use of Mua-upoko's environment
than they did that particular morning, the invaders from the north ensured
Papaitonga and Mua-upoko's sense of themselves became inextricably
linked. Where the same horror was repeated at the other lake, Horowhenua,
cows now graze to the water's edge. For as long as Papaitonga has its islands
and forest, Mua-upoko will know why many like the warriors Te
Kāhuōterangi and Kōkōta died. They'll also know why the ones they are
descended from could get away.

Once she was ashore she slid silently between the blades of raupō and
listened. She knew exactly where to go, where to crawl along between the
trees and the harakeke, invisible to the groups of men. It was her place; her
accustomed way of noticing everything—the way those who knew it before
her had taught her—made her intimate with it. Each place where she'd had
a healing plant explained to her had its memory. She knew where the dry,
open ground lay, the newly fallen trees, the bends in each stream, the quiet

pools with the black fish, the wet hollows with paru, the black mud. She knew where every accessible fruit tree was, which kahikatea were the most reliable bearers of fruit, the sunny slopes just out of the wind where kie kie's tiore and tāwhara were always ready first. She knew how to get to the inland clearings. Where the others would be, if there were any of them left.

Knowing Te Rauparaha's reputation, Mua-upoko strengthened their fortified island pā on Papaitonga and Horowhenua. Of Papaitonga's two islands, the larger one is natural, simply an extension of an underwater ridge from the headland, Te Kōpuru. The other, Papa-whaerangi, artificially built up above lake level with canoe-loads of soil and mussel shells from rubbish heaps, still feels besieged. Waves are eating it away where the pallisades once stood. Scattered among the shell fragments are shards of rounded umu stones brought from some distant riverbed. Mua-upoko's karaka grove has sprung into a dense forest.

TKM 25.3.1953 someone has carved into the largest tree. *MW 1943, BHK 1950* another one is inscribed. Every second tree has them: *BABY VALANCE. BANT UPPER HUTT. KA OX 23 OHAU 1956.* Duckshooters. No one can thrill at the sight of Brown Teal as Walter Buller did—'I have lately seen a flock of two hundred or more on the Papaitonga Lake; but they have become very shy, and it is almost impossible to get near enough for a shot'—but judging by the shotgun cartridges, Papa-whaerangi is still a ready-made maimai a century on.

The karaka forest of the other island has more signs of people—kakahi shell heaps, rounded cooking stones, even a decaying whale vertebra; and in the sunnier garden grove of old cabbage trees, more recent beer bottles and shotgun cartridges. The same cabbage trees, only smaller and slenderer, are blown out of focus in an 1890s photograph of the elegant ladies who perhaps planted the bright orangey *Montbretia* patch. Stuck up into the sky, a carved Māori canoe rises strangely out of their midst.

NGA RANGI-O-REHUA WATCHING OVER AN 1890S PICNIC.

Buller had the canoe, Nga Rangi-ō-Rehua, erected there. If you had stood with him in the 1890s on the high ground where he planned his mansion, he would have swept his arm around as though the lake lay in the arms of a pristine forest that stretched away for ever. Turned toward an implied audience, Nga Rangi-ō-Rehua rose above it like a centrepiece in Milton's *Paradise Regained* —'Statues and trophies, Gardens and groves presented to his eyes'. And if you failed to comment on them, he would have pointed out the 'specimens of Māori industry' in his illusory—and, as it was to prove, momentary—landscape theatre:

> On the island there was a famous obelisk, carved out of a great river canoe about seventy years ago, and called 'Ngarangiorehua'. It was originally erected at Pipiriki, in the Upper Wanganui, to mark the burial-place of a noted chief; then it stood for ten years or more in the Maori cemetery at Putiki, near the town of Wanganui; and was finally transported to Papaitonga, where it is erected to the memory of the ancestress of Major Kemp te Rangihiwinui, the late owner. These singular monuments are now becoming very scarce, and the history of the present one gives it a peculiar interest.

Nothing shows a person's values better than the manner in which they organise their living spaces. By the 1890s a wealthy settler like Walter Buller, relishing the presence of the past in his scenery but seeing Māori's fading from the landscape as Darwinian proof of his settler culture's right to it, could afford to romanticise them. After years of trying, he finally extracted a 'promise' from Mua-upoko to sell him Papaitonga in 1886, just before he left for 'Home . . . to represent the Colony at the Colonial and Indian Exhibition' in England with a selection of the great works of Māori craft on board. Some he sold when the exhibition at London's Imperial Institute ended; others, like Te Takinga, the magnificent pataka his brother-in-law Gilbert Mair obtained from Taheke, the Ngāti Pikiao marae near Rotorua, he brought back to install at Papaitonga.

Ever sensitive to the disadvantage of birth in a place with a name like Tangiteroria, Walter Buller craved the acceptance of English society. Four years in England gave him the opportunity. The new knight and director of the Imperial Institute became a committee member of 'one of the smartest and yet quietest of riparian resorts'. If there was one quintessential expression of British superiority to deflect Sir Walter Buller's gaze, it was the great landscaped estates with their parkland, lakes and islands; like England's Stowe and Rousham, filled with Italian marbles symbolising the lost glories of Rome. Its river's natural meandering reaches enhanced with lakes and wooded islands, copses and Italianate ruins, the exclusive Albany Club at Kingston-on-Thames was, as a New Zealand newspaperman observed, 'much frequented by boating men and maidens . . . on account of its healthy surroundings and pretty scenery'. In the manner of the classic English estate, it was a type of scenery made famous in the 18th century by Capability Brown and Humphrey Repton. Strolling through its statued grounds, musing on the faraway New Zealand landscape of flax swamps and burning bush, muddy roads and grim settlers' cottages, Buller must have considered the possibility of creating something like it himself. It need be little different from what Capability Brown himself had once said of one of his Hertfordshire 'pleasure grounds': 'Nature has done so much, little was wanting, but enlarging the River.' In Papaitonga's case, the wooded lake and islands were already there, but some ruins would be necessary.

Buller also saw something elsewhere in England that dazzled him: Tring Park, Lord Walter Rothschild's vast Hertfordshire estate. Farmer and financier, Rothschild was also an eccentric explorer and animal collector. Favourite client, in fact, of Buller's export business in New Zealand's primitive birds—Buller traded his entire collection of skins to Rothschild, and procured hundreds more to satisfy the eccentric young aristocrat's appetite for nature's peculiarities. Before they fell out he helped Rothschild build the best collection of birds in the world. Not all of it was skins in museum drawers. Set in a landscaped park among paired zebras pulling gigs and exotic animals wandering at will, Tring's famed water bird 'reservoirs' were renowned among Victorian and Edwardian ornithologists. Rothschild had a special passion for kiwi, and provided unlimited funds for Buller to charter special expeditions to indulge it. Tring's acres of aviaries had a flock of kiwi! 'In the Hon Walter Rothschild's beautiful collection of New Zealand birds at Tring Park,' wrote an admiring Buller, 'there are two partial albinoes of this species.'

Tring Park was laid out by Charles Bridgeman, a landscape designer who loved the grand scale and glades cut into natural woodland. The main influence on Bridgeman was the theatrical landscaping of the famous Stephen Switzer. Switzer's designs were distinguished by the same open, elevated view over a spacious countryside and dramatic descents to lakes that had thrilled the generations of English aristocrats who toured Italy's estates.

But above all, he brought a sense of history to English landscape design, just as gardens in 18th-century Rome had, wherever possible, used classical ruins:

> . . . *large prolated gardens and Plantations, adorn'd with magnificent Statues and Water-works, full of long extended, shady Walks and Groves . . . private Recesses, and some little retired Cabinets . . . all the adjacent Country be laid open to view . . . the Eye should not be bounded with high Walls, Woods misplac'd . . . and the Feet fetter'd in the midst of the extensive Charms of Nature, and the voluminous Tracts of a pleasant Country.*

Buller may not have read Switzer's *Ichnographica Rustica*, but he knew picturesque views could encourage the mind to explore history. Obtaining magnificent statues would be the least of his problems. As he collected birds, he had long hoarded any Māori curiosities he could lay his hands on. 'It seems to me,' he once explained, 'that everything relating to the early history of the land of our adoption should be carefully recorded and preserved for the student of the future.'

Buller's dream of making Papaitonga a beautiful, admired place succeeded so well it rebounded on him. By the early 1900s, when the government began saving scenery, picnickers could reach its ferny shores with 'ease and pleasure . . . without restriction all year round', albeit across a landscape of dead and dying trees. Settlers went to these bush, lakes and waterfalls and history's poignant spots for entertainment, which is why, when the government's Scenery Preservation Commission first met in 1903, clearing a space in the forest for picnics was one of its first resolutions. Nowhere in the country was scenery as admired as Papaitonga's.

Waiting outside when the arbiters of scenery arrived was an apprehensive Percy Buller, Sir Walter's son. Notwithstanding the picnickers, who'd always been allowed, Papaitonga, he protested, was 'an unalienable heritage of the Buller family, and . . . would remain so'. Nevertheless, Joseph Ward, the Prime Minister, sent the Inspector of Scenic Reserves to report on the place. He was awed by 'a magnificent large Pataka or Maori storehouse splendidly carved and in perfect condition. The carved walls of the verandah of this finished piece of Maori handiwork is finely decorated with bunches of albino feathers of the Kiwi and Kereru or Wood Pigeon . . . the most artistic and beautifully finished pataka I have met with'. Sir

Walter Buller's Papaitonga, he wrote, 'furnishes a good illustration of the expressed opinions of the Commission that cleared areas with dwellings thereon in good order in bush country fronting rivers and lakes vastly improves the scenery'.

Such artful deception was the essence of both Buller's Papaitonga and the scenery preservation idea. Studded with the masterpieces of a dying race, tricking picnickers into believing it stretched wildly away for ever, it was just enough to screen off the safe, ordinary landscape of food production. When Walter Buller's grand-daughter from Bath, in England, drove up in a Morris Minor one day in 1972, all she could talk about was how little Papaitonga's

WALTER BULLER'S LANDSCAPE THEATRE, FROM THE SITE OF HIS NEVER-BUILT MANSION, 1890s.

forest had changed from the faraway place in the 1890s photographs with which she had grown up. As a scenic place it had survived three-quarters of a century of private ownership after Buller's death; nine years after she saw it, it became part of the national estate.

Not knowing quite what it had on its hands, the government called for submissions on Papaitonga Scenic Reserve. There was an immediate Māori response—not from Mua-upoko, but from the Ngāti Raukawa hapu who took Papaitonga from them in the 1820s, still inhabited its southern shore and, from their marae Kikopiri, maintained their claim to it.

In 1864, 127 years earlier, Ngāti Kikopiri's ancestors had come close to selling Papaitonga to the government's Land Purchase Commissioner, Isaac Featherston—and a young magistrate named Walter Buller. Four months later some 80 Raukawa men confronted Buller at Otaki demanding their £100 payment, only to be told Papaitonga 'now belongs to the Queen', and that 'the surveyor would soon be there'. He wasn't, and the sale died. Raukawa in those days were sheltering the Mua-upoko survivors of Te Rauparaha's raid. South of Lake Horowhenua there was hardly one. Of Mua-upoko's Papaitonga, little more than 'a small whare and eel-fishing weirs' remained. At the Waiwiri, Papaitonga's outlet to the sea, Ngāti Kikopiri built their own pā tuna—Te Karaka, Te Kahikatea, Whakamate, Te Rere and Te Karamū. Mua-upoko's 20 or so poha were abandoned, their names lost to memory, forgotten until clearing and straightening of the Waiwiri in the 1930s exposed them.

Yet within nine years of Kikopiri almost selling Papaitonga, Mua-upoko had built defensive pā, fired shots and burnt Raukawa whare, and had the Native Land Court hurriedly convened. Declaring Mua-upoko unconquered, it ordered Ngāti Raukawa to sign an agreement of 'final settlement' on the strip of the plain with Mua-upoko's precious forest lakes. Mua-upoko, for their part, were persuaded to 'convey by way of gift' a section to the descendants of Te Whatanui who had given them sanctuary. A Royal Commission in 1896 into the legal mess the Horowhenua land-dealing—not least Buller's—had become, didn't fail to note that 'there is no permanent water except swamp on this subdivision, and it will be noticed that the land does not touch either the Hokio Stream or the Horowhenua Lake from which places a considerable amount of the food supply of the Natives come'.

Ngāti Raukawa have never really accepted the Land Court decision, contesting Mua-upoko's rights to Papaitonga ever since. The government's belated purchase of Papaitonga in 1981, from a Ngāti Raukawa farmer curiously enough, was an opportunity for Ngāti Kikopiri to reiterate claim to it. Their links, they said, were 'beyond question or repudiation'. They had 'since time in memoriam [sic] upheld and enjoyed Traditional rights to fish' and collect kai and materials like kie kie from the bush around it. Ngawini Kuiti, who led the offensive, wanted to see again the clear deep lake she had dived into as a child. It was her great-great grandfather, Waretini Tuainuku, who recounted Te Rauparaha's routing of Mua-upoko in 1823 to Walter Buller; her grandmother, Hinga Waretini, who told Leslie Adkin about the old names. She could see my anxiety at the glistening sheets of mud that narrowed the gap to the tapu islands each summer and the raupō that followed it. She wanted action before it was too late and the mud began to stay over winter too.

'You know what I think? All that mud? The lake's dying.'

After first allowing it, the government refused Ngāti Kikopiri permission to gather kie kie from the new reserve, but built a boardwalk to which the public were flocking. Kikopiri, though, had little concern for scenic beauty and picnics. Their first business was with names. Their tupuna had known Papaitonga as Waiwiri. But there were two other names which simply had to be annulled. Not only were the islands 'urupa, respected and regarded as Tapu . . . not recommended as appropriate places for sightseeing or picnics . . .', the Māori names they were given on every government map were offensive; they were Buller's labels of dispossession.

'Motu Kiwi', he called the big tapu island 'which constitutes the kiwi reserve . . . ideal spot for the lover of nature'. And using his knowledge of the ancient 'rites, forms and observancies' of tapu, as much to humiliate and frighten Mua-upoko as preserve rare birds, he called the other 'Motu Ngarara'—Demon Island—after the feared, primordial guardians he landed there.

> To prevent any chance of Maori depredations in the breeding-season I have also placed on the island three large live tuataras, kindly supplied to me by Captain Fairchild. The fame of these lizards, of which the Maoris have a most unaccountable dread, has spread far and wide. I have named them after three noted dragons of the past, Peketahi, Whangaimokopuna and Horomatangi; . . . the Kiwis could have no better guardians, for with the dread of the ngarara no Maori will every willingly set foot on the island.

Confused with the flow of corpses and correspondence from his man in New Zealand, Lord Rothschild had given the Great Spotted Kiwi a North Island distribution range in one of his kiwi essays. In pointing out Rothschild had 'fallen into the error', Buller felt compelled to explain they 'were liberated there by myself'.

> Some months ago I received a fine pair from the South, and after keeping them for some time in my Kiwi enclosure in order to study their habits, I liberated them on a wooded island, a little over an acre in extent, near my homestead at Papaitonga. I placed on the island at the same time a pair of the small Grey Kiwi (Apteryx owenii) and, a short time previously, a single North Island Kiwi (Apteryx bullerii), kindly presented to me by Mr Drew, of Wanganui, for that purpose. The locality is admirably suited to such an experiment, the ground being similar to that which the Kiwi frequents in its natural state, and well covered with natural vegetation. Being on an island, surrounded by a fresh-water lake about 15 acres in extent, and all within my private property, they are not likely to be molested in any way.

Hearing the birds' shrill night calls across the lake, he planned to add a pair of kākāpō to his new 'island community'. However, one died and the other escaped before he could. He believed, though, he had 'successfully introduced' the large spotted kiwi to his North Island island, and that all three species 'may be looked upon as fairly established there'. Contradicting his earlier conviction that 'the task is a hopeless one', he lectured on the principle that 'expiring species always [last] longest on islands, and we ought to draw a lesson from experience and place the birds on islands'. Papaitonga is one of the first places this strategy was used, and from its successes on islands like Kapiti and Little Barrier it has become a hallmark of New Zealand nature conservation. However, its obsession with endangered species and small reserves still swamps more ecological strategies.

Not only Pākehā ornithologists thought the island sanctuary a great idea:

> Manakau, 5th February, 1897
> Friend, Sir Walter Buller, Salutations! I have in my possession a live Kiwi, one I brought with me lately from Whakarewarewa, Rotorua. I have thought that it would be an excellent thing to have on your island at Papaitonga. If you desire to have it, then come at any time and fetch it from my place here at Ohau.
> From your friend, TAMATI RANAPIRI

'It is very pleasing,' Buller remarked, 'to find a Maori taking so practical an interest in the preservation of one of the vanishing forms of native bird life. But the writer of the letter is an exceptionally intelligent man, belonging to the Ngatiraukawa tribe.'

He was not so gracious about Mua-upoko and their naive, primitive ways. 'Get any stray Muaupoko to sign,' he wrote to Hector McDonald, knowing he didn't have enough names on a land deal. 'Don't say anything to the Muaupoko . . . then bring them out in a body in order that I may "Korero" with them.' Walter Buller was too astute an observer not to have noticed Mua-upoko feeling about the islands, but while a 'perfect necropolis of human bones' added curiosity to his country estate, he did not want the nuisance of a wāhi tapu.

> The beaten Muaupoko, stripped of everything and reduced in numbers to a mere remnant, who took refuge in the mountains, never dared to impose the spell of the tapu on the scene of their

discomfiture and entombment . . . one of the most cruel passages
in Maori history . . . No better proof, perhaps, could be given of
the complete conquest of the Muaupoko at that time by the
Ngatitoa and Ngatiraukawa than the inability of the survivors
ever afterwards to enforce the observance of this rite. The nearest
to it is what I have myself done in this present year of grace.

Buller delighted in the dramatic quality history had given his property.
Quoting the missionary, William Colenso, he once entertained the gentlemen
of the Wellington Philosophical Society on 'The Ancient Institutions of Tapu'.
As 'the foundation of Maori society and the bulwark of tribal existence', tapu,
he told them, regulated, 'or pretended to regulate', everything. 'Through it,
their large cultivations, their fisheries, their fine villages and hill forest, their
fine canoes, their good houses, their large seine-nets, their bold carvings, and a
hundred other things were accomplished—without possessing either iron or
metal . . . their fowl, and fish, and forests were preserved . . . the tombs and
graves of their dead—objects, held sacred by even the most untutored savage—
were preserved inviolable.' He even showed his audience parts of two human
skulls from two such graves. One was from a place, 'so strictly tapu that it was
considered unsafe for any European to trespass upon it, to say nothing of
interfering with the human relics'. The other, Buller said, was 'a heavy cranium
. . . from the island of Papaitonga lake . . . [which] although the scene of a
terrible slaughter and practically the cemetery of the Muaupoko tribe, has never
been tapu at all'.

Yet what of the kiwi and the guardian tuatara he put on the island?
Buller suspected rightly that the cause of the demise of New Zealand lowland
forest birds was ecological. But as these tiny cabinets of curiosity in his wildlife
park proved, human fiddling with wild birds can be as fatal as a bite from a
weasel. Endangered birds are still transferred from their home habitats to islands,
a century later. Not everyone is unanimous in support, but at least it is now
done on the basis of rigorous research into the risk of predators and the birds'
territory and habitat needs. On Buller's islands, none of his 'endemic forms'
survived. Maybe someone took them off after he left for England; or Mua-
upoko tapu exacted their reprisal. More likely though, while Buller fantasised
about his country seat in New Zealand and Rothschild wandered his rows of
glass cases, they succumbed to rats who snuck across with a picnic party, or to
stoats who smelled them and swam out.

Staying in forest, the track from The Lookout drops down into another wet arm of boardwalk and flax, before climbing back under the trees of another sandstone headland. After meandering under the beautiful kohekohe that cover the old seacliff, it enters a dark gully forest. Kahikatea, pukatea and fronds of nīkau arc over a stream with rare black mudfish. On the other side, light appears through the trees and the swamp forest opens suddenly and unexpectedly into a farm landscape.

Until 1895 the farm was a forest, Ō-tomuri, revered by all who lived around it. When its huge, spreading rātā flowered, tui, bellbirds, parakeets and kākā converged here. Buller called Ō-tomuri a 'kaka resort'; half a century after Mua-upoko's defeat, their kākā-snarers' old vine-ladders still hung from the trees. If there was anywhere where it was hard for someone like Buller to ignore the way birds came down from the mountains and across the plain to particular trees precisely when nectar flow began, it was Ō-tomuri. Not long after Buller had obtained Papaitonga, a southerly whipped up a fire on his neighbour, Jillet's, bush block and Ō-tomuri vanished. Only a grove of karaka, planted centuries ago in a clearing and still standing today, survived the flames that swept right through to the lake. Every one of the great rātā was incinerated.

Secure in Ngāti Kikopiri testimony that they'd seen the fire lit on Jillet's block, Buller took Jillet to the Supreme Court. By 1895 there was already a sufficient country-city dichotomy for urban people to have a growing, romantic concern for forest scenery. The new Wellington Scenery Preservation Society appeared in support of Buller. Jillet's lawyer argued his innocence, that it was just 'another fire lighted by the Maoris', and that the claim on Ō-tomuri's merits by Buller and the scenery preservationists who supported him were 'purely sentimental'. The Chief Justice clearly found the case a hard one, as well, as he was quick to point out, as very unusual. Papaitonga, he told the jury, indeed had 'exceptional advantages'. Even in a country like this, 'where bush-firing is a necessity, people must understand that if, in firing their own bush, they set fire to their neighbour's, either directly or remotely, they must pay for it'. It didn't convince the jury, but it did stimulate interest right in the middle of the speediest deforestation of a region New Zealand has seen, for preserving some of it. Prior to the fire, Buller himself had had far more of Papaitonga's forest cleared than he would ever protect. Now he declared he'd 'spare no pains to preserve it in all its native beauty as a heritage for those who may come after us', and published the letters of sympathy that arrived after the verdict—including, of course, the Premier's. Buller applauded Seddon's artistic tastes and his determination to withstand 'the Goths and Vandals in our midst'.

Amongst the scenery preservationists, Edward Tregear's presence in the Supreme Court rekindled a curious connection. Tregear's friend, or 'beloved patron and socialist soulmate' as he has been called, was Seddon's Minister of Labour, William Pember Reeves. Reeves was, among other things, a poet who shared Buller's love of wild scenery and misgivings at its vanishing. His *Passing of the Forest* was one of the earliest signs in Pākehā literature of a concern for the indigenous—'gone is the forest world . . . Gone is the forest nation . . . Gone are the forest birds' has become an anthem for the New Zealand conservation movement. It's no wonder that, in the small society in which they lived, Reeves and Buller knew one another, and despite their ideological differences, the Fabian poet found his way to the gentleman naturalist's country estate.

While Reeves, in the midst of a depression, was trying to avert a tidal wave of poverty, Buller had by 1895 spent the equivalent of hundreds of thousands of dollars on Papaitonga—without even beginning his mansion. I never look at the arm of the lake below the sweep of Ō-tumuri forest without picturing the two of them that Victorian afternoon, down there in Buller's splendid boat—itself 'a perfect picture in appearance'. Buller, conspicuous consumer, rowing the leader of a political movement that regarded the 'excessive individualism' of the rich as enslaving the poor, across his 'silent mere'—its shiny mud now filling with raupō and impossible to row across.

Buller named the lake arm Pember Bay in honour of the visit. Reeves' celebratory poem soon graced the pages of *The New Zealand Graphic*. Adjusted in the wake of the fire, it reappeared:

> *Safe from the mountain tempest's wild alarms*
> *Safe from the driving sea-wind's bitter spray,*
> *Placid, enfolded in the forest's arms*
> *Lies Pember Bay.*
>
> *Did some brown lover in his fancy's youth*
> *Name thee in accents musically, slow,*
> *Soft Papaitonga 'Beauty of the South',*
> *called long ago?*

Midway between the mountains and the deep
Secure from upland cold, from salt winds keen,
Bathed in sweet air and sunshine thou dost keep
A golden mean.

Dark clouds may brood on yonder peaks and spurs,
Chill winds may chase the sea foam flake on flake,
But here is peace. Nought ruffles, nothing stirs
The tranquil lake.

Nought shakes the ferns, whose interlacing fronds,
Like sea birds wings, uplift their giant pinions.
Nought stirs the brakes, whose creepers myriad bonds,
Guard green dominions.

Look, while the sunset clings to yonder range,
Look, while the lake gleams silver in its way,
And pray that though all beauty else may change
This scene may stay.

Here the wild birds from ancient coverts pressed,
May seek asylum by this silent mere;
For though no other glade or wave give rest,
They find it here.

Though in an hour the forest fire ends all
That nature can in patient ages do
Though, 'neath the axe the straight tall trees must fall
The wide land through.

Yet in this sacred wood no axe shall ring,
These winding shores shall sanctuary give,
Where in cool thickets happy birds may sing,
And verdure live.

Long Papaitonga, may thy ferns grow fair,
Thy graceful toe-toe droop and sway.
And never tree or bird know scathe or scare
By Pember Bay.

Buller loved Reeves' lines, and included them in his final work on New Zealand's birds alongside Kipling's assertion that New Zealand was 'the most lovely country on the face of the earth', and his own words about its 'magnificent and silent forests . . . laden with luxurient epiphytic growth; the semi-tropical richness . . . the ever-present glory of tree ferns . . . the never-ending coils of "kiekie" . . . the native "ngaherehere"—a sylvan medley of matchless beauty'.

Reeves, New Zealand's original Labour Minister, has been called its first intellectual. As the welfare state drew its first breaths, he considered care of 'the ancient coverts' like Papaitonga's 'sacred wood' to be 'essentials of refinement' of a civilised society. The vulnerable in the new society— nature or the poor—struck a similar chord in his Labour Secretary, Edward Tregear.

When diplomatic duties took Reeves to Britain, Tregear, far from immune to 'the flinty impassivity and matter-of-factness with which nine out of ten young colonials regard the spiritual side of life', missed the passions of his 'dear chief and friend'. The wild landscape was a constant presence in their correspondence. If Tregear wasn't advising the 'lover of dear Dame Nature' of the rātā seedlings from the West Coast he had dispatched for him, he was reporting on 'charming pieces of forest' he saw in his travels or commenting on how speedily bush-burning was 'ruining the hem of the old lady's garment recklessly every year. The match of the devilish teamster, lighted for the fiendish folly of seeing the fire tear through . . . is worse than the axe of the settler who wants to feed his sheep on landslips. Miles of blackness, alas, miles of white skeleton trees, when a year ago was the exquisite undulation of hills clothed with forest.'

Reeves and Tregear commiserated about the labour colony—the 'socialistic experiment', as some called it—they had created alongside Sir Walter Buller's country estate. Soon after Reeves landed in England, a letter arrived from Tregear who had been 'up at the State Farm last week', because since Reeves had left, public criticism about their experiment had been growing. The Prime Minister, Richard Seddon, never liked the idea. His Minister of Lands, John McKenzie, detested it. Now Tregear himself wanted 'a rougher place' where 'men can be sent for hard slogging'.

As social reformers, Reeves and Tregear were shocked by the speed with which New Zealand was, for all its promise of freedom, filling with the failed, the oppressed and the workless. The root of the problem, they were sure, was land; 'the landholder,' as Tregear put it, 'as the master of the landless . . . the divorce of the worker from the means of sustenance'. To solve this they planned a series of 'State Farms' outside the new cities where, in the words of Tregear's bureaucratic reports, they could examine 'the possibility of destitute persons succeeding in living in co-operative societies under fostering Government care'. A rural solution to a city problem, the idea came from Dutch labour colonies earlier in the century. 'A State Farm,' Tregear wrote, 'is to comprise about 1000 acres of land fit for agricultural purposes and to this will be drafted the surplus workmen of the towns . . . applying at the Labour Bureau . . . clerks, stewards, firemen, tailors, printers etc., who crowded out of their regular employments are in a state of destitution.' If the co-operative principle worked, Reeves and Tregear believed, it would price private enterprise off the market.

An obvious problem was where to site the experiment. By the 1890s, in the wake of the advent of refrigerated shipping, there was already a shortage of easy land for 'sunburnt, sinewy men, whose earnest wish for work has been proved by the independent way in which they sought and found it'. About the only district where they could avoid 'the landholder as the master of the landless' and where flat country was still cheap, in bush cover and Māori hands, was Horowhenua.

As it happened, the search for the right acres coincided with Buller purchasing Papaitonga from the Mua-upoko chief, Meiha Kēpa Te Rangihiwinui. The Native Land Court had vested the huge Horowhenua block in Kēpa's trust when it was retrieved from Ngāti Raukawa in 1873, but this had fomented a dispute with another, younger Mua-upoko chief, Warena Hunia. Kēpa's was the only name on the block's title. Buller persuaded his friend Kēpa that he individually, and not the tribe communally, was absolute owner—and thus able to sell him Papaitonga. Meanwhile, in almost exactly the same way, Hunia was being coaxed to clear his debt to another Pākehā by selling the block with his name on it—to the government, for its labour colony. Within months, Hunia had sold the government the land next door to Papaitonga for Reeves and Tregear's 'State experiment', and a pleased Tregear was reporting that 'fifty men, eight women, and twenty-five children were on the ground—the men cutting roads through the forest, felling bush for burning, planting orchards . . . ready for the permanent homestead to be laid out'.

Buller had probably imagined some rich settler as neighbour, not the uncouth inmates of a labour colony. Pitting Mua-upoko against Mua-upoko, he did his utmost to stop the purchase. Confronting a Royal Commission into his actions, Buller denied embarrassing the government over its purchase of the State Farm. But his warning that it was illegal, followed by his friend Kēpa leading an angry deputation of Mua-upoko chiefs to Wellington, rebounded on him. Accusations flew about just how *he* had obtained his lake in the forest. Widely believed to have 'taken the land of the Maori', as Edward Tregear bluntly put it, Buller was soon the centre of a scandal. Summoned in front of parliament, he was told he 'ought to be in gaol for his dealings with the natives'.

Papaitonga became the symbol of two clashing ideologies: the conspicuous consumption displayed by Buller's country estate and the Lands Minister John McKenzie's hatred of the wealthy taking more land than they needed. A fiery Highlander whose family were refugees from the Clearances, McKenzie was the most passionate of the government's campaigners for 'Lands for the people'. He unleashed a chain of events that would end with Buller exiling himself to England, abandoning his kiwi experiments and the government gaining the best part of his collapsing country estate.

New Zealand of the 1890s is remembered for radical labour laws, social reform and women's suffrage. In ordinary life, though, it was a divided society. Sir Walter Buller didn't confine his Darwinism to birds and Māori; he told the government that 'subsidising the survival of the unfit', for example, simply increased their ability to reproduce their kind. He had disguised his humble origins on a non-conformist Wesleyan mission farm and recreated himself as a landed Englishman. By the 1890s his appointments and status, his ornithology and wealth, kept to a minimum contact with the social and intellectual strata he considered beneath him. Papaitonga, his 'country seat', was a central pull in it.

Buller knew that the landless people the government intended to bring up from Wellington would resent his wealth and scorn his passion for birds and scenery. Behind his dedication to beauty and refinement was an urge to hover above the squalor of the folk moving in beyond the trees with their pitiful tents. In this new settler society, with guns in every house, Buller knew his lake's flocks of teal and the newly arrived exotic water birds would be irresistible to State Farmers finding themselves beside a forest of cooing pigeons, with the quiet lake of a gentleman's estate through the trees.

Reeves and Tregear never doubted their experiment's social benefits, but they knew that the State Farm was part of the relentless campaign against nature. Closer subdivision of the land and village settlements—giving the 'landless' what wealth had given the landed—meant more men to 'strip the woods away':

> And he is mightly as he hews again,
> Bronzed pioneer of nations. Ay, but scan
> The ruined wonder never wrought again,
> The ravaged beauty God alone could plan!
> Bitter the thought: 'Is this the price we pay—
> The price for progress—beauty swept away?'

So they issued instructions that a strip of forest be left before Buller's boundary. Conveniently, there was a swampy gully.

Buller wanted Papaitonga to be talked about as a place of birds, a parkland for leisured, aristocratic pursuits: 'Since His Excellency the Earl of Glasgow was a guest there, and enjoyed some good sport, in 1892, no shooting has been allowed on the lake except for taking specimens, and, as a consequence, in the shooting season thousands of Wild-Duck, Teal, and Wigeon congregate there, feeling perfectly secure from molestation of any kind.'

The same year as Glasgow's visit, destitute families began arriving at the State Farm block, subsisting with calico tents in the forest until they could erect cottages from its timber. By 1894 Buller had his Egyptian geese and Teneriffe quail: '. . . all the new birds are doing well'. By the following year, the year of the Ō-tomuri fire, the State Farmers had felled a third of the forest next door, sold the timber, burnt, stumped and sown it, built fences, roads, a school house and a village of other buildings—and escaped the worst of the depression in the bargain. Within a year it was a thriving dairy farm, but as Tregear himself realised, 'quite unsuitable now for a labour depot'.

Despite Papaitonga's scenery, Buller's daughter, Laura, was 'awfully put out' at the prospect of living there, certainly in winter, but Walter, said his brother-in law, Gilbert Mair, 'is simply infatuated about the place'. 'The beauty of the district is fast being destroyed,' Mair wrote after a visit to Papaitonga in 1897. There were still plenty of birds for the Mairs to see, perhaps a thousand of today's almost-extinct brown teal in fact, but the day was ruined by trespassers—the 'beastly "State farmers"' as Mair called them, shooting at the head of one of the bays. The next day, 'Walter posted a Notice of Reward of £5 for conviction of any one of them'. Across the fence, the freshly cleared State Farm had far more men than it needed. Even Tregear could see 'you can't put 40 or 50 men on a dairy farm and keep them in useful work'.

By 1899 Leo Buller was telling his father he'd never known the once multitudinous brown teal to be so scarce. The start of the shooting season had been 'a hard day's tramp after birds but no luck. The only pheasant I shot fell in thick swamp.' More than habitat loss was to blame: 150 men had passed through the State Farm by 1900 when Reeves' and Tregear's social experiment was handed over to the government's agriculturalists. Men 'whose advancing years and domestic responsibilities have caused them to fall out from the foremost ranks of labour', as Tregear depicted them, they were hardly the bronzed pioneers that Reeves had had in mind.

Lying in the grass at one corner, broken and as forgotten as the grateful hands that made it, the remains of the State Farm's concrete entrance are still there. At the other end of the sweep of market gardens, dairy units and deer farms, a line of old kahikatea trees stands dark against the sky like an English hedgerow. Magpies scream from the high clumps of epiphytic lilies at men stacking piles of pallets up against the reserve fence beside the rows of cabbages.

Papaitonga Scenic Reserve is so tiny we expect it survived as a single block. The really observant, though, can see, beyond the end of Buller Road, a strip of forest younger than that on either side (although there is no more trace of the road that was here than of the contradictory aspirations it once divided). On one side the forest survived the 1890s as the lakeshore of a gentleman's country estate; on the other, because two influential men interested in nature saved it from their labour colony. Buller was in England when the 68-acre reserve appeared among the quarries, public school and hall sites, cemeteries, travelling stock reserves and gravel pits in a list of *Places permanently reserved under the Land Act 1892*. But he praised the way 'forest reserves like the beautiful belt of bush along the boundary of the State farm at Horowhenua are being defined and proclaimed'. The *New Zealand Gazette* of 7 January 1901 simply said it had been reserved for 'the preservation of native bush'. The famous botanist Leonard Cockayne came across it on a visit to his brother Arthur at the new experimental farm next door. Keeping his boots dry, he stood on the edge to see:

the tangle of roots on the wet floor and a densely jungly
undergrowth, hardly penetrable, which consists principally of the
following: slender stems of Freycinetia, *small* Dicksonia
squarrosa, *here and there sapling* Laurelia, Carpodetus, *with*
naked stems for their lower two-thirds, but above with short
flexuous branches . . . Where the ground is wet, rise up huge much-
buttressed trunks of Laurelia, *its far-extending roots putting forth*
abundant pneumatophores. Finally, there are the straight trunks
of Podocarpus dacrydioides *and their crowns full of* Astelia
Solandri *looking like huge bird's nests.*

'Happily,' he told readers of *The Vegetation of New Zealand,* 'a few remnants in an almost virgin state' like this tiny piece 'not far from Levin (fortunately a Scenic Reserve)' were still to be seen. He knew it was merely a few years since what he was describing had been common, when settlers breaking in country like this loathed watching the way the sun warmed the birds in the tree-tops but never reached down to where they were slipping in the dark, cold mud. By 1900 'coastal plain semi-swamp forest' belonged to a vanished world. Cockayne's task was to record it in the language of those who could match its latin plant names to relatives in other parts of the world.

Kahikatea: fruit-basket of the forest. When the big trees rock in a nor'westerly gale, you can feel their swampy ground move. Cloaked in their korowai of kiekie vines, some trees date back to when people first came here—when the land was wetter, the lake closer and te hōkioi, the vanished giant eagle, watched over the forest from high in their branches. Cockayne didn't mention such things, or the cooing kererū and the continuous chatter of birds that distinguishes the kahikatea forest from others in its vicinity. That wasn't his discipline. And I wonder if he even saw the other, tiny carnivores—curled up underfoot.

There has been a flood through the kahikatea forest. A film of fine, brown silt covers every seedling, leaf and frond near the forest floor. Yet only where rotting logs have banked up against the aerial roots of pukatea is any flow perceptible. Lying in one of the pools is a snail's shell, the diameter of a golfball and almost as circular, its owner dead. But a few minutes of peering into the swamp forest's primeval corners reveals dozens of its relatives who have survived the inundation, resting up for the day from a night's feast of earthworms and insects.

Walk over to the sandstone gullies on on the other side of Papaitonga and look in the same sort of place and you will find the same creatures are subtly different. Once you know why and what, in terms of time and landscape history is involved, you can never again read this stretch of country the same. I'd watched kererū leave Papaitonga's kahikatea and head inland to the mountains. I knew how its eels' ecosystem reached thousands of miles away to the tropical Pacific. Yet as I came to know Papaitonga intimately it was its giant landsnails that came to symbolise nature's plight here. When this vast sweep of life is confined to a tiny cell, it makes the centuries of our human preoccupations seem as brief as an El Nino summer.

On 5 October 1910, 20-year-old Leslie Adkin, a settler's son, took the train from Levin into the city to deliver a lecture to the learned men of the Wellington Philosophical Society. Adkin's unravelling of the Horowhenua Plain's geological history had thrust him into a sea change in New Zealand earth science. Ever since he could draw he had located himself on the plain by meticulous maps. Those he hung in front of the city's public servants and men of science, and later published with his paper in their prestigious journal, depicted different times since the early Pleistocene, showing how dynamic the Horowhenua's plain had been compared to its hill country. How, as oceans warmed and ice melted, it changed from a vast open flatland joining the North Island to the top of the South to a steep, indented coast with islands poking out of a shallow sea; and then, as the rising mountains dragged it out of the sea again, it became a plain once more.

Adkin looked down at the plain as he and his father burnt their way inland. As stumping and plowing revealed more and more of its past, he realised that without youth and dynamism, the plain could never have supported the mosaic of lagoons, lakes, swamps and forests Māori described to him. Until Adkin's study, few on the plain, or elsewhere, had thought beyond improving its productivity. His theory has never been refuted. It wasn't a wise geomorphologist that proved him right though, but a species of snail.

The essence of Adkin's story was dynamism. Water courses and lagoons came and went. One river, it seemed, had even flipped from a northern to a southern track on its route from the mountains to the sea. Until recently, the Ohau had meandered northwards out of the Tararuas, emerging with streams from the Manawatu end of the plain before flowing into the low-lying basin occupied today by Lake Horowhenua. Then it suddenly spilled south into the course to the sea that it takes today.

Twenty years later, the zoologist A.W.B. Powell was well into a study of New Zealand's giant carnivorous landsnails so comprehensive that the genus to which most of them belong has since been named *Powelliphanta*. Distributed around the broken traces of Gondwana, with origins back late in the Palaeozoic or early Mesozoic, their family of meat-eating molluscs is probably the oldest on earth. Their intricacy of forms and puzzling distributions suggested a remarkable history of gradual evolution and geographic isolation. Powell suspected the explanation for their seemingly endless colour forms lay in the geological ancestry of the country itself.

Surmising that continuous land was necessary for landsnail dispersal, Powell concentrated on the parts of the country that had avoided glaciation, particularly the broken hill country of Nelson and Marlborough. He soon saw a logic in the snails' distribution. Every population he encountered had a unique pattern of colour banding; each shell within it was virtually identical. Yet only a ridge away, across a valley, the snails had another, subtly different, pattern. 'Geographic features, such as mountain ranges, river systems and islands,' he wrote, 'have played or are still playing an important part in the segregation and evolution of species.' Every landsnail, in other words, carried its landscape's history in its genes. Faced with a land that was forming new mountains and rivers faster than the snails could cross them, isolated populations of snails evolved into new species.

Powell searched every kind of forest. In the summer of 1927, in country quite unlike the Nelson-Marlborough mountains, he came out of one bit of bush particularly excited, having found an abundance of obviously related snails. But they were on the other side of Cook Strait—under decaying leaves here at Papaitonga. Convinced that New Zealand's giant landsnails were essentially hill and mountain animals, Powell had an immediate answer to why those on the 'Pleistocene plains around Levin' were almost identical to species of the northern South Island. They were, he said, an anomaly. 'This low country habit has no doubt been inherited' from the ancestors of the only other giant landsnails he had seen in lowland environments, around Whanganui Inlet in North-west Nelson.

So absorbed in how the Horowhenua species might throw light on what he called 'the species problem in New Zealand landsnails', Powell didn't exactly explain how connection between obviously related but geographically separated snails could be possible. It had to be a 'comparatively recent' land link, and it had to be with North-west Nelson, because that was the only other area he'd seen the giant snails inhabiting the lowlands.

The acid-test of genetic connection was the similarity in shells. Although on record saying it 'cannot be denied', Powell would soon question this suggested link with North-west Nelson, suspecting instead that there were greater affinities with Marlborough Sounds species. A Marlborough Sounds link made the Cook Strait land bridge hypothesis more realistic, but it took a geologist to prove it. Picking up on Powell's observation of the 'striking resemblance' one of the forms of the Horowhenua landsnail, *traversii otakia*, bore to some of the hybrids between *obscura* and *bicolor*, two species from high in the outer Sounds, Martin Te Punga showed what was needed to have created the link: a narrow isthmus across the strait in a zone where *obscura* from the northwest Sounds could interbreed with *bicolor* from the southeast. New geological evidence of D'Urville Island rocks in Manawatu Pleistocene deposits gave him just the proof he needed.

At first Powell had formally grouped his Horowhenua landsnail in a series of North-west Nelson species, even mapping it as the solitary aberration somehow stranded away from the rest, in the North Island. He did give the new species its own name, *Paryphanta traversii*. His research spurred others into a snail survey of the Horowhenua Plains, and the Prouse cousins' packages of snails in Powell's mail began to reveal a very different story. Far from being a simple species, they displayed the same kind of 'intense localisation' as Powell had found in the South Island mountain and hill country; and although the plain had few such 'topographic boundaries', the tell-tale colour banding was, if anything, even more complex. Snails less than a kilometre apart, in the different swampy arms of Papaitonga for example, could have strikingly different shell colouring.

The mountains above their plain revealed new forms of *traversii* to the Prouses too. But on the plain, where the snails had an unprecedented intricacy of colour forms, the destruction of what only 30 years before had been a 'once almost continuous forest' meant that any exact reconstruction of the snails' distributions was virtually impossible. So rapidly did they appear to be evolving, what's more, that this sudden, 'induced isolation' seemed to be already leading to genetic differences. Powell was familiar with the gradual separation and evolution of populations in hill country such as the Marlborough Sounds. Or in Hawaii, where, faced with constant creation of topographic boundaries, landsnails were likewise evolving into a myriad of forms. But why, on such a seemingly homogeneous plain was each snail population so different? By 1940 he had recognised and formally named five 'forms' of *Paraphanta traversii*. The dramatic removal of the plains forest meant its 'once-compact snail populations now exist as a series of artificially-isolated colonies'. But he needed evidence of another kind to know that they had been far from genetically uniform in the first place.

It was probably Powell's snail collectors who told him about the extraordinary scholar of land and history who farmed just up the road. By the time Powell met Leslie Adkin when visiting the Prouses late in 1945, and Adkin explained his unravelling 35 years before of the plain's geological history, Powell had read his 'excellent' paper. The answer to his puzzle was 'at once apparent'. What had seemed bewilderingly complex was beautifully simple. 'There have been two prior courses of the Ohau River,' he wrote, 'and snail populations along its banks have been subjected to a "give and take" operation on at least three separate occasions during and since the Pleistocene.'

Sometime after their first ancestors had crossed the ancient low-lying link with the South Island, rising sea levels confined them to the Tararua hill country where each form evolved. Not so isolated they could no longer interbreed, they came together again as soon as a new lowland plain emerged in the late Pleistocene. The ecosystem that made it possible had been in existence less than 10,000 years—the same time Europeans have been cultivating plants and breeding animals for food production.

The mixing agent was water. Rivers in hill country stay in place for thousands of years, but not on young sandplains. 'It seems evident,' Powell concluded, 'that the Ohau River has formed a fluctuating barrier to the free dispersal of the snails of the coastal plain, even when the area was in virgin forest . . . Owing to past changes in the course of that river, a buffer zone of mixed colonies occurs.'

The discovery of mixed snail colonies at Papaitonga confirmed exactly what Adkin had suggested in 1910—the lake had once been a lagoon at the Ohau rivermouth. Each progressively southern course of the Ohau brought down flood debris from a different combination of hill country catchments, and with it different landsnail subspecies. Each swampy arm of the lake had slightly different snails because each had once received different genetic combinations when the lake was the Ohau's course to the sea and yet still had the 'continual dampness' to which Powell said the snails are so sensitive. Able to survive inundation but not to seal their shell to conserve moisture—and thus ill-equipped for the dry, intervening sand ridges—the snails have stayed effectively where the water delivered them.

Buller, too, knew about them, if not with Powell's insight. He would have been among the scientific audience to whom W.T.L. Travers said landsnails displayed, 'as Darwin pointed out', greater puzzles of distribution and dispersal than any other group of animals. Reminding them of Darwin's experiments with the power of landsnails to resist sea water, Travers postulated water transport to explain the Horowhenua snails' extraordinary similarity with those across Cook Strait. The great irony though is that their ceaseless genetic diversity is precisely what obsession with exact taxonomy prevented so many Victorian Darwinists like Buller from seeing. Not so Darwin. 'The problem' with his theory, he said, lay in 'the tendency in organic beings descended from the same stock to diverge in character as they become modified'—as though he had Papaitonga's snails in mind, rather than Galapagos finches.

Had Māori been as fond of landsnails as the French, or as the pigs now ravaging their numbers throughout the country, the Māori landscape of the Horowhenua would reflect it. The snails would be, as eels are, rudimentary to concepts of intimacy with the land. As they knew other migrators' homing instincts—kuaka's, titi's and pīpī-wharauroa's—brought them so insistently and precisely across the ocean, Papaitonga's eel fishers knew each lake and swamp had subtly different eels, and that the lives on which their own wellbeing depended hinged around a greater, live *system*, a network of relationships and processes.

HINAKI HEREHERE, HOKIO STREAM, 1920S, (PĀ TUNA, RUATANIWHA, IN BACKGROUND).

Early European settlers in this stretch of country found it convenient to disparage the Māori passion for its harakeke and kahikatea: '. . . to the old-time Maori bush country in general formed a possession of little value, except in so far as the streams running through it held eels.' To others who knew it in the days when 'cuttings from swamp to swamp abounded', it was evident that 'eel-preserves' were as valuable to Māori 'as gold-mines are to Europeans'. Nothing gave a negotiator for Māori land so much trouble. As William Fox learned from Mua-upoko's relatives Ngātiapa, disputing Ngāti Raukawa's claim to the Rangitikei sand country:

> To European minds, cultivation may seem a more important exercise of ownership than habitual fishing in eel-ponds; but in New Zealand it is just the reverse . . . If the Ngatiraukawa had been as thick over that land as the eels are in its ponds, the undisputed exercise of the right of fishery in the hands of the Ngatiraukawa would have been proof that the mana of the district was still with them. To enjoy the right of fishing, the right to the adjacent land is essential; and there is no ingredient of so much weight . . . to prove the continuance of the Ngatiapa Muaupoko mana . . . as their holding on to the eel-ponds.

Kēpa te Rangihiwinui understood that the genius of the sand country—which his Mua-upoko could no more allow other Māori to possess than trade to the Pākehā—lay in its eely lakes, swamp forests and streams. Not for nothing was a watery grove of kahikatea in the midst of it called Mauri, the same name as the pou that, with ritual and karakia, was placed at each end of an eel weir to invoke Tangaroa's goodwill.

When Kēpa strode down Hokio Beach with the judge of the Native Land Court in 1873, he carried two pou to stand in the sand dunes to mark the strip from sea to mountains with the sand lakes and eel weirs from which Mua-upoko had been forced 50 years before. For all Kēpa's European ways, he knew his people's ancient reliance on their fishing grounds and forests was vulnerable to what settlers were doing to them; and with a father who was one of the few who had escaped from Te Rauparaha's guns, he knew Papaitonga was sacred for more than the quality of its eels. As a war hero, mail carrier and policeman, Kēpa had influence with the Pākehā government which empowered the vanquished and landless Mua-upoko to repossess the mana of their precious eel fisheries. The same image underlay his rapport with Buller, and led him so fatefully into debt to him. Caught between two worlds, convinced the new Pākehā ways would change their Horowhenua forever, part of Kēpa tried to get Mua-upoko to adapt, while the other part of him began staking a claim to arrest the clearing and draining.

Mua-upoko were the real losers at Papaitonga, and right across Horowhenua. To Buller, the plain's metamorphosis from forest to English grasses was destined. 'This,' he said, 'seems to be one of the inscrutable laws of Nature.' What had happened in other parts of the world 'must inevitably happen, and indeed is happening here. The aboriginal race must in time give place to a more highly organised, or, at any rate, a more civilised one.'

As soon as he saw Papaitonga in the 1860s, Buller was determined to get it—whatever the means. 'It was the *lake* I was hankering after,' he told the Horowhenua Commission in 1896. 'I was charmed by the scenery, and there and then asked the Maori owners, the Muaupoko, to let me have a piece of land on the lake . . . I told them I would give any price they liked as I wanted a home there.' No matter how insistent Buller was that Kēpa was free to sell without wider Mua-upoko agreement, Kēpa knew he was merely kaitiaki, trustee, not absolute owner. And he wasn't deaf to the talk—*kua kite-matou i te tinihanga ō taua roia*—that his lawyer friend was intent on cheating Mua-upoko of their land.

The completion of the railway across Mua-upoko's forest plain in 1889 guaranteed an influx of European settlers. Desperate for money, Kēpa headed for Wellington with an offer of Mua-upoko acres as soon as he heard of the government's plans for a village settlement. He wanted a part in the inevitable, but he had conditions. What has become Levin was to be called 'Taitoko' after his father. A tenth of the town sections were to be reserved for Māori, 100 acres for a garden, and a square and schools for Māori and settler children. And beyond the new town to which he knew Mua-upoko would drift—as they did—he wanted 'the Lakes, Horowhenua and Papaitonga, and the streams issuing from there to the sea, and a chain round the borders of the Lakes, . . . reserved so that they may not be drained . . .' But by the end of the bargaining, anxiety about his finances had Kēpa signing a deed that made no more mention of 'Taitoko' than it did of eel streams and lakeshores.

There was another chance to sell land the following year when his friend Buller, full of ideas for his lake in the forest, came back from England. As Buller put it, Kēpa 'on my return to the colony . . . gave effect to his promise by giving me a lease'. By May 1892 Buller had, for four pounds a year, a two-acre lakeshore section and, for six pounds, a lease on the lake and all the forested land right back to the railway. This time, Kēpa had only one condition: 'the right at all times to erect eel weirs . . . to put down eel baskets at the outlet of the Waiwiri [Papaitonga] Lake . . . for the purpose of catching and taking eels therefrom, and to that end will be allowed full liberty of ingress and egress at all convenient times and seasons.'

If Buller didn't mind his old friend from the Land Wars coming onto his country estate to catch a few eels every now and then, the man of property was hardly thrilled when he opened his new deed to find 'a reserve, two chains wide, was marked off around the edge of the lake and designated "Right of Way"'. Extracting a statutory declaration from Kēpa that it was an error, he spent the next four days trying to find out why it had happened. The Survey Office protested the 'misconception' originated with the plan of Papaitonga they'd received from the Native Land Court. Then, even before Kēpa could return the declaration, Buller went straight to Percy Smith, the Surveyor-General, with the word that Kēpa 'was anxious that the Certificate of Title held by him should be cancelled'.

Smith and Buller shared a passion for the landscape and its surveillence as it vanished. The year Buller got his lake the two of them were elected governors of the New Zealand Institute, the forerunner of the Royal Society of New Zealand. Citing an 'arrangement made with the Surveyor-General', Buller soon had his problem on the desk of the secretary for Crown Lands. Within days, Smith was instructing clerks to amend Buller's certificate of title 'by excluding the so-called right-of-road around the Waiwiri Lake'. Three weeks later Walter Buller had his country estate free of encumbrances and Mua-upoko had lost their last hold on the lakeshores that had fed their ancestors for centuries.

Secure title was essential for what Buller had in mind. It was one thing to symbolise the colony's 'old primeval grandeur' and savagery's brief time in it with burial canoes and carved storehouses, but he had other visions that needed Māori gone. As soon as he had title and had taken 'a mile's tramp to no purpose' through it, he was hiring a clearing gang. 'I hope you will be careful about the logging after the timber is down,' he instructed, 'or we might have a bad burn . . . see that your men are careful to cut all kareaos [supplejack] clean away . . . any left intact will interfere with the burning . . . save all the tree ferns and nikaus.' It went on until he finally left for England in 1899: 'McLeavey and Hudson have fallen out over the underscrubbing . . . I hear the men are making a good job on the bush.'

The new clearings became another smiling farm, as enclosed as anything Buller had seen in England. 'The Natives have no permission from me to run any of their stock on any of my land,' he told Henson, his new estate manager, 'the sheep ought to fare much better than they did when the place was a common and swarming with other people's stock.' As well as Māori to be moved, there was the new flora and fauna to be brought in. Raising his voice 'against so insane a policy', Buller had been one of the most vociferous opponents of acclimatisation of 'vermin' like rabbits and weasels. But it was a different matter when it came to embellishing Papaitonga in the fashion of England's great estates:

> *Sir Walter Buller on his visit up the Coast last week took with him a large number of valuable waterfowl . . . and these have all been placed on the Papaitonga Lake . . . several pairs of the English Mallards, . . . the small call-duck . . . the beautiful Iceland shell drake, the red-backed Egyptian goose and the Barnacle goose . . . several pairs of Hungarian partridge and of smaller Teneriffe quail . . . to get these desirable birds acclimatised and distributed throughout the country, it is to be hoped that the settlers and Maoris alike will do their best to protect them.*

> *Morris said . . . that I was to have the whole brood of Cygnets for my New Zealand lake; . . . the executive of Kew Gardens has given Sir Walter Buller a brood of fine young white swans to be placed on his lake at Papaitanga . . . They will go out by one of the direct steamers . . . a nice addition to the introduced birds.*

> *Could you possibly manage 1 American Char or 'Rainbow Trout? . . . I shall go up to Papaitonga by Monday afternoon's train taking the 5 young trout with me for the lake.*

Ornamentals and fruit trees were planted in hundreds. Bert Richards, whose father managed the estate for Buller's sons, saw what Buller intended. Bert's earliest memories are of a Papaitonga when everything beyond it seemed 'all Maoris and bush—bush, bush as far as you could see'. We wander under Buller's firs, cypress, cedar, oak, Scots and Norfolk Pines and along a sprawling row of chestnuts that were already big trees when he gathered nuts from them just before the First World War. Beside them, on the lake side of the grove, is the knarled solitary olive Buller planted to symbolise the Horowhenua's fecundity.

'The variety's gone though,' he says. The big trees only hint at what Buller planted. 'The grounds were laid out grandly . . . Right down to the

A WILD ISLAND IN A
DOMESTICATED SEA, 1980s.

lake edge. He had big plans, Buller. But all he ever got round to building was the house where we lived. That you see left the ideal site for a grand mansion . . . so he could look down to the lake through his trees.'

Not all Buller's introductions were foreign. A solitary kauri is all that survives of *Te Kari a Maui*, the native garden where 'rare plants and shrubs from other parts of New Zealand have been introduced and planted with the intention of making it an epitome, as it were, of the indigenous flora'. Today most of it is a thicket of Wandering Jew, the *Tradescantia* that has become one of New Zealand's worst forest weeds. Bert suspects Buller brought it in for edging paths: 'My father tried to get rid of it by piling it up on the wire-netting of the bird enclosure.'

Bert leads me along the lake shore to where, when he was a kid, the big aviary stood forlorn and empty. When Buller himself was at Papaitonga the aviary was at the centre of the action. He mentions it in an 1893 paper, and its construction, Bert is sure, was part of that initial flurry of activity in 1892. And as soon as the aviary was ready, it would seem, Buller went looking for the bird that he had once labelled 'hopelessly doomed', but would best symbolise Papaitonga's security.

Buller knew of huia that had been caged for years. As a young magistrate in Wanganui he'd kept a pair in an aviary, sent others to English zoos, even visited them there. In 1892, due in no small part to Buller's own artful lobbying of the governor who signed the proclamation, huia became legally protected. Yet only days before the proclamation, Buller told Lord Rothschild, he was dispatching 'parties of Maories into the woods . . . to obtain a live pair'. Legal protection was important, but having huia in 'his own private collection . . . before they have finally passed away' more so.

Buller obtained his forest lake in May 1892 but it was early July before he had all Māori access rights removed from the title deed. Six days later he was lecturing the Wellington Philosophical Society about the birds that 'under the changed conditions of existence, are passing away'. His preoccupation was the just protected huia and the 'deep shade of its forest home . . .

invaded by the settler's axe'. In his next lecture, in January 1893, he spoke of a huia hunt he had undertaken with the surveyor, Morgan Carkeek, 'a few months ago' into the ranges where Carkeek had seen abundant huia a few years earlier. If 'a few months ago' meant spring 1892, huia would have been nesting, and Buller would have been taking advantage of their 'extreme docility' in the wild. 'The female bird allowing herself to be handled on the nest' meant young were easily obtained for aviaries. All a second trip revealed, though, in a 10-mile search of 'almost impervious' Akatarawa forest and several nights camped out—obviously an arduous experience for the then 54-year-old Buller—was a solitary huia near their camp one morning.

Buller plainly intended to do more than just look at huia. The same spring, the Liberal government suddenly changed its policy on island bird sanctuaries, withdrawing funds for the two for which Buller and others had been pushing. Buller immediately wrote to the Premier advocating 'systematically stocking' Little Barrier Island 'by catching Huias Kiwis Kakapos Crows and Thrushes'. His own lake's islands too, he believed, were 'admirably suited' to the experiments necessary to understand the habits of endangered birds.

By 1892 huia, more than any other bird, had come to symbolise New Zealand's birds' inability to coexist with the settler culture. As a young man Buller had handled hundreds before on-selling their skins to European collectors. Despite the missionary-naturalist William Colenso having seen huia feeding in coastal karaka trees, Buller had long considered *Heteralocha acutirostris*, as he had described it in his *History of the Birds of New Zealand*, a mountain bird—immune, in other words, from events on the plains below. After seeing the Horowhenua forest's sudden destruction repeat the earlier vanishing, over the mountains, of the 'Forty-mile Bush'—once a favourite Buller source of huia—Buller's *Supplement* to his famous book described how 'Huia loves the mountains, but is driven down by the cold in winter to lower forests'.

No huia made it to Papaitonga's aviaries, and thus none to the tapu islands for which, presumably, they were intended. As its exotic water birds fell victim to State Farmers' guns, Buller's picturesque fantasy got caught in the conflict of ideologies. There was no love lost between Buller and the fiery Minister of Lands, the highlander John McKenzie. His response to learning how Buller had managed to get his lake in Mua-upoko's forest was a Royal Commission, its costs to be paid for by Kēpa and Mua-upoko. Its interminable hearings ended with a completely confused Commission castigating Buller for the harm he had done Mua-upoko, and handing it to the courts to sort out. McKenzie followed it with a Bill suspending all Horowhenua titles, mortgages and leases such as Buller's. None of the protracted court battles produced any evidence against Buller. But McKenzie had exacted his own vengeance:

> The beauties of the Country are to be opened up! The Minister of Lands does not love Sir Walter Buller . . . To let the public see the kind of man who, owing to defect of Liberal legislation is still at large, it has been decided to form a road into the Muhunoa [Papaitonga] Lake, and what is better for the public, and worse for the owner, to carry a road around the lake. Landowners will learn it is not well to fall out with those in power . . . The natural scenery gives the value to Sir Walter Buller's 12 acres. The Minister, foiled in his attacks, sent a survey party to lay out a road round the lake, so as to spoil its natural beauties. He was informed that apart from the vandalism, a road could not be made under £20,000 and would be of no service. To this he retorted to the survey officer, 'I don't care what it costs, so long as I spoil the looks of it'.

In the event, the only damage was a few trees removed so the surveyors could line up their theodolites. Ever since 1895 anyone looking at a title plan of Papaitonga would have seen Buller's name and the straight line boundaries of the block he obtained from Mua-upoko. But just as visible is a chain-wide surveyed strip and the facts from the *New Zealand Gazette* about the 'Laying off of Roads' around the lake, and the government's taking of land for the purpose. But while McKenzie held any legal power in the matter, the lakeshore was not really Buller's—it was Mua-upoko's, the phantom of Kēpa's naive and fatal belief that, as they had eventually resisted Ngāti Raukawa's claim on their eel lakes, they could resist the Pākehā's.

Over his head in debt to Buller, Kēpa died the morning after the final verdict upheld his right to have sold Papaitonga. But not until Buller had had him alter his will to sign over everything but his military regalia—and Kēpa had whispered his final ōhakī, a tragic, ironic urging for Mua-upoko to keep their land from the Pākehā. Eventually, early in 1899, Buller was able to re-register his title to Papaitonga, and at a May auction just before he left for England, acquire the rest of the slice of the plain in which it lay.

Weeds grew over the aviaries, the kiwi experiments were abandoned and stock wandered through the rescued forest. Buller's 'specimens of Maori industry' showed that totara ruins are not as easily preserved as Italianate marbles. Bert Richards saw them after the dream had faded: Te Takingā the pataka, Nga Rangi-ō-Rehua the burial canoe, Te Ranga the huge, ancient Te Arawa war canoe lying half sunk, Te Karere-a-Māhuri the smaller canoe rotting on the lake shore. By the time the truck from the museum in Wellington came and took them away, six years after Buller's death, to where they are today, they were all deteriorating rapidly. Bert watched as Te Ranga was cut up into three bits and dragged out with a steam winch: 'The Roera boys came across from Kikopiri, and paddled each bit to the winch for them. They were war-whooping and having a great time.'

———————

Sir Walter Buller's theatrical screen of forest around the lake was enough for it to seem that he lived in a landscape still undefiled by humanity, a wild forest stretching away from his oasis of manners, but not to absorb the realities of the new neighbourhood. By the time of his death faraway in England in 1906, Papaitonga was already showing the signs that cause its Māori kaitiaki to say it is dying.

On a late summer's day, it is hard to believe this is the same deep, clear lake in the forest where W.G. Adkin took his family picnicking little over 100 years ago. The tree ferns they admired are still there, but now the water they hang over is merely a shallow film. It is *water* that made the landsnails what they are, the wai Māori that makes Papaitonga the richly diverse place that attracted early people here and, for centuries, sustained the thousands who inhabited its edges. Water in which every season the hinaki herehere, intricately woven weirs of supplejack and flax, caught the tuna-heke in their hundreds as they set off each autumn to spawn in much warmer and infinitely more dangerous waters—somewhere, it is believed, off Fiji. Water is also the reason that Mua-upoko, unaccustomed to muskets, died the way they did. Without the lake and its islands, Walter Buller wouldn't have hankered after this land. Yet, without his protection, private and priveleged as it was, the ancient kahikatea forest would never have been kept from the State Farm.

In 1912, 69 years before the government bought Papaitonga for a scenic reserve, Buller's son Leo came back from England to sell his dead father's estate. His friend, the local MP Willy Field, lobbied the government to buy it. But the flurry of telegrams—*Buller leaving for England Friday naturally anxious regarding Papaitonga . . . What is position please?*—was in vain. As Leo packed, a surveyor taking soundings out on Papaitonga was discovering how vulnerable sand country lakes were to farm drains: 'The lake is very shallow . . . The bottom consists of fine soft mud, and at the time of my visit there was a stiff breeze blowing and the water was very dirty . . . drainage operations were carried out some time back but the water level of the lake began to fall in consequence and they were discontinued . . . the Horowhenua County Council Engineer has taken levels towards the sea from the lake which go to prove that the lake could be drained if a large drain were dug through the swamp.'

Ever since the arcadian imagery of the placards for the Village Settlement—*the lovely lake . . . admirably adapted for Regattas, the charming sea beaches, the great forest covered ranges of hill and mountain, the most entrancing of picture landscapes . . . the abundance of fish and game within a few minutes walk of the town*—the sand lakes have been some of the Horowhenua's key assets for the European culture. The government's surveyor had no doubt Papaitonga was 'a desirable National undertaking'. But he recommended against its acquisition as a reserve—for it to survive as a lake, he believed, either the entire belt of sand country in which it lay would have to be obtained, or a dam built right across the big swamp, Repo-roa. If the government wanted scenery, there were 'other less costly sanctuaries' on which to spend its money.

Mua-upoko have reason to believe that the health of their lakes depends on what happens upstream and reason to see its health in spiritual terms. Mua-upoko saw their lake's life-support system ravaged when its forest vanished in the 1890s. They are seeing it ravaged again a century later as, to meet market gardeners' demands, bore after bore is drilled down into its water-table. Comparing maps since the 1890s and aerial photos, as they optimistically sand-bag illegal farm drains downstream, Papaitonga's conservation managers have revealed a stable lake up until the 1940s and then substantial retrenchment since horticulture and bores have proliferated. As Papaitonga's kaitiaki grow more and more anxious, 'underground water scientists' insist the impact on Papaitonga is minor, but to anyone who understands the lake as part of a greater living system, and the water that flows across the sandplain from the mountains as its mauri, the profligacy with water rights is slowly killing it. Papaitonga will only survive as a lake, says the Mua-upoko tohunga Joseph Tukupua, if its intimate connection to the mist and rain of the Tararuas is cared for.

All through the 20th century, engineers have been forcing the sand-plain's streams out of their beds, out of any flaxy hollow where nature had intended water to lie, until the plain's drains match the patchwork grid of the surveyors' plans. Yet all the time, voices have been calling for care of Papaitonga that, in our culture, only the government can provide. If Papaitonga is to reach into the next century as a place for kererū, eels and landsnails, we have to find ways for them to persist alongside human land-use. They must have prospects beyond the fences, and someone will have to take a stand for the processes and life support systems that underwrite their existence. The key will be water.

<hr />

Driving north. A glowing western sky. The evening traffic is heavy on the sand country straights so we turn off to the lake. At the fence the children run under the silhouetted trees in a race to The Lookout, to savour the moment when the sun fills the swampy hollows and Papaitonga becomes a temple of light. Suddenly they stop, immobilised by the close rush of wings above their heads. Gliding onto a low branch just out of reach, a ruru pauses, looks penetratingly at us and flies off silently into the forest.

There was kinship in that split-second encounter and the sense that the bird had seen us before, yet only this time made its move. A moment of revelation that it was a shaman, besieged in this last trace of a once-wild, forested sweep from here to the mountains. 'A fountain of energy flowing through a circuit of soils, plants and animals' as Aldo Leopold described it. Something, he said, we can see, feel, understand, love or 'otherwise have faith in'. Yet something in which being a wild animal has, because of us, become a very different matter for that ruru than for its ancestors.

As the children disappear down through the trees and out across the flax, and the forest settles down again, I think of the many years it was before I realised what the intimate presence of nature—other, wild, species—in my own childhood had meant. The power of places like this is how they keep alive the possibility of people being what Aldo Leopold urged: ordinary citizens and members of an ecosystem. Certainly few on this plain are. Few ever give a thought to the other species on it, let alone its life as an ecosystem, how to tell its story and mind it.

Papaitonga was once described as 'religiously preserved'. It is not surprising that some cultures see other species as spirits—that ruru, to many Māori, are kaitiaki. Western culture in countries 'hitherto undisturbed . . . where civilization is inevitably and legitimately spreading', has long used a religious term for places like this. It has believed, as Walter Buller hoped here, that 'the only chance that native wild life'—like New Zealand's 'archaic birds'—'has of surviving is if it is possible to establish a Reserve or *Sanctuary* of some kind in the district concerned'. Like the root sense of religion, conservation at its most profound binds us back to the sources of energy that are the source of life. Not that we can recreate Leopold's fountain of energy, but we can go back through history to rediscover that ultimately it is only courtesy of *other* life, other species, that we inhabit the world.

Leopold on the other hand, believed that ultimately the human struggle to maintain biodiversity is going to be won or lost in finding ways to coexist with agriculture's domestic ecosystems. As the humans in a new landscape gain an understanding of the 'processes by which the land and the living things upon it have achieved their characteristic forms (evolution) and by which they maintain their existence (ecology)', they begin, he said, to think in terms of 'duties to ecosystems'.

For a demanding society that sees land as a trade commodity, that has always told itself how little history there is in New Zealand, anywhere that conserves what nature intended is a revelatory place. Yet in landscapes like this where the protected pockets of wild nature are far smaller than the range of key species, the business of conservation is beset with enormous problems, not the least of which is the exclusionary way it, itself, operates.

Radical a century ago, the Papaitonga of Walter Buller's imagination still limits ours. Buller had a fine-tuned sense of scenery, just as he knew an immense amount about huia and kererū. But his imagination responded no more to the jig-saw puzzle of their ecosystem than it did to the prospect of Papaitonga as an auspicious Māori place. Perhaps because it was the missing piece in Darwin's theory, the missing piece in Buller's jigsaw—the really creative force was that little-understood array of species (humans included), processes and relationships we know as *biodiversity*.

Deteriorating, tapu, tiny, with no room for mistakes, how do we do justice to such contested ground? Do we perceive it as a crucible that has shaped how we think about conservation? As one of New Zealand's most precious lowland forest wetlands? As a mere bit-part of a wider ecosystem of which most needs to be rebuilt? Or as it is labelled, a *scenic* reserve, a late Victorian art form, perpetuating Walter Buller's fantasy as the first scenery preservationists wanted? Should we first listen to history, learn to recognise a travesty when we see one, and re-interrogate the past for ways forward? Do we then embrace the landscape Ngāti Raukawa imagine, Mua-upoko's emotional, sacred one or the even more mythical, people-less one before history?

It is a century now since William Pember Reeves called Papaitonga a 'sacred wood'. If a sacred place is, as Gary Snyder suggests, one that helps take us out of ourselves, one in which, as we enter, we make contact with the real world, Papaitonga is undoubtedly one. It could be yet another century though before it is renowned for such qualities.

If any place holds the prospect of rediscovering what it means to belong to the greater, sacred community of nature, it is not going to be in mountain national parks but here in the lowlands where we spend most of our time. Yet it seems hard to imagine that a culture as seduced by creature comforts as the one that came up the railway in the 1880s to remove nature will ever develop a reverence for it and then translate that reverence into practice. Our scientific enquiries into the natural world and our determination, so explicit here, to banish the wild as primeval and useless have shrivelled more ancient, spiritual intuitions. Even when we recognise our intimacy with the other life about us, we now struggle to express it. Part of Papaitonga's magic, though, is that just before it was too late the colonial paradigms about nature's fate shifted, a healing tide flowed against its annihilation and an example of nature's design for the land survived.

We can hear the sea as the sun slides away behind the islands and the birds go silent. Walking back through the dark trees I think how so much of this country is changing so rapidly. Except, possibly, the way kahikatea's leaves decompose when they fall in the forest, its fruits ripen each autumn and its kererū flock to them. Before we reach the fence we can hear the traffic again.

CHAPTER FIVE

THE HEAD
OF THE INLET

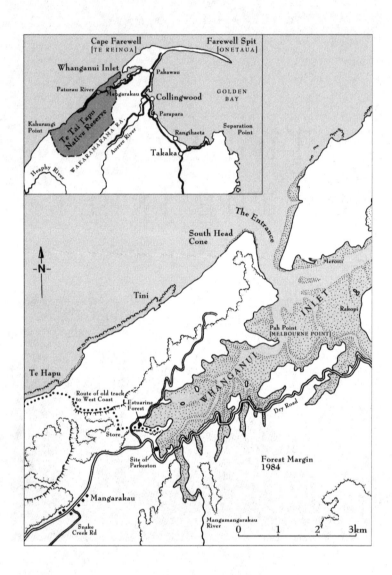

Cape Farewell
[TE REINGA]

Farewell Spit
[ONETAUA]

Whanganui Inlet

Pakawau

Paturau River

Mangarakau

Collingwood

GOLDEN
BAY

Te Tai Tapu Native Reserve

Kahurangi
Point

Parapara

W A K A R A M A R A M A R A.

Aorere River

Rangihaeta

Separation
Point

Heaphy River

Takaka

The Entrance

South Head
Cone

Meroiti

-N-

Tini

W H A N G A N U I   I N L E T

Rakopi

Pah Point
[MELBOURNE POINT]

Te Hapu

Route of old track
to West Coast

Estuarine
Forest

Dry Road

Store

Site of
Parkeston

Forest Margin
1984

Mangarakau

Snake
Creek Rd

Mangamangarakau
River

0   1   2   3km

FIRST THING IN the morning, autumn's light just touching the tips of the forest, the serenity of the bay—to a city dweller—is unforgettable. Only the canoe wake betrays the stillness, and the illusion that the big trees are keeping their distance. Ashore, a heron breakfasting along the band of raupō in front of them wishes I would keep mine. Stepping into a run and flexing its wings in great downward arcs, it sweeps noisily out over the calm water.

I sensed Whanganui Inlet was an auspicious place the moment I first saw it. I keep coming back, not just on romantic, rejuvenating jaunts; more for practical advice from real nature. The inlet has given me a new awareness of the country I live in. Something has survived in its silences, something I'd been taught to believe had vanished like the huia, swept away in the vortex of colonial history. Yet in such tranquility it is impossible to ignore the message that no matter how cautiously I enter, I represent trouble. I'm the marauder, the hunter with shotgun, a lone member of the swarming species.

New Zealand's most low-lying country, estuaries and tidal inlets, has become its most altered. If ecology tells us anything, what's more, the signs are that worse is yet to come. Once, before we brought our farms and towns to this kind of ground, there must have been countless places like it, all around the coast. Had Europeans settled New Zealand in less of a rush—and with less anticipation of a low country spread waiting them—a few more forests of big trees might still stand on its tidal flats.

For all they evoke of the presence of the past, the tall trees are unassuming. Kahikatea, rātā, pukatea—loaded with shiny, flaxen clumps of epiphytes, they appear to stand at the water's edge. But, like the same pattern of plants at Petone that—momentarily—had the New Zealand Company believing their desperate search for a great alluvial plain was over, it's an illusion. At Petone, the low line of forest that seemed to come down to the harbour's edge turned out to be behind an invisible belt of swamps and hollows. Just as unapparent from out on the water, the bands of manuka scrub and sun-bleached raupō and rushes in front of these big trees are actually broader than the trees are tall. Spread between the tide and the trees is a diversity of life we've made a rarity—sea rushes lapped by the sea at one end, shaded palms and delicate ferns beneath them at the other, and in between, a succession of plants, each progressively less salt-tolerant. Yet, unless your gaze is led by the quirks of ecology, you might notice none of it.

Ecologists talk of such places as communities, but any sense of a co-evolved alliance between its plants is more illusory than real—another fantasy about nature, grown from our urge to divide and classify. As easily as our eyes pick out concentrations of colour and texture, we are tempted to see zones and boundaries—as if, to be able to inhabit them, the plants of places like this must organise themselves into something like societies. But the species this place attracts are no more than co-habitors, with a shared affinity for the edges of tidal inlets. What seems coordination, a special natural system to keep the sea from the trees, is revealed on close investigation to be just a collection of plants thrown together by fate and their ancient histories.

The last spring tide has left its calling cards among them: salty, white encrustations like hand-painted bands on every cylindrical rush leaf. Seen from a distance, the bands curve around the head of the inlet like a Plimsoll line. On that kind of tide I could glide the canoe right into the thick of the rushes and step out dry. Not today. Well out from the first line of shore plants, the falling neap tide maroons me in soft, cold mud. Sinking with each step, I slide the canoe toward the trees, leaving a trail infinitely less delicate than the inlet's herons and crabs. In behind the front line of rushes, twigs and logs, feathers, bones, shells and crab carapaces stranded by the tide responsible for the Plimsoll line are held up by the rushes.

This is more than just a shoreline. There seems wisdom and order in this miscellany of life at the land's edge. The big trees are only slightly above the reach of a spring tide, in 'height above sea-level' terms, yet their very existence proves that the sea has not been near them for centuries. White skeletons of manuka mark the sea's most recent push inland—a spring tide, decades ago, driven in by a gale perhaps, ending yet another attempt by the forest to expand across the mudflats. Beneath the gaunt manuka trunks, the vegetation suddenly changes from rushes to salt-stunted shrubs, low and spindly at first, but rising in height with each step inland until you disappear beneath them. Many are coprosmas, almost every one, it seems, bears the large, fleshy, bright green companion leaves of mistletoe among its own tiny-leaved canopies. Underneath the shrubs, young plants seeded from the taller forest trees give you the feeling that, with half a chance, their young would overwhelm everything else were it not for the salty soil. Each autumn, hundreds of thousands of kahikatea and pukatea seeds, flicked by the wind or dropped by gravity and birds, must rain down from the big trees. Yet not one has become a seedling.

A few more steps inland, and manuka's tight, tiny leaves are replaced by a multitude of broadleaved shrubs, small trees and entanglements of kiekie and supplejack. Close to the big trees the floor is littered with jumbled masses of epiphytes that storms have thrown down from their upper reaches. The ground is also dense with kahikatea and pukatea seedlings, but none of the other big tree species. Rātā has an altogether different strategy for perpetuating its kind. Unable to establish as seeds on the forest floor, it has evolved a way of beginning life nearer the sky. Every century, as the old forest ages, rātā is increasing its presence, by germinating its seed among the epiphytes high in the kahikatea and pukatea, establishing a foothold for its vigorous vines to descend. Taking root in the fertile soil, they eventually dominate the old trees. Here in the tree-less tidal zone, the rātā has simply mimicked the strategy on low, shorter-lived shrubs. Strange, multi-trunked little rātā are now scattered through the scrub.

A bit more shoving against plants and I am looking up through lianes of kiekie to towering trunks, arcing palm fronds which reflect deep shafts of sunlight and, far above, masses of epiphytic lilies, ferns and orchids. The damp floor is a sprawling jumble of aerial roots, which rise every now and then in great buttresses. The impression of tropical rainforest is no delusion: 30 million years ago, before the days of birds—when reptiles did the flying and seed dispersal—before the land that has become New Zealand broke away from the rest of the ancient Gondwana continent, it was mainly low-lying like this, forested and tropical. Almost every plant here, and its interaction with others, derives from these tropical rainforest beginnings.

'Primeval' was how Whanganui Inlet was first described to me. Embellished no doubt by the other name in this stretch of country, Te Tai Tapu—the sacred, or as some locals prefer forbidden, coast—the image I created in my mind's eye was of a timewarp, a glimpse of coastal New Zealand before people came. The stories that drew me to it also made me so cautious about its tide that I spent my first evening watching the speed with which it came in, crept up each arm of the inlet, paused, and was sucked back across the mudflats, into its channels and out to the open sea. Next morning, to avoid a stranding, I timed my exploration around the brief hour the inlet was other than a swathe of mud. My reward was to encounter its bay of big trees from the water.

As I floated motionless, surrounded by forest, Whanganui indeed seemed one of those 'safe and commodious harbours' the first Europeans were so keen to find. The bark of a farm dog, cutting through the silence from paddocks miles away on the other side of The Entrance, brought me back to the present. North, beyond Pah Point, the Pakawau Hills lay in blue haze. West, across the emerald calm of the inlet, were the limestone bluffs from whose summits you can see down the West Coast in fine weather. East, different country altogether: low granite hills of beech forest, tried for farms but left in burnt stumps. South, the illusion of fertile plains that is in reality the largely unfarmable scrub and flax-covered peat of Maungarakau Swamp where the inlet used to go to the sea many thousands of years ago. Then, with merely a different ripple, and a flick of the eelgrass under the canoe, the tide turned. Imperceptibly at first, forest began drifting past and I felt the pull toward the swells of the Tasman Sea.

Neck-twisting at the inlet scenery one evening, too close to The Entrance, an ebbing tide did catch me. It was clearly impossible to reach the spot where I'd left the van, so I took the next best option. An hour bent against the flow left me stranded in water too shallow for paddling, and still moving in the opposite direction. Knowing time wasn't on my side, I ran with the canoe until the film of water was too thin to slide it any more. Alternately pushing and dragging, I made it to the nearest landing, the gravel beach of Coal Point, a headland that guards the little bay of trees like a crab's pincer.

Weary from the effort, I sat down and gazed back at my tracks. The last of the sun sparkled off old bottles poking out of the mud, sand-blasted by a century's storms. Two rusted bits of a horse-drawn plough littered the beach. All around them were water-worn jet-black pebbles of coal. Offshore in the mud, I could see the last remains of the jetty from which they were spilt. A primeval place?

Coal Point would barely be 50 metres across. It's nothing much, a low-lying flat of tide-winnowed gravel at the foot of a steep spur, barely a metre above highwater. But in an environment like this, that's enough to focus human interest. Apart from an even smaller flat across the bay, there is nothing else like it in this southern part of Whanganui Inlet. No other shoreline that isn't steep, hard rock. Nothing loose for the tides and winds to dissolve and re-form, breakup or extend. Nowhere else for people.

Whanganui Inlet supports more species of shellfish than any other New Zealand estuary with which it has been compared. Every strandline carries the evidence in the myriad whelks and cockles among the leaves and driftwood of the enclosing forest. They are common enough among the wrack of Coal Point, as you might expect given their abundance in the surrounding mudflats, but strangely outnumbered by pipi which live miles away in the sandy tidal flats by The Entrance. It

SHELL MIDDEN, COAL POINT.

wasn't the tide that brought the pipi shells here. Sure enough, if you look under the rank fescue where recent spring tides have been at work at the edge of the flat, shells, almost all of them pipi, are spewing onto the beach. Following the edge of fescue, my fingers black with the unmistakeable smears of charcoal, I discover most of the flat, here at least, is a shell midden—the rubbish heap of a long-ago settlement.

By the time I return to the canoe, the tide is well on its way out. At a safe distance, a pair of herons stalk the retreating film of water. Feeding like gourmets, they step delicately over what looks like the arcing parallel lines of a railway without rails. Months later, when the railway comes up in the memories of one of the men who laid it out, I can tell him I've seen it—bits of it anyway.

My questions rekindle memories. Countless trucks of white pine for butterboxes, silver pine for posts, bales of flax and woolclips rumbling along now-vanished rails. Flat-bottomed cutters from Nelson with names like *Maid of Italy* waiting alongside the mudflat jetty for men to tip wheel-

REMAINS OF 1930S TRAMWAY, WHANGANUI INLET.

barrows of coal into their holds. Stories of hard miners and boatbuilders. Songs echoing off the bluffs. Mudflat rugby matches when low tide and Saturday afternoon coincide. Billy Addison clearing Coal Point's bush to build a shed and yards. A century on, his posts and rails, a saddle even, rotting into the leaves of another forest. The potatoes that grew so well on the little flat, and the pipi shells that digging for them brought to the surface. 'The Maoris,' said someone, 'had been here.'

Just because the land has revealed something to you, however, doesn't mean it can be easily explained. Lying in the mudflats at Coal Point, there is a perfect circle of round stones—the trace, undoubtedly, of someone's efforts. Archaeologists I have taken to see it have walked around and around it, photographed and puzzled over it, but in the end we were none the wiser. Every one of its thousands of stones—all quartzite from nearby rivers, hard as you can get and infinitely more rounded than any stone in the inlet—was gathered and brought here. Precisely why, though, remains a mystery. I've heard people argue it is the collapsed foundation of an ancient Māori fish trap. Others insist that despite its perfect symmetry it is nothing more than a pile of ballast from one of last century's coal cutters.

Reading the landscape—like using a tiny net in a big river—you can catch only some of the infinite detail. The rest is washed away beyond memory and possession. Unequivocal facts are elusive. As Whanganui Inlet becomes a place where respect for nature means withdrawal, it becomes a place of contested values. It attracts my senses with its primeval, land-before-people meeting of forest and water—yet amiably unhidden, as though last century was yesterday, is the abundant sign of its human history.

Nevertheless, you wouldn't see an environment like this in Europe. Even in New Zealand, for such a large tidal inlet to have sneaked through the 19th and 20th centuries completely un-urbanised is an aberration. That's why so much of Te Whanganui has been designated a marine reserve. Assuming some moral duty to minimise human presence, the government that has more often got behind the campaign against nature has brought logging to a standstill and reserved the last forests, and is now doing the same to the inlet itself. That has upset those who had grown used to 'backblocks' subsidies like the 1930s Depression labour that carved the Dry Road around the inlet, and used to 'the Haven' as their unfettered domain, who have known it as a place whose hills have smouldered in the search for gold and coal and the creation of pasture—or, as the urge took someone once, just to rid the place of wasps. They know well of the endless succession of flax, timber and cattle that has gone down the inlet to sailing barques, scows and steamers. Now they are being told this is one of New Zealand's very few estuaries still in its natural state. Soon after the talk about a marine reserve started, they put a sign up beside the Dry Road:

> WESTHAVEN HUMAN RESERVE
> No
> BIRDS, D.O.C. OR BIRD BRAINS

They are being overtaken by the growing passion for nature that is drawing more and more urbanites like me to seek the last traces of the original land. With nature now more novelty than nuisance, an out-of-the-way territory for quiet exploitation has become sudden wilderness. Curiosities in its primeval shadow, the tramway rotting into the mudflats and the shell heaps of the vanished people who called it a sacred coast, seem less important to those grappling with the prospect of a sustainable future than the notion of an unpolluted, native estuary.

Frederick George Moore liked to call himself 'the first white man in West Whanganui'. His wasn't a planned arrival in one of his New Zealand Company's 'spots of natural advantage'. Almost as soon as he arrived at Port Nicholson in 1840, he was off, heading out of Cook Strait to seek the Taranaki the company said was of such 'great importance to explore'. Blown south in a gale, he went for the gap that suddenly appeared in the cliffs south of Cape Farewell, and found himself in a 'good, smooth, landlocked harbour with sufficient water, reasonable holding ground and grand scenery'. He took a sample of 'the best coal found in New Zealand', whacking bits off the veins that stuck out of the mudflats like rows of black teeth. He claimed it was a place of fertile soil, and he didn't neglect to add that his West Whanganui 'will one day be deemed one of the best ports on the West Coast of the Middle Island'.

He imagined the life people led in such an environment:

> *In the waters of the harbour and on the shores of the adjacent*
> *coasts there was a plentiful supply of good fish—mussels, pipis,*
> *oysters, crayfish, etc. ducks of all sorts abounded while . . . the*
> *forest and bush was full of pigeons, wild pigs, kakas, woodhens*

*and song birds, food everywhere for the simple catching . . . plenty
of edible fern, raupo roots and nikau. With on all sides a charming
fairylike landscape of hill and vale clothed in great beauty and
profusion peculiar to the more fertile lands of N.Z. Here Rewi
and kind family were face to face with bountiful nature free as
the winds, well housed and apparently happy and innocent of the
crooked ways of civilization and its luxuries, they had already
cultivated a garden and had Indian corn, potatoes, melons of
various sorts and some taro.*

It would seem the harmonious scene had been so for centuries Riwai
Turangapeke and his band of Taranaki Māori were only there at all though
by dint of the musket. Of their cultivated plants, only taro—one of the
handful of survivors of the ancient voyagers from tropical Polynesia, and
sole survivor of the gardens of the Ngāti Tumatakokiri, the people the
Taranaki Māori had overun merely a decade before—had not come by way
of 'the crooked ways of civilization'. Ngāti Tumatakokiri's gardens, if not
the traces of where Moore said 'they had built and fortified a pah', lasted to
merit a mention on an 1860s miner's map. A new forest grows over them
today, but from the same sunlit clearings, Pah Point marijuana is now slipped
away to markets as lucrative as those that fired Moore's enthusiasm.

European interest in Whanganui Inlet has the haziest of beginnings.
The Māori-Pākehā beach whalers at Tory Channel were rumoured to have
gathered its coal well before 1840. Moore's 'West Whanganui' lingered on
as source of easy coal and a site for gatherers of rural Māori statistics, but
no town or port arose. His account of it in 1840 is no more than a roman-
ticised, late-in-life reminiscence. He knew full well that what he had escaped
in Britain was already streaming ashore with the New Zealand Company:
'God spare the Maori from such fates . . . and the Colonists from grasping
all the land, the unjust seizure of which, by the few privileged is the source,
beginning and ending of all human poverty and misery over the surface of
the Garden of Eden.'

As the only harbour along Te Tai Tapu, the stretch of coast where
Europeans first realised New Zealand was 'a very fine country'—and already
inhabited—the inlet came within the reach of some of the most influential
European explorers. Abel Tasman didn't detect much promise in the 'very
high double land' he saw from somewhere off Punakaiki in 1642. And if the
West Coast terrain changed as they travelled north, the impression of a

'very desolate', unpeopled domain did not. Then, north of Kahurangi Point, everything transformed, and from the lowered coast 'about a mile from the shore, in various places we saw smoke arising from fires made by the natives'. In 1992, 350 years later, a spate of sand-dune erosion at the mouth of the Turimawiwi River briefly exposed one of the kāinga: a series of huge stone ovens with shell heaps nearby. At almost every rivermouth or gap in the cliffs from Kahurangi, past the inlet's entrance to Onetaua, or Farewell Spit, are the traces of other Ngāti Tumatakokiri kāinga—Kaukauawai, Raukawa, Te Wahi Ngāki, Patu Rau, Te Hapu, Rākopi, Kaihoka.

The Dutch sailors' mile offshore was close enough for the entrance to Whanganui Inlet to be invisible. Had they noticed the break in the cliffs that saved Frederick Moore and the low-lying country that the Frenchman Dumont D'Urville's sailors discerned beyond 185 years later, the explorer's imperative would have taken them in out of the swell. They would not have been surprised to find it occupied. Abel Tasman had been told to expect 'many excellent and fertile regions', and 'well-populated districts in favourable climates and under propitious skies'. Had the *Heemskerck* and the *Zeehaen* entered Whanganui, they would have been challenged by cousins of the same people who, a few days later on the other side of Golden Bay, were to frighten them away from New Zealand with fewer on board than when they arrived.

D'Urville's enthusiastic sighting of Whanganui Inlet was in 1827, the year of Ngāti Tumatakokiri's demise. A glimpse of flat land beyond the swell and breakers at The Entrance compelled a closer look:

> *We believed we could see on the coast a vast basin capable of offering a good anchorage, and I had great hope of being able to enter it next morning to examine that part of New Zealand . . . M. Gressian mounted on the cross trees to obtain a more exact view, He assured me that the basin was very extensive, but, unfortunately communicated with the sea only by a narrow channel, completely barred by breakers. I was consequently obliged to renounce my hopes of entering. We gave it the name of 'Harbour-barred'.*

Had there been calmer seas and a convivial meeting on the mudflats, and with Dumont D'Urville's eloquence, Whanganui Inlet might have become a very different place in the European imagination.

As Barry Lopez, the American nature writer, says, what you think of a landscape you're travelling through depends on your disposition to it, what you imagine and know of it. Frederick Moore could afford, in 1840, to describe Te Whanganui in words that almost pant with excitement, to honour its inhabitants' way in the world, free of prejudice, to tell it as he thought it was. But by the time the New Zealand Company had someone take a serious look at it, six years later, candour of that kind was not so easy. Even with recognition of the short supply of the wide, alluvial spaces of coastal New Zealand in 1839, idealism persisted. By 1846 though, only a few of the company's settler crowd were still deceived.

Land disputes with Māori had erupted at every new settlement. A British government inquiry, three years in the effort, had established that only a minuscule fraction of the 20 million acres the Company claimed in Cook Strait had been fairly acquired in the first place. Almost everywhere the Commissioner, William Spain, went, Māori challenged the Company's title. And from Tuamarina in the Wairau, Te Rauparaha sent the bluntest of messages—22 dead settlers, including a Wakefield—not to take more land. Yet demanding, uppity settlers continued to arrive to find their promised land unsurveyed or non-existent.

At Petone in 1840, the swampy, forested, impenetrable edge of the land had been an unpleasant surprise. To Charles Heaphy, though, its towering kahikatea trees quickly came to symbolise the colony's most fertile soils. Inevitably, a remark on some promising piece of ground would refer to the 'lofty pine wood . . . that appeared to occupy the whole breadth and length of the Hutt Valley'. Heaphy's West Coast journey with Kehu and Thomas Brunner has become famous as an odyssey of eaten dogs and sodden, exhausted spirit that for sheer privation rivals anything in colonial history. Early in the trip, they came through the gap from Golden Bay into Te Whanganui. Kehu, Kai Tahu and former slave who was showing the way, was no doubt apprehensive at entering others' territory.

The tide was in when they reached the inlet and a Ngāti Rarua family cutting flax offered them a canoe ride. Gliding across the channels, the meeting of tide and trees would have been more beautiful than any Heaphy had seen. Given the picturesque Mount Taranakis and coastal profiles for which he is remembered as colonial artist, we might expect him to notice the 'charming, fairytale landscape' that struck Frederick Moore, and so moved a goldminer, Harry Washbourne, a few years later: 'When I first saw the Inlet, I thought it the most beautiful scenery I had ever seen.' Yet his journal contains nothing more than a terse mention of the 'long and tedious walk' across the mudflats which the canoe enabled Heaphy's party to avoid.

Heaphy had more than scenery on his mind. A harbour of hospitality for his friend Frederick Moore was to him a gauntlet to be run. 'Either by cajolery or bullying,' he seethed, 'they consider the traveller a fit subject for plunder, and leave no method untried.' The very same 'kind' Māori Frederick Moore was still envying 30 years later—so kind that by the time he sailed away, their chief's daughter had been 'made *tapu*' for him—were to Heaphy 'the most extortionate natives' he'd ever met. As they slipped past Pah Point in 'Captain Cook's' canoe, a chief flourished an axe at them. Furious at the sight of its Pākehā cargo going by without his permission, Niho, a leader of the invasion 20 years before, demanded they come back. Calling for money, another canoe-full of men, alerted by all the yelling, quickly appeared. Paddling fast into shallower water, the travelling party got away. Avoiding the muddier bits—as they would have learnt to do— they were forced to slip and slide the last few kilometres 'along the flats of the southern arm to its termination'.

From a distance, you wonder just where in the surrounding wall of forest Heaphy and his party 'ascended the hills'. He would have glanced up each arm of trees that reached into the inlet, wondering what problem might confront them next. Only 25, he was already a skilled observer of new country. He would have known these sorts of hills and that their 'birch' trees signalled impoverished, useless clay soils. Alert for any prospect of the level country likely to give 'superiority over the owners of ordinary land', to his eyes each new valley of grey mud would have meant the possibility of a river and its attendant alluvium for farms.

Mud-spattered and no less relieved than Heaphy to reach the forest, I am soon stepping up into the same worn groove of clay they did, and vanishing, like them, between the trees. Kehu would have known about this one ridge out of the inlet that kept you clear of bluffs, liane-filled gullies and trouble—the old track which generations of pounamu carriers came down on their return from the West Coast. Soon, hundreds of gold-seekers would hurry along it, until the settlers cut their zigzag over to Te Namu on the coast, and a bullozer funded by the 1950s woolboom, Ralph Irons on the county grader in its wake, cut through the ridge and scraped out today's road.

Following Kehu up the ridge of his escape, Heaphy would have looked down through the trees at the tide sliding out of the inlet. It is, to me, one of the most beautiful sights on the New Zealand coast. Perhaps by 1846, though, the looker-at-land had had enough of muddy inlets and the wet thickets that clung to their edges, or was holding optimism in reserve for futher south. 'The hills nearly all around it are too steep for cultivation otherwise in the native manner,' he wrote, 'with the exception of a flax valley of about 2,000 acres, at the southern extremity, there is little land available to Europeans.' Available and cultivable, in those days, to an agent of the New Zealand Company anyway, was one and the same thing. Where Frederick Moore is the fascinated new chum, Heaphy is the jaded inspector of a land-use and occupancy survey, in peripatetic mode in awkward, incompletely mapped country. Something more important was over the horizon: the final coast remaining unwalked by Europeans.

'The valley of the Wanganui' turned out to be one of the very few areas 'of a nature that would render much of it available for cultivation' that he saw on the entire West Coast. Even so: 'It is not worthy of the attention of the Company; but possessing the advantage of a contiguous harbour, may, ere long, be settled by squatters.'

It is surprising that the New Zealand Company hadn't sent someone like Heaphy to check out the inlet earlier. Perhaps at that early juncture they couldn't raise settler interest in a place so wild and harbour-barred— until, that is, the jolt of Spain's report in 1846. Spain deemed illegal harbour after harbour, coast after coast of the Wakefields' deal with Te Rauparaha, on Kapiti Island in 1839. 'I was particular in my enquiries of Rauparaha,' he said, 'as to what lands he had sold to Colonel Wakefield on the Middle island as well as the Northern Island.' In only one place was the New Zealand Company's holding not disputed:

> ... while he acknowledged the receipt of a considerable quantity of property, he would not admit that he had ever sold or intended to sell any other place than 'Taitapu' by which name the Natives, I believe, designate a district in Massacre Bay, forming part of the Nelson Settlement.

But what stretch of country, precisely, was 'Taitapu'? Names, as Apirana Ngata once said, can be like charged particles. The knowledge of why this coast was given such an auspicious title, whether its name means sacred or forbidden, and just where it reaches, is in the mists of time. To

Spain, Taitapu was an unknown space with a Māori name. The remotest of Te Rauparaha's Cook Strait conquests, it may not have been much more to him either. Was Te Rauparaha, to get some of the newcomers' guns, selling them a harbour he knew their sort could use, but as far away as possible? Or, angered by their purchase of Whanganui-a-Tara from Te Ati Awa without his authority, had he sold the fork-tongued Englishmen his version of a pup?

On the first sketch maps that emerged from the first surveyors, 'Te Tae Tapu' is a very specific and distinctive district. What Charles Heaphy called 'the sandy beaches and low hills of the Taitap country' begins at the inlet and its limestone coast and suddenly ends at the 'precipitous cliffs' of granite just beyond of Kahurangi Point. The Taitapu of Tamihana Te Rauparaha's account of the 1820s tribal massacre, however, is more like what today is Golden Bay: 'So the killing went on along that coast as far as Whakatu, Waimea, Motueka, Taitapu and even to Whanganui. The descendants of mankind were decimated, the remnant being as mere castaways left as slaves.'

More reliable, and the proof I think, is his uncle's proud recital in 1839 of the places he had conquered a decade before—so fatefully interpreted by the Wakefields as a land sale. Recalling Te Rauparaha's passion for the new guns, Jerningham Wakefield wrote that he 'dictated to me the native names of all the places on both coasts to which they had any claim, whether by conquest or inheritance. The operation took some time as I made him repeat some of the names several times in order to write them down clearly, and as he showed me the position of each on the map.' As carefully as he listed the 'six single-barrelled guns, five double-barrelled guns, . . . twenty muskets', the spades and axes, the flushing coats and trousers, shaving boxes and razors, the young Wakefield meticulously recorded each one. He began with the most distant: 'Taitap, Wanganui, Onetaua or Cape Farewell, Pakawao, Takaka, Taomiti, Motueka, Waimea, Okatu, Okapuerka . . .'

Rankling at the list of mispronunciations, Te Rauparaha's biographer, Patricia Burns, considered Taitapu a general name for Golden Bay. For it to be so, though, Te Rauparaha would have had to have made a mistake—the only fumble in an otherwise geographically perfect sequence from the West Coast to Canterbury.

As clearly as he named it as the piece of the coast from Whanganui Inlet south to Kahurangi, and distinguished it from Golden Bay localities like Pakawau and Takaka, Te Rauparaha insisted he'd sold Te Tai Tapu. He and Te Rangihaeata told Spain they'd parted with only two places: 'Taitapa, in Blind Bay, forms the solitary exception to his denial of any sale of land to the Company's agent. Rangihaeata has also . . . admitted having disposed, by the transaction at Kapiti, of his rights in Wakatu, in Blind Bay.'

Te Rauparaha was just as insistent that the list he'd dictated to the Wakefields in 1839 was of the Cook Strait places he'd acquired by conquest, not a sale list. It was three weeks before the Wakefields sensed they might have been duped. Jerningham Wakefield noticed how 'ill at ease' Te Rauparaha looked the next time they met and he came on board the *Tory*. Looking his brother William in the eye, 'he asked for some grog, and then took an early opportunity of stating, in the most bare-faced way, that he should sell some land to the vessel from Port Jackson as he wanted more guns, and had only sold us Taitapu and Rangitoto; that is Blind Bay and D'Urville's Island!' Even then, the Wakefields were anxious for confirmation. Obliged by the weather to shelter at Kapiti two years later, William's other brother, Arthur, his Māori not much better than Jerningham's, 'visited Te Raupero and Hiko who acknowledged positively the sale of the Taitap to you in 1839'.

'Run no risk of misleading others,' the New Zealand Company directors had cautioned the Wakefields. As 'the Taitap' began to trip so easily, if perplexingly, off New Zealand Company lips, it became an emblem of the confusion and chaos around their land purchases. While Te Rangihaeata's Whakatu became the site of Nelson, Te Tai Tapu, after Spain's

Te Matu, The Great Wood of Motueka, SARAH GREENWOOD, 1852.

verdict, became Massacre Bay, or Golden Bay as we now know it. Te Rauparaha's Ngāti Toa were paid for agreeing to their 'full and final giving up and making over' of their claim to 'Taitapu'. Takaka and Motupipi chiefs received money for land at 'Whanganui'. No one from the inlet country was there.

Once the New Zealand Company took hold of a piece of level ground, their surveyors and axes didn't wait for land commissioners. No more than their squatters—Frederick Moore and Charles Heaphy among them—waited for proper title. Revered forests like Te Mātu, The Great Wood of Motueka, and The Wood of Nelson appeared briefly in the earliest paintings and plans and then were gone. With them went the centre of the Māori landscape that Dumont D'Urville so admired: the food-rich country of edges—kahikatea woods, flax swamps, coastal lagoons and rivermouths. Aggrieved, Tasman Bay Māori argued to Spain that they had stipulated the Company retain Te Mātu as well as 'the pas and cultivations'. Spain was unmoved, saying that quite sufficient of the forest had been allotted to Native Reserves. When Governor Fitz Roy issued the Company a land grant, Māori were allocated 10 per cent of the land, yet all they were allowed to keep for their own use were

> . . . the pahs and burial places, and grounds actually in cultivation by the natives situated within . . . Wakatu, Waimea, Moutere, Motueka and Massacre Bay; the limits of the pahs to be the ground fenced in around the adjoining houses, or huts without the fence; and the cultivations, being those tracts of land which are now used for the natives for vegetable productions, or which have been so used by any aboriginal natives of New Zealand since the establishment of the colony.

Even then the Company objected. Their appeal to the Secretary of State for the Colonies slashed native reserves in the Town of Nelson, for example, to a quarter of what Spain had allowed.

Beyond the gaze of settlers, Whanganui Inlet's forest remained as Frederick Moore saw it, 'clothed in great beauty and profusion'—and still in native hands. Only 10 kilometres away as waders fly, another estuary and its new grid town, Collingwood, was proposed as the capital of New Zealand. Within eight years of Charles Heaphy dismissing 'the valley of the Wanganui' as no place for Europeans, the Superintendent of Nelson, Mathew Richmond, was trying to acquire it. Its 'importance . . . to the

Nelson Settlement', he wrote to the Governor, 'can scarcely be overrated'. Not only did it 'extinguish the Native title to a tract of land . . . needed to complete the Nelson Block', but 'more especially, it contains those elements of wealth and prosperity to the settlement which I brought under his Excellency's notice.'

What Richmond meant, of course, was minerals. And the longer they were known about, 'the more difficult it would be of acomplishment . . . for I found the Natives had already been aroused by the reported value of the minerals upon their land, and if they were advised that it would be more to their interest to retain the ownership, the present opportunity might be lost of acquiring it'. When indeed the Whanganui Inlet end of the block was purchased, Richmond's clerk, John Tinline, instructed the surveyor Thomas Brunner, to lay off a tiny 10-acre 'reserve' for one of the Ngāti Rarua chiefs. Before he did, he was asked to 'consult with the wishes of the Native Matiaha as to whether he will prefer it at the small pa called Toiere, on the south shore of that harbour, where he is now living, or on the opposite side of the harbour where he has got his cultivations'.

Richmond was 'grieved to find so many pas deserted . . . so miserable in appearance . . . so few inhabitants'. Unable, he alleged, to 'resist the appeal' of the old peoples' reluctance to leave the places where they had buried their fathers and children, he 'promised that reserves should be made for them'. Tinline saw the result three years later. 'With reference to the native reserves in general,' he reported from Massacre Bay in 1855, there was 'a universal feeling of complaint amongst the Natives on the subject. Not only is it asserted that they are too small, but the limited and undefined powers over them of the Natives in occupation gives much dissatisfaction.'

It was far from a lone observation. Te Rauparaha, said Frederick Tuckett, considered the 'profession of reserving lands for the Maories was all gammon, humbug and lies'. It was just another of the Wakefields' duplicitous devices; any philantropy in it was for the Company's settlers and speculators rather than the natives. Te Rauparaha wouldn't have been in the least surprised that, over a century and a half later, his descendants and other Nelson and Wellington Māori are still trying to get fair market rent for their 'Tenths'. Others in the 1850s however still clung to the idea of separate areas for what Donald McLean, the government's Chief Land Purchase Commissioner, called native 'subsistence'. Regardless of Tinline's observations, McLean was gazetting 44,000 acres for the purpose. Te Tai Tapu Native Reserve, he said, was:

> *... more a provision for their future wants than as needed for immediate cultivation ... together with what they elsewhere possess, of sufficient extent for their present and future requirements, even if they have a considerable increase of cattle and horses ... it is situated within natural boundaries, requiring no outlay for surveys, and lies on a part of the West Coast as yet remote from European settlers, but which the Natives were particularly anxious to retain.*

When Ngāti Tama, for example, signed for the 'one place excluded from . . . sale and reserved for our use, viz., the land beyond the Wanganui, commencing at Mangamangarakau; thence to the sea side at the westward; thence inland to the first ridge of the hills which look eastward to the sea', it was with agreement that the government could make roads through it for themselves and European settlers.

All colonisation, says the ecologist Paul Colinvaux, is aggression. He has invoked the principles of ecology to explain the way humans, like virtually no other species before, have spread over most of the world, and the imperative of 18th- and 19th-century Europeans in particular, to seek out new lands so distant from their home territory. Rarely does goodwill or benevolence on the part of the coloniser allow any of the sought-after resources to remain with the colonised—as when Britain, at the height of its imperialist powers, included the notion of 'reservation of lands for the benefit of the natives' in its plans for New Zealand. Most 'history', Colinvaux argues, happens according to rules at which no ecologist should be too surprised; one thriving culture wrings wealth from the land by cleverness and industry, needs another's land to swell its success, and goes and gets it. Colonisation is simply the natural process of niche expansion, a successful invader establishing a foothold in a new space, multiplying numbers and driving out the resisting culture. As any pā landscape reveals, Māori, by the 18th century, were well used to it.

The origin of the New Zealand Company's reserves idea lay in Edward Gibbon Wakefield's attempt to distinguish his *Theory of British Colonization of New Zealand* from imperialism's murderous behaviour in the American and Australian colonies—to add some colour, as Keith Sinclair has said, to the view that his company was a humanitarian venture. Māori were peripheral to his vision of a reproduced England, but he allowed that, if confined to small sections in each settlement, Māori would benefit from the civilisation around them. Few Europeans, even those close to the Company, saw much virtue in the reserves idea. When Wakefield's brother hastily left England, without the Company's much-sought government charter, he was no less an agent of empire heading to what was seen as a primitive darkness than anyone before him had been. 'If the advantage of the Natives alone were consulted,' his fellow directors' Instructions cautioned, 'it would be better, perhaps, that they should remain for ever the savages that they are.'

The 'Sacred Coast Native Reserve', as we could call Te Tai Tapu, was British colonisation of New Zealand at its most benevolent: 80 per cent of the total acreage of Nelson Province that was set aside for Māori use—12 times the combined size of all the native reserves (few greater than 50 acres and none larger than 200) that would be set aside on the entire South Island West Coast. More surprisingly, it was set up at a time when its inhabitants, Taranaki people in the main, were leaving the coast of their 1820s conquest. The 'striking contrast' that Charles Heaphy noticed in 1846 between the people of Whanganui Inlet and those elsewhere in Golden Bay lasted barely a decade. Heaphy attributed the difference to the inlet people 'having so little intercourse with Europeans, the ruggedness of the path preventing them from carrying their produce to market, and the coast being too much exposed for the safe passage of canoes'. Hoani Tatana's family, for example, like most who had come south with Te Rauparaha's taua, responded to the homeward pull of turangawaewae and Pākehā temptations: 'I was born at Taitapu, West Whanganui in 1845. We lived there with Riwai. The reason we left Taitapu was to be nearer Nelson.'

To settlers who saw native reserves as good ground left empty and uncultivated, and the provincial administrators who had to deal with them, this was tantamount to self-dispossession. Alexander Mackay's 1865 census reported only 'about ten Natives living on and near' Te Tai Tapu, or the 'West Whanganui Native Reserve' as he called it, but '. . . others were interested in it'. No matter how 'particularly anxious' its natives had been in 1855 to keep it theirs, their thinness on the ground could not be ignored.

In 1870 the Commissioner for Native Reserves calculated the big reserve had 'ostensibly 120 and five-sixths acres to each Native'; 25 years after his encounter with their extortion, Charles Heaphy was a factor in the landscape again. So many native reserves that came across his desk seemed to have 'been lost sight of', or 'remained unutilised'. The vast and increasingly empty one at West Whanganui was remote as well, and there could be a blessing in that. Better, he said, to have one large single reserve: 'It may not be premature . . . to draw attention to the advantage that would accrue from a consolidation of the more scattered reserves being effected, when practicable, whether by the simple consent of the natives, or if necessary, by legislative enactment.'

What its Māori wanted to do with it was, by 1870, the least of Heaphy's concerns. Native reserve it might be; he preferred the label 'unextinguished' Māori land. While it had 'a few small sheltered areas fit for cultivation in the Native manner', he wrote in his *Report on the Native Reserves of the Province of Nelson,* 'it is chiefly valuable . . . in containing a coal field; which, lying along the shore of the harbour, promises to become much importance'. Practical development of the Whanganui Coal Field, Heaphy advised, 'would subserve equally the Native and public interests of Nelson'. He even suggested aiding it by 'judicious expenditure' of the native reserve trust fund.

Minerals led the first European to his glancing contact with Te Tai Tapu; and over 200 years after Tasman, the same dream of 'many rich mines of precious and other minerals' underlay Heaphy's resistance to Māori sovereignty over it. Within six years of the ink drying on the deed of Te Tai Tapu Native Reserve, gold had been found, it was believed, in 'considerable quantities'. Miners on the Aorere diggings rushed the new field when the Te Tai Tapu's Māori broke the news in Collingwood and demanded each miner pay a licence to enter.

Fearing 'bad feeling and . . . more serious evils . . . between the two races', the government's man at Collingwood immediately pasted up notices warning Europeans against a rush on Te Tai Tapu. In response to James Mackay's proclamation that it was still land 'over which the Native title had not been extinguished', the miners boasted that they were going to mine regardless. While he waited for instructions from the Governor in Wellington, Mackay rushed back and forth from the inlet trying to talk its owners down from a licence fee that, to him, was objectionable. The Governor was simply relieved the West Whanganui natives were willing to permit 'the peaceable pursuit of gold-mining on their own land', so Mackay found himself agreeing to an annual fee of one pound from every miner crossing the inlet. Within a year, Riwai Turangapeke and Pirimoana Matenga

Te Aupouri's compliance had earned them £93, of which £10 10s went on tax and printing the licences. Mackay extracted another £20 to pay the Ngātiawa and Ngāti Tama owners of the southern parts of Te Tai Tapu.

The sudden money had Ngāti Rarua expressing 'their determination', as James Mackay put it, 'not to admit the other tribes to the reserve'. Riwai Turangapeke also managed to get a cart, plough, pair of oxen and two cows for the other 20,000 acres around Whanganui Inlet, payment for which had been been overlooked since the reserve's designation in 1856. Down at the head of the inlet, their new money very soon had another, irresistable demand on it. Strategically placed to intercept any mud-covered miner coming off the inlet, or bush-weary miners about to face it, Riley's Store was as difficult to bypass as was crossing the inlet without a fee. Harry Washbourne said he'd 'seen some pretty rough and primitive places supposed to supply food and lodging for the public, but this one . . . a large Māori whare with a chimney at one end and a door at the other with a bare ground floor . . . stood on its own'. You could buy food here—small potatoes that doubled in price if you preferred them cooked—and liquor.

The forest has crept back and reclaimed the store's site, as it has enveloped the tramway cutting of half a century later. In spring, though, on the sharp, still mornings of that time of year, you might notice, as I did, a sickly sweet, non-native-tree smell emanating from the forest. Long before I saw the big shiny leaves, a furious stream of bee-traffic led me to the laurel tree where Riley's Store once stood. It was low tide, and glinting from the mudflats, at hurling distance from the big laurel, were hundreds of bottles, some still intact. Harry Washbourne had noted a liquid 'in the refreshment line . . . I do not know the composition but it was called "Rum"'.

Well into the 1870s Ngāti Rarua at Whanganui Inlet earned money from goldmining rights to their big reserve. Soon after the gold find, they leased the stretch of country at the head of the inlet to a German, Charles Weisenhavern, for a coalmining venture. Within 16 months, Arnold Pachten, Engineer of the Whanganui Coal Mining Company, had relieved him of it. Over the next seven years, the lease would earn each of Te Tai Tapu's owners —Riwai Turangapeke, Pirimona Matenga, Wiremu Katene te Manu, Wirihana Rauakitua and Raniera Matenga—eight pounds, enough to have cash coming in, and horses.

That, however, is about as good as it got. Initially, Te Tai Tapu Native Reserve almost seemed theirs. Māori control weakened dramatically in 1873, as it did in all native reserves, with the Native Land Court's establishment.

Then, in Te Tai Tapu's case, Oswald Curtis, the Superintendent of Nelson, issued a proclamation bringing the big native reserve under the jurisdiction of the Goldfields Act and out of native authority. In the furious 1880s trade in Māori land, the Native Land Court was a bottleneck: no block could be sold until the Court determined its owners. Inevitably, once it did there were eager buyers. By 1880 Riwai Turangapeke had moved to Motueka and was dead. Yet his and other Ngāti Rarua, Ngāti Tama and Ngātiawa hapu still kept connection with Te Tai Tapu. On 27 October Henare Wiremu and representatives of Ngāti Rarina, Ngāti Pukauae, Ngāti Pareteata, Waipuia, Ngāti Hinewairoa, Ngāti Kurahui and Ngāti Arawaere, submitted a claim for legal title to their land. Within weeks, the surveyor Arthur Carkeek had seen the lay of it and finished his pen and ink sketch. Riley's Store was on it, along with many miners' creek names, and as well as the centuries-old track across to the coast, there was a new, proposed one where today's road goes south to Patarau.

Nothing happened for three years. In 1882 Frederick Moore, with a Wellington lawyer, Alfred de Bathe Brandon, tried to realise his 1840s dream with a new West Wanganui Coal Company. Golden Bay settlers had already selected the parts of Te Tai Tapu's 'locked up and unrenumerative' acres they wanted, knowing that as soon as the great reserve had passed through the Native Land Court it would be re-surveyed into sections and offered for sale. In November 1883 Major W.G. Mair heard the Māori claimants. Carkeek made another sketch map that the chief surveyor ruled sufficient for Native Land Court purposes. Within nine days, it had awarded Te Tai Tapu to them. But the ink on Mair's judgement had hardly dried before a Mr Holmes was enquiring of Alexander Mackay, the Commissioner of Native Reserves in Nelson, about 'the Te Tai Tapu Block'.

While the documents last, says V.S. Naipaul, we can hunt up the story of every strip of occupied land. Preserved in neat copperplate script in a big leather-bound registry book, Holmes' letter was one of hundreds of requests to purchase native land that poured into Native Affairs offices through the 1880s. The actual letter, like the succession of correspondence that followed it, has disappeared. Within six weeks, the request led to Te Tai Tapu's title papers being forwarded to Wellington, to one Alfred D'Bathe Brandon the Younger. Te Tai Tapu Reserve's unsurveyed boundaries and 'vague description' had caused problems before when gold was discovered in the 1860s. The government's native agent at Collingwood, James Mackay, had tried to rectify it with a sketch map of the area. This time not even that would suffice, so Carkeek was sent back to the inlet to get a measured grip on Te Tai Tapu's wild acres. Some of the places he had to haul his iron spikes, mallet and theodolite must have made him wonder at the people who were 'so particularly anxious to retain' such impossible country. The place he named after the only European feature in the inlet landscape, however, was easily accessible.

Finding trig 'Δ Store' today means a scramble through roadside second-growth. Out of sight behind cutty grass, on an old timber-loading platform bulldozed out of the clay, a truckload of fertiliser bags and possum netting awaits the new season's marijuana planters. Beyond it, as untouched and primeval as Heaphy and Brunner and centuries of Māori travellers would have known it, a ridge of open beech forest circles around above the head of the inlet and its big estuarine trees.

After half an hour's climbing in the forest's cool, I'm yearning for a view of the inlet. Just as I'm imagining Carkeek wanting to catch his breath and ease the weighty Victorian theodolite to the ground, the ridge levels off. Walking to the edge, I can see down into the tops of the huge pukatea and rātā beside the mudflats. Beyond them, the inlet stretches away like a lake to his other triangulation points—the old kāinga site on Pah Point and the strange granite knob of Knuckle Hill.

I run my eyes over the forest floor, kick a few brittle branches aside, and there it is, a piece of round iron, no wider than the few centimetres poking out of the beech leaves, as though he had whacked it in only a few weeks before. I bend down and touch it. In answer to the European needs in the antipodes—definition, distinction, difference—surveyors like Arthur Carkeek moulded and manipulated the landscape itself as much as our perceptions of it. Most places where they lined up and hammered in their pegs were never the same again. Here it's as though everything has stood still. The same ancient trees under which he stood and drove this spike into the clay make the century or more between him and me seem but a moment.

On the Crown Grant that Alfred D'Bathe Brandon secured from the Governor in 1885, Carkeek's carefully measured lines revealed Te Tai Tapu Native Reserve to be twice the size it had been thought. According to the prospectus of Taitapu Gold Estates Ltd, the government was paid £10,000 for it. Brandon had been a director of the New West Wanganui Coal Company, the failed venture of Frederick Moore, the so-called 'first white man' at the inlet. The syndicate of buyers behind him, politicians in the main—'influential members of both Houses', as the local newspaper described them—quickly resold it on the London market for £110,000. Floated on the London Stock Exchange as a mining proposition, it attracted 300 shareholders.

For a century, a succession of land speculators, mining and timber companies stripped and logged most of what had been Māori reserve, and subdivided its coast into farms. By the 1970s it was rare to see a valley still forested right down to the sea anywhere in New Zealand. Surveying from the air because the loggers refused them entry, ecologists found that Te Tai Tapu still had some. When the logging rights expired, exactly 100 years after Alfred D'Barthe Brandon got his Crown Grant, the government paid the last Taitapu Estates Ltd $650,000 for what was still left of it in forest. In the following decade other pieces of land subdivided off by the company, but still in forest, were rescued—including the estuarine forest at the head of the inlet. Then, along with the vast wilderness of Northwest Nelson's mountains, they were included in the new Kahurangi National Park.

History, however, ensures no neat ending. The descendants of the first settlers who had been waiting for bits of Te Tai Tapu for farms say the 'the Taitap was sold twice', first in 1839 by Te Rauparaha and then again in 1883. They also believe something shady—'insider trading, call it what you will'—happened in 1883. The Māori, they say, were done out of their land. There is no doubt that Ngāti Rarua were offered money, and that, somewhere along the line, someone else made a lot of it. Harry Moffat, who had an early miners' store in Te Tai Tapu, said he advised Ngāti Rarua against selling. Then, he says, someone approached the government, a syndicate came in with a better price, 'the block was put through the Native Land Court, and the purchase was made'. Yet the descendants of Henare Wiremu, Rore Pukekohatu and Tapata Harepeka insist none of the 2/6d per acre—or £10,000—went to any Māori. With money of that kind, you don't have to rely on government archives for a record of it being distributed, to whom and how much. In Te Tai Tapu's case there is nothing. Until it is sorted out, they don't want any of Te Tai Tapu in any National Park.

Other Māori though, had also been at the 1883 Native Land Court hearing. They had spoken about Te Tai Tapu and a connection between people and place that made that of the Ngāti Rarua claimants seem as brief and ephemeral as the land-grabbing Pākehā, but more brutal.

N A T I V E   L A N D   C O U R T ,   N E L S O N ,   1 8 8 3 :

I claim Te Whanganui because I am descended form the original possessors. I claim on behalf of the hapus I belong to. I occupied previous to the time of fighting. They fought without warning or provocation. Ngati Rarua with Ngati Toa came over . . . The conquerors allowed some of the conquered to live of whom I am representative. If they had killed them all, they would now be able to have undisputed possession. There are other witnesses who are descended from the survivors.

Hoani Mahuika, like the others who spoke, came from afar—the Manawatu, the Wairau and Westport. Wirihana Maui recounted: 'I was taken as a slave to Wairau and have not returned. Some of our people lived as slaves at Whanganui to Motueka.' Few denied they had been conquered, but as one said, 'The land was taken without cause. Our fires were on the ground when we were conquered.' The Ngāti Rarua claim on the inlet country made members of this hapu feel they were being denied part of their reality and they wanted the Court to know some facts.

Most of the canoes that had brought about Wirihana Maui's people's destruction were not of the tribes making the claim, but of Te Rauparaha's Ngāti Toa. Yet to Meihana Kereopa the mean facts of the 1820s conquest meant little: 'I claim the whole. I claim through my ancestors who had possession before the conquest. My mother and I left through fear of being eaten. This is the first opportunity of claiming.' The inlet country was filled with symbolic meaning, but so obscure had his own tribe become that he had to distinguish himself through others with descent from Kurahaupō waka: 'I belong to Rangitane, Ngātikuia and Ngāti Apa . . .'

Many Māori by the 1820s dealt with the new European influence within their own tribal boundaries. Others, determined to occupy distant territory, now had the technology of wholesale slaughter. The muskets of 1827 were so effective that, by the 1880s, virtually no one called themselves Ngāti Tumatakokiri. Every authoritative voice told me it was an *extinct* tribe, yet a tiny handful of people still call themselves so today—some who have found their way back along the slender threads of history to the inlet of their ancestors. Little has survived of their time there. Unlike other more settled shores, the marks of people on this coast are quickly scoured away by tides or hidden in returning forest. Yet the evidence in the ground, in place names and karaka groves, dispels the myth that has persisted in local histories ever since Heaphy's sparse 1846 Māori head-count, that Te Tai Tapu was 'forbidden territory'.

An old man eking out his last days in the remains of the Pah Point kāinga was the only Māori living at the inlet in 1899 when the first white settler, John Richards, finally got his bit of 'the Taitap'. But Richards would have seen plenty of evidence that another culture had been here before his. Digging a post hole back in the 1930s, his son Jack came across a lump of obsidian the size of a football. Hidden nearby in a limestone crevice was a bundle of unfinished adzes. Jack's daughter, Joyce Parkinson, remembers her childhood task of scooping bucket-fulls of grit for the chooks from the Māori shell heaps. 'Up and down the beach there were piles of blackened and broken stones, and heaps of pipi and other shells in many places along the sandhills from the Paturau Rivermouth to Gilbert Richards's house . . . below the old Paturau river bridge there was a band of broken shells a foot deep.' Some heaps were huge, with species that must have been carried miles.

The karaka trees growing only in certain places, inevitably near shell heaps, didn't escape their notice either. Kati Wae Wae have inhabited the West Coast, Te Tai Poutini, for three centuries, yet they acknowledge the planters of the karaka groves along its northern reach to be the people their ancestors tried but failed to conquer. Like the Ngāti Rarua, Ngāti Tama and Ngātiawa people who claim mahinga kai along Te Tai Tapu, they attribute karaka and shell heaps to Ngāti Tumatakokiri.

Unless you coincide with a couple of carloads come over from Motueka for kaimoana, or someone checking out their interest in Rakopi and Tauaro, the tiny bits of the inlet still in Māori hands, you don't see many Māori on this coast. Some of the descendants of those who supplanted Ngāti Tumatakokiri believe Te Tai Tapu to be an ancient name of great mana. Its meaning, they think, lies in the limestone bluffs carved by ancient sea levels and rivers flowing acidic out of beech forests between Kahurangi and Raraka Tana, the South Head of the inlet. And in the high, dry caverns in the forest where, every now and then, settlers chasing stock stumbled over burial remains. There is nothing to show that before the mining and logging it was in any way a Māori place, yet almost everywhere people could live—beside water, out of the wind—are signs.

South of Whanganui Inlet, Heaphy encountered merely some 100 Coasters in 1846. Only a tiny number lived between the inlet and the next habitation at Kararoa, way to the south beyond Punakaiki. Abandoned taro and kumara gardens between Te Whanganui and Kahurangi suggested more had, but not enough to alter Heaphy's grim impression of the West Coast as 'uninhabited', 'one long solitude with forbidding sky and impenetrable forest'.

Until recent archaeological evidence from Bruce Bay in South Westland, there was little to counter this view. A few excavations well south of Whanganui Inlet, at the Heaphy and Buller Rivers, revealed a coastal profusion of small, local subsistence economies centred around fishing and birding, including moa-hunting. These early southern people depended more on local, native plants and animals than on gardens. Most of their needs from the forest—tree fern pith, young fern fronds, the tiny fleshy fruit of the podocarp trees, kahikatea, matai and rimu, and a host of other foods and materials—would have been available from its edges. As well as forest birds, they hunted mollymawks, shags and shearwaters, and from the lagoons and estuaries, eels, grayling and whitebait. Fur seals along with shellfish were gathered from the shore, but judging from the remarkably few fish remains, these people rarely ventured off the beach.

The picture now emerging of the first Coasters is that they were here early in the era of migration from tropical Polynesia, and that marine resources, offshore as well as littoral, were a significant component of their diet. They are likely to have had trading connections with the warmer, more populous north, and they had a strict preference, like Aotearoa's other early settlers, for the environments to which humankind has always been inclined—rivermouths, lagoons and estuaries. It conforms to the prehistoric settlement pattern throughout Polynesia; evidence so common around the lagoons of the more intensively and earliest settled islands like Tonga that it is 'considered by Tongans as part of the soil itself'.

Te Tai Poutini is certainly not Tonga. When people began settling the west coast of Te Wai Pounamu, probably some time between 1200 and 1400, the country was considerably warmer than today. Yet far easier living environments, still little exploited, existed in the warmer, subtropical north and drier east. There was little of the pressure on resources that, two centuries later, began forcing weaker tribes inland and south into colder and less desirable environments. For long periods, every year, it must have been a bleak, trying coast to live along. Why then, were these early bands of people here?

Some who have pondered the question say the answer lies with moa-hunting, the function ascribed to the Heaphy River site when it was discovered in the 1960s. Perhaps a better reason lies in the one esteemed resource unique to the West Coast.

One certainty of Pacific history is that the original colonisers of The Great Harbour of Kiwa have always been great cultivators and traders, their plants, objects and materials constantly muddying the boundaries of European concepts like Melanesia, Micronesia and Polynesia. They came to Aotearoa with a reverence for stone and an abiding need for it. From their earliest geological surveys came stones surpassing anything Polynesians had seen—tangiwai, pounamu and pākohe. Contrary to the idea that pre-19th-century Māori were many separate nations with no sense of these islands as one entity, esteem for the new stones quickly spread their entire length and breadth.

Most revered of all, giving the great southern island its name, was pounamu. Trade and exchange systems in pre-musket Aotearoa hinged around it. Every piece of pounamu that ever swung from an ear or neck, or became an auspicious adze or mere, came from Te Tai Poutini, the West Coast. Some undoubtedly travelled to the northern markets by canoe, the Coast's wild seas notwithstanding. For many, though, pounamu was so precious it demanded safer passage. Unless they travelled east across some high pass in the Southern Alps, the bearers of pounamu faced two equally arduous options: through Northwest Nelson's forbidding mountains, or along their western coast, parts of which are so exacting they are still in the wild state. Some took the route that countless tourists now take as the cut-and-benched, bridged and hutted Heaphy Track. Most took the so-called Poutini or Greenstone Trail, swimming their precious cargoes across the same rivermouths and lowering them down the same, scary flax ladders of Heaphy, Kehu and Brunner's Great Journey.

The passage of pounamu dominated the stone trade, but it was more than a south-to-north affair. Other kinds of stone, usually shaped into the adze forms some archaeologists call Archaic—to distinguish them from the more recent Classic—have been found along the West Coast. Almost without exception they are of varieties of pakohe that have been brought south from D'Urville Island and around Nelson. Only along Te Tai Tapu, the Coast's northernmost reach, has stone from outside the region—obsidian from the North Island's volcanic country—been found.

Trade routes need control points and vigilance. Anyone moving pounamu along Te Tai Poutini had to pass certain places where the land funnelled movement—or take the exhausting evasive action of weeks in

Miners, Te Tai Tapu, Frederick
Tyree, 1840s.

bleak, wet, forested mountains. The village
that was at the mouth of the Heaphy River
about the year 1400 might have been such a
place. Its inhabitants used argillite from
faraway quarries in the hills behind today's
Nelson. They were strategically positioned
to see anyone coming through, but could
sustain themselves from their surroundings—for long periods if necessary.

Somewhere, north of the mountains,
closer to the calmer waters of Golden Bay
and the populous coast across Cook Strait,
there had to be another site like it. The location was obvious, as Harry
Moffat, an 1870s goldfields storekeeper, knew so well: 'Then comes a tidal
inlet eight miles long to be traversed when the tide is out, then you come to
a deep, wide channel and you are dependent on a Maori seeing you bringing
his canoe to ferry you over.' Even when only a handful of people inhabited
Whanganui Inlet, as Heaphy found in 1846, it was almost impossible to
avoid being challenged and charged to cross. Many miners who did try its
deep, dangerous channels were swept out through The Entrance and
drowned.

There are periods when Whanganui Inlet seems just too bleak for
human comfort. But only half a day's walk away are the rich mudflats and
relative shelter of Golden Bay. Weather notwithstanding, you would expect
the West Coast's largest inlet and its ecologically diverse environs to be an
important Māori place. Archaeologists have revealed plenty of shoreline
habitation, but nothing comparable to the Heaphy River site. Onaira Noa,
where Niho put the frighteners on Heaphy's party, may be such a place. As
its European name, Pah Point, suggests, its cliffs' sheer drop to the water
would have been perfect for defence. You can see the ridge of the pounamu
trail meeting the mudflats. But you'd need to be closer to intercept anyone
coming down it.

When what longer-lived locals call the Dry Road was cut around the
inlet in the 1930s Depression, the men with picks and wheelbarrows took
away a spur in its southeast corner. A few telltale white pipi shells can still
be seen slipping down the road cutting and in the returning forest, but what
was perhaps the biggest Māori site at Whanganui Inlet was destroyed. Phil
Skilton saw it in 1913, before the gorse came with the road gravel and covered

any bit of bare ground: 'You can see bits of it still, at the head of the Haven. It was a big Maori settlement, a really big one.'

Everyone who lived at the head of the inlet knew the other shell middens too, on the only two bits of flat ground at Parkeston and Coal Point. Parkeston was never much, a place of stores where the tramway out to Pah Point met the mudflats, where people gathered, used the post office, got drunk and set off again. Gooding's Guesthouse was the focus for miners from the Golden Blocks, and

PARKESTON, FREDERICK TYREE 1890S.

Golden Bay locals like Phil Skilton and his mates on pigeon-shooting trips. Phil was keen on the Goodings' daughter, Sue, who always knew where the birds would be, around the mudflats in the same kahikatea forest she and her sister gathered tiore, the delicious, white flesh of the kiekie flower, better than any vegetable—even those from the shelly grit of the old goldminer Joe Malone's fantastic garden, walled up against the big spring tides.

Parkeston is but a few bricks and rails in the scrub today, yet it attracted people in a way Pah Point didn't. And to anyone as observant as Ken McKenzie, it was evident others beforehand had thought likewise: 'The Maoris, they'd been there before us. The whole place was one mass of shells and charcoal.'

Ken's parents last dug their garden just after the First World War. Their house, like Joe Malone's and the Gooding's, has long gone. But digging beneath the rank tall fescue, I find mutton chop remains still lying in the shelly soil where they were tossed out among the vegetables and buried. Below the depth of Ken's father's shovel, undisturbed for centuries, are tightly packed wads of shells and charcoal, identical to the middens across at Coal Point.

Were they all just summer fishing camps or gardens, or something else? For anyone needing to keep an eye on things, and live well while doing so, the head of the inlet was a perfect site: a sunny, north-facing spur with a view of the ridge off the inlet, two guarding pincers of flat land and, right alongside, a kahikatea forest full of birds. I can imagine the sentinel eyes, the ready canoes and the now-vanished knowledge of the sheet of water that came in and out each day, controlling everyone and everything.

'Working the tide', Jack Nicholls always called it. His life revolved around its cycle—before cattle were mobbed across the inlet, when 'the Taitap' was all forest and thick coastal scrub right down to the sea, and all the flats were white pine and pukatea, when the children at Parkeston had to swim the inlet with horses to get to one or other of the saw-mill schools. His horse-drawn coach, *The Mudflat Express*, had an 11-year run till just before the Dry Road went in in 1937. 'Never once caught by the tide', he carried whatever needed a ride, in whatever weather. 'Close to it on many an occasion, but just kept ahead. On one occasion I had to leave three women passengers, mail, anything perishable in Fisherman's Bay. Then I bolted through to Parkeston with the empty cart, standing on the handrails in the deep places.'

He sits on the edge of the worn-out pakihi terrace in the sunroom at Collingwood's geriatric hospital, wheelchair positioned seaward. It is cold and showery outside. Every time the sun breaks through the cloud over the Whakamarama Range, he looks up from his hands and squints out the window as it briefly illuminates the mudflats.

He reacts straightaway to the photos I've brought, especially Frederick Tyree's one with his father and other flaxies in front of the Parkeston store in 1904. Nicholls had recently arrived from the North Island, was just about old enough for his first job helping with the carpentry at Prouse's flax mill and the wharf. He was there when the *Marora*, a big, three-masted intercolonial windjammer, came into the inlet to load white pine from Mangarakau Swamp for Australia. A scow had to tow it. Each trip the *Marora* loaded 250,000 feet of the tall timber. He looks emotionless at old photos of men perched on wagons of flax fibre and posed beside steam winches. But his eyes light up again at my own photo of the big kahikatea and pukatea at the head of the inlet: 'Pigeons . . . always there, every time.'

Few other memories have survived his stroke. Ten years before I met him, a romantic foray had him chasing a lady to Australia, his only long spell away from the mudflats. He treated his homesickness by writing the past into long letters to Joyce Parkinson, daughter of his old friend Jack Richards. How he came to 'the Haven' when Prouse and Saunders' swamp timber and flax operation had cut out in the Horowhenua, and they'd moved it, tramway and all, across Cook Strait.

The tramway, predecessor of the one whose remains lie in the mudflats today, was the settlers' lifeline: 'All the saw and flaxmilling gear came in by steamer, also all the draught horses that pulled the trucks along the tramway . . . After the timber and fibre boats ceased to come to . . . we used to charter the Fairburn, a scow, to take our wool to Wellington once a year.' Occasionally the tramway had another purpose. 'There were three Scotsmen at the Blocks in those days and when we celebrated the Coronation of King George and Queen Mary the three Scotties arrived and led the parade down the tramline from the school to the huge sawdust heap where the doings were held. The bush and hills rang with the strains from the pipes.'

Jack loved dancing. But with the closing of the Golden Blocks mine in 1912, the accordion player moved on and the dances at Maungarakau stopped. Then in 1919 even the mill closed, ending regular supplies from the timber steamers, *Waverley*, *Kennedy*, *Kaitoa* and *Waimea*. When the post office closed in 1925, Jack and *The Mudflat Express* got the mail contract.

Other than the tides and practical details like the tramway rails Prouse and Saunders brought across from the Horowhenua swamps being rewarewa, or honeysuckle—a tree which, while common up there, didn't grow around here—Jack's letters don't mention nature much. When they do, it's not about forest fragmentation or vanishing wildlife: 'We had plenty of boats in those days and used to do a lot of fishing so fish was plentiful on the menu. When the tide was in we used to go floundering in the Inlet by Parkeston with Acetylene gas lamps and a spear and used to get plenty . . . Pigeons were also plentiful and open season of course in those days.'

By Jack's time, of course, kererū had been protected for years, with a £50 fine if you were caught with one. But despite the 1895 law, the Golden Bay *Argus* announced shooting seasons on kererū and kākā well into the 1900s. Today, even though all over the country kererū are dying faster than they are breeding, there is talk again of allowing them to be hunted. They are still common at the inlet, perhaps because of the amount of forest that's survived—a shadow of what Phil Skilton knew though.

> *When I first came over to Westhaven, before Benara came, the flats right down to Patarau were all white pine bush—big whopping trees. It was just a natural forest. Prouse and Saunders had bypassed it and were milling rimu for house timber. What pukatea they could get they were taking for cheese crates.*
> *When I went back on the Dry Road in the '30s, the white pine had all gone. No more pigeon tucker. And no more pigeons.*

The Road to Paturau,
MANGARAKAU, 1950S.

Benara had taken the lot.
    No wonder the Maoris like that
tree. We used to eat the fruit ourselves.
In autumn, the ground was covered
with them, but you would never eat the
blue end-bits.

At 93, not long before he died, Phil's family
took him over to Westhaven for a last look.
He could hardly recognise the place. The
swampy flats at Maungarakau were still
there, but gone were the tall, close trees
blocking out any view. Everything seemed burnt or covered in gorse, a plant
that had not been there at all in his days. He suddenly realised what he'd
taken for granted: 'I wasn't bush conscious in those days. It was everywhere.
Everywhere. And most people hated it.'

In autumn, before the 1820s and the musket, Phil Skilton's 'whopping
great trees' would have been frequented by people with snares. It would
have been the same in early summer when rātā flowered. Some trees would
have had special names. Under strict tapu, the forest's mauri would have
held sway, its mana protecting the forest's fertility and fruitfulness. Once
the mauri was awakened by rites, someone would have been here every
day, climbing trees, checking snares, removing birds and resetting them. So
long as the snaring season lasted, one local iwi, Ngāti Kuia, prohibited their
bird snarers from eating any kererū during daylight. Ngāti Tumatakokiri,
their tribal relatives, would have evolved their own rituals here—techniques
and protocols that have vanished with them.

In 1827, in a bay head very much the same as the head of Whanganui
Inlet and not far away, Dumont D'Urville was struck by the difference
between the 'funereal silence' of the hill forest and the coastal flats 'so full
of life'. Te Whanganui's inhabitants, sentinels for the stone trade perhaps,
would have known its subtleties: coastal flats were alive with birds because
that's where their preferred food plants were. When agriculture took away
the mosaic of forest edges and swamps, the whole country fell silent.

Surrounded by settlements for centuries, the grove of big kahikatea
and rātā could have been burnt anytime. Kahikatea swamp forests may look
wet, but despite what some ecologists say they are extremely inflammable.
When Harry Fisher felled and burnt the Prouse's hill block above the head

of the inlet in the early 1920s, the updraft created by the fire sent burning heads of kiekie vine up into the sky. Driven by the nor'westerly, they drifted inland, over the bluffs, setting Maungarakau Swamp burning for weeks.

Once when I was at the inlet, a farm fire, whipped along by a southerly, got away in the manuka at Long Gully. I could smell it out on the mudflats. Heating up, it raced across Maungarakau Swamp and into old kahikatea and pukatea—the last, sad survivors from the days before Benara Timber. Crackling and spitting, oblivious to the water beneath, it swept through the cutty grass beneath the big trees, and up their cloaks of kiekie, the updraft bursting out and incinerating every crown.

By the 1930s most of New Zealand's kahikatea had gone. Virtually all the lowland swamp forests were cleared, and Australia's dairy industry was also getting its white pine from the central North Island. Benara, an Australian company, leased the timber rights from The Westhaven Harbour Land, Coal and Timber Company. 'This is the only place in New Zealand where there is any quantity of White Pine left,' proclaimed their 1933 prospectus. Te Tai Tapu, or Taitapu Estates as almost everyone called it, read like an exploiter's paradise:

> A huge rich forest of softwoods, enormous deposits of superior quality coal, auriferous areas containing bodies of rich ore awaiting development, valuable flax and dairying lands and pastoral area . . . splendid stands of White Pine, within one mile of the Harbour, very thick and tall, all on flat lands and valleys— all easily logged. This, in the opinion of experts is the best White Pine timber in the South Island. For five chains, each side of the mill there is half a million feet of standing timber . . . one conti- nuous block of White Pine, in wonderful condition for milling.

To move the wood to Australia, Benara needed a new tramway. Ron Walker and his mates, Harry Harvey and Harvey Fisher, were taken on to cut sleepers and lay it—12/6d a day, but only on the days they worked. They laid the Maungarakau Swamp section first and then moved home to Pah Point—or Melbourne Point, as it was now called. Ron's wife, Ivy, daughter of one of the original tramway's teamsters, had grown up there. When her mother sang in the garden, everyone could hear her—as though the inlet was an opera house.

Cut wherever they could be found, the hundreds of sleepers were laid along the line of boulders that had held down the tramway's wooden predecessor. Many have since been eaten away by the mudflats' toledo worm, but some still have even their bark intact. 'We got them out of the bush as we went—eight foot long and eight inches by four. Yellow pine if we could get it, birch, rimu mostly. A long muddy job. Always wet-footed. Getting home when the tide chased us.'

The estuarine forest at the head of the inlet was too far away for its trees to be felled and was close enough for its pigeons to be on the menu, although it had plenty of long, straight timber. Its kahikatea and pukatea would not have withstood the toledo anyway.

No sooner was the tramway laid than the *Port Waitaki* was steaming in through The Entrance. Ron Walker and his mates became timber-stackers, working day and night in the rush to fill it, the tides allowing only an hour or two off. One million feet of white pine went out for starters, a forest of kahikatea to be turned into picture frames, kitchen utensils, scrubbing boards and butterboxes for Australians. By the early 1950s Benara had moved virtually all the kahikatea off the Maungarakau flats and across the Tasman. They were boom years for anyone with first call on nature's wealth.

The Cowin brothers needed a road to break in the limestone country they had acquired above the inlet. Wool prices were so good in 1953, just before Benara cut out, that the brothers brought themselves a bulldozer. The county procured a backblocks subsidy to grade it. High above the inlet, in the grader, Ralph Irons almost ended his days there. As he was finishing a steep hill section, his grader started slipping out of the cut. The thick forest acted like a net and caught it before it gathered speed. Once the road was through Don McKay and his Benara felling gang were right behind: 'If you'd told me they'd have had the timber out of there as soon as they did, I wouldn't have believed you . . . You should have seen the timber. There's no longer white pine like that today.'

Were it not for that road, says Don, the estuarine forest's big white pines would still be there. Extracting them took only a few weeks; Don and Ken MacKenzie cutting a snig line through the cutty grass and dragging the big kahikatea out onto the mudflats. 'It was really swampy, but we probably got about 60,000 cu feet from it. Most would have gone for butter boxes. 12x1's, you could cut a lot that way.'

The smaller kahikatea were winched up onto the road, Ken pulling the bigger logs across the mudflats with an old Fordson tractor. The tramway took them to the Mangarakau Mill. Fed from nutrients coming down off the limestone country, the kahikatea were the biggest trees he'd seen. 'Huge logs. Four to five foot through. The bukatea was not the best. Big, but hard on the saws. The salt air off the inlet over the years did it to them. In the end we used them in axeman competitions.' But the saddest fact is that the estuarine forest was never Benara's to log. Ken McKenzie in fact logged his own family's land, for someone else's profit, without knowing it.

'The McKenzie Country', some sceptical locals called the dark forested hills of Taitapu Estate when Ken's father and uncle arrived from the North Island's East Coast to clear them for a cattle station. They came south with enough optimism to buy a bit of the big estate Ken's father managed—and dreamt of farming one day. So often was his father away in the bush that Ken had to carry the mail and man the telephone at the Parkeston Post Office. With the job in those days came inside knowledge of the continous feuding between the settler families. If someone wasn't grazing cattle illegally, they were sneaking out valuable silver pine posts, padlocking roads or trying to stop neighbours getting their bales of flax out. Some feuds boiled over and the police were called.

The McKenzies' dream quarreled into collapse; Ken's father and uncle sold up. But one piece of land, from Parkeston around to the estuarine forest, ended up disputed, with the Public Trust. It was 1989 before it was released. A vigilant conservationist spotted the sale notice, and the newly formed Department of Conservation, having been told nothing like it survived anywhere else, bought it for the nation.

From a distance, the zone of rushes seems to completely seal off the estuarine forest from the mudflats. But behind the smooth waving carpet, a crumpled corduroy track of broken logs lies in the mud. Benara's snig line quickly drives away any feeling you are in a timeless, wild sphere.

Where Ken McKenzie's tractor dragged the big logs, smashing the pukatea's aerial breathing-roots and the great elbows and knobs that snake across the forest floor (some so far from their parent trunk, it is impossible to work out to which tree they belong), is still a line of destruction. Where the big kahikatea stood until 1953, the forest opens out into a wet thicket of punga and cutty grass. It is like finding a jewel box empty, a hole smashed in the glass.

Out on the mudflats, though, the feeling that always creeps up on me is that we are back early last century and I'm the first European to see it. The road and the logger's mess may almost not be there, even when I've just pushed my way from them to the mudflats. There is none of the constant human murmur of other big harbours. With Taitapu Estates' and its loggers gone, there can be hours between motors resounding across the inlet. But this is silence I suspect that people have caused, that would not have existed when the parrots, pelicans, and the host of other vanished birds whose bones lie in Te Tai Tapu's caves, were here.

Years after the Cowin brothers cut the road up to their Te Hapu block above the head of the inlet, Gilbert Richards and his son Bill took it over. Most of their interest was miles away, where Gilbert's father, the first European settler in Te Tai Tapu, cleared the sandy Patarau hills. They still lived in his spartan clifftop house among the macrocarpas; a stock and station agent's calendar on one wall, a print of a storm at Prussia Cove on the Cornish coast on the other, reminders of agriculture's priorities and their smuggler ancestry.

After Gilbert's stroke he'd promised his family he'd never take his old Datsun truck out of first gear. But he still used it to move sheep between the two blocks, traction being such a problem on the climb across to Te Hapu that, until they gravelled it, he drove everywhere with a permanent load of sand on the tray. One afternoon, way out on the mudflats, two kilometres away, I heard a dog barking and a horn echoing on and on around the bluffs. I let it go for a while, then seeing no one, I decided whoever was so anxious to find me was running out of patience. Slipping and sliding across the mudflats, I reached dry land out of breath and pushed up through the cutty grass to the road. Around the first bend, I came face-to-face with a mob of shocked sheep and an annoyed dog. Gilbert was at the wheel behind them.

Way out toward The Entrance, the line of water is coming in again. I start back to where the canoe is waiting, thinking of the things I had not noticed before. Where once I saw only special plants, heard kererū's wing beat and saw its white belly-feathers overhead, I now think also of the people who lie in long-forgotten places up beyond Te Tai Tapu's bluffs: their pipi shells, the tramway, the iron spike in the forest still marking out a vanished Māori reserve. I think of the long time before the first people canoed in through the breakers into its sheltered shallows, or came through the gap from Pakawau and saw it. Then the time of the stone traders up and down it. The generations of fishermen and bird snarers. Heaphy stepping through the mud, and then a new century of forest vanishing. Jack Nicholls with his horse team and the mail. A Polynesian and then a European culture have both brought their thousands, settled and used this place, and then left. It makes you wonder if the 'reserving' of its forests and mudflats will be as permanent as we think, or just time out before another culture has its turn.

I came to Te Whanganui as a biologist, but I needed history to begin to understand it. I misread the inlet until I could see under the skin of its primal beauty to its human layers, feel its intractability, know what it suffered. Without history, how easily primeval fantasies seduce and strand the conservation idea in colonial sensibility.

As its 'first estuary-based reserve', the inlet has a unique niche in New Zealand history. Often in the inlet's silence, I have been conscious of a sense that Te Tai Tapu was never meant to be one of those estuaries where factory waste kills fish, where people dump plastic, disposable nappies, supermarket trundlers and old car bodies, a place so sick people get infected if they cut themselves on its mudflats' shells. I believe there *are* places where the land has expectations we must meet, where people can live only briefly. Perhaps, in the efforts to make the country's 'largest unmodified estuary' a place for conservation, in keeping wild some of the fertile flats that Heaphy called 'available', the sacred coast's expectations are being met.

Certainly it wasn't called sacred in the sense of Benares on the Ganges, so dense in auspicious human events that culture has worn nature away. If Te Tai Tapu was so named, it was patently as a place of nature, the place known throughout the country, before the days of the musket, of whose huia this waiata of Ngāti Toa sings:

> *Ka puihi tonu atu ki te tai-uru*
> *Ki a Tamai-rangi e*
> *Tae a wairua te motu-huia*
> *Ō Tara-rua i runga,*
> *Ki Wairarapa e, ki Te Tai-tapu,*
> *Ki a Te Ahuru e.*

A lament for their home of Kawhia, it reveals that the mana of Te Tai Tapu and its precious groves of life was something known far and wide.

Te Whanganui's hills may be ravaged but biologists say its marine environments resemble the estuaries of last century. And that presumably, along with the lack of urban stormwater, reclamation or trampling stock that's the customary fate of this sort of place, is why it contains many birds like banded rail that are now rare elsewhere in the country, and such a diverse abundance of animals in the mud itself. Its real value though lies not so much in the 6,000 individual invertebrates estimated in each clinging square metre or in the 30 marine fish species that use the inlet at some stage in their life history. It is in the mockery that their intricate ecological networks make of the laws that have rendered the New Zealand coast a no-man's-land between territorial and marine authorities.

No one anymore can explain this coast's 'sacredness' to us. But can any place be more sacred to a culture like ours than a harbour where we can see the flow of the tide meeting unrestrained the flows off the forested hills; where we are ephemeral; where we can see the myriad, unownable processes that nourish an estuary and keep it healthy?

Somewhere near here the culture that came across the world seeking 'Commodious harbours' first discovered New Zealand was inhabited. Maybe, in choosing this harbour to be one coast where we coast-dwellers let nature be, we are finally groping toward a colloquoy with it—one that perhaps Ngāti Tumatakokiri understood. Not as some outdoors museum, holding the past fixed as if in preservative, nor just, as the advocates of Te Tai Tapu Marine Reserve argued, a spawning ground for fish, a storehouse where nature is kept to be used, but as a place where nature's life-support systems are as healthy as they were before us.

I look behind me at the head of the inlet, the dark greens of the big kahikatea and pukatea below the beech forest, and between them and the brown rushes, the brighter green of the raupō, its leaves not quite yet turned by the cool autumn air. They merge with distance into bands of colour. Between us arcs the muddy line of my footprints, another human trace about to slip into history like thousands before it. Beyond Te Tai Tapu's bluffs, a bank of clouds is coming across at the clear sky. Way out to sea another sou'westerly is moving in.

THE SANDPLAIN
FOREST

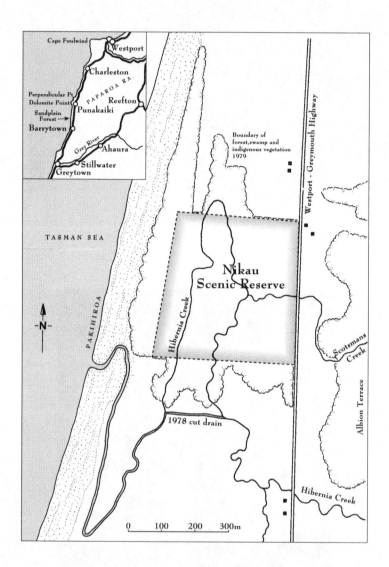

Cape Foulwind
Westport
Charleston
Perpendicular Pt
Dolomite Point
Reefton
Punakaiki
Sandplain
Forest
PAPAROA RA.
Barrytown
Grey River
Ahaura
Stillwater
Greytown

TASMAN SEA

Boundary of
forest, swamp and
indigenous vegetation
1979

Westport - Greymouth Highway

Nikau
Scenic Reserve

Hibernia Creek

PAKIHIROA

-N-

Scotsmans
Creek

Albion Terrace

1978 cut drain

Hibernia Creek

0   100   200   300m

CHAPTER SIX

Very fair travelling today, along a great stretch of beach, in places
great quantities of black sand and garnets, all bush and scrub
down to high water, camped near a Bluff, bad place for fresh
water, had to walk some distance to get it.

WILLIAM SMART, *Diary*, 22 FEBRUARY 1863

T HE WIND OFF the waves whips sand around my ankles. Dotterels
scatter away in front. The sea is menacing, but I can imagine someone seeing what lies landward as just as terrifying. Windshorn so
perfectly a machine could have been involved—a low, inpenetrable forest
confining human activities to the thin seam between it and sea. Under almost
every battered log, seedlings wait ready, like advance guards at a perpetual
frontier. Inland, further from the salt spray, a taller forest, rising in height,
stretches away across the plain to the hills.

Or so it seems. A few hundred metres away, cars hurtle along the
tarseal straights of the Greymouth to Westport highway, many of them
bearing tourists to and from the scenic delights of Punakaiki. On most days,
gazing south from The Blowholes for a glimpse of Mt Cook they see the
same low sweep 'all bush and scrub down to high water' William Smart
saw. A primeval foreground for countless photos of mountains, forest and
sea, it looks as though eagles might still sweep low over its windshorn trees,
and geese and pelicans glide into its lagoons. When the big swells are bursting
ashore, whipping up a salt haze, even from the high limestone bluffs of The

Razorback the sandplain of the Barrytown Flats can seem wild and unentered. Whenever the haze clears, its forest is revealed as no more than an
island amid the surveyed order of paddocks and fences.

Once, land like this was so commonplace that hardly anyone thought
to keep a piece. It's not at all easy any more to imagine the freshly cut and
burnt landscape that rapidly replaced the experience of being hemmed
between wild sea and trackless forest, nor that New Zealand's plains ever
could terrify.

The sandplain has little of the spectacle of The Blowholes and none
of its tourists, and unless ecology (the salvation of diversity, possibility
and potential as Edward Abbey called it) leads you here, no cultural signpost
will. There is not much of it: a few hectares untouched by our 'improvements' for anyone who needs to imagine New Zealand at the very beginning.

In flat country like this we have become accustomed to ourselves
and our consummate, opportunist weeds being in charge, but here our impact
is substantially diluted: a line of gorse and a few pieces of milled and squared
timber amongst the driftwood. Between them native, akeake seedlings assert
themselves—a forest taking its chances, advancing its frontline troops down
the gravel slope where tomorrow a big sea could dowse everything in salt
spray. Either the akeake establish a new forest among the tidal debris, or
the fantastic power of the sea slams into the frontline forces and annihilates
them. To us nothing much has happened. The next morning a beach and a
forest are still there; dotterels still call one another as they have for millenia.

The proximity of seed sources is clearly a factor in the forest's urgency
to be here, but the logs may be the key to creating the ground it needs.
Most of the logs are forest debris, sloughed out of the watersheds of the big
rivers further south. Without them, the artist Michael Smither believes, New
Zealand's sandy, gravelly coastlines would be utterly different. The logs,
he reckons—or more correctly, the forested hinterland that is constantly
supplying them—furnish a dune's or beach ridge's foundation. Working in
concert with storms and tides, gravel and sand, they provide the bulwark
from the sea that enables a sandplain like this to develop. His theory's broad
hint is that the beach erosion taking place all around the New Zealand coast
is the result of the dramatic reduction in log supply since the 19th century
when forest clearance got going in such a big way.

The beach William Smart walked along in 1863 is now forest. Under
brittle leaves, 100 metres inland from the tide, I once found a solid, ceramic
insulator of the sort used in Victorian telegraph lines. The sea couldn't have

thrown it there—the metal was corroded but its glazing was as perfect as the day it was packed. The only explanation could be the line of wire the 1860s blacksand goldminers who followed Smart had strung over headlands and along the backs of beaches between their new towns of Brighton and St Kilda and Greymouth. Smart and his friends would have seen waves breaking where I walk among young tree seedlings, and great piles of logs all along the beach. The sea has added a few more storm ridges since then, and gorse. The gorse turned up straight after his discovery of beach gold further south, with the rush of men who followed. Beginning as hedges to keep stock in, it wasn't long before its tough, yellow seeds got among the tumble of West Coast rivers and currents. Today, along the entire West Coast, one looks in vain for a beach or a lagoon where gorse hasn't squeezed out the locals nature intended for the land's edges.

Yet for a land returning to forest, gorse is a great asset. As an edge-dweller, its pioneering skills leave the natives in its wake. Less than generous in their supply of nitrogen, New Zealand's soils require its plants to evolve myriad ways of converting atmospheric nitrogen into nitrates, but none come anywhere near the efficiency of gorse's root nodules and their resident bacteria. More than anything else, too, it is gorse that keeps people out of the sandplain forest. I had always thought the prickly and almost inpenetrable buffer would keep the beach the quiet, forsaken place I knew. Then one day, looking up from the beach just like William Smart, I saw a swathe wide enough for a vehicle cut through to the forest. I followed a line of crushed trees and broken cobbles to a hole so deep I could see the sand under the beach ridge. A few weeks later a drilling rig appeared on the sandplain, in the paddocks alongside the island of forest.

The drilling began in the middle of plans to amalgamate all the wild country from the sweep of scenic, limestone coast to the Paparoa tops, the Pancake Rocks—and the sandplain forest—in a new national park. Paparoa National Park was meant to close the gap on the one big problem with New Zealand's protected area system; the neglect of lowland ecosystems. One of the few places where the new 'sea-to-mountains' national park actually touched the shore, and a last survivor of a unique lowland ecosystem, there was a passionate campaign to secure the sandplain forest as part of the national park. Once ornithologists discovered how many of the region's birds overwintered in its sheltered basins of lowland forest, the new park caught the imagination of the New Zealand's embryonic conservation movement and soon had the public support it needed.

However, while Paparoa National Park ensured the lowland limestone basins were no longer zoned for logging when it was gazetted in 1987, the sandplain forest—richer in birds than any other Paparoa forest—was not included in it.

Until its forests became a political issue, the Punakaiki coast was known only for its Pancake Rocks and their blowholes. Then suddenly, late in the 1970s, Coasters were pitched against conservationists in a struggle over which parts to keep and which to dismantle and turn, however temporarily, into material wealth. From Puketi in Northland to Haast in South Westland, the Forest Service was besieged by the conservation movement until it relented. Forest after forest labelled 'merchantable' on maps was given up; mill after mill closed. Without this national movement, none of the forests whose towering rimu and kahikatea are now among New Zealand's most sacred groves—Pureora, Whirinaki, Oparara, Okarito —would have escaped the chainsaws.

An ill-conceived government scheme to harvest the region's lowland forests for a giant Japanese pulp mill had catalysed the offensive on the West Coast. When the West Coast Beech Scheme was hatched in the early 1970s, 'the Coast' was the last part of New Zealand in which you could walk in continuous forest from the sea across plains to the mountains. For natural historians it was still a region where scientists knew virtually nothing about whole suites of ecosystems. The government agreed, in principle, to a system of reserves—and some new jobs for naturalists.

Like other scientists, naturalists prefer to think of themselves as paragons of independence and objectivity. But natural history in New Zealand has been a beggar's game ever since its first practitioners assisted imperialist possession of the new southern land by naming its plants and animals. What's studied, what's said to be special, has always had to be tailored to the times. Even Leonard Cockayne, whose exhortation to save 'these sanctuaries from the dim past' must be the clearest fusion of natural science and protection, was party to a Royal Commission recommendation as unanimous as it was powerful, to remove any forest from the productive plains 'forthwith'.

As a consequence, we know a few things about timber lines and offshore islands, but little of the workings of New Zealand's lowland forest ecosystems. From the few traces left, naturalists can only hint at their precarious complexity. When all the land that an ecosystem needs has been taken—as agriculture took the coastal plains—when all the myriad linkages between its plants and animals have been broken, then the ecosystem just isn't there anymore, although its constituent species may survive piecemeal in others.

In the 1970s conservation suddenly became a raison d'être for New Zealand naturalists. Teams of ecologists descended on the West Coast's forests as intricate and forceful arguments were prepared for both logging and protection. After years of careful bird-counting, day after day, season after season, in different ecosystems, patterns emerged that proved what had been suspected ever since Victorian bird-watchers like Sir Walter Buller saw the colony's 'primitive' birds reel at the clearing of the plains: that most followed food and warmth from forest to forest. Some, like kererū, tui and bellbirds, flew miles in search of a meal, completely vacating some inland valleys in winter. If their life-support systems were to be safeguarded, representative slices of the West Coast would not be enough: connecting corridors would also be needed. The key pieces would be the lowland plains and basins—right where the foresters believed the Coast's best timber stood.

The new research showed that each winter the lowland basin whose timber the Forest Service was eyeing at Punakaiki contained more birds than any other area in mainland New Zealand. With other scientists' revelations about the basin's pristine cave system—about to be the site of even more profound ornithological discoveries—the bureaucrats were soon drawing boundaries for New Zealand's first 'sea-to-the-mountains' national park.

THE NORTHERN END OF THE BARRYTOWN FLATS, 1980S.

In fact, it was only possible to burst out of a protected forest onto a wild beach in two tiny places. One was the sandplain forest. It was already conservation land when the national park idea came along, and its mosaic of forest and wetland had the highest winter bird counts of all Paparoa lowland environments. Nonetheless, it was what New Zealand's National Parks and Reserves Authority called an 'outlier': an 'island' of primitive landscape within the human ocean.

By the 1970s too, naturalists and conser-vation managers alike were beginning to be influenced by the lessons from ecological history: that although 'expiring species always last longer on islands', as Walter Buller liked to say, islands, if too small, had their problems. For more than a century the naturalists drawn to islands and their biological curiosities had done little more than confirm what men like Charles Darwin and Alfred Wallace wrote: islands contain fewer species than mainland areas of the same size, and that small islands contain fewer species than large islands. Then, in 1967, two young American ecologists, Robert MacArthur and Edward O. Wilson, published a small technical book whose concerns with the problems of small, isolated populations would lead to the framework of study now known as conservation biology. Their *Theory of Island Biogeography'* was concerned with mainland islands. However, the same principles would, they wrote, 'apply to an accelerating extent in the future, to formerly continuous natural habitats, now being broken up by the encroachment of civilization . . .' Mathematically arcane it may have been, but its essence was simple: two off-setting processes, extinction and immigration, determine the biological diversity of any island.

MacArthur and Wilson's theory appeared at a crucial time for New Zealand's lowland forests. Applying it to the fragmented remains of nature that lay in colonial agriculture's wake, ecologists lamented the small size of most existing reserves and advocated protection of the few large tracts that still survived. Forest birds like kōkāko and kākāriki would be lost, they suggested, from most forest patches less than 2,000 hectares. Their preoccupation with large areas was not unnoticed by scientists and government land planners. Nor was the corollary that the small, isolated 'pocket handkerchiefs' of wild nature that proliferated in New Zealand's lowlands were—like leftovers from someone else's meal—nuisances not worth bothering about.

To check that New Zealand's nature reserves presented 'a picture . . . coherent and representative of the original' to future generations, biologists were, by the 1970s, developing scientific criteria to rank each region's reserves. But size and continuity took supremacy over the type of ecosystem the reserve represented, so by the time the 20-hectare sandplain forest was ranked alongside other West Coast forest reserves, it didn't compare very well at all.

It was years before the significance of sandplain was officially recognised, its new guardians finding it 'hard to understand it was so lowly ranked . . . in the first place'. By then, a national park had been created alongside, excluding the sandplain 'for reason of its small size and isolation . . .'

On 6 June 1984 the persuasive lawyers of a mining company appeared before the National Park and Reserves Authority. The government, they said, would create a problem if it included the sandplain forest in the new national park. They wanted it removed.

One hundred and twenty years after William Smart's excitement at the black sand he ran through his fingers, Grampian Mining, a subsidiary of New Zealand's largest company, Fletcher Challenge, knew the sandplain was one of the best deposits of ilmenite in the world. A succession of companies before them had set up on the Barrytown Flats with plans to mine. This time, though, it looked serious. Moving south from the Punakaiki end, huge floating dredges with underwater suction would completely turn the landscape over, extract and concentrate the heavy materials, and spew the rest back. Out in front, other machines would be felling and mashing the vegetation. The heavy metals would be pumped in a slurry to a separation plant that would extract the precious ores like ilmenite and gold. According to Grampian's data, the highest grade ilmenite ore was directly beneath the strip of forest and swampy creek meanders that was scenic reserve. They asked for its reserve designation to be cancelled so they could prospect— and then mine it. In exchange, they said, they'd be happy to give the government a nearby block of hill country they'd managed to acquire.

Within a few days, the company's lawyers were reiterating to the Director-General of Lands 'the substantial advantages' of the land swap. It could even enlarge the area of the proposed national park, while retaining the sandplain forest as a reserve 'could have the effect of preventing the economic development of the ilmenite resource in that area'. Few of his

West Coast staff had ever been near the reserve, yet a meeting with the company's executives quickly had them persuaded that a small rectangle of fertile flats surrounded by farms had no place in a national park. The man in charge of West Coast Crown land said 'I appreciate their concern', and suggested that the reserve's legal title need not be changed until the commercial plant was built and mining was underway. Meanwhile, even though it might 'generate a lot of "heat" from the conservation groups' he would ask his senior ranger to assess the sandplain forest's 'survivability' and compare it with the hill country offered in exchange by the company. 'We are dealing with hard-nosed businessmen,' he said, 'so we need a factual, unemotional, unbiased report.' As rumours flew around the Coast of the hundreds of people the ilmenite plant might one day employ, he wrote to Wellington asking his head office to do what the miners wanted, and take the sandplain forest out of plans for the national park.

The next time I pushed through the gorse and out of the wind under the strange trees, many were branded with Day-Glo, as though condemned. From others, brightly coloured tapes flapped in the wind. This was more than some duckshooter, shotgun under arm, marking an illicit passage to some secret, out-of-the-way hide. I soon saw there was a pattern to them. The sandplain forest had been gridded for prospecting.

Inland, the mining company's intentions were even more obvious. The evening silhouettes of the nīkau palms had been joined by that of a drilling rig. At the foot of the old seacliff, new buildings rose out of what had been milking yards. Gathering blackberry, an old wooden farm gate lay in the grass where it had been flung by whoever put up the new, high security, galvanised-iron one. The mining company's project manager was living in the old house that had come with the dairy farm, but he said to meet him at the new laboratory.

An arc light lit up the empty yard. Peering inside, I could see a family of sparrows splatter-bombing the huge space's long benches and rows of crudely numbered barrels. Ushered though its sparseness into the city comforts of the manager's office, I soon saw how the numbers worked. Stretching the length of one wall was a gridded aerial photograph of the Flats—the dark tones of the sandplain forest standing out from the light-coloured pasture that surrounded it on three sides. Each numbered barrel contained sand drilled from a grid intersection. And you didn't have to be a mining engineer to read the tracing of circling contours pinned over it. Just as a coastal hydrographer's chart discloses water depth, it spelt out the ore concentrations sand-miners understand. The project manager knew I knew. 'Don't worry,' he said. 'We're going to mine, all right. That reserve of yours could have a $100 million dollars of titanium under it.'

One of the things all New Zealanders should ponder, but few do, is their relation to and attitude toward the coterie of surveyors, land commissioners and balloted selectors that was called 'land settlement'. How its relentless nonchalance about nature left so few areas like the sandplain forest, and how easily it could have left none. Yet other than the reserves ranger at Punakaiki and the few biologists who knew it, no one appeared unduly worried when the miners included the sandplain forest in their licence— regardless of the fact that they had no prospecting rights over it. If they were anticipating a fight for it with the wardens of the nation's heritage, they must have been surprised to find them more interested in having it prospected, and the ilmenite plant up and running, than keeping it in wild forest.

Quis custodiet ipsos? Custodes! Who guards the guards? asked Juvenal, the Roman satirist. In the end, we are our own wardens. Instructed to supervise the cut-lines and drilling, the reserves ranger resisted the very idea, knowing the sandplain forest had been specifically excluded from any prospecting. Soon others were challenging the miners. When she tried to seek evidence of the ease with which the wardens of the nation's heritage would revoke a reserve protection if miners asked for it, the vigilant editor of *Mining Monitor* was told to invoke the Official Information Act. Buoyed by a newly elected government's promise of environmental reform, two biologists who knew the calibre of the reserve took their concerns to the politicians.

The new Minister of Environment and Conservation was appalled at what he heard. Calling an immediate halt to the land swap and admonishing those who had entertained it in the first place, he demanded the sandplain forest be returned to the national park proposal. His Wellington officials had already told their colleagues on the Coast 'it would probably be unwise to pursue any further suggestion of an exchange. . . . The principle is a bad one and clearly the . . . reserve does have qualities which distinguish it from any of the land available for exchange.'

'This matter is turning into a bit of a political hot potato,' Lands and Surveys' man in Hokitika wrote to his bosses in Wellington. He was annoyed at politicians intruding into his domain. Other interests quickly entered the fray. The miners alerted local newspapers to the high-grade ilmenite lying under the reserve. The West Coast Regional Development Council lobbied the new government; the Minister of Conservation was cautioned that he was threatening 'a major industry' and that, until the company actually applied for a mining licence, the issue of the reserve and the impact of mining on it 'are questions which cannot be addressed'.

The bureaucrats tried to argue that the exclusion of the sandplain from the new national park had not been connected to pressure from the miners. The National Parks and Reserves Authority, they said, had 'closely looked at the boundaries it would see as being desirable if a park is to be established'. As a result, it had made a number of changes. One of them was to exclude the sandplain forest. It was important, the new Minister was told, 'to get the park established with the reluctant agreement of the region rather than jeopardise the wider issue through having an argument about a small separated area which already has reserve status'.

Those who had been assured the sandplain forest was as good as theirs were having to be persuaded of other realities. Now the officials who had been so keen to swap it for a piece of hill country were describing it as 'the only example of successional vegetation from the sea to near the foothills that originally existed on the Barrytown Flats. This sequence of vegetation and the habitat it provides . . . conforms to the department's policy of reserving representative samples of the cover that gave New Zealand its original vegetative character. For these reasons the reserve is an important part of the country's protected area system.' Then their head office in Wellington told them 'to sit back . . . and see what develops'.

———

Out of the gorse and wind, I drop into a landscape of tight-leaved shrubs and piles of countless, rounded stones. Although they may be lichen-covered and long inert from the flick and surge of waves, there is still a sense of stored energy about them.

On a clear day, when summer heats up these old beach ridge hollows and dries out their few spring ponds, they seem like another country. And as is so often the case, there is always some form of life ready, designed to respond. One of the tight-leaved shrubs, undistinguished to all but the most vigilant botanical eyes, is a corokia. It is common enough across the mountains in drier, eastern country, but nowhere else on the West Coast has it ever been seen. The vigour of its few envoys here suggests their presence can be explained by the endless trial and error of plants, the perpetual contest they wage with the physical environment in trying to expand their range. But in the end, it is mysterious. My eyes peeled for one of them, I blunder into signs of other life attracted to the warmth of the hollow: a spade and a grubber, plastic bags, water bottles; and a trail of thrown-back gorse ending in a pile of bags of fertiliser, potting mix and marijuana plants hurriedly dropped among the flowering flax and the crimson, asparagus-like spring tūtū.

As the spring planters have learnt, the Punakaiki coast is warmer than any to the south, or most of the country to the north. Geography, in the form of what Māori call Tuterakiwhanau, blesses this auspicious part of the West Coast with mildness. Its secret lies partly in the fact that the mountains rising behind don't reach as high as those further south, are without the perpetual snows that each winter night send freezing air across their plains, and block the same freezing air from the higher mountains inland. It also lies in the warm, life-rich, oceanic current that Punakaiki's earliest people called Te Mahunui, which makes its first New Zealand landfall here.

You can interpret the ecology of the Punakaiki coast that way if you wish, or you can explain it as the rununga of the Atua: the place where Tane, Tawhirimatea, Tangaroa and the other children of Raki and Papatuanuku all meet. Once it was manifest in a phenomenon now rarely seen other than on the offshore islands: the massing of hundreds of birds in one place for the first taste of spring. He ua kōwhai happened every year, one reason this part of the West Coast, where rivers emerge from limestone gorges to meet the sea, in fertile aprons of sand and lagoons—where Te Tai Poutini's first kōwhai burst into flower—is named *te puna kai ki*.

The route inland is a sudden, steep gravelly scramble through flax, unexpected in the prevailing flatness. At the crest is a forest full of orchids getting through their brief life before the heat of summer saps the moisture from its stony ground. It is an extraordinary forest compared with others in New Zealand. Akeake, horoeka, porokaiwhiri, tārata, mahoe, kōhuhu, karamū, kōwhai, māmaku, te kouka, rimu, matai, totara, miro, heketara, rātā; so many tree species in the canopy, none more dominant than another, it is impossible to label it, as botanists like to do, with reference to just one or two. In 1826, on similar beach ridges at the head of Wellington Harbour, Thomas Shepherd saw a low windswept forest of 'a great many beautiful shrubs'. Heaphy drew it in 1839 just before it vanished under settlers' fires and axes. When I saw the sandplain forest, I knew what they had seen.

The ridge's waterworn cobbles seem too dry to support a forest—yet each trunk is covered with epiphytic ferns and orchids and, every now and then, vigorous young rātā vines that will eventually become the sprawling, multi-trunked rātā once so characteristic of forests of rivermouths and coastal plains in this part of New Zealand.

The gravel ridge forest slopes away inland again—prolonged wetness replaces clinky dryness, the long list of trees reduces to kahikatea, kōwhai and houhere. Moss instead of lichen covers the stones, most of it one species, lying loose and rootless waiting for the water that will float it through the forest. A specialist moss, evolved for hazards of floodplains, it must have arrived here as a spore or fragment on the muddy feet of some water bird flown in from some similar floodplain elsewhere. It is an unobtrusive reminder that if nature has created a particular species for flooded forests, those forests must have long been an element of the New Zealand landscape.

Just as suddenly the cobbles disappear under silt, the trees end their reach, the sky opens and I step out into in a wet swathe of flax. The silence makes it hard to believe I'm in the same stretch of country as the wild sea and beach, but it lasts no longer than my slowly deepening wade. Objecting to my leaping from clump to clump of any sedge that looks like it will take my weight, a pair of pukeko set off a chain reaction in the kōwhai.

I hear the unmistakeable slow beat of pigeons' wings before I see them. Other birds, preoccupied by the new kōwhai buds, warily adjust their position: dozens of white underbellies, all along the lagoon edge. The way they catch the light as they reach out for buds makes the landscape seem fecund with some strange gigantic fruit. A hunter with the skill of one Charles Heaphy watched in the 1840s could take 30 or more in a morning without the long-spear leaving his hand:

KERERU FEEDING IN NIKAU.

The pigeons are probably feeding in low trees or are about water-holes, and are scarcely frightened at the appproach of the hunter, who quietly steal under them . . . The spear is then quietly directed amongst the foliage towards the breast of the bird, which takes little notice of the operation. When the point is within half a yard a sudden thrust is made, and the bird is transfixed.

The spring gathering of kererū is a remarkable sight, now rarely met. One day the lagoon lies, like everything else, with the leanness of late winter. Then kōwhai's flower buds begin swelling. As though word of the sudden food basket has gone out around the region's kererū haunts, the lagoon is theirs for a week or so—until tui and korimako make life miserable for them. The air is rent with their arrivals and departures, their wing beat slowly building as they cross the sandplain and head up into the Paparoa hills. Sandy Bartle has been observing birds at Punakaiki for almost 30 years. From the hills above the sandplain forest he has many times seen kererū lifting out of the flats and without hesitation heading inland. Most of them fly so high above the forest that their intention can only be to cross the ranges.

It is a very different picture from the National Parks and Reserves Authority's description of the sandplain forest as 'isolated'—its plants and animals forever cut off by a sea of farmland—an 'outlier' of nature of the sort to be 'avoided' in a national park unless there's a 'sufficiently compelling argument to overcome the inherent objectives of fragmentation'.

But it is different, also, from the spring flocks of birds on the move that suffuse Lindsay Matthias' memories. 'Birds?' he asks. 'There's a fiftieth of what used to be here. Years ago, you'd see pigeons constantly in and out of the hills.' He puts much of it down to stoats and weasels, but there's no doubt that once the bush on the Flats started to go, the birds did too.

From where he keeps his caravan up against the bush above the All Nations Tavern at Barrytown you can see across the Flats to the sea—but there is hardly a native tree in sight. When Lindsay came over to Punakaiki as a toddler in 1922, when the Punakaiki River was called Deadman's, the sandplain was all bush and swampy watercourses full of kōwhai and flax. Jack Hill and his brother Henry were back from Gallipoli and just beginning to clear it. Within a year, Lindsay's father could inch his Model T truck through the long tunnel of bush to begin a delivery service to Greymouth. It was a life of close and constant attention to such details as the sudden arrival of weka in the district: 'We didn't have Māori hens here then. But Bill Fischer raised some eggs with a bantam, and now they're everywhere.'

Recollections like these are vital if we want to understand the speed and scale with which our culture rearranged life for New Zealand's birds. Yet they count for little in the scientific world of natural history. Nothing is valid unless an expert has measured or said it. Not until the 1930s did an ornithologist lay the blame for the dramatic demise of New Zealand's native birds squarely on European settlement's selective destruction of the rich plains forests. 'Birds deprived of lowland forest into which they were accustomed to descend in winter,' said Robert Falla, 'have become extinct or very scarce.'

> *Lowland forest areas were speedily reduced, swamp regions were steadily drained and man-made pasture areas took their place . . . lowland forest areas which had distinctive advantages for some birds not possessed by hill country and mountain forests disappeared almost completely.*

Although cautious not to offend, Sir Walter Buller came close to declaring the sudden vanishing of huia to have the same cause. Nature's basic ecological pattern is no different in New Zealand from elsewhere: species numbers, whether birds, insects or plants, are inevitably greater in the coastal lowlands than in the mountains. New Zealand, furthermore, has a pronounced and geologically active physical character—mountains sharply divided from the lowlands which they constantly supply with new, fertile soil and forest-building material. Add to this the fact that most of New Zealand's native ecosystems have evolved to be frugal rather than profligate in their use of scarce mineral resources, notably the phosphates that birds seek, and it is not surprising that many New Zealand forest birds evolved a lifestyle mobile enough to fly out of the hills to where the best food is, down on the riverflats and plains.

By the 1970s the Western Paparoas was the only district in warmer, northern New Zealand still with the range of ecosystems that confronted the first Europeans. Government biologists sent to identify localities for conservation reserves soon revealed it to be 'in stark contrast to many earlier assumptions about the region . . . from the time of the early explorers . . . a dank and uniform blanket of beech trees and "empty" of birds . . . like the less savoury parts of Middle Earth in *Lord of the Rings*'—as one put it. There were many in the West Coast timber industry who dismissed the biologists as 'at best, irrelevant'. But by 1978 a common theme was emerging: 'low altitude, warm forest holds more species, and in higher numbers, than the forest of adjacent hills and cold, montane valleys. Some species prefer the warmer forest throughout the year, while others require it seasonally.'

As the biologists were finding few kererū overwintering in the inland valleys at Reefton and Inangahua, a young English ornithologist working on his own at Punakaiki was recording a simultaneous increase of them feeding on hinau, miro and pigeonwood, and in spring, on the coastal kōwhai groves.

Whenever Derek Onley walked the two kilometres past the sandplain forest to the shop, he listed every bird he heard. Soon patterns began emerging. Different species and numbers in different forests, and at different seasons in the same forest. Some, like those on the sandplain and the even higher-fertility talus of the limestone gorges, contained more birds than scientists had ever recorded in South Island forests. 'Great care must be taken,' Onley wrote in the ornithologists' journal *Notornis*, 'to include these favoured habitats in any reserve proposal.'

Around him, wildlife officers were saying 'it is not going to be easy to stop those who wish to cut the last remnants of low altitude forests on the West Coast'. Presented with a government proposal to protect a surviving piece of the coastal plain south of Hokitika, still in Crown land, the Westland County Council tersely advised their 'complete opposition'.

Countering the talk of 'winter refuges' and 'wildlife corridors', the head of the Forest Service complained that the region's merchantable forest would be barely sufficient or insufficient to honour long-term sale commitments because 'ornithologists wish to make even further inroads . . . It is as simple as that.' Despite him, the forests where Onley made his revelatory bird counts were saved from logging. By the time the new 'sea-to-the-mountains' Paparoa National Park was opened in a storm-lashed ceremony at Punakaiki's Blowholes a decade later, telemetry and radio tracking were proving what generations of foresters had denied: a kererū seen high in the hills could have spent the morning 40 kilometres away, feeding on kōwhai by coastal lagoons.

———————

At the inland edge of the lagoon I push muddily out of the thicket of flax and tight, small-leaved shrubs, up onto a dry, sandy rise and back into the low light of a forest world—a dune forest though, very different from the droughty gravel ridges across the water. Here only one tree species dominates, the aggressive little rātā which had centuries before bludged a lift from the shrubs on the gravel ridges. Before the press of wind and sea yielded, the driftwood logs beneath rotted, and ridge after ridge of new gravel pushed the sea away.

In the flat, my sense of direction has slid away. Tangled supplejack vines confront me on all sides. Cobwebs cling to my face as I look up into the huge, arcing fronds of some of the southernmost palms in the world, and down at their young miko scattered everywhere across the forest floor. The ground is damp and covered with ferns and mosses. A thin soil has even begun to form. Peel away the rotting leaves, however, and it is still raw, young beach sand from the sea. A truly pristine forest, we might say.

Inland, the old dune slopes imperceptibly down toward damp. Rātā's big, spreading crowns give way to kahikatea and rimu and the wetter ground of a creek's course into the lagoon. Once, when the rātā forest was wind-blasted sanddune scrub, the sea would have pushed the sluggish surge of the tide up it. Now it's hard to believe it is a coastal sand country place.

From late November into December, the rātā's canopies are alive with tui and bellbirds and the ground beneath the nīkau palms is littered with their spent, scarlet flowers. I lay under them once, contemplating the nīkau, musing on Tom Robbins' flippant wisdom that what Alexander von Humboldt considered the very emblem of the exotic was, of all trees, 'obviously the stand-up comedian'. Many times before I had lain back on the mounded ground watching pigeons grazing their way through the epiphytic delicatessen overhead, and crumbling its dry leaves between my fingers. This time, my fingers closed on something colder and harder and brought out a sea shell.

Startled, I scraped a circle free of leaves. What for years I'd assumed to be sand the sea had left was a heap of almost pure shell. Thousands of bivalves retrieved from the surf by human hands, packed tightly together, every one of them tuatua, their ocean white stained brown by forested centuries. More scraping, more shells, all obviously older than the rātā. Increasingly charcoaled fingers uncovered split and reddened fire stones, not flattened like the cobbles on the beach ridges but rounded as though the fire-makers had carefully selected them from a stream. Beside the heaps, uneven ground, as though dug and mounded—for long-ago dwellings perhaps—broke the dune's smooth, curving back slope.

In my mind hundreds of people suddenly inhabited the sandplain: countless backs bent out in the surf, scooping shellfish into flax bags and bringing them here, beside the hāpua, out of the wind. Obviously their sandplain was different from what we see now—no rātā for them to lie under;

not much more than coastal scrub; the lagoon beside still tidally connected to the sea, with birds that we know only from bones in limestone caves. Then the people vanished and the older claim of a forest asserted itself.

Nowhere in the ecological literature about the West Coast will you find a reference to people being anything but an ephemeral factor in its landscape until Europeans came last century. Elsewhere in northern New Zealand on sandy coasts like this, those who'd like to imagine and preserve primeval nature—the more virginal, the more virtuous—cannot ignore the evidence of an almost contiguously inhabited littoral.

Two years previously, about a kilometre south, when the bulldozers had halted for the night, Derek Onley went across the road to have a closer look at how his neighbour was spending his Land Development Loan. For the best part of a week, the machines had pushed their way along the sand dunes, flattening the forest. Wandering among the crushed trees, watching the birds scavenge for insects in the wreckage, he was drawn to a patch of ground whose whiteness stood out in the swathe of dark sand. Once he saw one ripped-apart shell heap, the rest, dozens of them, some enormous, all along the same sand dune, were not hard to find.

Onley had heard rumours of an ancient Māori presence at Punakaiki, and seen the limestone caverns where greenstone and argillite adzes had been found, but nothing like this. He rang around for an archaeologist who stopped the bulldozers, as the law required, while each heap was recorded. Someone found an argillite adze a few weeks later. The solitary charcoal sample that was sent away to be subjected to the mysteries of carbon-dating showed the shellfish gatherers were living here in 1500 AD. Who they were and whether a few of them lived here for a very long time, or a large number briefly, it couldn't say. Nor could it explain why, although the same sand dune extends for miles along the Barrytown Flats, their rubbish heaps are confined to only a tiny part of it. Nor whether their presence right below one of the New Zealand mainland's largest and most accessible muttonbird breeding colonies was a coincidence.

Kati Wae Wae, the local Kai Tahu hapu, claim mahinga kai rights to the sandplain today, ensure the treasured tuatua beds remain secret, and guard them against the prospect of the muddy mining sludge that could end up fouling the beach. It took hui after hui for them to decide they would resist the sand-miners' persuasions. But in the waiata the old hakui down the coast at Arahura composed in celebration, it was not so much Pakiroa's tuatua as the revered titi of the forests above that were remembered. Kati

Wae Wae trace their origins in Aotearoa back 25 generations to Paikea, who left Mauke in the Cook Islands and arrived at Whangara on the North Island's east coast. But they have only been here, on the Coast, since the late 1700s. Moving south through Cook Strait, fighting and intermarrying with Ngāti Mamoe and Ngāti Ira, they invaded Te Tai Poutini and supplanted the Ngāti Wairangi, a tribe from Taranaki, to gain control of the pounamu trade. Most of the invaders returned over the mountains to Kaiapohia. Kati Wae Wae's name signals the people who stayed; Runanga, the rivermouth settlement just down the coast, the meeting that decided to stay.

Kati Wae Wae know the shell heaps aren't theirs, but whoever they belong to, they say, was once here in great numbers. The tribes they cite in their whakapapa—Ngāti Kopiha, Ngāti Wairangi, Ngāti Apa and Ngāti Tumatakōkiri—are merely the tip of the historical iceberg. James Stack went back further in the 1860s when he pieced together the different tribal genealogies he'd recorded, back to the late 1500s and a people called Waitaha being overrun by Ngāti Mamoe over two centuries before Kai Tahu's arrival—a century later than the carbon-date on the sandplain charcoal.

Convinced that only a tight-lipped approach to their ancient connection with the land gives them the pride and power to resist others' claims on it, Waitaha, the water bearers, have long kept their songs to themselves. But in the 1990s, when provoked by the high-profile Kai Tahu claim to Te Wai Pounamu, whose every mountain contains ancestral Waitaha bone, they finally spoke, revealing this prolific stretch of coast to be one of their most revered places. Their firstcomers, descendants of Rakaihautu of the waka Uruao, who is said to have settled these islands over 60 generations ago, made their final landfall here. Close to where they discovered the God Stone, pounamu, Te Punakaiki became a place to which generations journeyed.

So skilled did Waitaha become at watching what kererū, titi and karoro revealed about how the land lived, they called themselves Bird People. They learned what ornithologists have only recently measured statisically, that kererū have a preference for older forests. How the dark beech forest waters are only safe after running through country like Te Punakaiki's sandplain, and how waters from the limestone hills behind gave strength to their bodies and produced good crops when taken to their gardens. Had we seen their sandplain 500 years ago, we might have been surprised by the number of its species they used to subsist within it, their detailed knowledge of each one's ecology and their tuned response to the seasons.

Then something ended it all. The huts disintegrated over their excavated hollows. Storms collapsed the timber stands where bodies were left with the elements until the time came to wash their bones clean and bury them in the sand. The relentless wind swept sand and seeds over it all. A forest of spreading rātā grew over the kāinga nohoanga. Ferns and mosses covered the shell heaps. Waitaha's garden clearings became no more than a disturbance in the forest, the kind of ecological vacuum which nature will not abide for long. If today's growth rates are any indication, it wouldn't have taken even a century for all human sign to disappear under trees and give it the countenance of a totally uninhabited coast that it had to the first Europeans to pass offshore in 1642. The quintessential original, unpeopled land of conservation mythology.

The Waitaha elders' reticence recalls the atmosphere of secrecy in which Carl Jung said America's native Pueblo preserved their ancestors' knowledge from outsiders. Of the kind of evidence archaeologists like there is nothing whatsoever to authenticate their firstcomers' anchorage in the Porarari estuary. But the accounts of their awe at its wall of forest and birdsong, its sheltering caves and their planting of the karaka trees still to be found there, have brought Te Punakaiki out of hiding. About their sacred sites within it, though, Waitaha maintain silence—a silence momentarily relaxed to halt a plan for a tourist boardwalk across the the sandplain and its tapu creek.

New Zealanders with an affection for nature never have their minds far from the fabled land of birds into whose estuaries the first humans brought their canoes. The evidence is that it was one of the most extraordinary ecosystems in the world: a forested land whose big animals were virtually all birds, some 70 species of them found nowhere else, more than a third of them flightless, and almost a quarter nocturnal. Many occupied the essentially ground-dwelling niches for which, in continental ecosystems, mammals evolved; 40 per cent were fated to vanish soon after the first people—and the Asian rat that had travelled the Pacific with them—came ashore.

Waitaha's traditions also preserve the response to the new land of the rats they had caged and nurtured on the voyage. Guardian of the Heights, Waitaha called kiore, so awed were they of its ability to find trails and survive where others failed. Yet as sure as they began to feel the spirit of Punakaiki's forests and waters, their rats were wreaking havoc.

Trevor Worthy and Richard Holdaway reckon they have found the earliest known kiore remains in New Zealand at Punakaiki. It could pinpoint Waitaha's date of arrival exactly—if they had enough funds for the extravagant business of carbon-dating. What matters in *their* landscape is the prodigious array of birds that lived here and then suddenly vanished. Worthy and Holdaway first discovered the 'missing fauna', as they called it, in limestone caves in Northwest Nelson. Their search for more limestone country, lowland preferably, brought them to Punakaiki. Not surprisingly, most species are forest birds, many of them—moa, snipes, kākāpō, parakeets, kōkakō, yellowheads, wrens, saddlebacks—now either extinct or nearly so. But the most abundant of all were petrels and prions, sea-going birds that nested in the forest and whose bones were more likely to make it into caves than the arboreal songbirds'. Before kiore came, the landscape teemed with petrels and prions, and, gliding voracious among the millions that flew in from the sea each night, the now vanished laughing owl.

Waitaha had special esteem for the places of the laughing owl like Te Ata Po. Worthy and Holdaway had to learn to recognise them too. From meticulous analysis of the owls' roosts they have extracted a landscape history reaching back 17,000 years, before people entered the Pacific, when the Punakaiki limestone country was a forested island in an otherwise open, glaciated landcape. Before the sandplain began building, when the cliff behind it was the beach and the sea swept into the forested basins behind Punakaiki.

For virtually all those 17,000 years, the crushed bones of prions and small petrels dominate the amassed layers of laughing owl roosts. Then the uppermost layers show something unprecedented hitting the birds of Punakaiki and suddenly transforming their ecosystem. Petrel and prion bones almost vanish, replaced by the chewed remains of kiore. It was the beginning of the end for 'one of the most remarkable plant-animal communities in the world . . . a largely forested landscape dominated by birds'.

The few petrel species that could fight off kiore had only a few centuries grace before even more predatory rats began slipping off European ships and venturing inland. Today, if Punakaiki is remarkable to people anxious about New Zealand's birds, it is because, despite predators that have routed even kiore, a petrel species still finds it possible to live here.

Out of the corner of his eye early one morning, my son Mat saw one in a roadside drain as we drove past the sandplain forest. Disoriented the night before by the security lights the ilmenite miners had just installed outside their new laboratory—as its ancestors were by Māori fires—the big, black bird struggled lamely. It was in sight of home—it had a navigational guidance system trustworthy enough to bring it back in any weather to the very spot where it was born after seven years skimming waves around the Roaring Forties—yet it may as well have been an ocean away. We looked after it until it seemed stronger. Then Mat carried it through the flax to an open spot at the top of the Razorback, the bluff above where William Smart camped in 1863. But the damage was permanent: the next day a German tourist picked up its corpse from the strandline on Punakaiki Beach.

When I was Mat's age in the early 1950s, one of the best things each week—if you were interested in nature—were the ornithologist Robert Falla's broadcasts to schools. I'd seen petrels and shearwaters scudding behind the old Cook Strait ferry *Tamahine*, but anything I knew about them—that they were also muttonbirds, say—I knew from him. A few months after the end of World War II, New Zealand children heard Falla describing the life of muttonbirds: how, in spring, their parents come in from months on the southern oceans; how they lay their eggs in burrows in November, and raise their young through the summer months, ready for an autumn departure—that is, if they can escape the rats, stoats and long-reaching human arms that descend on the colonies in March to gather the chicks that are so plump they're larger than their parents.

At Barrytown School some listened with disbelief. *Spring* was when you went muttonbirding in their part of the world. 'There's muttonbirds up the back of Richards' place right now,' said Barry Fischer. The teacher took notice and suggested they go up and get some.

Tom Richards was then farming the Flats just below the petrel colony, at what, ever since the goldminers, had been Scotsman's Creek. Whenever the school bus stopped at their gate in winter, the children could hear the muttonbirds low overhead in the dark, dawn sky. The Fischer children from up at Punakaiki knew the sound well. Before their neighbour, McAlpine, came and cleared the bush, petrels of another sort had lived just above the coast road among the big blocks of sandstone. They vanished after one of McAlpine's fires brought a slip down.

The class wrote to Falla, saying he might know a lot about some muttonbirds, but obviously not theirs. The big black birds were gone all summer, but every autumn, like clockwork, thousands of them came back to raise their chicks in the burrows in the bluffs above the Flats. Just in case, they sent him one.

Falla couldn't believe what tumbled out of his mail. Black petrels just didn't behave like that: breeding one season in one part of the country, and another season elsewhere. With his friend Edgar Stead, he was on the Coast as soon as he could be. Forty years later, Barry Fischer's mother still remembered the excitement when Barry brought the two ornithologists down out of the bush. Stead was up with the petrels again the next breeding season confirming that they were different from anything ornithologists knew. What hungry blacksand-miners knew as the huge muttonbirds they tracked each winter to burrows above their diggings, what Kati Wae Wae and Waitaha before them knew as titi, Falla was soon naming *Procellaria westlandica*, the Westland Black Petrel.

Sandy Bartle has known what he calls the Westland Blacks for most of the time science has known about them. It was his own childhood friendship with Falla, in fact, that led to his passion, and his painstaking all night vigils near the colony to which Falla and Stead were first taken. He is waiting for them most Aprils when they come into the limestone bluffs to nest, and each November when, no sooner fledged, the latest crop of black petrels are staggering up tree trunks, flapping their wings and heading out to sea—to their first meal on their own and several years way beyond New Zealand's borders before each and every one returns.

One winter night, as the light went out of the sky, I waited with him high on a bluff above the sandplain forest. A strong breeze was blowing off the Tasman and I remember the smell of the sea and the anticipation of excitement as I swept the horizon with binoculars. A few black shapes skimmed into view, and suddenly there were tens of thousands of them massed along the lines of breakers like midges around rotting kelp. Then the sky reddened and, as though from some elemental signal out of the ocean's world, they headed our way. Closer and closer they came, circling over the sandplain and back out to sea, a few calling as they swept low over us—some of them birds Sandy had been recording for 20 years—then, like an eddy becoming a current, they poured over our heads into the dark wall of Paparoa forest.

Centuries before, Waitaha would have watched this nightly river of birds over their huts. To some, the petrels would have encapsulated the ancient mysteries of Waitaha's newfound country. Others, noticing how winter fires seemed to bring the big titi in close, would have developed techniques of lighting fires below the bluffs on misty nights to attract them into nets.

Preserving titi in fat-and-kelp pōhā was something Waitaha learned from places like Punakaiki. Other bird knowledge, like the noose snare and pigeons' habit of flying to the nearest streams for water, had come with them from Polynesia. For a people to whom pigeons were as valued as Waitaha's songs suggest, who gathered such large seasonal catches that means had to be developed for preserving the extra supply, the sandplain with its early flowering kōwhai must have been an enormously precious place, even once the kōwhai finished and pigeon numbers thinned out.

Weak from eight months' slipping in the rain on rocky shorelines, but loath to abandon a European diet, even Kai Tahu's almost inedible—'for want of proper cultivation'—potatoes, Thomas Brunner had insight into the West Coast's sudden, seasonal productivity:

> December is a glorious month of dietary amongst the natives on the coast . . . The rivers, large or small, abound in eels, hawera, upukuroro, haparu, patiki, and parauki; the fruit of the ekiakia [kiekie] is then ripe, called by the natives tawara, and is very luscious, more like a conserve than a fruit; the honey of the flax blossom is also in season, called korari, and, when mixed with fern root, also makes a species of confectionary; the natives also . . . make taro ovens of the mamakou, and of a species of the ti, the stem of which is the eatable part, and is called koari; it is very sweet and pleasant to the taste.

Brunner's white companion on 'The Great Journey' was Charles Heaphy. By 1846 the New Zealand Company had searched almost everywhere for more of the coastal plains in which they'd sited their Cook Strait settlements. Only the West Coast kept their hopes alive. Māori stories and sealers' conjecture about large rivers with 'a considerable tract of level land' on their banks, yet but a solitary native footprint seen in the sand, had to be followed up. 'It became especially a matter of interest,' Heaphy wrote before setting out, 'to know whether the reports of the natives respecting a level country, which they compared to Taranaki, were accurate.'

The first few weeks produced merely fragments of flats hemmed in by hills 'quite useless for agricultural purposes'. Things looked up at 'the triangular flat of wood' where the Buller poured out of the mountains: 'about

180 miles of available land, of good soil, but covered with dense forest, that near the coast being of rata and low bush, similar to the wood in the lower portion of the Hutt valley'. But Heaphy never did find his South Island Taranaki. He poked around abandoned gardens, but kept his distance from the few Māori he did meet, hungrily eating their inanga, and the potatoes and dogfish that followed 'without cessation', but declining their 'affectionate salutation of rubbing noses'. Their 'uninhabited coast', he had decided, was inferior country for settlement by an agricultural people 'the undulating pine forest which everywhere closes round one' barely worth claiming. 'Along the Pakiroa [Pakihiroa] beach, however,' he felt it worth mentioning, 'is a strip of level land about nine miles long and a mile deep, containing perhaps 6,000 acres, and covered with rata, bush and flax. It appeared to be swampy; but after so much rain as had then recently fallen, it was difficult to form a just idea of its availability.'

Curiously, it was to Taranaki, to childhood brushes with wet, rundown, forest-edge dairy farms, that my mind slipped when I first saw the sandplain: the way the red algae covered the posts and the mossy, numbered gates, how dew lay on the Yorkshire Fog in the morning, and punga, kamahi and foxgloves grew around the fences and out of the windrows of lichened stumps.

Fred Stewart grew up in it as it took shape, clambering over the burnt logs as the grown-ups sowed the grass seed among the burnt rātā stumps. The first pasture in the spongy forest humus set butterfat records that, in the 1920s, beat even Taranaki's. Just down the Flats at Canoe Creek there was still a miners' settlement winning gold with its big blow-up dredge. 'All the years we've been here,' he says, 'they've have been wanting our land for mining.'

The mining company claims that to have its suction dredge working its way through his paddocks will be the best thing that ever happened to them. Fred and most of his neighbours who have seen the lifeless gravel tailings left behind along the riverflats of the Grey and Taramakau are disgusted at those who've yielded to the miners' dollars. 'They've just bought out Rae's,' he says as if what's happening is beginning to get beyond the locals' ability to control it. 'He got enough from them to buy himself a farm up in Nelson. That's what's going to happen all along here. And straight away, the land goes back . . . for farming, I mean.'

For two generations, nobody seriously questioned Heaphy's assessment of the land's inadequacies, but it was undoubtedly a factor in the government's cunning West Coast Purchase 14 years later. For a mere

£300, James Mackay persuaded Kai Tahu to sell their 'trees, minerals, waters, rivers, lakes, streams and all appertaining to the said Land or beneath the surface of the said Land and all our right title claim and interest whatsoever thereon To Hold to Queen Victoria Her Heirs and Assigns as a lasting possession absolutely for ever and ever'.

Once William Smart and his friends had climbed over from Canterbury in the summer heat of early 1863, it took them three weeks to work their way north to Charles Heaphy's Pakihiroa beach. They'd had to replace their worn-out leather boots with parara, flax sandals, and were rationing their Pākehā food. They found they could make a bitter tea from the coastal piripiri, and 'we knew we could get plenty of mussels off the rocks if we got no birds, and in places we could get the tops of nikau palm which grows near the Beach line'. But had they been differently disposed toward the land, hunger would not have been an issue.

There were hardly any locals who could give them such advice. The ancient pounamu centre, Arahura, was down to '2 huts with some old Maori women and children nearly eaten alive with fleas and sandflies'. Mawhera was little better, the old chief Heaphy and Brunner had met, Tarapuhi te Kaukihi, telling them how, before the old pā where today's Greymouth stands was washed away by the sea, 'a great many natives' had lived there. But if anything symbolised the sense of abandonment, it was at Te Miko, just north of Punakaiki, where Heaphy had so famously sketched his dog being pulled up the cliff. Tingling with the thrill of their findings, Smart's party spent 'nearly all day in the bush . . . instead of going down the flax ladders as the Maories told us the old ladders were rotten'. Back at Mawhera, Smart showed Tarapuhi his bags of beach sand. 'He has no knowledge of Gold,' he wrote in his diary that night, 'but says he has seen similar stuff to what we showed him in several creeks and rivers.'

Within three years of William Smart claiming that not a single white man was to be found south of the Buller, hundreds were living on the terrace above the sandplain forest. Canoe Creek, a few miles south, supported 1,500 more and several hotels, and Seventeen Mile, where the beach gold boom began in 1879, another 2,000, together with 11 hotels and a casino. They named the gold-bearing terrace above the sandplain Albion, after old England, and the tapu creek that becomes the lagoon, Hibernia. Alongside were Scotsman's Creek and Welshman's. It had become a miners' coast—as its owners' land deeds declare it is still.

Colonial governments did not like to see either people—Māori, settlers or miners—or land beyond their control. As soon as the West Coast's native title was extinguished in the 1860s, the sandplain, like the rest, became Crown Land. It stayed that way right through the early mining rushes until 1894 when a reformist Liberal government, while intent on breaking up the vast pastoral estates, responded favourably to a delegation of miners wanting a large grant, 'with the right to the whole area from sea beach to foot of range . . . at a nominal rent for gold mining purposes'. For years, the sandplain was known as 'McMillan's' after the miner who acquired it. In deference to his trade's solitary occupation of its flats, the Crown grant gave him freehold, not only to the land surface, but to the minerals beneath it. The same, Victorian, rights have persisted from owner to owner, with every sale and subdivision since.

Had the miners not deemed the forest such a cursed obstacle to progress, today's highway might not have been quite as uncompromisingly straight as it is. Denis Ryall, the publican at the miners' tavern at Canoe Creek, wrote to the Mines Minister in 1880: 'It is known that the district is one of the most promising on the West Coast to mining enterprise, were miners able to penetrate it, but its extraordinary growth of tangled scrub and bush frustrates the efforts of struggling working men to encounter it.' Eventually, in the winter of 1882, the county's road overseer came up and agreed 'the bush in its natural state' prevented access to 'good paying ground' because it was 'almost imprenetrable . . . owing to the close nature of the undergrowth, which is thickly interwoven with supplejacks'.

MINERS AND THEIR NEW COAST ROAD, 1900.

By 1885 the blacksand-miners had their road, the Inspecting Engineer for the Goldfields reporting, 'the present extension will afford . . . miners working on the terraces, gullies and creeks . . . a more convenient means of obtaining their supplies and will tend in a great measure to open up this portion of the district'. The 'County Track' is on the earliest surveyors' maps of the 1890s—a perfect line cutting through the sandplain forest between the terraces and the shoreline. In 1896, as a token of his success perhaps, Denis Ryall had a photograph taken of himself and his mates posing on it in their Sunday best under huge, spreading rātā. Their expressions are like those worn by victorious tunnellers finally through to the other side.

Most goldminers stay no longer than what they have come to find. A few stayed on when farming families like the Stewarts began to arrive. Right into the 1940s, the government's paper grid towns and side roads carried names like Barrytown Gold Dredging Limited. Their surveyor's comments told the changing landscape as well as anything:

> *Fairly thick bush, rata, kiekie, supplejack and nikau palms . . . Supplejack, rata, gigi and hinau . . . Bush . . . bush . . . old shingle bank covered with scrub . . . flax and thick scrub . . . Swampy with bush . . . patches of good land . . . Lagoon and old workings . . . raupo swamp . . . Fair land with rough scrub . . . mostly flax swamp.*

The flats around the sandplain forest were cleared by someone who hated doing it. Desperate for work, Arthur Sheldon came to the Barrytown Flats in 1920 after farm labouring in Canterbury, to work with his share-milking brother at Canoe Creek, but left within months after an argument over the way his partner kicked the cows.

> *And you know, I was just leaving the place and along on his bike came Apted, who owned the land up at McMillans with his friend Charlie Dale. He said, 'Come up to our place and work.' I had only the things I stood up in, but I stayed there eight years. The agreement was that I'd have some of the land at McMillan's, I had twenty four acres there, freehold. It was always called 'The 24 acres'.*
>
> *I don't like chopping trees down. But I had to make a living. I dropped all that bush for Apted and Dale, from Lawson's Creek to the Razorback, both sides of the bush reserve. But I didn't like doing it.*
>
> *I'd start with the birds in the morning, wet or fine. We'd never stop. The whole place was really wet before those drains went in. And full of white pines. All them were cut down and burnt.*
>
> *Charlie would come over sometimes, but he didn't help much. It was for me to do really. Yet if I'd had my way I wouldn't have cut the big kahikateas. I said we could keep them and have grass growing around them. It would look beautiful. But Apted and Dale said they had to come down so they came down. And you know, not long after we'd burnt the last of the big white pines,*

ARTHUR SHELDON, ON THE
FLATS AT 'MACMILLANS', 1920S.

*Wilde's sawmills up the Punakaiki River were calling
out for the same timber.*

*The nikau palms they let me leave. But
everything else was cut as close to the ground as we
could and then burnt.*

Silhouetted by the last of the sun, Arthur's nīkau
palms can make you feel momentarily in the tropics. His
house by The Razorback is still there beside the coast road,
surrounded by its bungi hedge, but eventually he had to
leave the Flats for an old people's home in Greymouth.
As for the sandplain forest: 'a bloke called Keown, a
miner, lived in a clearing on the edge of it. He had it for
bees. That's really why it was never cut down. And it was
always so wet in there . . .'

Fred Stewart and his fraternity weren't content, of course, with mere
clearings in the bush. Nor were they very happy with the regularity with
which the creeks from the Paparoas poured across their pastured flats. When
John Coates complained to the Westland Catchment Board about Hibernia
Creek flooding his farm, they simply sent in a bulldozer to flatten its nīkau
and kōwhai groves and a ditch-digger to cut off its tapu meanders through
the forest next door. By 1978 it was illegal to put in such a drain without a
water right. But the Catchment Board was a law unto itself. Ever since, the
tapu creek has barely been able to flow.

The first time I saw it, before it succumbed—like most creeks of its
kind on the Coast—to the drainage engineers, every surface below eye-
level, every twig and leaf, right across the sandflat, carried a film of life-
sustaining silt. Now only in floods does it look like a stream and then it is
never out of its channel. For a while the huge, old spreading kahikatea and
rātā, with their crowns of epiphytic orchids, ferns and lilies, the huge tree
ferns and palms, and the thickets of kiekie and supplejack, so dense that
you lose sense of where in the flatness you are, won't miss their regular
feeds of silt. Yet without the floods which wash in the silt off the limey
hills, none of them would be here.

Had it not been for the fact that Nīkau Scenic Reserve was alongside
the breeding grounds of the first new mainland bird to be found by science
for the best part of a century, the sandplain forest almost certainly wouldn't
exist. Early in the 1950s a Lands and Survey field officer came to the

Barrytown Flats 'investigating the closing of areas surrounding the nesting grounds of the black petrel'. Some thought that the little of the forest that had covered the Flats a generation earlier which still stood was more than enough. The Barrytown schoolteacher's reaction to the fuss his pupils' letter about the muttonbirds had stirred up was to go out to his swampy block of white pine forest at Lawson's Creek and fell a swath of the big trees. Not long after, the Power Board dropped some more.

Fortunately, the scientist who recognised the Westland Black Petrel as a new species was not one to be satisfied by having its vital statistics latinised in the literature and a few museum specimens. Robert Falla's concern coincided, what's more, with new government willingness to reserve bits of bush. In the petrels' neighbourhood, the only decent piece of bush left was on Jack and Henry Hill's place, next to the Richards' at Scotsman's Creek where Falla had first seen his new birds. The two brothers had seen enough bush burning and were anxious to see some of it kept. Henry and Jack had also had their eyes on a strip of sandy, well-drained Crown land that had been surveyed off for a coastal subdivision. A straight exchange, they told the field officer, would suit them fine.

The field officer reported the walk through the bush to the Coast to be 'particularly delightful' and, before he wrote his report, came back for a closer look. 'The block contains very attractive bush and is worthy of preservation,' he wrote. 'The owners have not stocked this bush in recent years as is evident by the prolific undergrowth . . . This bush cover opens out to wet swamp, flax and scrub along the sea beach frontage.' 'The recommendations may be worth investigating,' replied the Director-General of Lands from Wellington.

Today, the Hill brothers lie in the Barrytown cemetery down the road from the All Nations Tavern. 'Hard workers,' say the few still in the district who knew them. On their farm practically all the time; never in town much. There was a 'big write-up' about them once in the halcyon days when the Hills' beloved Jerseys produced the best butterfat on the Coast, when the Overland Dairy in Greymouth sent a horse team up each day to about 20 farms on the Flats—one cream can on each side for balance fording the rivers.

After a succession of reports, the Minister of Lands approved 'Reserve 2009' and the department began talking about surveying and fencing it. Before that though, the Grey County Council had to agree to the closing of the paper road that had been surveyed beside it. By August 1957 the

Director-General of Lands wanted to know why everything was taking so long. But it had been a wet winter on the Coast and so hard to get labour that the department had not even had a quote for it. It was the best part of another year before they did.

Then, in 1958, they found out that William Dennehy had flax-cutting rights to the land and, with it, the right to form roads and tramways through the bush if necessary. The Hill brothers had said so, but were nevertheless accused of not disclosing it. No matter that Dennehy himself was dead, and flax hadn't been cut from around the lagoon for years, the Hills were obliged to preserve any flax and keep their stock out of it. The Barrytown flax mill was still operating, and until the agreement expired in 1961, the Hills' swamp could not be made into a reserve.

For most of Fred Stewart's life, flax was carted to the mill by horse teams, hung and spread out on the rails to dry. Dennehy had one of the biggest blocks. 'All of it Dennehy's,' Fred says, 'from there right along the Crown land behind the beach, right through that reserve to our place at Lawson's.' Dennehy isn't remembered with affection. 'He knew that we all thought he *owned* it.' And he wasn't going to be the one to tell them otherwise. 'Our fires got away with a southerly once and he tried to claim damages. But when we went to the lawyer about it and found out it wasn't his land, he couldn't do a thing.'

The Director-General of Lands told his commissioner in Hokitika that it was 'indeed unfortunate . . . a proper search of the title was not made by your office', and issued instructions for the new reserve to be gazetted as soon as the flax-cutting rights expired. In the meantime, he said, 'it would be a wise precaution if you could arrange to keep an eye on the land and if there is any evidence that the cutting rights are likely to be exercised it might be possible, by a tactful approach to the District Public Trustee, to arrange for any flax to be taken out with a minimum of damage to the bush. It might even be that this Department should assist with the provision of access to the flax if this would mean minimising damage to the bush.'

While the government waited, foreign jute came onto the market, then new synthetics. Mills amalgamated in defence and the Coast's flax was forgotten. The tracks into the flaxy lagoon grew over and the forest and swamp gradually returned to what they had been before the fires and the flax-cutters' knives. By the time ecologists became aware of the sandplain forest in the 1970s, it seemed as wild and primeval as any coast they'd seen.

The commissioner did not forget Reserve 2009. In September 1961

he wrote to Grey County Council proposing it be named '"Nikau Scenic
Reserve" . . . because the reserve contains—in addition to rata, kamahi,
mahoe, supple jack and many native shrubs—nikau palms which look well
from the road'. With the county's agreement, the sandplain forest, the lagoon
and the gravel ridges were gazetted protected land. In the Hokitika Lands
and Survey office, Miss Watson was asked to prepare a new card for this
addition to Westland's scenic reserves.

It was the autumn of 1964, John and Henry Hill in their late sixties,
when they were asked to tender for the reserve fencing contract. They were,
they replied, 'not over keen'; they had a contract logging up after a bush
burn, and the Public Trustee was still trying to get the money owed them
for erecting the original fence along the boundary with their place. John
Hill died four years later and the following year, Carpentaria Exploration
Company Proprietary Ltd of Queensland applied for a mineral prospecting
warrant over the sandplain forest. Lands and Survey and the Punakaiki
Scenic Board agreed, but on condition it was all out of sight and 'no
interference was made with Nikau palms and other native bush'.

Conversation at the All Nations, the last of the old Barrytown gold rush
hotels, has never drifted far from mining and new ways—like water buffalo—
of making the Flats spawn profit. Now it's likely to be punctuated by the
new national park up the road and the strange ways of the thousands of
foreign backpackers it's attracting to this strip of the Coast.

Down on the beach, improvised sluices and sieves wait, ever hopeful
of a storm winnowing a new slurry of gold. But it's the bigger players in
the wings that are on everyone's lips. A sudden shift in world titanium prices
and their investment could take off. European and American sanctions on
South African ilmenite are no longer likely to trigger it; but Tamil separatists
halting sand-mining in Sri Lanka could; or environmental militants closing
down Japan's huge and grossly polluting titanium extraction plants.

Up the road by the sandplain forest, the sand-miners are ready. 'Cape
Canaveral' the locals call the three-storey tower rising out of the gorse and
rushes which now overrun the old dairy farms. The German tourists flocking
to the national park can't believe such a wildly beautiful place is being
destroyed by something so ugly. The mining company claims it's merely a

pilot operation, yet their steelwork now dominates a landscape in which the tallest, most impressive things used to be kahikatea and rātā trees.

The miners have purchased the dairy farms around the sandplain forest and, with their Victorian titles, the right to mine their own land right to the edge of the trees and the farcical fence that straddles the lagoon. They know that in country like this nature's patterns are particularly sensitive to the meandering ways of water, and that they can't extract the ilmenite without ravaging them. They'd have preferred to send in a bulldozer, run it back and forth across the dunes until the old trees were flattened and crushed, dragged into piles and burnt. Eventually, though, they accepted the argument of ecologists that the piece of native bush in the middle of their prospecting grid was considered too precious to the country for them to either buy or mine. When they finally applied for their mining licence, the sandplain forest was excluded from it.

The government's response was to warn the miners not to assume the other remaining piece of the Flats still in Crown land would be theirs to mine. Scientists, they said, considered Maher Swamp one of the last big lowland wetlands of its kind left in New Zealand. The miners fought the prospect as long and hard as their predecessors the decade before had tried to acquire the sandplain forest, hiring their own ecologists and arguing that the feasibility of their whole operation depended on Maher Swamp. But when they could not put a precise figure on the amount of ilmenite beneath its flax and raupō, Maher Swamp too was taken out of their plans.

The decision set off resentments that quickly escalated to threats and house-burnings and left Punakaiki a polarised community. For years the sand-miners had ensured their ambitious plans were front page news on the Coast, raising expectations of hundreds of new jobs and of 'useless' swamps brought into production. Maher Swamp's and the sandplain forest's exclusion from the operation signalled that, whatever Coasters thought conservation was, it wasn't something safely confined to unfarmable country like the Paparoa mountains. The government was listening—if they weren't—to people like the judge who said that 'mankind should not change the whole of the physical environment in which he lives; that here and there representative samples of the natural environment should be preserved intact'.

As in most people's lives, the historian Alexis de Tocqueville observed, the circumstances of birth deeply affects the development of nations. It may take many centuries for the European culture in New Zealand to discover just how far what it did to the land was from any long-term guarantee of sustainable harmony. When it does, any surviving trace of the richest pieces in the jigsaw of these islands' native ecosystem will have a value we today can barely imagine.

To become what Kirkpatrick Sale calls 'dwellers-in-the-land', to understand what he calls *place*, 'the immediate specific place where we live; the kinds of soils . . . under our feet; the source of the waters we drink . . . the common insects, birds, plants . . . the particular cycles of the seasons; the limits of its resources; the carrying capacity of its lands and waters; the places where it must not be stressed; the places where its bounties can be best developed . . .', we need land in its wild natural state. In the future, when more is known about 'sustainability', some of our most precious national landscapes are going to be those where, as an old friend of mine once wisely said, the life forces of nature and culture have been allowed to go on expressing themselves. Without reference points like the sandplain, people will never know how they're changing the land, let alone how it was before their predecessors came off the ships.

For obvious historical reasons, national parks simply don't contain fertile, coastal country like the sandplain. The Punakaiki coast that Waitaha recognised as auspicious is one of the few prospects for a national park that could, yet not without the sandplain forest. Ecologically, the plant and animal species that contribute the living parts of ecosystems distribute themselves along the different environmental gradients such as fertility, temperature, moisture. For every gradient that has been measured in the Punakaiki lowlands, the sandplain forest stands out, distinctive and without comparison.

It is now recognised that any attempt to halt further decline of these ruined ecosystems must begin with remnants. The sandplain forest has been identified as one of the most important. But for West Coasters who see the flat seam between the mountains and the sea as a precious agricultural resource, to listen tolerantly to talk about keeping some bits wild for plants to keep reproducing themselves, for seed and pollen-dispersing birds to fly to for winter food, for nutrients to cycle and their energy and water to flow as they did before we came, is contrary to everything the European spirit of finding plains and settling them has been about.

The first time I saw the sandplain and its succession of sand dunes and storm beaches gone under forest, the giant kahikatea at one end and, at the other, low coastal scrub shorn smooth by the wind, a dozen shades of green, I knew I had encountered a special place. I remember the intimidating press of the wind on the beach and the roar of the sea drowning out every sound. And then, only 100 metres away, the lagoon, cold, clear and calm in the pale winter's morning, only the big trees stirring.

It still seems as forsaken as ever. A national park has appeared around it. Miners have bought up its neighbouring dairy farms but their laboratory stands locked and shuttered, the trial extraction plant silent. While they have prospected and the world price of their ilmenite has been creeping up, the pasture has been yielding to rushes and gorse, and if you look closely enough, the first signs of returning forest. But there is tension in the landscape. I fear what might be around the corner and whether the tiny rectangle of wildness will be able to cope.

'The end of Nature', Bill McKibbin calls the collapse of life-support systems into remnants. He fears that we are reluctant to attach ourselves to remnants for the same reason that we don't usually choose friends from among the terminally ill. But there is nothing reluctant about the way the descendants of the people who inhabited the sandplain 500 years ago invest it with meaning and spirit. So resolute have they been to keep it quiet and empty, the last time I walked through to the lagoon the track was so overgrown I lost it.

NECESSARY
PROTECTION

Arts and letters, ethics and religion, law and folklore still regard
the wild things of the land either as enemies, or as food, or as dolls
to be kept 'for pretty'. This view of land is our inheritance from
Abraham, whose foothold in the land of milk and honey was still
a precarious one, but it is outmoded for us. Our foothold is
precarious, not because it may slip but because we may kill the
land before we begin to use it with love and respect. Conservation
is a pipe-dream as long as Homo sapiens is cast in the role of
conqueror, and his land in the role of slave and servant.
Conservation becomes possible only when man assumes the role of
citizen in a community of which soils and waters, plants and
animals are fellow members, each dependent on the others, and
each entitled to his place in the sun.

ALDO LEOPOLD, *A SAND COUNTY ALMANAC*

Fair earth, we have broken our idols
and after the days of fire we shall
come to you
For the stones of a new temple.

A.R.D. FAIRBURN, *ELEMENTS*

If we are to be properly humble in our use of the world, we need
places that we do not use at all. We need the experience of leaving
something alone. We need places that we forebear to change, or
influence by our presence, or impose on even by our understanding;
places that we accept as influences upon us, not the other way
around, that we enter in a kind of cultural nakedness, without
comforts or tools, to submit rather than to conquer. We need what
other cultures would have called sacred groves.

WENDELL BERRY, *THE UNSETTLING OF AMERICA*

CENTURY AND a half of European settlement banishing nature from
the lowlands has carved a divide in New Zealanders' minds. Seldom
now does anyone locate the spirit of the land in what a poet once
called 'the savage forests that from groins and armpits of the hills so fiercely
look'. The mountains, not the plains, are the location of New Zealanders'
passion for the natural world. It isn't wrong, but after getting to know some
of the few places where nature survives on the plains, I am sure it is
misleading.

New Zealanders are not mountain people. The vast majority of us
are coastal dwellers, edge-of-the-land or plains people inhabiting the grid
squares of the 19th century's surveyors, keeping our distance from 'the
uncolonized nothing . . . the peaks that plunge their icy heads into space'.
New Zealand may be named after a totally flat, agricultural province of the
Netherlands, but it has no Great Plains, no antipodean Nile, no Euphrates
delta. It has, though, been colonised as if it abounded in them. Proclaimed
a land of 'Planes and Vallies' by the men who found it for Europe, it was
soon attracting labels like 'the granary of the New Southern World'. Lobbed
into a void of knowledge, never checked, the myth persisted to shape the
schemes of colony-makers and make us the plains people we effectively
are.

'Thousands and tens of thousands of acres as level as can be found in
England . . . when the land is cleared, the plough shall go over nineteen
acres out of twenty,' an elated New Zealand Company colonist wrote home
from Taranaki in 1842. Elsewhere, others were chiding the Company for

'the want of flat land'. Yet three-quarters of a century later, the geologist James Bell was still optimistic. 'If New Zealand were ironed out,' he began *The Wilds of Maoriland*, 'it would make a fine, large country.' Perhaps it was Bell's uncommon sense of time that led him to 'picture even vaster flocks of sheep and cattle than we know today roaming over a flat country when, ages hence, the mountains have been worn down . . . to make new lands in the oceans'.

In *Terra Incognita Australis*, the antipodean utopia that Gabriel de Foigny had imagined centuries earlier, there was 'not one mountain to be seen; the natives having levelled them all'. The inhabitants of this 'great flat country, without forests, marshes or deserts . . . much more fertile and populous than any in Europe', lived on fruit that grows on trees all the year round. The words James Cook used to describe the promise of his new-found River Thames were almost identical to those with which the Renaissance writer St. Thomas Aquinas depicted his perfect country—'where the soil is so fertile that it nobly provides for all the necessities of life'. The intimate union of town and country Edward Gibbon Wakefield envisioned in his theory of British colonisation of New Zealand could similarly have been lifted from Sir Thomas More's *Utopia*. No utopian allowed land to go 'to waste'. 'Nature' didn't rate a mention.

'Every valley shall be made plain, every hill shall be made low . . . for our God', the Rev Richard Taylor urged his newly Christian natives. By the time New Zealand became a piece of empire, utopian ideals had been called on time and time again to 'tame Nature where she is most unbridled'. As Bell's *The Wilds of Maoriland* went to print in 1913, a Royal Commission was decreeing the clearance of the last of the plains' kahikatea forest 'forthwith', for dairy farms. The Department of Agriculture that year still referred to forests that had 'yet to be subdued'—but was becoming anxious at 'the depletion of virgin fertility . . . the greatly increased toll of wealth being extracted from New Zealand soils . . . the prodigious and alarming' wastage of nature's bounties. What a few years before had seemed limitless—nature's potential for each place as expressed through what we today call species,

CLEARING AND DYNAMITING THE FLATS, 1890S.

genes and ecosystems—was vanishing in front of the eyes of the 'pioneers of Empire'.

As much as limits are the least of the concerns of those who invade and exploit new territory, it is in the nature of human beings to discriminate. In the landscape like everywhere else the good is sorted from the not-so-good, the useful from the useless. By 1913 the only signs of nature on most plains were the blackened stumps that hadn't yet been dynamited. Plants the Europeans brought had changed the face of every plain they inhabited. It had begun even before the settlers of 1840 waited impatiently on the beach to possess their rectangle of 'entangled, impervious forest'. To Charles Darwin in 1835, it was a simple matter of the superiority of European life. Recalling slogging all day through fernland and forest, then seeing the fields and orchards of the Waimate mission station, he said it was as though 'the enchanter's wand' had been swept over the country.

Within less than two decades, English land laws, war and prejudice about the wild had been as effective as any enchanter's wand. 'As regards polish of cultivation,' wrote Charles Hursthouse, 'the garden's glories, the plough's court robes, New Zealand is much in the state that Britain was when Caesar landed; and if Caesar's Britain could now be shown to us, many a bright champaign country which we call beautiful, would vanish to reveal the gloomy forest and repulsive waste.' About as far as it was possible to get from their culture's homeland, yet still loyal to its resolute beliefs about how to use fertile plains, settlers like Hursthouse reserved the superlatives for the soil and the grass, the meat and wool it grew. 'The lands of the colony were fertile enough,' wrote Julius Vogel, 'to warrant the expenditure necesary to open them to the operation of human energy.' This opening, or Europeanisation as it has been called, required everything pre-existing on the plains to go, for the land 'to know them never again'.

Vogel, despite furious opposition, was the first politician to propose forest conservation. Yet of all factors working against nature, his 1877 Land Act was perhaps the most destructive. To create his Britain of the South's 'essentially agricultural' grid landscape, it took to the lowland forests like a scythe. Selectors—those applying for land or licensed to occupy it—were obliged to 'bring it into cultivation' immediately or forfeit it. Ten per cent of suburban land and five per cent of rural acres had to be cleared of forest in the first year. Within four years, a rural selector had to be cultivating 20 per cent of his land. His town counterpart had to 'have enclosed the whole of his allotment with a substantial fence, and . . . cultivated at least three-fourths of it'. By law and threat, our ordinary countryside was shaped.

By 1893 people with a concern for nature, like the Rev Phillip Walsh, were noticing how for most New Zealanders the 'wealth of ferns' had 'vanished with the bellbird and the tui, and must now be sought amongst the far-off mountain ranges'. One of the few who spoke out about what was happening, Walsh could see that although 'familiar enough to older colonists, [it] hardly comes within the observation of later arrivals and of the younger generation of our town populations—namely, the deplorable destruction of almost all forms of indigenous vegetation which is taking place throughout the country'.

Within two generations of 1840, the seed James Cook sowed in the utopian dreams of men like Edward Gibbon Wakefield had created a land-scape whose people had virtually no contact with nature; who believed, what's more, they no longer needed it. But the Rev Walsh knew that one day their descendants would. 'We want something nearer at hand,' he said, 'something we can see and enjoy as a portion of our daily life. We are familiar with the blue-gum and the Pinus insignis, with the Norfolk pine and macrocarpa. But of the indigenous vegetation most of us know very little indeed.'

The historian W.H. Oliver has made the point that the forefathers of the modern Pākehā were too busy reshaping the land to let it—or Māori—reshape them in any way. We can't, as he says, blame them individually for what we find missing today. 'Until landscape became saturated with memories of birth and childhood, love and poverty and war'—until, as Peter Hooper said, we had made for ourselves our own, not England's, past—the new culture was blind to Aotearoa's unique natural life. But with so many immigrants for so little plains country, the forests couldn't last that long. Those modern New Zealanders who need nature as neighbour are lucky their country didn't turn out to be the country of the New Zealand Company's mind—'full two-thirds capable of being beneficially cultivated . . . the average nature of the soil, a rich alluvial'. Had it been, New Zealand would now look like Holland or the endless, farmed grid of the American mid-west.

Is it too much to call this a campaign against nature? The wholesale levelling of the plains forests, like the 'extinguishing' of their native title, could scarcely have happened without the connivance of governments. Only by settlement, said Julius Vogel of his 1877 Land Act, could 'the Maori difficulty' be met. Barely a decade from a war won with difficulty, anything native on the plains became effectively an enemy of the state. As a result the *selective* taking of land, picking out the fertile eyes of it for settlers, leaving Māori to eke out an existence on the remains, is at the root of Māori economic disadvantage a century later, still visceral in land claim after land claim: 'What was confiscated was the best of Tuhoe's flat and fertile land'.

Vogel intended a *new* landscape—rational, rectangularised, beholden to agriculture. Landscapes can be potent like that. In 1939 the Nazis prepared a plan to make Poland the East Areas of Germany—using exclusively German native plants once they had eliminated its people. The Teutonic German, they said, must be made 'to feel himself, to be at home'.

Connection with nature is expressed by every religion, every prophet and every scholar of myth. The sad fact of New Zealand's lowlands is that they were found, possessed and gutted by a *foreign* culture at a point in its history when what Thomas Berry calls the mystique of industry entranced it more than the mystique of nature. That culture's spread out of Europe has had global consequences: the explosion in humanity's numbers and unprecedented devastation of natural ecosystems. Only now are those of us who dwell in its aftermath beginning to attach value to the vestiges that survived.

Every country, argues the eminent conservation biologist Edward O. Wilson, possesses three kinds of riches—material, cultural and biological. 'Animals and plants are part of a country's heritage; they are the result of millions of years of evolution in a particular place; they are at least as valuable as language or culture.' Of the many risky things happening in our times, he believes the riskiest is the loss of ecosystems as the human species dismantles the natural world in which, over millions of years, its brain has assembled. Yet one of the problems of the modern conservation ethic, as he himself has pointed out, is the way natural selection works on people. We think mostly in personal, physiological time. We find it extremely hard to value ecosystems with which we have no generational experience. Our minds can travel back and forth across hours, days and working lives; longer time scales are not so easy. The plains forests may be all cut, their fertile soils degrading under our agriculture, but if it happened more than a few generations back, or the effects are unlikely to devastate for a few more yet, hardly anyone notices. Few dispute that 'changing useless swamp into rich farm land' will 'produce ever increasing wealth'. And as surely as the 19th-century landscapes of nature as neighbourhood have slid into myth, obligations to future generations fail to compel.

On 22 January 1990 the people of Wellington celebrated the site where it is said the first recruits to Edward Gibbon Wakefield's utopian dream stepped ashore. The day was not about land so much as the meeting of cultures that had taken place on Petone Beach 150 years earlier. Everyone spoke of the way Māori and European co-operated. But their dreams of 1840 were 1990s dreams.

No one swept their arm around to where the sand hills had been, and behind them the forest. Speakers recounted the first southerly felling the settlers' tents and overturning the boats they slept under, but not how, with Te Atiawa's help, the forest provided the trees and supplejack vines to build shelter. And food too. It was as if before the survey lines there was nothing; the wild land was just a blank slate on which history happened.

Fifty years earlier in January 1940, there were freezing works behind the beach full of export carcasses ready for England, instead of computer companies. The orators on the flag-draped centennial stage were full of rhetoric and confidence in the empire the place and moment symbolised. In a similar ceremony on another floodplain so tied to empire some still call it the Thames, a local member of parliament unveiled a plaque to Cook the navi-gator and spoke about 'untidy Maori pa', 'curious brown men' and 'mighty trees'.

Nineteen-forty was only five years on from the Labour Party exorting New Zealanders 'to utilise to its maximum degree the wonderful resources of the Dominion'. Even less meaningful to New Zealand life than the finiteness of nature's resources or the need to conserve them, the Treaty of Waitangi lay forgotten, rat-eaten, in a Wellington basement. The plains that had been the larder of Māori life had become the centrepiece of the attempt to replicate rural Britain in the South Pacific. In places as remote as the Mōkau River and the head of Whanganui Inlet, the dairy industry was marking the last bits of plains forest for farms, and their kahikatea for mills hungry for butterbox timber. By 1947 the New Zealand Forest Service was reporting the national kahikatea resource in the past tense.

As New Zealand celebrated a century of European conquest, Herbert Guthrie-Smith in a new preface to his famous *Tutira* was dismally reconsidering the story of the clearing of the forest and its replacement by alien plants and animals that he had told so assuredly 20 years before. It was in part a question of ethics, he wrote , of 'simple right and wrong, one increasingly clamatory in years'. But it was also, he believed, a matter of who he was, the contest between Scots forebears impelling him to 'Destroy your fern! Clear off your woods' and an Irish ancestry telling him to 'Admire, conserve, let well alone'. 'Have I then,' he reflected, 'for sixty years desecrated God's earth and dubbed it improvement?' 'Nor, being of philosophic mind,' he added, 'am I absolutely happy on another score—my substitution of domestic breeds of animals for native lizards and birds; my substitution of one flora for another.'

While Guthrie-Smith pondered his 'contribution towards more quickly melting New Zealand through erosion into the Pacific', another observer of nature was reproaching New Zealanders for their apathy toward the destruction of what was to her an avian paradise. Writing to the Society for the Preservation of the Fauna of the Empire, Perrine Moncrieff described a 'sylvan Parthenon' collapsing as human impact destroyed 'whole links in the chain-armour defence of the forest'. Central to the forest's wellbeing was the timeless, intimate coexistence of its birds and plants: 'the one inter-acting upon the other so delicately that, without each other, neither could flourish'. Everywhere she looked, nature's ancient ecosystem was showing signs of stress and breakdown.

Today, conservation ecology puts new words to Perrine Moncrieff's worries. Forests are ecosystems with intricate nutrient cycles and energy flow pathways. Biological corridors facilitate the movement of wide-ranging, seed-dispersing species like kererū, and enable genetic exchange between populations and migration in response to climate change. In South Westland, as far as you can get from the 'Convenient Situations' of the New Zealand Company, we have managed to save something of the full sprawl of forest— out from the cold mountains across the watery plains to the sea. Elsewhere, we know that when the smoke of Victorian settlers' fires cleared from the plains—'the glorious sight presented by the tall pines, of fire right at the top, some of them dotted all over with brilliant lights resembling spirit lamps'—more than just trees and birds had disappeared. Breaking open an energy system which had been millennia in the making, New Zealand agriculture's mining of soil carbon had started to destroy a vast genetic library, subtly different in each part of the country.

With these insights, the natural life of New Zealand presents itself to us, not as a meaningless clamour of myriad plants and animals, but as a mosaic of life *systems*, as complex as they are delicate, caught up in the unique and comprehensive unity of the country itself. Each system has evolved a unique pattern of life which is intimately related to systems adjoin-ing it. Wherever plains occur, in other words, they connect ecologically with the rivers and hills alongside, in parallel with their geomorphic evolution from them. It is in this sense that human settlement's tearing-out of the plains' forests and swamps has so disrupted the wider ecosystem. Birds seen in the hills in the early afternoon could have spent the morning in coastal swamps. As speedily as weasels and stoats switched off each district's dawn chorus, the first crops of grass on the plains rendered the hills and mountains quiet.

As New Zealand entered its second century of European control, it became harder and harder for some people to reconcile its agricultural prosperity with the estrangement from nature it had brought about. Another who looked into the forest in the early 1940s revealed something more than a vanishing paradise for birds—a fascination for the timeless life of these islands. 'To stand on the edge of the primeval forest,' wrote Monte Holcroft, is to encounter 'something that is not ours, something that has never belonged even to the Maori, but has known centuries of an undisturbed stillness, or has contained some dream of life too strange for our minds to grasp . . . something to be feared.'

Holcroft called that unsettling quality he felt in a West Coast plains forest remnant *the primeval shadow*. Like the 'spiritual grandeur' of Janet Frame's dark-foliaged bush—'the forest and the land are clearly the parents, the ancestors making their presence known, and what else may people do but rebel against a life of such dependence?'—he believed it would have immense cultural consequences. Until they found a reconciliation with the forest, Holcroft forecast, New Zealanders would remain cut off from any real depth of spiritual life. When nature's primordial forces were recognised,

KORU.

the forest would become 'an unexpected source of power in an adventure of the spirit'. Then the fern frond might symbolise something more than the awful wild and become the iconic koru of A.R.D. Fairburn's 'coiled spring . . . fit instrument to play archaic tunes'. Then the groves of totara, rimu and kahikatea at Whirinaki, Okarito and Pureora—still to be rescued from the chainsaws—would come to be called New Zealanders' cathedrals.

Europeans had always been unsettled by New Zealand's landscape. Dumont D'Urville was aware of a 'solemn, almost sinister atmosphere' pervading the country in the 1820s—then, as Perrine Moncrieff said, under a forest mantle 'right to the water's edge'. It was, he said, like a state of suspended evolution, as if one were transported to that point in time 'when nature, having produced the members of the plant kingdom, still waited for the decree of the Eternal to bring forth living creatures'. Another traveller noticed the same forces 150 years later. While he didn't overlook New Zealanders' singular passion for eradication, J.B. Priestley considered the land's primal forces offered an urgent message, 'sinister, strangely menacing, suddenly revealing another and terrible aspect of the New Zealand scene'. It was certainly not Auberon Waugh's Britain of the South 'exactly like England . . . the same green fields everywhere for producing the same New Zealand butter and Canterbury lamb we ate here'. Nor the repeat performance of Europe that last century's settlers pretended. 'Some Nature god of the South Pacific,' ventured Priestley, 'Warning us that we were deceiving ourselves if we thought we were in another Eden.'

Holcroft was aware of the ancient 'struggle against the forest' locked away in the dim regions of the human psyche, 'an unconscious memory of the primeval journey from the cave to safe pastures'. In their escape from Britain, he suggested, the colonists were effectively returning to the forests of their prehistoric origins. Behind their ruthless, almost religious, crusade to implant a disciplined British landscape in the South Pacific was determination to supress any re-emergence of their animist past. Yet Holcroft's primeval shadow is trapped in its own language. His 'wild profusion of native trees, ferns and parasitic growths' transmitting some primordial memory to immigrant Europeans is no different from what early settlers like Charles Hursthouse called 'the primeval dress of nature' and dismissed as 'savagery'.

There are, in other words, *two* shadows over New Zealanders and their landscape: the primordial forces of nature that Holcroft and Priestley sensed; and the 19th-century mischief with which immigrant Europeans took over the country and, disallowing Māori their native sense of it, labelled it as primeval waste awaiting cultivation. Both treat nature as if numb to our presence and blind to our behaviour; enabling it to diminish and still, at times, terrify us, reminding us, Māori and Pākehā, of how momentary the human grip on these islands has been. As surely as they guided the Victorian campaigns to annihilate nature, they guide the passions that have been saving native forests from chainsaws since the 1970s.

The 'empty places' that led Monte Holcroft 'straight back to the unknown' are like Cook's wild and conveniently vacant plains. Prior to the predations of rats and stoats, his primeval shadow's 'sharp edge of silence' may simply not have existed. It resembles 'the balance of nature', a cultural metaphor deeply rooted in the Western psyche but revealed as a fallacy by any New Zealand swamp that preserves the evidence of ever-changing climates and forests. The primeval shadow undeniably evokes what Thomas Berry calls the mystique of the land, but it is ultimately a colonialism. As long as it lingers it will alienate New Zealanders from nature—and Pākehā from Māori.

Intuitive in pre-missionary Polynesian knowledge is the *unity* in living matter, humans included. Nature abounds with spirits. And, without romanticising early Māori, this knowledge gives some clues to the human ecology of these islands prior to Europeans. A taste of it—*the Land with all Wood and Waters*—is preserved on a Whangaroa land deed signed just weeks before the Treaty of Waitangi. More substantive evidence is the simple, unambiguous picture that emerges when you plot all the archaeological evidence of pre-19th-century Māori. River mouths, estuaries, dune lakes, lagoons and inlets were where the great majority lived up to 1840. Māori were, in other words, essentially the same edge-of-the-land dwellers Polynesians have always been.

The Treaty that historians have led us to understand in terms of law and land ownership, government and te tino rangitiratanga, is as much as anything about the human ecology of northern New Zealand in 1840. The need for the Treaty arose in a particular landscape, and it would be a mistake to read it by that landscape's late-20th-century appearance. But historians are not renowned for their insights into landscape and its ecology. 'The Land with all Woods and Waters' looked nothing like the estuary and river country we see today. With its kahikatea, harakeke and birds, it functioned differently—as differently perhaps as its native inhabitants from today's Māori.

This fertile, flat, coastal country was considered, in 1840, the best land. Its 'forests' were the taonga whose wellbeing the elders who assembled at Te Ti early in February 1840 wanted spelt out in the Treaty of Waitangi—refusing to sign until it was. Even then, of course, that wasn't the end of it. 'No No No, Mr Governor, you will not square out our land and sell it!', Kaitoke, a Hokianga chief, told William Hobson the following week. Here, with fish and birds, were most of the plants that had found their way into the Māori diet; once, that is, the failed tropical root crops were distant memories. Yet the ardour with which Māori welcomed European potatoes suggests it was hardly a Garden of Eden. Extracting food from the forests and swamps, like felling trees and building canoes before metal axes, was hard work, demanding energy and time and suffused with ritual and limitations. It succumbed to the new order as fast as Māori adopted cows, cabbages and fruit trees.

<hr />

I the undersigned, a Chief of New Zealand acknowledge to have received from Simeon Lord Esq. One musket and other Articles for which I engage to deliver the Bearer One Ton of New Zealand Flax or Mooka on Demand.

Farming, the London Missionary Society believed, would remedy Māori's primitive, pagan dependence on nature. But while Māori in the early 19th century became Christian farmers in large numbers, the new economy and its enforcer, the musket, also radically altered the Māori landscape, shifting people down into the coastal swamps into the path of fearful new diseases. The ecosystem whose spars and flax so impressed James Cook was precisely where Māori first became apprehensive of European intentions.

Conflict followed Cook into 'the Land with all Woods and Waters' like a shadow. The sounds of guns and axes rang out as early as 1771, when Marion Du Fresne, seeking new masts to replace the ones ruined in the South Indian Ocean, gave up on the burnt, scrubby trees of Tasmania and anchored instead off the tall, wet forests of a New Zealand river mouth. A believer in the goodness of 'the natural man' living close to nature, Marion settled his men in three timber camps in the bush. Blind to Ngāpuhi tapu, they rambled about the wooded estuary at will, shooting game and catching fish. After a few days, it began to seem the visitors intended to remain there always. Inside a few stealthy hours, Marion and 27 of his men were dead. To the lieutenant, Crozet, to whom there was no such thing as the Good Savage. His retaliation left some 50 Ngāpuhi dead and their villages destroyed.

By 1820, when Richard Cruise sailed into the Bay of Islands on the naval store ship *Dromedary*, Ngāpuhi had converted their landscape's spars and flax into their muskets. Cruise heard about many more deaths than French ones. The *Dromedary* was seeking more of 'the stick of first rate quality' that had found its way from Cook's new River Thames to England's naval yards in the 1790s. Kahikatea was one of the trees they hoped to find in proximity to water. They did: 'The Kaikaterre . . . growing to an immense height is found in swampy ground . . . on the banks of rivers, and is . . . easy to procure.' Three miles up from the mouth of the Waikare, a shore party took to smaller boats. The speed with which each village knew they were coming impressed Cruise as much as the towering trees. Between the villages and their 'small spots of cultivation . . . the ground . . . appeared never to have been disturbed'. Beyond the Waikare, up the Kawakawa River, they found what they wanted: 'a profusion of kaikaterre spars, of the largest dimensions . . . for naval purposes, growing close to the water's edge'.

Drawn like a magnet to the 'the Land with all Wood and Waters', the spar-getters, traders and missionaries of the early 1800s did not lie back and discuss landscape aesthetics with the natives. The Treaty's Māori signatories were not blind: 'We all tried to find out the reason why the Governor was so anxious to get us to make these marks . . . and when we met the Governor, the speaker of Maori [the interpreter] told us that if we put our names, or even made any sort of mark on that paper, the Governor would then protect us, and prevent us from being robbed of our cultivated land, and our timber land, and everything else which belonged to us.' In the event, they signed knowing what they were doing; as they knew, by 1840, the concept of selling land. What they failed to appreciate was just how many Pākehā were going to come.

Robert FitzRoy, the aristocratic master of the *Beagle* on which Charles Darwin visited New Zealand, saw the problem coming as early as 1835. 'The Natives,' he told the British House of Lords, 'live almost entirely upon the Sea Coast . . . the Part of which is immediately around the Harbours, which is also the Part which would be of most Use to Settlers.' FitzRoy made no mention of the plants and animals that were part and parcel of these fecund coastal environments. Darwin, travelling as his dining companion, noticed European weeds spreading like quicksilver around the Bay of Islands flats. Most of his observations, however, remain lost with his New Zealand notebooks. He was never one to miss much of a place's ecology, and undoubtedly saw here the same British birds he had observed on the missionaries' farms at Waimate outsmarting those from the primeval forest. New Zealand seemed only to confirm the theory beginning to brew in his mind that life is a jungle in which only the fittest, the superior, survive.

'The land is the people; break up the land and you break up the people.' No symbol more graphically expresses the land's shattering than the devil monster that started coming out of English ships once the Treaty was signed. Taipo, the people were soon calling it. Its three, all-seeing eyes more than made up for the lack of a body above its three spindly legs. So speedily did the land change once the surveyor's theodolite turned its eyes on a stretch of country, that when people saw it coming, they expected it to destroy everything forever. In the late 20th century New Zealand society is being propelled to recognise the repercussions of the events of the 1840s on Māori health and wellbeing. But few of us have a clue what, *ecologically*, the land at the centre of them was like.

'No, we are not agreeable to give up our land,' insisted Aperahama Taonui of Hokianga—named by missionaries for the biblical Abraham—in 1840. 'It is from the earth we obtain all things. The land is our father; the land is our chieftainship. We will not give it up.' In the British government's Instructions to William Hobson, Lord Normanby had written of the need for the 'free and intelligent consent of the natives expressed according to their established usages first

Theodolite with surveyor, **AORERE, C.1900.**

being obtained'. There were some willing sellers. Only a few weeks before the Treaty's signing, several chiefs who the British thought would sell were enjoying themselves at the Governor's garden party in Sydney, but they left unsigned the version of the Treaty he put in front of them the next day because it ceded much more than their sovereignty to the British Crown. It ceded their natural capital.

For any chief signing the Treaty on 6 February 1840, the clause that gave Māori 'the full, exclusive and undisturbed possession of their Lands, Estates, Forests, Fisheries and other properties', or 'unqualified exercise of chieftainship over their lands . . . and over their treasures' was more important than the one preceding it that created a government. Hobson only secured their marks on the parchment document because his version had benefited from the insight of people like Henry Williams about the integral relationship Māori had with the landscapes in which they lived. To many rangitira gathered at Waitangi, though, many scarcely able to hold a quill let alone read critically or write their name, the ink marks they made may not have been much more than a souvenir of the event. The contract that mattered—the agreement they believed had been reached orally—never left Waitangi.

At the other end of The Fish of Maui, where impatient settlers waited at the edge of a plain for the New Zealand Company's surveyors to cut their lines through a swamp forest, Henry Williams had another job to do. He had a land speculators' republic to up-end.

A presidential palace had pride of place in the grand town the Company planned to call Britannia. When they were refused a charter for it, they sent their land purchase agent, surveyors and colonists non-stop across the world. 'The emergency of the events at Port Nicholson', Hobson called their claim of autonomy when it reached him in the Bay of Islands within weeks of the signing of his Treaty. Months passed before the chiefs around Cook Strait saw his Treaty. They signed unanimously, the missionary Henry Williams telling Hobson it had been 'with much satisfaction . . . that a check was put to the importunities of the Europeans to the purchase of their lands, and that protection was now afforded them'.

Hobson was not trying to get the New Zealand Company off their floodplain—he simply wanted to *control* its capture of arcadia. Eventually, in July 1840, the Company yielded its brief bid at sovereignty, explaining that its hasty action in setting apart 'the most valuable sections of land' had been for public purposes. Hobson, acknowledging its acquiescence, hoped that 'under the Divine Providence the resources of these valuable and important islands may be speedily developed'. Then he got on with the business of choosing the best site from which to lead the country. Eventually, though, the forces he represented would bow to the New Zealand Company's strategic choice of Cook Strait as the place to govern New Zealand.

Hobson's choice was as ecological as Wakefield's: close to level land, water, timber and flax. But it was hundreds of miles away, back in Cook's great harbour. He wrote to the Secretary of State for the Colonies extolling 'the fertility of the soil which is . . . available for every agricultural purpose, the richest and most valuable land in the northern island being concentrated within a radius of fifty miles'. To verify his acumen, he enclosed a fresh report from the river which England's famous navigator had praised 70 years earlier:

> *The breadth of this magnificent valley . . . of the Thames . . . the most eligible situation for the settlement of an extensive agricultural population . . . the whole of this immense tract is available . . . the banks of both rivers are covered with an uninterrupted belting of wood . . . ; clumps which have rather a beautiful and picturesque*

appearance, and contrast strongly with the apparent nakedness of the surrounding plain . . . with very little labour, and merely by opening out the natural drains, all these flax flats might be made available; they in general contain the richest of the soil.

As Hobson wrote, George Clarke, Protector of Aborigines, was on the banks of Cook's River Thames, persuading its kaitiaki to lift its ancient tapu. He was readying it for settlers—for a rout that didn't stop until every big tree, even the burial kahikatea of the old river people, was down.

The modern environmental movement with its accent on ecosystems has done much to promote the world view that everything is connected to everything else, and that you cannot remove one piece of the jigsaw without repercussions—new, unforeseen problems—elsewhere. The first rule of the tinkerer, Aldo Leopold entreated, is to keep *all* of the pieces.

We know that New Zealand's national parks and nature reserves fail in the lowlands. Colonial resolve to create a replica Britain isolated the tiny scenic remains of nature from anything of their kind, increasing the rate of change in the environment far beyond what their constituent species had experienced during their evolutionary histories, and beyond the rate of genetic adaption. It's a fact of history we can't change. Until the passionate campaigns of the 1970s saved Whirinaki and Okarito, almost all 20th-century conservationists, timid before the authority of agricultural and timber interests, focused their effort on islands and high-elevation wildernesses.

As 'progress' in Western culture is so often measured by the technological innovations by which humans have gained more and more of the planet's productivity, nature is usually considered to be life operating independently of us. The Western approach to conservation sets nature aside as large tracts of land in a state of imagined innocence—national parks and other 'reserves'. Particularly highly valued in this scheme are forests said to be 'virgin' or 'pristine' or 'primeval'. The people who have nurtured traditional, spiritual ties to these forests know the reality to be different.

Conservation in New Zealand is no more multi-cultural than it is innocent endeavour without a compromising history. It obtained much of its land by stealth and confiscation in the years of government-led devastation of taha Māori. It is prevailed upon by preservation, an ethic rooted in dogma about an ephemerally occupied, but otherwise empty, land whose 'many types of ancient forms' needed to be saved in their 'old primeval grandeur'. Conservation began in the minds of men who viewed Māori as a vanishing race whose attitude to nature reflected a primitive stage in human progress, irrelevant to modern needs. Their settler culture was utilitarian, but liked ferny glades, waterfalls and forest clearings for bush picnics. The scenic reserve—conservation's main agent in the colonial landscape, and in most New Zealand lowlands today—was just another masthead on which the empire could fly its banners over this new garden. A century later, it is one of the most resilient and dominant, and at the same time politically constraining, symbols in the European landscape tradition. A direct steal from 18th-century Europe's aesthetics of the picturesque, the heart of the scenic reserve idea lay in the beautiful, awesome and sublime. But it marginalised *ordinary* nature, just as it made the sacred ancestral places left to nature's forces into curiosities.

The idea that Māori society before European contact was a model of ecological prudence has come under pressure in recent years. The country the first Europeans saw wasn't a pristine wilderness, but neither was it a run-down desert, burnt from one end to the other. Confounding the evidence of moa butchery-grounds and rubbish heaps with now-extinct birds' bones at the bottom but little more than shellfish at the top, are countless 19th-century European journals, sketches and paintings showing how close Māori lived to healthy-looking forests and swamps. Like many indigenous societies, Māori traditionally depended on a limited resource catchment, augmenting it by manipulating the landscape. Strong incentives to nurture and sustain biotic diversity were closely integrated with moral and religious belief systems. 'He may be a bit primitive,' said Elsdon Best, 'but he knows the functions of seeds and the varied manifestations of Dame Nature in the wao nui a Tane.'

Maori Village, King Country,
W.G. BAKER, 1860s.

It is in this context that Māori knowledge of nature, like any other accrued over time, is significant to conservation. Sometimes, alone in a forest in early summer, when I can imagine the smells of its trees at the water's edge and the distant sound of the sea as daily sensations—when I can sense 'the immense, flat forest . . . so peaceful, so well suited to meditation' that William Yate experienced on the Hauraki Plains in 1832—I can begin to understand it. Those brief moments when the forest shadow of another New Zealand is so strong that consciousness slides off into another world have, I am sure, a spiritual effect.

One hundred and fifty years after their ancestor Aperahama Taonui declared the land and its forests his father, Te Mahurehure of Hokianga protested the government's plans to rid Waipoua Forest of possums by aerially poisoning it. They knew a sacred, indwelling spirit was responsible for the forest's fruitfulness. Waipoua's mauri, they said, would be destroyed, and when the mauri of a river, person, bird or forest goes into decline, everything does.

The pragmatic Polynesians who came ashore a millenium ago brought with them a deep-seated sense of shared origins and even blood kinship with all life and all elements of the cosmos. Like *whenua*, a word that means both *land* and *placenta*, *mauri* is older than Māori, older than Polynesia itself. As *ma'uri* it was in existence by what linguists call Proto-Polynesian time, meaning *be alive (not dead)* as it still does today in some Western Oceania languages. In Vanuatu, the wild, western coast is known as *tahi mauri*, compared to the 'deathly' still eastern *tahi mate*. *Ko na mauri*, the common greeting in Kiribati, conveys the same sense of life and health. As *ola* or *ora* became the ordinary Polynesian equivalent for *life*, *mauri* took on the metaphysical connotations of life force or spirit.

'Know that by nature,' said René Descartes, 300 years ago, 'I do not understand some goddess of some sort of imaginary power . . . I employ this word to signify matter itself . . . There exists no occult forces in stones or plants.' From Descartes descends the Western doctrine that reduces nature to senseless, valueless and purposeless objects. Securing Westerners from nature, it makes it next to impossible for them to regard nature as anything but a storehouse of material of which we are the 'masters and possessors'. But it made it easy for the New Zealand colony's London decision-makers to speak of Māori's spiritual fusion with nature as 'barbarous and superstitious customs' and Māori as rude inhabitants who 'attached no idea of value to unoccupied land'.

From the time of the 1820s missionaries, seven generations of law, science and public policy invalidated Māori spiritual knowledge of the natural world. Even a seasoned ethnologist like Elsdon Best, who called mauri 'the unseen presence' in the forest, denigrated it as 'primitive, super-stitious feelings'. Then as soon as 1985 legislation let the Waitangi Tribunal interrogate the past back to the events of 1840, the animist Māori world of guardian spirits, life forces and sea gods re-emerged. Without these spirits, the Tribunal found (in its very first decision), the foreshore and waters of the Manakau, for example, could not be managed properly. Keri Hulme ends *the bone people*: 'The old people's belief that this country, and our people, are different and special . . .' Maybe, she ventures, 'that thing which allied itself to us is still here . . . it sleeps now. It retired into itself when the world changed, when the people changed . . . but I am afraid for the mauri! Aue!'

Many Pākehā now dissociate themselves from the European ethos of conquest and its rationalised landscapes of square paddocks and dead straight roads. Many have an intuitive affinity for the idea of mauri, and are probably not surprised that, 1,000 years before the first Polynesians began landing here, the most striking thing the Romans noted about the people who were to become the first English—the Anglii tribe of the North Sea low country—was their passionate worship of nature and Earth. They lament the fading of what Albert Schweitzer called mankind's capacity to foresee and forestall. They ask: 'What is this place about? How do we fit into it?'

A sense of place is a fundamental human need. When poets, painters and novelists compress a sense of place into its essence, it is inevitably that connection between people and the land's non-human life—a connection whose sparse presence in Pākehā art and literature is symptom, perhaps, of the land's native spirit vanishing before the immigrant culture could evolve bonds of affection for it.

At its most meagre, a sense of place is the intuitive human skill we depend on to interpret the landscape and differentiate one place from another. Like the *genius loci* or 'spirit of place', it is about the forces that determine the uniqueness of each place; the immediate sensory vividness of plant textures, smells and animal sounds that Gerard Manley Hopkins called 'inscape'. What D.H. Lawrence called 'a great reality' is nebulous, impossible to measure, intensifying as we fuse with the country and learn to read it. But something, as he said, humans yearn for deeply.

Like Alexander Pope with his famous maxim 'Consult the Genius of the Place in all', Lawrence identified in particular with a locality's *elemental* nature. Both knew what most of us know instinctively but deny, that any place has its own nature—its own potential—without us. Pope's concern was with the havoc the nouveau riche were wreaking on rural England; Lawrence's came from the mass migrations of Europeans 'uprooted from the native soil, planted in strong aboriginal earth' of their new worlds. But he allowed that 'a new fierce salt of the earth in their mouths, penetrated and altered the substance of their bones . . . Their subtlest plasm was changed under the radiation of new skies, new influence of light, their first and rarest life-stuff transmuted . . . through hundreds of years, new races are made, people slowly smelted down and recast.'

Those who saw Lawrence write say he started with the landscape and looked and looked at it until gradually its 'spirit' expressed itself:

> For every great locality has its own pure daimon, and is conveyed at last into perfected life . . . Every great locality expresses itself perfectly, in . . . its own birds and beasts, lastly its own men, with their perfected works . . . It is so with all worlds and all places in the world. We may take it as a law. So now we wait for the fulfillment of the law in the west, the inception of a new era of living.

Wendell Berry, a modern prophet in the new cultures that Lawrence was anxious about, considers this the key to ecological sustainability. You cannot act well in a place, he says, until you have understood what nature intended for it: '. . . in country originally forested, the farmer must study the forest, because to be healthy, the field must be an analogue of the forest; in analogy its nature is remembered. The nature of the original forest is, so to speak, "the genius of the place", which one is obliged to consult, not by human prescription, but by natural law.'

Slowly Pākehā are coming to the sense of place Aotearoa forced on Māori—'Whata ngārongāro he tangata, toitū he whenua.' After the human frenzies there remains the ancient land. There is an indwelling yet little talked about primordial power in these islands. Obvious to those who contemplate the eruptions, floods and earthquakes within the brief span of European civilisations, is the hard truth that ultimately nature rules the land they inhabit.

Most New Zealanders, though, like many other members of the technological global culture that faces the 21st century, have but the barest comprehension of what nature intended for their place. Many ecological thinkers like Paul Shepard now fear that they have become too dislocated from nature for a new oneness with it to be possible. In his remarkable book *Nature and Madness* he argues that an intimate regard for nature is 'as native to the human organism in its adolescent years as any nutritive element in the diet'. Cultures like New Zealand's will ultimately pay a severe price for their colonisers' rapacity. Lacking close, regular, dependent contact with wild nature, and so prevented from instilling a sense and knowledge of it into their youth, they are, he believes, truly mad. I think of the dark, brooding quality that Sam Neill says distinguishes New Zealand films. Was 'this willingness to take no prisoners . . . always the potential for violence' seeded in the Victorian destruction of forests?

A century after British settlement, what John Beaglehole called New Zealand's *genius loci*—'the tenderness of place, the sense of intimacy . . . mingled with an habitual and inseparable surrounding'—was his chief concern for the country. While it 'pastures its soul in fields classically English', its true identity was where 'the bush perpetually and in silence renews its green, inviolate life'. It was another half century before a historian recognised 'the Pakeha discovery of the precious ecology of this country'.

This is why the survivors of the plains are priceless. Not just as remnants, last traces, the end of nature. Nor as outdoor museum pieces— curious islands of history fenced off from the rest of the countryside. But as guides to a sustainable future, reminders of the patterns of nature from which the land's wealth comes, sources of renewal for rebuilding similar ecosystems one day. If the last stands of one of empire's most ravaged ecosystems wither and die, something will truly have been lost.

A 1940s story, a true one I think, expresses this. The children on a Manawatu floodplain dairy farm grow up thinking the long drains, the macrocarpa and pine shelter belts and paddocks define their permanent world. Then one day they discover water in a line of post holes thay are watching being dug. In some, buried flax leaves are still intact. Later, a plough turns up a buried log like the stumps of the pukatea trees at the back of the farm. Yet it is not until they discover a circle of blackened river stones that they 'create in their mind's eye a swamp with its standing flax rising above the raupo, and see it forested at the fringes and crossed with the tracks of men. They people their vision of the past, becoming conscious of a longer and earlier history, so indefinitely long it loses itself in the recesses of their imagination. A new sense of place . . .' But the 'older past' has been 'rubbed out' by their fathers and grandfathers, 'like words rubbed off a slate'. The story is called 'Immigrant to Native'.

That is the challenge for conservation in New Zealand posed by the last bits of flat, wet forested ground at Mōkau, Papaitonga, Te Tai Tapu and Punakaiki. What appear to be mere accidental survivors of colonial damage symbolise to Māori the connections between natural Aotearoa and the ancestors who added to it, as they derived from it, their uniqueness. Two cosmologies—'two landscapes'—coexist in New Zealand. One senses that nature and people are separate, the other that they are inseparable. Caught between them, the business called conservation has to find ways to keep alive both the primordial scent of the land before people and the ancient wisdom that people conserve nature best by using it. It must find itself in the common ground between the archaic life of a New Zealand forest and the comparative milli-second of human intimacy with it.

———

As the 21st century dawns there is fervent Pākehā opposition to conservation becoming one of the spheres in which New Zealand endeavours to become a bicultural society. Any suggestion that the Treaty of Waitangi gives Māori rights to harvest plants and birds on the conservation estate is disputed with claims that it 'strikes directly at the preservation basis of our conservation legislation'. Yet, as New Zealand realises it is no longer an empire's enterprise, it is evolving a sense of land and country different from that which led the 'extinguishers of native title' and the scenery preservationists of the early 1900s. In the wake of the ideas that sent Columbus across the Atlantic 500 years ago and eventually revealed finiteness to humankind, we are beginning to grapple with our limitations as a species. Land is still the great New Zealand subject of colonial times, but nature's gods are starting to call us to account for neglecting their ancient prohibitions.

'The country was a Paradise,' said Thomas Arnold. 'Paradising', says the mythologist Mircea Eliade, is the key to understanding the Western sensibility in strange, new environments like the 19th-century Pacific. Australia aside, its prelude was inevitably the garden. Even so, one early 1800 English traveller was 'impressed enough' by what he saw being achieved across the Tasman, 'even under the worst auspices, and in a country filled with the dregs of our own'. 'How much more then,' he asked, 'must New Zealand flourish, which is itself a beautiful garden, and capable of being rendered the most delightful spot on earth'? Ever since 17th-century thinkers like Francis Bacon secularised the idea of history as a journey, European culture has fed its spread across the world with visions of stepping ashore into a pre-prepared paradise of benevolent nature. 'The land,' said the prophet Joel, 'is as the Garden of Eden before them, and behind them a desolate wilderness.' If New Zealand's 'primeval solitudes' were everywhere apparent, so was country whose fertile flats skirted with trees already looked like 'English pleasure grounds'. Every farm servant's 'beau ideal of a new country', noted Thomas Cholmondeley, was the gentleman's park. New Zealand—frightful forests, savages and their sparse cultivations notwithstanding—was the picturesque ready-made and waiting. 'Picture to yourself this scenery,' said an awed Jerningham Wakefield. And between the grids of his settlement company's dream city, ready to grab the best land while its guards slept—ready to go to war for it if need be—gardens are as prominent as fortresses.

As advertisers use the tree to symbolise rootedness and stability, invaders use the garden to express their intentions and accomplishments. From the Edenic propaganda of the New Zealand Company, the idea of New Zealand as a garden grew like a virus. In Britain, it had instant effect, attracting arcadia seekers in hordes. But 'instead of the breadfruit tree', instead of 'Elysian fields and Groves adorned with every beauty of Nature', a complaining shipload arriving at Nelson saw merely 'the flax tree in a Swampy piece of Ground'.

To promote its venture, the New Zealand Company launched a London newspaper. In one of its first issues was an article, 'Of the Powers given to Man for the Formation of Future Nations', by a cleric from Trinity College, Cambridge—the one, perhaps, whose words about England's moral duty to carry the knowledge of the true God to the ends of the earth preface Edward Gibbon Wakefield's *The British Colonisation of New Zealand*. 'God,' he wrote this time, 'has empowered man . . . to fashion nature . . . as to draw from her hidden elemental forms of far greater beauty and utility than, in her present state of imperfection, are offered to us by nature herself.'

The Company's mission, the cleric told recruits, was divine. He couldn't think of 'any race that ever attained to a higher degree of culture, or as a nation emerged from barbarism' without a cultured race coming, so to speak, to its rescue. What was about to happen in distant New Zealand could be compared to a gardener's 'grafting of a gentler scion upon the wilder stem'. He didn't disguise the source of his analogy, and quoted the famous garden scene in *The Winter's Tale*. Scorning artifically bred flowers, Perdita, a true nymph of arcadia as she has been called, takes a stand on 'great, creating Nature'. But Polixenes wears her down with his plea to improve on it with some civilised elegance:

> *Yet nature is made better by no means,*
> *Which you say adds to nature is an art that*
> *Nature makes. You see sweet maid, we marry*
> *A gentle scion to the wildest stock;*
> *By bud of noble race. This is an art*
> *Which does mend nature—change it rather—but*
> *The art itself is nature.*

Whether Polixenes or Perdita is his champion has been disputed ever since Shakespeare wrote the play.

Few really big ideas are truly original. During the crucial months of 1838 as Charles Darwin finally assembled *The Origin of Species*, the writings of the Scottish economist Adam Smith were beside his bed. As *The Winter's Tale* formed in 1611, Shakespeare was reading Montaigne's essay 'Of the Caniballes'—civilisation less an evolution within nature than a contest against it. Whereas Europe's explorers inevitably described the natives of their new-found lands as lesser breeds, 'savages' still in a state of nature, Montaigne turned the tables and asked who the true savages really were:

> *They are even savage, as we call those fruites wilde, which nature*
> *of hir selfe, and of hir ordinarie progresse hath produced : whereas*
> *indeede, they are those which ourselves have altered by our*
> *artificial devises, and diverted from their common order, we*
> *should rather terme savage. In those are the true and most*
> *profitable vertues, and naturall proprieties most livelie and*
> *vigorous, which in these we have bastardized, applying them to*
> *the pleasure of our corrupted taste. And if notwithstanding, in*
> *divers fruites of those countries that were never tilled, we shall*
> *finde, that in respect of ours they are most excellent, and as delicate*
> *unto our taste; there is no reason, arte should gaine the point of*
> *honour of our great and puissant mother Nature. We have so much*

by our inventions, surcharged the beauties and riches of hir
workes, that we have altogether over-choaked hir: yet where-ever
hir puritie shineth, she makes our vaine, and frivolus enterprises
wonderfully ashamed.

'Of the Caniballes' is as much a celebration of nature in the Americas
prevailing over formality, order and artifice: 'Whoever contemplates our
mother nature in her full majesty and lustre is alone able to value things in
the true estimate.' Shakespeare had drawn on it before, in Gonzalo's utopian
speech in *The Tempest* about the natural new world's superiority to civilised
Europe. As much as a metaphor for taking God and civilisation to improve
the ends of the earth, as Edward Gibbon Wakefield dreamt, Shakespeare's
concern, like D.H. Lawrence's 400 years later, was with those far from
Europe falling victim to its imperialism. The prevailing interpretation sees
Perdita, champion of original virtue, as his heroine with her loathing of the
cultivated plants as 'nature's bastards'. 'Of that kind,' she scoffs, 'our rustic
garden's barren, and I care not to get slips of them.' Polixenes is the villian.
Underlying his bid to introduce 'civilised' plants to the wild garden is the
prospect New Zealand conservation biologists know so well—the
indigenous about to be overwhelmed.

The New Zealand Company may well have become a 'gentler scion
upon the wilder stem'. The soil of the Hutt Valley, said William Wakefield,
equalled that of 'an English garden'. In the event, the notion went right out
the window. But under different circumstances—more flat land, fewer
shiploads of surveyors and impatient settlers landing theodolites and cows—
New Zealand's plains may not have been so suddenly overrun. What if, for
example, Thomas Shepherd, the 1826 Surveyor of the New Zealand
Company had stayed among Petone's 'most beautiful sorts of trees and
shrubs'? His mentor, the great landscape architect Capability Brown, had
earned his nickname from his skill in discerning that 'the art itself is nature'
and drawing attention to it in new lakes, islands and carriage ways. Shepherd
always noticed a new place's pattern of plants, for there, he believed, nature's
promise lay.

Even with Wakefield, it could have happened. He and his chief
surveyor had instructions to 'provide for the beautiful appearance of the
future city . . . rather than the immediate profits of the Company . . . make
ample reserves . . . such as a botanical garden.' As the Hutt's suburban,
quarter-acre sprawl preserves the boundless country of the colonial mind,

the ferny gullies of Wellington's Botanic Garden—now almost sacred land—
keep the curiosity of history alive. But wherever level land was found, other
dreams took the stage.

———————

There is a painting that captures the moment; I first saw it as a child in the
1950s when thoughts of 'my country' were beginning to form. A river
bank of trees with which I've never lost a sense of connection. On first
encounter it was like news from a strange country, but labelled as my own.
Through that river of trees I first became aware of other New Zealands
beyond my experience.

Men, rowing a long-boat, are coming up the
river. They pull collectively against the flow with
an unmistakeable aura of having located something
they've been looking for. I can hear their voices in
my mind, as vivid as the chorus of birds in the river
bank trees and the forest's scent of early summer.
It is not a fantasy landscape. It is strangely familiar,
full of optimism we have all felt, like the sunlight
that opens an awaited day.

*Cowdie Forest on the Wairoa River,
Kaipara,* **Charles Heaphy, 1840.**

William Wakefield, top-hatted in the stern, and the avid men in
'Cowdie Forest on the Wairoa River, Kaipara' are the 1839 advance guard
of the New Zealand Company searching for level land on a tidal arm of
Kaipara Harbour. The artist, Charles Heaphy, was hired to record moments
like this. Despite his prosaic title, he leaves you in no doubt that the meeting
of great trees and water impressed him. He painted it from memory some
days later, but he has captured the strangeness of its life to European eyes,
even if his trees barely look like kauri. Yet was that really his purpose? His
painting intimates menace in the forest's dark interior, emptiness discovered
and big changes coming—as indeed they did. And here are the stiff men in
the *Tory*'s long-boat in Eden, in the garden, caught in the act with that
speculative, nature-cleaving optimism.

They don't look like tourists, off on a picnic, their quest purely
aesthetic. But were any of them, I wonder, in conversation with 'The Land
with all Wood and Waters' they pulled into? As an ecosystem it has since
vanished completely. Did they feel any regard for it, any reciprocity or

comfort? Was their moment of novelty tinged with any apprehension at what lay ahead when all that wild life around them would be gone? Or was the land just another vacant primeval lot, with survey lines to be cut and forest to be downed and fired for settlers' smiling farms uppermost in their minds? How long did they think it was all going to last? It would be interesting to be able to call out across the water and ask them now.

'Cowdie Forest on the Wairoa River, Kaipara' is only a watercolour painting, an ephemeral object. It could have vanished instead of becoming a national treasure. Most of our history is of its kind. The ultimately precious things, though, are not in the cabinets of curiosities but out there between the fences—the past's living presence, the 'very beautiful and terrifying mysteries' the painter Colin McCahon saw beyond the scenery.

Nothing, as the novelist John Fowles has observed, can stop man's worst self, his vicious notion of what freedom, his freedom, means. As progeny of colonial power, victims of colonisation themselves, Pākehā have always related ambiguously to their own colonising activities. The utopia in the minds of the men in the *Tory*'s long-boat has dominated our demanding national character from the outset—so that, emotionally, many of us are still colonising New Zealand, still imagining it as the land 'where the tall Forest and the Plains around, and waters wide with various Wealth abound'.

There are many New Zealanders for whom that utopia has never ceased to exist. They believe the attempt to replicate England on New Zealand's plains was the best thing that ever happened to them. Others' utopia is in the great, life-supporting systems of nature and the indigenous, metaphysical terms of belonging to them—ihi, mauri and wairua. Yet to those whose ancestors' bones were up in the branches of the river kahikatea that James Cook glided under, that were felled when it became the Thames and its eel weirs were blasted away to make it an agricultural highway, the spirit of the plains has gone. It cannot be recreated, no more than the land of birds before the coming of people. But neither should ever be forgotten.

Even in their borderline predicament, the survivors remind us of a possibility still with us; to heal the ecosystems which the secular world has been so carelessly tearing apart, rather than lose heart at the scale of the damage. Sources for restoring other places like them and using them again, the last of ngā uruora are more than fenced-off outdoor museum pieces.

I sometimes see them as temples of Pacific ecology, places that, for all their elusiveness, evoke the kind of fertility and freedom in which nature is still something vast, majestically pursuing its course without human interference—nature as measure, as Wendell Berry says. In a way, the remains of ngā uruora reveal more about us than about themselves. We cannot deny what predetermines our ways with land, nor that instead of gently grafting onto these islands' native life we have caused grievous damage. Ultimately, to coexist, *we* have to change, to accept that nature isn't a factory contructed for us—accept that we are part of it, not its masters.

Affection for nature may be growing where we have allowed its wildness space, but cultures don't suddenly change their basic commitment. The productive lowlands will enter the 21st century governed still by Pax Britannica. All across them, even the advocates of a republic continue to loyally perpetuate the great colonial effort to replicate Britain in the South Pacific. The lowlands' real significance to us *culturally*—the marvellous possession our forebears created from primeval space, privatised and enclosed—continues to render the native ecology of any place irrelevant to the use of it.

Meanwhile, collapsing ecosystems and deteriorating soils are within a short distance of all of us. Like the prospect that New Zealand agriculture faces the new century with over half the country being farmed unsustainably, they are facts that confront every New Zealander. Few soils under pasture grasses are, by nature, grassland soils. Merely 150 years ago, they were under the moist, microbe-rich, decaying leaves of trees. The strongest case for conservation is that we depend for our economic wellbeing on nature. We cannot live sustainably in a soil-based economy such as ours isolated from the natural ecosystems that created the land's wealth, or in ignorance of them. In the fading twilight of the campaign against the forest, any survivor now has value.

The discovery of nature's finiteness is a new turning for the European culture from which most of us come—a reality the men of empire in the *Tory*'s long-boat could not comprehend. The world we inhabit is a less certain one than theirs, more anxious about supplies from nature than humanity ever has been before. No longer is the quickening daily loss of plant and animal species across the planet seen as peripheral to human concerns. The loss of species, or 'biodiversity' as it has come to be called, is now causing the same global trepidation as climate change. New Zealanders tend to relegate 'ecocide', like genocide, to other, safely distant parts of the world. But the human process that is gutting the rainforests of the Amazon basin and Sarawak is no different from the scorched-earth colonial policies that took similarly ancient forests from the lowlands of New Zealand.

We have come to a crossroads. The air over New Zealand is still as close as can be found, anywhere in the world, to what air was like before humankind came along. But the site of our fresh beginnings has become a landscape of warnings. Where the first of us walked on a plain of great trees to which 'we could see no bounds', our blindness to limits and our belief in nature as a collection of free goods has taken the richest ecosystems to vanishing point. 'Protected', but still disintegrating, the last bits hover at the edge of existence, tiny islands besieged in a sea of new ecosystems with which they are not evolved to coexist, ever-dependent on what the humans around them decide to do.

A culture, said W.H. Auden, is no better than its woods. The last traces of ngā uruora—at Papaitonga and Mōkau, Te Tai Tapu and Punakaiki, and the other fragments like them—are places we will need if we ever start treating the land as though we intend to stay. Remote strangers to most of us, too small to drift while we reconcile oursleves to their value, they are the storm-warnings that, while nature's life pervades Aotearoa's wild mountains, in the lowlands its death is just a breath away. They are testimony too that rebuilding the native ecosystems of the plains will be as hard as bringing nature out into the open of our ordinary lives.

There was a time, back in the 1960s and '70s, when I was inclined to view the survivors as accidents—bits overlooked by the great scythe that took the trees off every plain, every river flat. My education as a biologist had taught me to see them as pristine and unpeopled. Nothing prepared me for what I now know—that each of them is an inhabited ancestral place, with mana enough to have survived the land laws and land clearances of the 19th century. There are, I imagine, many more like them, wāhi tapu whose Māori still wait for Pākehā who behave as though the colonial era is over to recognise what it has done to the Māori landscape. At the very least they want restoration of the mana of what, by stealth and proclamation, was taken 'here and there . . . [to] make the countryside more beautiful to travel through and be a source of pleasure'. Mana that comes from their ancestors sensing something sacred in the land and its water, its plants and birds, and keeping them in such a state that 'scenery preservationists' coveted them. Like rahui and tapu, mana cannot be left out of nature's care. No more than tūāhu, urupā, wāhi tūpāpaku can be left out of the sagas of ngā uruora's survival.

After the colonial preoccupation with land description, and then the greater insight of ecological enquiry, says Brian Elliott, comes the subtler quest for moral, spiritual and emotional connection. In lowland New Zealand, though, it has been paralleled by nature's relentless vanishing from sight and mind. And, as we have become a culture poor in people able to read country and feel it, we have been losing our capacity to know the life forces that sustain nature. Yet no piece of New Zealand has been colonised so long that its native spirit is a reality no more. Even in the most Europeanised plains like Manawatu or Canterbury, traces of forest—or archived paintings and settler diaries—reveal nature's intent, what ancient Europeans also knew as a place's 'genius'.

When the Treaty of Waitangi was signed almost all plains ecosystems were composed exclusively of plants and animals native to the country. Had the Treaty actually served the role its Maori signatories supposed, native forest would, I suspect, be far more common in today's lowland landscape. Even more so, had our countryside been shaped by gradual expansion from the coastal villages of whalers, traders or ticket-of-leave convicts rather than the myriad, expectant recruits of grid-settlement schemes who descended on it in droves last century. Instead, almost every tree, every bird, every living thing on the coastal plains—outside the lowland forest reserves of South Westland and a few tiny remnants elsewhere—is foreign.

While the inevitability of the encounter is impossible to ignore, few ecological transformations illustrate so clearly the rapid, ruthless triumph of Europe over antipodean nature that Charles Darwin foretold. Māori or Pākehā, the very reasons we are here in these islands are ancient biological ones, integral to the imperative of *Homo sapiens* to expand and spread and the evolution paths it had been taking, in the south Pacific on one hand, and in western Europe on the other, centuries before our ancestors decided to move. Successful animals and plants are continually on the move, expanding their range. Yet rarely has a group from one part of the world travelled quite so far, to invade an ecosystem so inherently different, and replace it so rapidly.

In cultures breaking their ties with Europe, it is easy to repudiate a notion such as the *genius loci* as jaded and romantic, 'a token of lost Eden, a nostalgia for lost innocence', as an Australian has described it, which 'deflects us from the ramifications of our current modifications of the land'. I think this is wrong. How can any innate sense of country—'an Intimate New Zealand'—be otherwise? Any stretch of country, no matter how pervasive agriculture's marks, has an indwelling life force, waning or waxing, which distinguishes it from any other. I know many landscapes made auspicious by things that have happened, where the spirit of place that Māori call mauri is very much a human thing. In some, nature, primitive to a fault, has been taken away as deftly as missionaries took the music of kōauau and puririhua, the summoner-of-rain. They no longer function as they did when kahikatea, harakeke, kererū and kākā prevailed; neither does intricate human knowledge of them. Something vital is missing. Something, with now so little prospect of resurgence it is as though it has died. Something, I dare suggest, of its mauri.

Kahikatea riverflat forest, **TE IA, MAUNGATAWHIRI, 1862, PHOTOGRAPHED EARLY IN THE WAIKATO WARS BY JOHN KINDER, A MILITARY CHAPLAIN.**

The plains forests have come to within the final few acres of vanishing point—tragic in one sense, yet magic in another. We may no longer feel insignificant in their shade, but as much as they are evidence of our power over nature, they are reminders that every bit of land, agricultural, urban, suburban, is, as the poet Gary Snyder says, part of the same territory—never totally ruined, never completely unnatural. Always restorable.

Whatever our fantasy, the survivors are in our hands. We can continue to act as conquerors—stay bound to dogma that wild nature has no place in land that can produce profit—and let them slide into the chasms of history and myth. Or we can heed those who say it is our destiny as a country to continually revisit the past. And keep alive a sense of native plants, soils, climatic cycles and life forces as necessary ingredients of how we actually live. It will be a daunting task. Formidable forces are ranged in opposition: greed, indifference, the many among us who see land as property and ecology as political enemy.

We still have the chance. It will be as much a matter of spirit and ritual as of ecology and policy. True 'future eaters', as Tim Flannery calls us, we have exploited these islands' richest ecosystems with all the violence that modern science and technology could summon. We will need more than that to keep their survivors alive. Rediscovery will need to turn into re-enchantment. The last emblems of the verdant country that drew our first comers ashore must lead us toward a concept of survival for ourselves: that we must live with the rest of nature or die with the rest of nature.

Abbreviations and short titles of frequently cited publications and other sources

A Sand County Almanac: Aldo Leopold, *A Sand County Almanac: Sketches Here and There*, Oxford University Press, New York, 1949.

Adkin, *Diary*: W.G. Adkin, 1880-1900 diary, in possession of his grandson, J.G. Law, Ohau.

Adkin, *Horowhenua*: Leslie Adkin, *Horowhenua: its Maori place-names and their topographical and historical background*, Dept of Internal Affairs, Wellington, 1948.

AJHR: Appendices to the Journals of the House of Representatives.

Anon. Missionary, *Royal Admiral*: Anonymous Missionary, 1801, 'The Missionaries' Journale in the *Royal Admiral* from Port Jackson to Matavai, Taheiti'. Microfilm of typescript copy of original MS. Microfilm LMS 328, University of Auckland Library.

Bagnall, *Diaries*: Edward Albert Bagnall's 1884-1900 Turua diary; Homer Socrates Bagnall's 1886 Turua diary (courtesy of Dorothy Bagnall, Auckland, 1987).

Bagnall, *Turua*: Dorothy Bagnall, *The Bagnalls of Turua, 1864-1984*, the author, Auckland,1984.

Banks Endeavour Journal: J.C. Beaglehole (ed.), *The 'Endeavour' Journal of Joseph Banks, 1768-1771*, 2 Vols, 2nd Edition, Public Library of NSW and Angus and Robertson, Sydney, 1962.

Best, *Forest Lore*: Elsdon Best, *Forest Lore of the Maori*, Dominion Museum Bulletin No.14 and Polynesian Society Memoir No.18, 1942. (Reprint Government Printer, Wellington, 1977.)

Best, *Maori Forest Lore*: Elsdon Best, quoting Tuhoe elder, Pio, 'Maori Forest Lore; being some Account of Native Forest Lore and Woodcraft, as also of many Myths, Rites, Customs and Superstitions connected with the Flora and Fauna of the Tuhoe, or Urewera District', Pt 1, *TNZI 40*, 1907, pp.185-254.

Best, *Maori Eschatology*: Elsdon Best, 'Maori Eschatology: The Whare Potae [House of Mourning] and its Lore; being a Description of many Customs, Beliefs, Superstitions, Rites, &c. pertaining to Death and Burial among the Maori people,and also some Account of Native Belief in a Spiritual World', *TNZI 38*, 1905, 148-239.

Best, *Oruarangi*: Simon Best, 1980, 'Oruarangi Pa: Past and Present Investigations', *NZJ Archaeology*, Vol.2, pp.65-91.

Bevan Ford, *E koe ano*: John Bevan Ford, 'E koe ano!', in Ian Wedde and Gregory Burke, *Now See Hear! Art, Language and Translation*, Victoria University Press, Wellington, 1990.

Bidwill, *Rambles*: John Carne Bidwill, *Rambles in New Zealand*, Orr and Co., London, 1851.

Bigge, *Report*: John Bigge, 1820, *Inquiry into the State of New South Wales*. British House of Commons Paper 136. Original in Public Record Office, London (C.O. 201 Vols.118-142) MS transcription by James Bonwick, in Mitchell Library, Sydney ('Bonwick Transcripts').

Brunner, *Expedition*: Thomas Brunner, *Expedition to the middle of the Middle Island*, in Taylor, *Early Travellers, NZ*.

Buller, *Birds*: Walter Lawry Buller, *A History of the Birds of New Zealand*. First Edition, van Voorst, London, 1872-73; Second Edition, the author, London, 1887-88.

Buller, *Illustrations of Darwinism*: W.L. Buller, 'Illustrations of Darwinism, or, The Avifauna of New Zealand considered in relation to the Fundamental Law of Descent with Modification', *TNZI 27*, pp.79-104.

Buller, *Observations, Tapu*: W.L. Buller, 'Observations of some peculiar Maori Remains, with Remarks on the Ancient Institution of Tapu', *TNZI 27*,1894, pp.148-154.

Buller, *Notes on Birds*: W.L. Buller, 'Notes on New Zealand Birds', *TNZI 25*, 1893.

Buller, *papers*: W.L. Buller miscell. papers (scrapbook, letters, cuttings, etc) qMS BUL 1866-1898, WTU.

Buller, *Supplement*: W.L. Buller, *Supplement to the 'Birds of New Zealand'*, publ. by the author (for the subscribers), London, 1905.

C.O.209: (Colonial Office) New Zealand Original Correspondence to the Secretary of State, 1830-1847, Vol.1-51, 60, at Public Record Office, London.

Clarke, *Report, River Thames*: George Clarke, 1846, 'Report on the River Thames in New Zealand', from *Extracts from the Final Report of the Chief Protector of Aborigines in New Zealand*, printed privately (15pp), Mitchell Library, Sydney, CY POS, pp.679-692.

Captain Cook's Voyages: Captain James Cook's Voyages Round the World, Jiques and Wright, London, 1824.

Collins, *Account, English Colony:* David Collins, *An Account of the English Colony in New South Wales,* London, 1798, Mitchell Library, Sydney, Q.991/C 926.

Cook Journals I: J.C. Beaglehole (ed.), *The Journals of James Cook: 1. The Voyage of the Endeavour,* Cambridge University Press, for the Hakluyt Society, Cambridge, England, 1955.

Cook Journals II: J.C. Beaglehole (ed.), *The Journals of James Cook—Voyage of the Resolution and Adventure 1772-1775,* for the Hakluyt Society, Cambridge, England, 1961.

Cowan, *Up the Mokau:* James Cowan, 'Up the Mokau', *Weekly Graphic & NZ Times,* 1911.

Crook, *Wildlife, North Westland:* I.G.Crook, 1978, 'Wildlife Surveys and the Future of North Westland Forests', *Wildlife: A Review,* p.17.

Crosby, *Ecological Imperialism:* Alfred Crosby, *Ecological Imperialism: the Biological Expansion of Europe, 900-1900,* Cambridge University Press, Cambridge, 1986.

Cruise, *Journal:* Richard Cruise's 1820 *Journal of Ten Months' Residence in New Zealand,* repr. Capper Press, Christchurch, 1974.

Darwin, *Origin of Species:* Charles Darwin, *The Origin of Species by Means of Natural Selection,* John Murray, London, 1859.

Davidson, *Prehistory:* Janet Davidson, *The Prehistory of New Zealand,* Longman Paul, Auckland, 1984.

Dieffenbach, *Travels:* Ernst Dieffenbach, *Travels in New Zealand,* 2 Parts, John Murray, London, 1843.

DLS: Department of Lands and Survey.

Dreaver, *Horowhenua County:* A.J. Dreaver, *Horowhenua County and its People,* Dunmore Press, 1984.

D'Urville, *New Zealand:* Dumont D'Urville, *New Zealand 1826-1827, from the French by Dumont D'Urville,* transl. O. Wright, Wingfield Press, Wellington, 1950.

Fairburn, *Ideal Society:* Miles Fairburn, *The Ideal Society and Its Enemies,* Auckland University Press, 1989.

Forest and Bird, *Indigenous Forest Policy:* Royal Forest and Bird Protection Society, *Policy for New Zealand's Remaining Indigenous Forests,* publ. with *Forest and Bird,* No. 218, November 1980.

Foster, *Lawrence in Taos:* Joseph Foster, *D.H. Lawrence in Taos,* University of New Mexico Press, Albuquerque, 1956, pp.136-140.

Future, West Coast Forestry: 'Seminar on the Future of the West Coast Forestry and Forest Industries, Hokitika, July, 1977', Proceedings and papers, New Zealand Forest Service, Wellington.

Galbreath, *Buller:* Ross Galbreath, *Walter Buller, the Reluctant Conservationist,* Government Printing Office, Wellington, 1989.

GBPP: Great Britain Parliamentary Papers.

Grey, *Moteatea:* Sir George Grey, *Ngā Mōteatea me Ngā Hakirara ō Ngā Māori,* Robert Stokes, Wellington, 1853.

Hawkesworth, *Account:* John Hawkesworth, *An Account of the Voyages Undertaken by the Order of His Present Majesty for Making Discoveries in the Southern Hemisphere . . .,* W. Strahan and T. Cadell, London, 1773.

Heale, *New Zealand and the NZCo:* Theophilus Heale, *New Zealand and the New Zealand Company; in answer to a Pamphlet entitled How to Colonize,* Sherwood, Gilbert and Piper, London, 1842.

Heaphy, *Expedition:* Charles Heaphy, *Expedition to Kawatiri and Araura,* in Taylor, *Early Travellers, NZ.*

Heaphy, *Narrative:* Charles Heaphy, *Narrative of a Residence in Various Parts of New Zealand. Together with a description of the Present State of the Company's Settlements,* Smith, Elder and Co., Cornhill, London, 1842.

Heaphy, *Native Reserves, Nelson:* Charles Heaphy, in 'Report on the Native Reserves of the Province of Nelson', 1870, in *AJHR,* D16, pp.37-40.

Heaphy, *Port Nicholson:* Charles Heaphy, 'Notes on Port Nicholson and the Natives in 1839', *TNZI 12,* 1880.

Horowhenua Commission: 'Report of the Royal Commission into the Horowhenua Block', *AJHR,* 1896, G2.

Howe, *Singer, Songless Land:* Kerry Howe, *Singer in a Songless Land: A Life of Edward Tregear, 1846-1931,* Auckland University Press, 1992.

Hunt, *Garden and Grove*: John Dixon Hunt, *Garden and Grove: The Italian Renaissance Garden in the English Imagination, 1600-1750*, J.M. Dent and Sons, London, 1986.

Hursthouse, *Zealandia*: Charles Hursthouse, *New Zealand, or Zealandia, the Britain of the South*, Edward Stanford, London, 1857.

Kawharu, *Waitangi*: I.H. Kawharu (ed.), *Waitangi: Maori and Pakeha Perspectives of the Treaty of Waitangi*, Oxford University Press, Auckland, 1989.

Lawrence, *Phoenix*: D.H.Lawrence, *Phoenix*, William Heinemann, London, 1961.

Leopold, *Round River*: Aldo Leopold, *Round River*, Oxford University Press, New York, 1953.

McDonald, *Te Hekenga*: Rod McDonald, quoted in *Te Hekenga: Early Days in Horowhenua*, G.H. Bennett & Co., Palmerston North, 1929.

McGurk, *Aurora letter*: Charles McGurk off the *Aurora*, early 1840 letter home, in 'Extracts from Colonists' Letters', *New Zealand Journal*, Vol.1, 1840; Louis Ward, *Early Wellington*, 1928.

Mackay, *Compendium*: Alexander Mackay, *A Compendium of the Official Documents relative to Native Affairs in the South Island*, 2 Vols, Government Printer, Wellington, 1873.

Mackay, *Collingwood letters*: James Mackay, letter to Native Secretary, Auckland, 12 Feb 1862 [quoting McLean's 7 April 1856 native reserve deed]; No.1 in 'Correspondence Respecting the Boundaries of the Native Reserve at West Wanganui'; to Native Sec, Auckland, 9 July 1863; pp.321-322 and No.6, in Mackay, *Compendium*.

McLean, *Papers and Documents*: Donald McLean, *Papers and Documents relative to the Purchases Effected in the Middle Island by Mr Commissioner McLean, in 1853-55*; in Mackay, *Compendium*, pp.300-301, 311-312.

McNabb, *HRNZ*: R.M. McNabb, *Historic Records of New Zealand*, 2 Vols, New Zealand Government Printer, Wellington, 1908 and 1914.

Marjoribanks, *Travels*: Alexander Marjoribanks, *Travels in New Zealand*, Smith, Elder & Co, London, 1846.

Mōkau DLS Box File: Unfiled papers on Awakino, Mōkau, Taumata Maire Purchases, found in old Box File, Māori Division, Hamilton office, DLS, copied by author, February 1987.

Mōkau Reserves, *HO files*: DLS, Head Office, Wellington files 407/1 (4/985); 407/59; 407/101

Moore, *Early Pioneer Days*: Frederick George Moore, Extract from *Early Pioneer Days in New Zealand*, typescript in Nelson Provincial Museum, Nelson.

Moncrieff, *Avian Paradise*: Perrine Moncrieff: 'The Destruction of an Avian Paradise', in *Preservation, Empire*, June, 1944.

MONZ: Museum of New Zealand: Te Papa Tongarewa.

Mundy, *Our Antipodes*: Godfrey Mundy, *Our Antipodes; or Residence and Rambles in the Australasian Colonies*, Vol.II, Richard Bentley, London, 1847.

NA: National Archives, Wellington.

Nelson NLC, *Minute Book*: Nelson Native Land Court, Minute Book, ML8 Reel 18, NA. Judge Mair, 15 November 1883, Judgement, 16 November (See also Nelson MB 2 Taitapu 154, West Whanganui 154).

Newport, *Collingwood*: J.N.W. Newport, *Collingwood*, Caxton Press, Christchurch, 1971.

Ngata, *Moteatea*: Apirana Ngata (ed.), *Ngā Moteatea* (3 parts): Pt 1 publ. for Polynesian Society by A.H.& A.W.Reed, 1928, Pts 2 and 3, transl. by Pei Te Hurunui Jones, Polynesian Society, Wellington, 1961 and 1970.

Nicholas, *Narrative*: John Liddiard Nicholas, *Narrative of a Voyage to New Zealand, performed in the years 1814 and 1815, in company with the Rev. Samuel Marsden*, Vol.1, James Black, Covent Garden, London, 1817.

NLC: Native Land Court.

NZCo: New Zealand Company.

NZCo, *Doc, 12th Rpt*: Documents appended to 12th Report of the New Zealand Company, 1840, MONZ Library.

NZHPT, *mf*: New Zealand Historic Places Trust, Monuments file HP8/14/1Pt7 and Captain Cook Landing Places, 107/11, Wellington.

Papaitonga, *Reserves files*: Lake Papaitonga Scenic Reserve files, DLS; Head Office 4/301(ex.138/28); Wellington District Office 13/102.

Parkinson, *A Voyage*: Sydney Parkinson, *A Voyage to the South Seas in His Majesty's Ship, The Endeavour*, ed. and publ. by Stanfield Parkinson, London, 1773; 2nd Edition, publ. by J.C.Lettson, Charles Dilly and James Phillips, London, 1784.

Patterson, *Queer, Cantankerous Lot*: Brad Patterson, 'A Queer Cantankerous Lot: The Human Factor in the Conduct of the New Zealand Company's Wellington Surveys', in David Hamer and Roberta Nicholls (eds.), *The Making of Wellington, 1800-1914*, Victoria University Press,

1990.

Powell, *Further Species*: A.W.B. Powell, 'Further Species of Paryphanta, Wainuia and Rhytida': *Records of the Auckland Institute and Museum*, Vol.3. No 2, 1946.

Powell, *The Species Problem*: A.W.B.Powell, 'The Species Problem in New Zealand Land Snails', *TRSNZ 77*, Pt 5, 1948.

Preservation, Empire: *Journal of the Society for the Preservation of the Fauna of the Empire*, Stephen Austin & Sons Ltd, Hertford.

Richmond, *Massacre Bay letters*: Mathew Richmond, Superintendent of Nelson, letter to Col.Sec., Wellington, 5 January 1852, p.189; 31 May 1852, p.290, in Mackay, *Compendium*.

Royal Instructions: The *Royal Instructions*, from the English Colonial Office in 1846 (C.O.209 Vol.47: pp.271-272), accompanied the Constitution Act 1846 that issued policies to Governor George Grey. GBPP, 1847/763, 64. No.43, Correspondence relating to the Affairs of New Zealand. See also *Ordinances of the Legislative Council of New Zealand,1841-53*, New Zealand, 1871.

Ryall *papers*: MS papers 1497 [Ryall family] Folder 3, WTU.

Savage, *Account*: John Savage, *Some Account of New Zealand; particularly The Bay of Islands, and Surrounding Country; with a Description of the Religion, Government, Language, Arts, Manufactures, Manners, and Customs of the Natives, &c, &c*, W.Wilson, for J. Murray, Fleet St, London, 1807. (Reprint, Capper Press, Christchurch, 1973.)

Schnackenberg, *Letters*: Cort Schnackenberg Papers, 1840-1854, Waikato Museum of Art and History, Hamilton.

Shepherd, *Journal*: Thomas Shepherd, journal in the log of the *Rosanna*, 5 March-12 November 1826, Mitchell Library, Sydney, CY Reel 479.

Sinclair, *History*: Keith Sinclair, *A History of New Zealand*, Penguin, Auckland, 1988.

Sinclair, *Origins*: Keith Sinclair, *The Origins of the Maori Wars*, Oxford University Press, Auckland, 1961.

Skinner, *Reminiscences, Taranaki*: William Skinner, *Reminiscences of a Taranaki Surveyor*, Thomas Avery and Sons, New Plymouth, 1946.

Smart, *Diary*: William Smart, Diary, University of Canterbury Library.

Smith, *History and Traditions*: Stephenson Percy Smith, *History and Traditions of the West Coast of the North Island*, Memoir of the Polynesian Society, Vol.1, Thomas Avery, New Plymouth, 1910.

Smith, *Journals*: William Mein Smith, 1836-1841, qMS, SMI, WTU.

Smith, *Journey from Taranaki*: Stephenson Percy Smith, *Notes of a Journey from Taranaki to Mokau, Taupo. Rotomahana, Tarawera, and Rangitikei, 1858*, in Taylor, *Early Travellers, NZ*.

Spain, *Report*: 'Mr Commissioner Spain's Report to Governor FitzRoy on the New Zealand Company's Claim to the Nelson District', March 31, 1845, No. 2, in Mackay, *Compendium*.

Spate, *Paradise*: O.H.K. Spate, *Paradise Found and Lost*, Australian National University Press, Canberra, 1988.

SPC: Scenery Preservation Commission.

SPC report, *Papaitonga*: W.W. Smith, Report on Lake Papaitonga to Scenery Preservation Commission, 23 Aug 1906, SPC Minutes, etc. LS/70, NA.

Tasman, Discovery: Abel Janszoon Tasman and the Discovery of New Zealand, Dept. of Internal Affairs, Wellington, 1942.

Tasman's *Instructions*: Abel Tasman's *Instructions for the discovery and exoloration of the known and unknown south-land . . . the islands circumjacent.*(from the Dutch Council of Batavia, 1642); Appendix E in *Abel Janszoon Tasman's Journal*, publ. N.A.Kovach, Los Angeles, 1965.

Taylor, *Early Travellers, NZ*: Nancy Taylor, *Early Travellers in New Zealand*, The Clarendon Press, Oxford, 1959.

TNZI: Transactions of the New Zealand Institute.

Tregear to Reeves, *Letters*: Tregear letters to W.P.Reeves, *Letters written, from 1895 onward, by Men of Mark in New Zealand to the Hon. William Pember Reeves, then Agent-General for New Zealand*, MS Micro, 182, WTU.

Turton, *Maori Deeds*: H. H.Turton, *Maori Deeds and Plans of Land Purchase in the North Island of New Zealand*. Vol.I, Government Printer, Wellington, 1877-1878.

Tye, *Hauraki*: Rufus E. Tye, *Hauraki Plains Story*, Thames Valley News Ltd, Paeroa, 1974.

Vogel, *Land*: Julius Vogel, *Land and Farming in New Zealand*, Waterlow, London, 1878.

Waikato-Maniapoto MLC, *Corres. file*: Waikato-Maniapoto District Māori Land Court, Hamilton, Correspondence File.

Wakefield, *Adventure*: Edward Jerningham Wakefield, *Adventure in New Zealand From 1839 to*

1844. 2 Vols, John W. Parker, London, 1845. (Reprint Whitcombe and Tombs, Wellington, 1908.)

Wakefield, *British Colonization, NZ*: Edward Gibbon Wakefield, *The British Colonization of New Zealand; being an Account of the Principles, Objects, and Plans of the New Zealand Association . . .*, John W.Parker, London, 1837.

Wakefield's *Instructions*: 'Instructions to Colonel Wakefield, Principal Agent of the Company', May, 1839: *The Company's Purchases of Land from the Natives 1839 to 1842*. F.No.1, pp.3F -15F, NZCo Papers, Carter Collection, MONZ.

Wakefield, *Despatch*: 'Extract of a Despatch from Colonel Wakefield, with Journal, dated Cloudy Bay, October 10, 1839', *Supplementary Information Relative to New-Zealand . . . and the First Report of The Directors*,[New Zealand Company], John W. Parker, London, 1840.

Wakefield, *Journal*: William Wakefield's 'Diary', 4 May-17 August 1839, on board the *Tory*, MS, WTU. See also Wakefield's No 2. Journal, 1839-1842, Typescript, NZCO 131/9, WTU.

Washbourne, *Further Reminiscences*: Harry Washbourne, 'Sundry Incidents', *Further Reminiscences of Early Days*, Betts, Nelson.

Westland Reserves, *local file*: DLS Hokitika District Office; 1950s entries, R.L.1112, f.65; 1960-1980s entries, 13/82.

Westland Reserves, *national file*: DLS Head Office, Wellington, 10/5/2.

White, *Ancient History, Maori*: John White, *The Ancient History of the Maori, His Mythology and Traditions, Tainui*, Sampson Low, Marston, Searle and Rivington Ltd, London, Vols IV & V, 1888.

Wilson, *Chart, River Thames*: William Wilson's 1801 *Chart of the River Thames in New Zealand*, in P.B. Maling, 1969, *Early Charts of New Zealand, 1642 -1851*, A.H. & A.W. Reed, Wellington, 1969.

Wilson, *Land of My Children*: Helen Wilson, *Land of My Children*, Paul's Book Arcade, Hamilton, 1956.

Wilson, *My First Eighty Years*: Helen Wilson, *My First Eighty Years*, Paul's Book Arcade, Hamilton, 1955.

WTU: Alexander Turnbull Library, National Library, Wellington.

Yate, *Account*: William Yate, *An Account of New Zealand*, Irish University Press, Shannon, 1970.

Notes and References

ngā uruora: 'The ordinary term for . . . fruitful forest is *whenua pua* . . . a whenua pua must necessarily have many trees of species that provide much food for birds. These lands are termed *uruora* and include tracts whereupon berry-producing trees such as the miro, kahikatea, maire, etc., are found in numbers, and such prized bird-preserves include valleys, flats . . .': Best, *Forest Lore*, pp.13-14.

Introduction

p.13 'a prison-scape for the incarceration . . .'; 'a garden and a pasture . . .': W.J.T. Mitchell, 'Imperial Landscape', in W.J.T. Mitchell (ed.), *Landscape and Power*, University of Chicago Press, Chicago, 1994, p.21.

Janet Frame is quoted in Susan Chenery, 'The Final Word' in *Sunday Star-Times*, 25 September 1994.

Phillip Adams's description of New Zealand was published in *The Weekend Australian*, 21-22 January 1988.

landscape: the term as used here integrates two senses: the pattern of landforms, plants, human structures, phenomena, etc that we 'see' when we look at a stretch of country; and the experiences, imaginations, beliefs and ideals which inform the looking and other interactions. See for example Paul Shepard, *Man in the Landscape*, Knopf, New York, 1967; Denis Cosgrove, *Social Formation and Symbolic Landscape*, Croom Helm, London, 1984; D.W. Meining (ed.), *The Interpretation of Ordinary Landscapes*, Oxford University Press, New York, 1979.

nature: In New Zealand—the islands that humankind reached last—the wild state prior to culture is a profound influence on the national imagination. That said, nowhere in New Zealand is now strictly natural, the boundaries between nature and culture increasingly blurred and impossible to police.

p.14 William Travers, 'On the Changes Effected in the Natural Features of a New Country by the Introduction of Civilised Races', in *TNZI*, 1869, pp.312-313.

V.S. Naipaul, *A Way in the World*, Heinemann, London, 1994, p.209.

p.15 Cicero: *De Natura Deodorum*, quoted in Thomas Glacken, in *Traces on the Rhodian Shore: nature and culture in western thought from ancient times to the end of the 18th century*, University of California Press, Berkeley, 1967.

Ross Gibson, 'Enchanted Country', *World Literature Today*, Summer 1993. See also Gibson, 'The Middle Distance', *Art Network*, 1987, pp.29-35.

p.16 Paul Theroux, *Sunrise with Seamonsters*, Penguin, Harmondsworth, 1985; David Hockney, *David Hockney and Stephen Spender, China Diary*, Thames & Hudson, London, 1982.

Chapter 1: The Immense Trees of Ooahaouragee

p.17 'Ooahaouragee' is one of several spellings in the literature of European exploration and colonial advocacy of 'Hauraki', an old Maori name for the district between Auckland and the Coromandel Peninsula, including the lower floodplains of the Waihou and Piako Rivers that are the locale of this chapter. This version is from the popular early 19th-century book, *Captain Cook's Voyages*.

p.20 *A Sand County Almanac.*

'an Industrus people . . . luxuries of life': J.C. Beaglehole (ed.), *Cook Journals I*, p.276.

p.21 'embedded in the Western worldview isolating us from nature': of the vast and growing literature on this subject, the books that have helped me most are Thomas Berry, *The Dream of the Earth*, Sierra Club and Natural Philosophy Library, San Francisco, 1988; Peter Marshall, *Nature's Web: An Exploration of Ecological Thinking*, Simon and Schuster, London, 1992; Peter Knutson and David Suzuki, *Wisdom of the Elders*, Allen and Unwin, Sydney, 1992; and Gary Snyder (with W. Scott McLean), *The Real Work*, New Directions Press, New York, 1981, and *The Practice of the Wild*, North Point Press, San Francisco, 1990.

p.22 'adorne its banks': *Cook Journals I*, p.206.

James Thorn MP, speech notes for the Opening of the Cook Memorial, 22 November 1941, NZHPT, *mf.*

'disheartening . . . dreadful thing': J.C. Beaglehole, 'Notes on a Little Tour to Coromandel and Mercury Bay mainly connected with the memory of Captain James Cook, 7 February 1967', NZHPT, *mf.*

'"Impossible" to fix its location': from extracts of letter from Capt. J.D. McComish, Sydney, NZHPT, *mf.*

p.24 'A factory for producing milk . . .': G.T. Alley & D.O.W. Hall, *New Zealand Centennial Surveys: The Farmer in New Zealand*, Dept. of Internal Affairs, Wellington, 1941.

'Mother Land': 1957 inscription on commemorative gates to the first shipment of refrigerated meat, Totara Park Estate, North Otago.

'immence woods': *Cook Journals I*, p.209.

Portmanteau of the ecology of invasion: Crosby, *Ecological Imperialism*.

Ralph Waldo Emerson, 'History', in *Emerson's Essays*, J.M. Dent and Sons, New York, 1906, p.8.

'Inexhaustible . . . rich alluvial': *The New Zealand Colonisation Company (1838) to be Incorporated by Charter, or Act of Parliament*, NZCo Papers, WTU, q.325.931. 77099.

p.25 Wakefield, *British Colonization, NZ*. His quoting of Cook (pp. 288-301): 'the banks of the Thames . . . best place for establishing a colony': Hawkesworth, *Account*; his 'space so ample', 'soil so fertile', 'immense surplus . . .', 'the fittest place . . .': Nicholas, *Narrative*; his 'of greater importance to Europeans . . .': John Savage, *Account of New Zealand in 1805*, J. Murray, Fleet St, and A. Constable, Edinburgh, Union Printing Office, St John's Sq., London, 1807; his 'for colonising waste lands': Savage, *Account*.

Sir Apirana Ngata is cited from John Bevan Ford, *E koe ano!*, p.117

'a very fine river . . .': *Banks Endeavour Journal*.

'Marchey such as we find about the Thames . . . river in England': *Cook Journals I*, pp.206, 207, 209.

'before we had named this river the Thames': *Cook Journals I*, p.207.

'the other day', 'the very end of the world', 'Sand-banks, marshes, forests . . .': Joseph Conrad, *Heart of Darkness*, Robert Bentley, Cambridge, Massachusetts, 1902, p.5.

'New Thames': *Cook Journals I*, fn, p.207.

p.26 Clarence Glacken in his remarkable *Traces on the Rhodian Shore: nature and culture in Western thought from ancient times to the end of the 18th century*, University of California Press, Berkeley, 1967, has suggested that living in the newly ordered Dutch lowlands had a powerful influence on Descartes' rationalism. Glacken also describes the influence of this landscape transformation on King James and the English. The drainage of England's Fens and the continental

Low Country is described in Wagret, *Polderlands*, Methuen, London, 1968; C.T. Smith, *A Historical Geography of Western Europe Before 1880*, Longmans, London, 1967; and Oliver Rackham, *The History of the Countryside*, J.M. Dent, London, 1986.

'So that not for a moment . . . doubt or dispute': Michael Jackson, *Rainshadow*, John McIndoe, Dunedin, 1988, p.4.

p.27 'Make small reserves of native forest . . .': Harry Ell MP, letter to Minister of Lands, quoted in Circular from J.W.A. Marchant, Surveyor-General, to North Island Commissioners of Crown Lands, 7 March 1903, NA LS 70/22.

'At 2PM the Boats returned . . .': *Cook Journals I*, p.206.

p.28 'Convenient Situations', 'observed with accuracy': Introduction, *Cook Journals II;* see also *Secret Instructions for Captain James Cook, commander of his Majesty's sloop Resolution*, from Lords of the Admiralty, 6 July 1776, in McNabb, *HRNZ*, Vol.1, pp.24-28.

Parkinson, *A Voyage*, pp.106-107.

'Should it ever become an object of settleing this Country . . .': *Cook Journals I*, p.278.

p.29 'Indeed in every respect the properest place . . .', 'Swamps which might doubtless . . .': *Banks Endeavour Journal*, pp.3, 4.

Banks' Lincolnshire youth: Patrick O'Brian, *Joseph Banks, A Life*, Collins Harvill, London, 1987; see also *Banks Endeavour Journal* (Introduction, pp.3-4, 7-8, 17).

p.30 Hawkesworth, *Account*. For an interpretation of 'Hawkesworth's Alterations' see W.H. Pearson, *Journal of Pacific History*,Vol.7, 1972, pp.45-75.

'At the entrance . . . We landed . . . We had not gone a hundred yards . . .': *Cook Journals I*, pp.206, 209; 'The finest timber my eyes ever beheld . . .': *Banks Endeavour Journal*, Vol.2, p.436.

p.31 'There could be no more striking sight . . . every glimpse of the outer world': Thomas Kirk, *The Student's Flora of New Zealand and the Outlying Islands*, Government Printer, Wellington, 1899, p.11.

'Immense' the kahikatea of Waihou may have been, but their forests were far from boundless. As Ernst Dieffenbach found out some 60 years later, `the valley of the Thames . . . with the exception of the banks of the rivers where the kahikatea pine grows to great perfection, . . . is occupied by fern, flax and manuka. This vegetation is interrupted by large raupo (typha) swamps which increase towards the mouth of the rivers where the country is low and subject to inundation', (Dieffenbach, *Travels*, pp.275-276).

p.32 Gordon Fisher is quoted from Tye, *Hauraki*, pp 111-112.

p.33 Barry Lopez, *Arctic Dreams*, Picador, New York, 1986.

Parkinson, *A Voyage*.

'A stick of first rate quality': Early European spar-getters: quoted in *Early History of New Zealand; Brett's Historical Series*, Part II, H. Brett, Auckland, 1890, p.242.

'The extensive flat . . .': Yate, *Account*; Yate's influence on settlement: his accounts of 'extensive valleys of rich, alluvial soil' are quoted prominently, for example, in 'The Commercial Prospects of New Zealand', in *New Zealand Journal*, 21 March 1840.

p.34 'But the scenery is most lovely . . .': Yate, *Account*.

The figures on the Royal Navy's 18th-century timber imports are from Clive Ponting, *A Green History of the World; the Environment and the Collapse of Great Civilizations*, Sinclair-Stevenson, London, 1991, p.432; the influence that James Cook's impression of the trade potential of the Waihou's kahikatea had on the choice of a site for a southern hemisphere British settlement is evidenced by J.M. Matra, 'Proposal for Establishing a Settlement in New South Wales', 1783 — 'it may be seen by Captain Cook's voyage that New Zealand is covered with timber of size and every quality that indicates long duration; it grows close to the water's edge and may be easily obtained. Would it not be worthwhile for some as may be dispatched to New South Wales to take in some of this timber on their return, for the use of the King's yards?': McNabb, *HRNZ*, Vol.1, 1907, p.39; 'The possibility of procuring from New Zealand any quantity of masts and ship timber for the use of our fleets in India . . .' was reiterated in the 'Heads of a Plan' from Lord Sydney to the Lord Commissioners of the Treasury that decided upon New South Wales as a convict colony, 18 August 1786: McNabb, *HRNZ*, Vol.1, pp.53-57.

p.35 Bidwill, *Rambles*, pp.74-76.

p.36 Kahikatea's linguistic inheritance: Bruce Biggs, *A linguist in the New Zealand bush*, in W. Harris and P. Kapoor (eds.), *Nga Mahi Maori o te Wao Nui a Tane*, an international workshop on Ethnobotany, DSIR, Christchurch, 1990, and B. Biggs, pers. comm., letter, May 1992.

'The bitter fruit of the tree of Uppsalan knowledge': John Fowles (with Frank Horvat), *The Tree*, Angus and Robertson, Australia, 1980.

Kahikatea's geological record, and that of its co-inhabiting species: Charles Fleming, *The Geological History of New Zealand and its Life*, Auckland University Press, Auckland, 1979; and

Stevens, McGlone and McCulloch, *Prehistoric New Zealand*, Heinemann Reed, Auckland, 1988.
p.38 J.C. Beaglehole's references to Ngāti Maru watching Cook's tree-felling, and to his dismay at the vanishing of the plain's kahikatea forests, from footnotes on p.436 of *Banks Endeavour Journal* and p.206 of *Cook Journals I* respectively. His love of wild, historic places was related to the author by his son, Tim Beaglehole, pers. comm., 1988.
'A ship of Moderate draught . . .': *Cook Journals I*, p.210.
p.39 'Proceeded up the River until near Noon . . . From this place . . .': *Cook Journals I*, pp.206, 208; 'Above this town the banks of the river . . .': *Banks Endeavour Journal*, p.435.
'Attall difficult': *Cook Journals I*, March 1770, p.279.
'Indians', ie 'Indian town': *Banks Endeavour Journal*, p.435.
'left wholly to Nature . . . *waste*': John Locke, *Two Treatises of Government*, Awnsham Churchill, London, 1690.
p.40 'All this chaffer about the rights of the natives . . . ': a NZCo settler, in *The Examiner*, Nelson, 10 June 1843.
'Impulse which prompts the colonisers . . .', 'Is it not the will of God . . .': Wakefield, *British Colonization, NZ*.
'Land, apparently waste is highly valued . . .': William Swainson, *New Zealand and its Colonization*, Smith, Elder & Co, London, 1859.
'ancient and acknowledged principle . . .', 'If native rights to the ownership of land . . .': House of Commons Committee, GBPP—Colonies, New Zealand, House of Commons Rep. Select Committee on NZ, Vol.4, Sessions 1841-1842, publ. July 1844, p.vi.
p.41 'A large class of writers . . .', 'This claim is represented as sacred . . .': *Royal Instructions, 1846*. The *Royal Instructions* contained directives which, if implemented, would effectively dispossess Māori of all land not directly used for cultivation, by designating such lands 'waste lands': Frederika Hackshaw, 'Nineteenth Century Notions of Aboriginal Title and their Influence on the Interpretation of the Treaty of Waitangi', in Kawharu, *Waitangi*, p.103.
'Entirely dissent' and quotes from *The Englishman's Register*: *Royal Instructions*.
'a people of hunters', '. . . the extent of land so occupied . . .'; *Royal Instructions*.
'the minds of the Natives . . .', 'by far the largest block of land . . .': Geo. Gipps, letter 7 March, 1841, Governor's Despatches, Vol.35, January-May 1841, A1224, Mitchell Library, Sydney CY POS, p.657.
p.42 'native fort', 'every winter the swamps from the entrance of Piako . . .', 'No probability of redeeming a country . . .', 'Heavily timbered with kahikatea . . .', 'might feel free to give up', 'The old man arose and vociferated . . . laid out to great advantage.': George Clarke, *Report, River Thames*, pp. 679-692.
p.43 'Those who have sold their land . . . clefts of the rocks': Colonial Office 209/53, Grey to Earl Grey, 2 August 1847 No.81 (quoted in Sinclair, *Origins*, p.65).
'must ultimately stand here': Grey's speech, in 'Turning the First Sod of the Thames Valley Railway, 21 December 1878', from Grey Papers, Stout Collection, Victoria University of Wellington, p.6.
p.44 'When you turn a bend in the river': G.S Cooper, *Expedition Overland from Auckland to Taranaki by way of Rotorua, Taupo and the West Coast, Summer 1849-50*, in Taylor, *Early Travellers, NZ*. Original in Auckland Institute and Museum. Typescript version (with Māori transl.), Grey Catalogue, Stout Collection, Victoria University of Wellington, pp.14-18.
'Hikutaia Outrage': *Particulars of Outrages Committed in 1869-70 by Natives . . . at Hikutaia, Thames . . .* Return to an Order of the House of Reps. 27 September 1871, NA Le1/1871/140.
'That is where they get the eels from . . .': from Pineaha te Wharekōwhai's evidence, in account of John Ballance's 1885 visit to Hauraki, *AJHR*, 1885, G1, p.11.
p.45 'in the most friendly manner immagineable': *Cook Journals I*, p.207.
'assault on the forests', 'all . . . the areas which are today valued . . .', 'They were doomed . . .': M.S. McGlone, 'Polynesian deforestation of New Zealand: a preliminary synthesis', in *Archaeology in Oceania*, Vol.18, 1983, pp.11-25; 'burning whole river catchments', 'widespread destruction of the swamp forests': M.S. McGlone, A.J. Anderson & R.N. Holdaway, 'An Ecological Approach to the Polynesian Settlement of New Zealand', in D.G. Sutton (ed.), *The Origins of the First New Zealanders*, Auckland University Press, Auckland, 1994, p.154.
'fine domestic grasses . . . lack of underbrush': Paul Shepard, *English Reaction to the New Zealand Landscape before 1850*, Pacific Viewpoint Monograph No.4, Victoria University of Wellington, 1969, p.3.
'enormous trees with the upward thrust . . .': D'Urville, *New Zealand*.
Aidan Challis, *Motueka: An Archaeological Survey*, N.Z. Archaeological Assoc. Memoir No.7, Longman Paul, Auckland, 1978.

'I can remember Pine Taiapa telling me . . .': Bevan Ford, *E koe ano!*

p.46 Richard Cassells' Waikato study, 1972: 'Locational Analysis of prehistoric settlement in New Zealand', in *Mankind*, 8, pp.212-222.

p.47 'With open arms': *Cook Journals I*, p.206.

James Hector's list of flax names: in *Phormium tenax as a fibrous plant*, Report of the New Zealand Flax Commissioners, Colonial Museum and Geological Survey Dept., Wellington, 1872.

p.48 'More rich in birds . . .': D'Urville, *New Zealand*.

'Benevolent nature hath supplied them . . .': *Cook Journals I*, July 1769, p.121.

'Charms of the plains . . .': L. Antoine de Bougainville, J.R. Forster (transl.), *A Voyage Round the World (1766-1769)*, trans. N. Israel, Amsterdam, 1772. (Reprint De Capo Press, New York, 1967.)

'flats fruitful and populous', 'people dispersed everywhere': *Cook Journals I*, June 1769, p.110, and July 1769, p.120.

'Transported into one of the most fertile plains . . .': Tongatapu, Tonga, 4 October 1773, *Cook Journals I*, p.252.

'The truest picture of an arcadia of which we were going to be kings . . .': *Banks Endeavour Journal*, September 1769, p.252.

p.49 The reference to Tinian and its influence on English estate landscaping is from 'The Room Outdoors', in *Landscape*, Winter 1954-1955; from Geoffrey Grigson, *Gardenage*, Routledge & Kegan Paul Ltd., London, 1952.

There is perhaps no better expression of the *Endeavour* party's great expectations of New Zealand once they left Tahiti than Joseph Banks' fantasy, a few days before land was seen, of their friends in England, watching them with the help of 'some magical spying glass'—'they would see that notwithstanding our different occupations our lips move very often, and without being conjurers might guess that we were talking about what we should see upon the land which there is now no doubt we shall see very soon': *Banks Endeavour Journal*, 3 October 1769, p.396.

Archaeological survey of eastern Hauraki Plains: Best, *Oruarangi*.

'early timber traders' maps and a hydrological survey . . .': James Downie, Master of the *Coromandel*, 1820 'Sketch of the River Thames in New Zealand Shewing the Coast Explored', in P.B. Maling, *Early Charts of New Zealand, 1542-1851*, A.H. & A.W. Reed, Wellington, 1969; 'Thames River from Tararau Point to Te Kari Island', surveyed by S. Percy Smith and Horace Baker, 'Trigonometrical Survey, Position of Buoys, Wharves and Wharves', by T.C. Baylon, Harbourmaster, Auckland Institute and Museum, 1880.

p.50 'We found the inlet end . . .', 'In our return . . .', 'We saw poles stuck up . . .': *Cook Journals I*, pp.206, 207, 209; 'about a mile up . . .': *Banks Endeavour Journal*, p.435.

p.51 'laboriously constructed', conceivably a pioneer settlement: Davidson, *Prehistory*, p.170.

Precise location of Cook's party's landing at Oruarangi: Best, *Oruarangi*.

p.52 Warner Hunter and family, pers. comm., Bond Rd., Hauraki Plains, May 1988.

p.53 1990s archaeological excavation of Oruarangi: Simon Best & Harry Allen, *Report on the 1991 Investigations, Oruarangi Pā (Site N49/28)*, prep. for Dept of Conservation, Waikato. Auckland UniServices Ltd., 1991.

p.54 Jack Golson, 1959, no comparative site . . ., 'It is a pity that the rich finds . . .': 'Culture Change in Prehistoric New Zealand', in J.D. Freeman and W.R. Geddes (eds.) *Anthropology in the South Seas*, T. Avery and Sons, New Plymouth, 1959. Also Davidson, *Prehistory*, p.6.

p.55 Traditional history of Oruarangi and Waihou: White, *Ancient History, Maori*, pp.140-145; Leslie Kelly, *Tainui*, Polynesian Society Memoir 25, Wellington, 1949, pp.173-181.

'at that time a new garment . . . procured the coveted flax': White, *Ancient History, Maori*, Vol.IV, pp.48-49.

p.56 'After many years another ship of goblins came to Hauraki . . .': Ngāti Maru oral tradition of 1790s' spar-getters, quoted from White, *Ancient History, Maori*, Vol.V, Chap.IX, p.126.

'After rowing about 4 or 5 miles . . .', 'The Natives call this town Kakramare . . .': Anon. Missionary, *Royal Admiral*.

p.57 'Hippah', 'As the object of going to the River Thames . . .': Wilson, *Chart, River Thames*.

Alfred Crosby, *Ecological Imperialism: The Biological Expansion of Europe, 900-1900*, Cambridge University Press, Cambridge, 1986.

Monopolistic rules of East India Company, and effect on trade from Australia in 1790s: see D.R. Hainsworth, *The Sydney Traders: Simeon Lord and his Contemporaries, 1788-1821*, Cassell, Australia, 1972. Simeon Lord himself had ships, the *Hunter* for example, trading Waihou kahikatea spars to Sydney and beyond to China.

p.58 'The potatoes and turnips are excellent . . .', 'Several canoes came alongside . . . to the wood', 'Since they had been here . . . opposite the ship': Anon. Missionary, *Royal Admiral*.

Spar timber ships in Waihou in 1790s: R. McNab, *From Tasman to Marsden: A History of Northern New Zealand from 1642 to 1818*, J. Wilkie & Co., Dunedin, 1914. The departure of other ships, *Hunter* and *Plumier*, for New Zealand and the Thames from Sydney, is recorded in *New South Wales Pocket Almanack and Colonial Remembrancer*, Government Press, Sydney, 1806.

'upwards of two hundred very fine trees . . .': Collins, *Account, English Colony*, p.410.

The *Fancy*'s arrival in Sydney and its secret departure with 'a commission from the Bombay marine' etc. (July, September 1794), ibid.

p.59 'in their usual enlarged style . . . these cannibals': Collins, *Account, English Colony*, quoted (by McNab) in footnote to letter of Lt. Gov. Paterson of NSW, to Secretary of State, 21 March 1795: McNab, *HRNZ*, Vol.1, p.197.

'Pore Mersable Place': Memo . . . entry, 30 September 1792, Dixson Library, Sydney; quoted by Robert Hughes, *The Fatal Shore*, Collins Harvill, Sydney, 1987.

p.66 Capt. Edgar Thomas Dell wrote a journal of his three months visit to the 'River Thames' and showed it to Governor Phillip Gidley King at Norfolk Island. Its whereabouts today are unknown. King advised Lt. Gov. Grose, of the *Fancy*'s visit: letter, 4 March 1795; King letterbook, Norfolk Island, 1788-99, Mitchell Library, Sydney, C187 CY POS 891, p.284.

'in perfect safety', 'on many occasions assisted . . .', 'the Natives regretted their separation . . . in a very luxurient manner': Gov. King's 1795 Journal, quoted in McNab, *HRNZ*, Vol.1, pp.551-552.

'to become the masters', 'an object worthy of his attention': Collins, *Account, Colony*, p 410.

'pretty much the same': Wilson, *Chart, River Thames*.

p.61 Missionaries being shown Joseph Banks' firing piece: Anon. Missionary, *Royal Admiral*.

'In going up the creek . . .', the careless Indians . . .', 'would produce anything . . .': ibid.

'their women had been inveighed on board . . . then carried off': 'The Church Mission to New Zealand' report on Rev. Samuel Marsden's travels to the River Thames, *Sydney Gazette*, 6 May 1815, Mitchell Library, Sydney.

'said to extend to the Southward as far as Cook's Straits . . .': Anon. Missionary, *Royal Admiral*.

p.62 'Remote in Southern Seas . . .': poem by 'E.H.', quoted in preface to Savage, *Account*.

p.63 Photographs of Turua, timber ships and stacks: in Tye, *Hauraki*, p.28. Also 'Turua: The Sawmills. The Kahikatea or White Pine Industry', in *The Resources of New Zealand*, Auckland Public Library, 1890s, pp.108-111.

Bagnall Bros. at Turua: Bagnall, *Diaries*.

'no single act of modern sorcery . . .', 'Now the settlers were able . . . wither and die': Roderick Finlayson, *Our Life in this Land*, Woolmore Printing Co, Auckland, 1940 (facsimile ed. Dennis McEldowney, 1985).

p.64 Gordon Fisher, quoted by Tye, *Hauraki*.

Shirley Metcalfe, née Bagnall, 'The Mill at Turua' from her story 'Three Rivers', extract in Bagnall, *Turua*, p.39.

p.65 Kahikatea ('the inferior species called kaikatina') etc., Bigge, *Report*. Evidence of Thomas Moore, Supt. of Sydney Dockyard, 2 February 1820. Bigge, *Report*, Evidence, pp.2079-2083. Bonwick Transcripts, BT Box 5, Mitchell Library, Sydney; Robt Elwes, Bigge, *Report*, 12 August 1820, Box 23, pp.4861-4864.; also Bigge to Earl Bathurst, 27 February 1823, in McNab, *Historic Records of New Zealand*, pp.587-594.

'derive all the advantages . . .': Samuel Marsden, to Rev J. Pratt, 7 February 1820, in McNab, *HRNZ*, p.481.

'immense forests of the wood called Cacitea': James Downie, log of naval storeship *Coromandel*, 1820, Mitchell Library, Sydney, CY39 CY POS 125.7.

p.66 Turua 'to all intents and purposes' an island, 'an abode of desolation': 'The Thames River: A trip to Paeroa', by the Wanderer, *The Auckland Star*, 14 January 1892.

'deep water close to the bank': in 'Turua, the Sawmills', *Resources of New Zealand*, p.109.

Shooting diary, 2 July 1891, 26 March 1894, etc.: W.G. Hammond, Diary, Hammond Coll., Auckland Institute and Museum, DU436 K39.

p.67 'the glory of the South . . .', 'happy home in fair New Zealand's Isles' etc.: John Grigg, 'My Own New Zealand Home', school song, Thames, 1875—sung by the children of the public schools of the Thames, at the turning of the first sod of the Thames Valley Railway, by Sir George Grey, 21 December 1878—in Auckland Public Library, GNZ MSS293.

'thousands of cattle . . .', 'hundreds of people . . .': *The Weekly News*, 31 January 1918.

'picturesqueness': *The Weekly News*, 14 February 1918.

p.68 'Formed of a Virgin Mould . . . exhausted Soil of Europe': British Home Office, 'Anonymous Proposal for the Settlement of New South Wales, 1783-86', in McNabb, *HRNZ*, Vol.1.

'splendid results': *The Weekly News*, 14 February 1918.

'useless swamp into rich farm land', 'a wilderness . . .' etc.: *The Weekly News*, 31 January 1918.

'into a single interacting whole . . .': William H. McNeill, *The Pursuit of Power: Technology, Armed Forces and Society Since 1000 AD*, University of Chicago Press, Chicago, 1983, pp.260-261.

'can never be replaced': W. Cook, letter to Rt. Hon. the Premier, 23 October 1901, *Proceedings of the Sawmillers' Conference together with Correspondence . . .*, in *AJHR*, 1901, 1. H50.

p.69 'to preserve the white-pine bush . . .': C.K. Beattie, letter to Rt. Hon. the Premier, 22 October 1901, ibid.

Statistics on run-down of kahikatea timber resource: 2nd and 3rd Annual Reports of the Board of Trade, *AJHR*, 1918, 1919, H44, pp.5-8, 5-6.

Bagnall Bros. winding things down: Bagnall, *Diaries*.

'No forest land . . .' (p.xx), 'As is well known . . . removal of the trees forthwith' (p.xxiii-xxiv): Recommendations, in 'Report of Royal Commission on Forestry', 1913, together with Minutes of Proceedings and Correspondence, *AJHR*, 1913, C12.

'close settlement', 'in view of the the pressing demand . . .': 2nd Annual Report of the Board of Trade, *AJHR*, 1918, H44, p.6.

Questioning use of 'the Dominion's white-pine': Annual Report of the New Zealand Forest Service, *AJHR*, 1939, C3, p.3.

'These forests stood in the main . . .': Annual Report of the New Zealand Forest Service *AJHR*, 1947, p.9.

p.70 'trees that had taken such ages to grow': Metcalfe, 'The Mill at Turua', in Bagnall, *Turua*.

'the sky looking quite black for a while . . .': Hazel Kingsford, quoted in Tye, *Hauraki*, p.40.

p.71 'The Land Ethic': *A Sand County Almanac*.

'that only the mountain has lived long enough . . .': 'Thinking like a Mountain': *A Sand County Almanac*.

Summary of conservation areas on the Hauraki Plains, from *Registrar of Protected Areas in New Zealand*, Dept. Lands and Survey, 1984; pers. comm. from Paul Champion and Keith Thompson, May 1989, and their 1988 report to Hauraki County Council (Speedy's Bush and Henderson Bush).

'average soil was a rich alluvial': *The New Zealand Colonisation Company (1838) to be Incorporated by Charter, or Act of Parliament*. NZCo papers, WTU, q 325.931 77099.

p.72 'the Nile at the time it overflows its banks': Clarke, *Report, River Thames*.

'It was manifest that a land which nourishes . . .': R.G. Jameson, *New Zealand, South Australia, and New South Wales—a Record of Recent Travels in those Colonies*, Smith, Elder and Co., London, 1841; quoted in Heale, *New Zealand and the NZCo*.

p.73 'I think it is plain . . .': Heale, *New Zealand and the NZCo*.

Bidwill, *Rambles*, p.73.

p.74 John Mulgan, *Report on Experience*, Oxford University Press, Oxford, 1985, pp.2-5, expresses eloquently New Zealanders' brief occupancy of their ancient islands.

Jonathon Porritt is quoted from 'Facts of Life', in *BBC Wildlife*, September 1994, p.57.

Chapter 2: The Perfect Vale

p.77 'It is certainly worth fighting for . . . hideous symbols of the Heathen': Mundy, *Our Antipodes*, pp.306-307.

p.78 'Leaving the little fort . . .': Mundy, *Our Antipodes*, pp.307-310.

p.79 A military road: Mundy's 'noble road . . . as long and straight as a French chausée' was a direct by-product of the land wars of 1846. A consequence of William Wakefield's 1845 protestations that Māori had possession of the best lands, the wars were precipitated by Ngāti Rangitahi's exclusion from compensation for the fertile Hutt Valley flats, and Ngāti Toa's grievance that Te Atiawa had received the bulk of compensation instead of them: W. Spain, Report No.1. Port Nicholson, 31 March 1845, *Brit. Parl. Papers for Colonies, NZ, 1846*, pp.12-43. See also David Millar, *Once Upon a Village: A history of Lower Hutt, 1819-1965*, New Zealand University Press, Wellington, 1972 (chap. 'Land Problems'), and M.K. Watson, *Maori Land and the Colonial System of Land Acquisition in Port Nicholson*, Geography Dept, Victoria University of Wellington, undated.

p.80 'gave a dash of home . . . odious accents': Mundy, *Our Antipodes*.

W.G. Adkin, *Diary*, 1882.

p.81 'elegant nikau palms . . .': John Johnson, 'Notes from a Journal' in 1846-47, in Taylor, *Early*

Travellers, NZ, p.121.

Arthur Ludlam, James McNab and the nīkau: 'Belle Vue Hotel stands in Locality once laid out as Popular Pleasure Gardens', Margaret Robinson, in *The Dominion*, 7 January 1952. (Quotes are from *Cyclopaedia of New Zealand*, Cyclopedia Co Ltd, Wellington and Christchurch, 1897-1908.)

'covered with high forest to within a mile . . .': Wakefield, *Adventure*, p.54.

'There is no need to remember swamp-grass . . .': Ruth France (Paul Henderson), 'Return Journey', in Allen Curnow (ed.), *The Penguin Book of New Zealand Verse*, Blackwood and Janet Paul, Auckland, 1966.

p.82 Robert Hughes, *The Fatal Shore*, Collins Harvill, London, 1987.

James K. Baxter is quoted from 'Conversation with an Ancestor', in *The Man on the Horse*, University of Otago Press, Dunedin, 1967.

'Petone did not look like the 'new pastures' they had been promised': Lieutenant John Wood, *Twelve Months in Wellington, Port Nicholson*, Pelham Richardson, London, 1843, p.9.

'We were all full of hope . . . dreary and inhospitable shore': Marjoribanks, *Travels*, p.11.

'You couldn't move for the forest': J. Campbell, letter to the Glasgow *Chronicle*, May 1840, *The New Zealand Journal*.

p.83 John Wallace's account of his and Richard Samuel Deighton's landing is from an article by Celia & Cecil Manson in *The Dominion*, Wellington, 25 January 1965.

p.85 Charles Heaphy's descriptions, Heaphy, *Port Nicholson*.

p.86 'A good Harbour': *Cook Journals II* .

p.87 'excellent harbour . . . land fit for cultivation . . .', 'about forty or fifty natives': Shepherd, *Journal*.

'less intimidating Sydney': Introductory Note, 'Colonising New Zealand, The First Ill-Starred Attempt', in A.D. McKinlay (ed.), *Savage's Account of New Zealand in 1805 together with Schemes of 1771 and 1824 for Commerce and Colonization*, L.T. Watkins Ltd, Wellington, 1939, pp.109-113.

'When you gentlemen first got your estates . . .': quoted from Ralph Neale, 'Thomas Shepherd's Dream', in *Landscape Australia*, Vol.10, No.1, 1988, pp.46-52, and from notes from Shepherd, *Lectures on Landscape Gardening in Australia*, J. McGarvie (ed.), Hort. Pampl. Vol.10, Sydney, 1836, kindly provided by Ralph Neale.

p.88 'Struck with astonishment . . .' and 'Whanga Nui Atra' description: Shepherd, *Journal*.

p.89 William Mein Smith's watercolour painting 'A Wet Day, July, 1853', WTU.

'Eritonga', 'the sandy downs of the coast . . .': Dieffenbach, *Travels*, p.73.

Waiwhetu synonymous with urban pollution: 'Pollution Disaster in Hutt Valley', *The Dominion*, 30 December 1987, p.1; 'Hutt pollution in World league', *The Evening Post*, 30 December 1987.

'Stinking Mudflat Mess . . .': *The Evening Post*, 25 August 1972, p.2.

p.90 Measurement of heavy metal levels: P. Stoffer, G.P. Glasby, C.J. Wilson, K.R. Davis and P. Walter, 'Heavy Metal Pollution in Wellington Harbour', *New Zealand Journal of Marine and Freshwater Research*, Vol.20, 1986, pp.495-512.

The material on tribal movements around Whanganui-a-Tara, and the taniwha, are summarised from Janet Bayley, *The Heretaunga/Waiwhetu River Mouth: An historical narrative*, Petone Settlers' Museum, c.1986.

p.91 Te Hao Whenua and formation of lower Hutt Valley: Graeme R. Stevens, *Rugged Landscape: The Geology of Central New Zealand*, A.H & A.W. Reed, Wellington, 1975.

'into a great fury, his tail lashing . . .': T. O'Regan, in David McGill, 'The Great Harbour of Tara', *The Evening Post*, c.1984.

p.92 The description of the 13th-century umu is from G.N. Park, 'A Maori oven site in the Tararua Range, New Zealand: a palaeoclimatogical evaluation', *New Zealand Archaeological Association Newsletter*, 13, 1970, pp.191-197.

William Wakefield's description of meeting Te Ati Awa and that Te Puni and Wharepouri 'begged' him 'to look at the place'; his examining of their valley: from Wakefield, *Despatch*, pp.27-62.

p.93 'commercial metropolis', Wakefield's *Instructions*.

'large tracts of flat land . . .': Wakefield, *Despatch*, pp.64-65.

'That harbour in Cook's Straits is the most valuable . . .', 'Of merely fertile land . . .'; 'In making this selection . . .', 'shores of safe commodious harbours, . . .': Wakefield, *Despatch*, pp.4F-5F.

p.94 'a sufficiency of level land form the wants of the colony . . .': Heaphy, *Narrative*, p.2.

Captain Cook's Voyages, p.74.

'Testimony': Wakefield, *British Colonization, NZ*, p.112-113.

Wilson, *Chart, River Thames*.

'Friday, August 16th 1839, Fine weather Saw LAND . . . wood in the interior': Wakefield, *Journal*.

p.95 'Cook dwells on not having seen land . . .': Wakefield, *Journal*.

'the scenery became more and more majestic . . .', 'The hills rise . . . feathered musicians.': Wakefield, *Adventure*. In January 1770 Joseph Banks, on ship a quarter of a mile offshore, had been similarly impressed by 'the most melodious wild musick I have ever heard . . .' *Banks Endeavour Journal*, p.456.

'a Boar and a Breeding Sow . . . Goats and Hoggs': *Cook Journals II*, p.169.

'all our endeavours for stocking this Country with usefull Animals are likely to be frusterated by the very people who we meant to serve': *Cook Journals II*, p.287.

Cook's successful introduction of pigs of Asian origin from Tonga, on his third voyage: C.M.H. Clarke and R.M. Dzieciolowski, 'Feral Pigs in the northern South Island, New Zealand: I. Origin, distribution and density', *Journal of the Royal Society of New Zealand*, Vol.21, No.3, 1991, pp.237-247. See also Cook's journal entry for 6 November 1773.

p.96 'so closely cover'd with Wood . . . could not penetrate . . .': *Cook Journals II*, p.237.

'hardly possible . . . to fail': *Cook Journals II*, p.578.

'as to Wood the land here is one intire forest': *Cook Journals I*, p.233.

'they live disperse'd along the Shores . . .': *Cook Journals I*, p.247.

'Making room for better plants': *Cook Journals II*.

'the several Gardens . . . several hundreds of Cabbages': Furneaux's Narrative, Nov 1772 in App.IV, *Cook Journals II*, p.741.

'without exception the finest harbour in New Zealand . . .', 'to leave No space . . .', 'sufficient flat land . . .', 'altogether the most miserable specimen . . .': Heaphy, *Narrative*, pp.2-4.

'land, with excellent water communication . . .', 'not adapted for colonization . . . plans of the Company': Heaphy, *Narrative*, p.3.

p.97 'formidable height': Wakefield, *Despatch*.

'noble expanse of water, surrounded by a country of the most picturesque . . .': Heaphy, *Narrative*, p.3.

'two inlets leading from Cook's Straits . . .', 'covered with lofty trees . . .': Dr Traill of Liverpool, quoted in Wakefield, *British Colonization, NZ*.

'where the River Haritaoua . . .', 'valuable productions . . . might be procured . . .': Wakefield, *British Colonization, NZ*, pp.111, 113.

Administration not the NZCo's forté: see Patterson, *Queer Cantankerous Lot*, p.62.

'imposing the greatest responsibility . . .': Wakefield's *Instructions*.

'the propriety of carefully avoiding . . . exaggeration': Wakefield's *Instructions*, p.11F.

'habitations in the wilderness' by Englishmen': Majoribanks, *Travels*, pp.25-27.

p.98 'a commercial metropolis . . . inhabited by Englishmen': Wakefield's *Instructions*, p.4F.

Samuel Cobham's Plan (Britannia): (A Proposed Plan of the City of Wellington in the First Settlement in New Zealand founded 1839-40.) Photo Collection, WTU, F51659, F137698.

'Britannia': for example, see Nancy M. Taylor (ed.), *The Journal of Ensign Best 1837-43*, Government Printer, Wellington, 1966, p.228; '. . . went to Britania [sic] and stayed a couple of days with Colonel Wakefield . . .': Edward Hopper, letter to Mrs Stanhope from 'Brittania [sic], Port Nicholson', May 1840, repr. in *1840 The Immigrants*, Petone Public Library Resource Project, with permission of WTU, undated.

'Unfortunately, these spots have been reserved . . .': George Duppa, letter, *New Zealand Journal*, 1840.

p.99 Britannia's similarity to the grid towns of the British colonisation of North America, e.g. Gravesend, New York, the second settlement in the English colonies laid out on a precise orthogonal grid, and the first to include within it a regular distribution of public open space: Thomas Campanella, 'Sanctuary in the Wilderness, Deborah Moody and the Town Plan for Colonial Gravesend', in *Landscape Journal*, Vol.12, No.2, Fall 1993.

Descent of orthogonal grid towns: Dan Stanislawski, 'The Origin and Spread of the Grid-Pattern Town', in George A. Theodorson (ed.), *Studies in Human Ecology*, Harper and Row, New York, 1961.

1683 Plan of Philadelphia: see Campanella's illustration, from Historic Urban Plans, Ithaca, New York (engraving in Olin Library, Cornell University).

Machiavelli's plan for an ideal military encampment, 1521, and Robert Barret's, 1598: see *Journal of the Society of Architectural Historians*, May 1961.

Roman occupation towns in Britain, e.g. legionary fortress at Caerleon, Wales AD 75, in Kostof,

The City Shaped: Urban Patterns and Meanings Through History, Thames and Hudson Ltd., London, 1991.

J.B. Jackson, on the human organisation of space, and values: *The Necessity for Ruins*, University of Massachusetts Press, Amherst, 1980, p.115.

p.100 'extraordinary fertility': Heaphy, *Narrative*, p.80.

'Rich, Alluvial Soil': on *Chart of Port Nicholson, New Zealand*, Capt. E.M. Chaffers, 1839, Wellington Harbour Board Collection.

'A Bird's Eye View of Port Nicholson': Thomas Allom, litho, 'Taken from the Charts and Drawings made during Col Wakefield's survey in October', 1839, F.G. Moon, London. ('A very beautiful landscape from a sketch by Mr Heaphey': *New Zealand Journal*, 2 October 1841.) Hand-coloured copy, in Nan Kivell Coll., National Library of Australia, Canberra. Similar copy in WTU, but trimmed and without publisher's imprint.

'the very highway between New Holland and the Western World', 'land exceeding in fertility . . .', 'What may be the termination . . .': Wakefield, *Despatch*, pp.44, 48.

'sold and parted with all right, title, . . .': Wakefield's 'First Deed of Purchase from the Natives', 27 September 1839; 'for the whole of the bay, harbour and district of Whanga Nui Atera . . .': *The Company's Purchase of Land from the Natives*. AppF, NZCo papers, F.No10.

p.101 'and to bring cattle and corn': Heaphy, *Narrative*, p.4.

The pro-military faction in the NZCo, and Light's possible appointment as Surveyor-General: see Patterson, *Queer Cantankerous Lot*.

'you should make ample reserves . . .': NZCo Directors' Instructions to William Mein Smith, *New Zealand Journal*, 1, 1840, p.13.

p.102 'a shore that hinders every communication with it', 'out and out the finest . . . be the commercial capital': Wakefield, *Despatch* (Oct 13-December 13, 1889).

'of the most valuable portions . . .': Wakefield's *Instructions*.

'commenced reconnoitering the flat ground as I think it will do . . .': Smith, *Journals*. Also Smith's Letterbook, WTU, Micro MS 264.

'a valuable acquisition . . .', 'At a short distance from the beach . . . in all aspects': Smith, *Journals*.

'a guarantee that a knowledge of the country will in all cases precede settlement . . . .': *New Zealand Journal*, 23 May 1840.

p.103 David Millar, *Once Upon a Village: A history of Lower Hutt, 1819-1965*, New Zealand University Press, Wellington, 1972.

'much interspersed with sluggish creeks', 'it impeded the rapid progress . . .': Smith, *Journals*.

'a great many of the streets would run through swamps . . .': McGurk, *Aurora letter*.

'a more correct survey . . .': Smith, *Journals*.

W. Wakefield's rebuking of W. Mein Smith: Wakefield to NZCo Sec., 27 February 1840, NZCo papers, NA; Smith's insistence of his authority, Wakefield to NZCo Sec., 25 March 1840, Colonial Office Archives, 208/127. Microfilm at NA.

'that his name would be coupled . . .': quoted in Patterson, *Queer Cantankerous Lot*, p.68.

Smith's replacement: W. Wakefield to NZCo Sec., 2 September 1840, NZCo papers, 3/1 NA.

'Jan 19. Captain Smith and myself . . .' etc.: Wakefield, *Journal* (No.2).

p.104 'The sand hummocks at the back of the long beach . . .': Wakefield, *Adventure*, pp.145-146.

William Molesworth's Leeds speech, 5 February 1840: *New Zealand Journal*, No.2, 22 February 1840, p.18.

p.105 'this being the first ship . . .': John and Harriet Longford, of the *Aurora*, 26 January 1840, *New Zealand Journal*, p.182.

'may guess what wilderness we had to go to . . .': John Lodge, letter to his father, 27 January 1840, *New Zealand Journal*, p.183.

'The soil is perfectly wonderful . . . the general concert': *New Zealand Journal*, p.183.

p.106 'rise at five, breakfast and out to the woods . . .', 'amazingly': Charles McGurk, off the *Aurora*, early 1840 letter home, in extracts from colonists' letters published in *New Zealand Journal*; Louis Ward, *Early Wellington*, Whitcombe & Tombs, Wellington, 1929.

'saw the first tent . . . supposed garden of Eden . . .', 'Remarks from New Zealand': *New Zealand Journal*, July 1840.

A blunder, '. . . worse than a crime', 'Bitter was the disappointment . . . continual storm': Heale, *New Zealand and the NZCo*.

'spots of natural advantage': Wakefield's *Instructions*, p.4F.

'many enquiries of the natives . . . whether these rivers ever overflowed . . .': Smith, *Journals*.

p.107 'Up the river today . . . floods on the land': Wakefield, *Journals*.

'The Hutt Valley Development Scheme . . .': Newspaper report, (source unknown) 1940.

'what damage the flood had really done'; 'the swamps would be thrown out': Wakefield, *Journal* (No.2).

Flood history: 'A History of the Management of the Hutt River, 1839 to 1989', compiled by Catchment Engineering, for Wellington Regional Council, May 1989.

p.108 'Alicetown residents, armed with picks and shovels . . .': W.B. Nicholson (ed.), *Petone's First Hundred Years*, L.T. Watkins Ltd, Petone, 1940, p.68.

'The settlers on arrival will be relieved from all the usual difficulties . . .': *New Zealand Journal*, 23 May 1840. The New Zealand Company realised before the settler ships left however that 'the surveys may not, when the ships arrive, be sufficiently advance to permit the settlers to take possession of their lands': John Ward, N.Z. Land Co., letter to Wakefield (Instructions for the Guidance . . . after the Arrival in NZ of the Ships about to Sail for the First Colony) 1839, NZCo papers, WTU, MS704, Folder 1.

'rather tedious to build these huts . . .': McGurk, *Aurora letter*.

p.109 'We had to build our huts ourselves . . .': a passenger in the *Bengal Merchant*, letter in *New Zealand Journal*, 5 April 1840.

'They are all working away in excellent spirits, . . .', 'eyeing with satisfied looks the rich land . . .': Edward Jerningham Wakefield, letter in *New Zealand Journal*, 22 February 1840.

'timber, brushwood, etc.', 'will produce anything': John Wallace, letter reprinted in *New Zealand Journal*, 1841, p.322.

'People are grumbling about . . . the want of flat land': letter, 'from a settler who went out in the Oriental, June 24–July 21, 1840', *New Zealand Journal*, 1841, p.311.

'What the cattle and sheep fatten on . . .' Lord Petre, letter in *New Zealand Journal*, 1841, p.250.

'For half a century sawmills operated . . .': letter in *Dominion,* 21 August 1937.

p.110 'Before dark, a considerable space of ground was cleared . . .', 'the energetic and combined movements . . .': Wakefield, *Journal,* 3 February 1840.

'not the least preparation had been made . . .', nor 'was even the site of the town yet fixed . . .', 'our dwellings appear to be built in a shrubbery . . . twice the size of English Pidgeons': Edward Hopper, 'Letter to Mrs Stanhope, from Brittania, Port Nicholson', May 1840.

p.111 'the dense forest which has enriched the soil for ages': George Duppa, letter to his father, *New Zealand Journal*, 1840 .

'the Fern tree which hangs its majestic leaves . . .': Edward Hopper, letter, *New Zealand Journal*, 1840.

Chapter 3: The Riverbend

p.116 'the river Mokou', 'from the native account . . .': Wakefield, *British Colonization, NZ.*

'valuable superiority over the owners of ordinary lands': Wakefield's *Instructions.*

Dorset, 'in my possession . . . to Mokou and buy that': letter to his brother, 29 March 1840, in *New Zealand Journal*, 29 August 1840.

p.117 'made visits of inspection . . .', 'baskets of water-melons . . .', 'In all my travels . . .', God spare the Maoris . . .': Frederick George Moore, *Early Pioneer Days*. Most is also quoted in Skinner, *Reminiscences, Taranaki.*

p.118 'the evidence everywhere . . . remain now': L. Cussen, surveyor, quoted in *AJHR*, (reports on King Country surveys) 1. C1, Sess.II 1884.

'very prosperous circumstances . . . natives called Nga-te-Meniopoto': Dieffenbach, *Travels,* pp.162-171.

p.119 'bird-nest-like masses . . . perched high up in the forest roof': after Lucy Cranwell, *The Botany of Auckland*, (republ. ed.), Auckland Institute and Museum, Auckland, 1983, pp.115-116. The naturalist Daniel Solander in 1769 noted its resemblance to tropical bromeliads. Like bromeliads, kahakaha's reservoirs sustain a host of tiny life, one species of which, a mosquito, breeds only in them.

p.120 Mangrove in Awakino estuary, H.D. Wellman, pers. comm., 1987.

p.121 Edwin Brooks, parātawhiti: quoted from *Frontier Life Taranaki, New Zealand*, H. Brett, Auckland, 1892.

'the gloomy and repulsive waste': Hursthouse, *Zealandia.*

p.123 S. Percy Smith's voyage up the Mōkau: 'Notes of a Journey from Taranaki to Mokau, Taupo. Rotomahana, Tarawera, and Rangitikei, 1858', in Taylor, *Early Travellers, NZ.*

Smith's map together with sketches and watercolour paintings are in an album held at New Plymouth Public Library.

p.124 Waiata, 'Ka ngau Mōkau . . .': quoted from Grey, *Mōteatea.*

p.125 Account of Maniapoto and Ngāti Tama fear of lightning from Aunty Mary Turner, pers. comm. Waitara, September 1987.

Old urupā map: undated map (late 1940s?) of the sandspit, Te Nau Nau, at Mōkau River mouth, divided into hapū areas: in Mōkau DLS Box File.

William Skinner's account of Rangi-ō-Hua: Skinner, *Reminiscences, Taranaki*.

'stories current on this coast of a people called Maero . . .': Smith, *History and Traditions*.

p.126 'undisturbed forest growth': Skinner, *Reminiscences, Taranaki*.

History of pā settlement: Davidson, *Prehistory*.

Tainui waka traditions: Leslie Kelly, *Tainui*, Memoir of the Polynesian Society 25, Wellington, 1949.

p.127 'when I was a youth . . . He aha te tapu?': Tanirau Wharauroa, quoted by Cowan, *Up the Mokau*.

p.128 'Karanga pa mai . . .': from the waiata *Ko te Tau a Mōkau mo Te Rauparaha*, quoted from Ngata, *Moteatea*.

Cautionary advice about Tauwhare and tapu: from Te Oriwa Stephenson, at Mōkau, 1986-1990.

p.130 Pepene Eketone's evidence, 'It was Takarei te Kaka who kept this piece of land out of the sale . . .': Native Land Court Minutes, Otorohanga, 28 July 1897, NA MLC, MB OT/28/295. The Court decided it did not have the jurisdiction to hear it, and left it over until authorised to deal with it on 4 February 1899, MB OT/34/128. The same NLC heard a partitioning of Tauwhare on 15 November 1911, MB OT/54/77.

'so sad about the Natives', 'We have time . . .': James Edward Fitzgerald, letter to Alfred Domett, 19 May 1883, WTU, MS papers 1632 [A Domett], 3.

The New Zealand Gazette, 9 September 1897, p.1615, carries a notice bringing three areas of 'the Mokau Reserves' under 'the Jurisdiction of the Native Land Court'. One is 'Te Mahoe or Tawari Reserve, otherwise Section 12, Block I., Awakino Survey District, containing 76 acres'.

William Skinner: recollection regarding Mōkau Native Reserves, New Plymouth, Mōkau Reserves file, New Plymouth Office of Dept. Lands and Survey, 1937, quoted in memo (L&S file, 20/349) to Under-Sec. Lands, 19 March 1937 citing Skinner's 26/2/37 meeting with Chief Surveyor, New Plymouth, in file dealing with several wahi tapu matters, incl. extract from Otorohanga NLC Minute Book No. 72/342-352, with evidence, on oath, from Skinner, DLS HO file, Series 22/3009 Awakino Native Reserve.

'several flats of rich land . . .', 'considerable improvement', 'As yet no offers . . .': Donald McLean, Inspector of Police, letter to Colonial Secretary, Auckland 27 March 1850, Item No.12 in series of letters in Mōkau DLS Box File.

p.131 'about two miles square extending along the banks of the river', the 'reserves', Te Kauri etc., 'a large tongue formed by a bend of the river . . . burial ground': George Cooper, letter to Civil Secretary, 24 October 1852. Item No.12, in Mōkau DLS Box File.

'Until the chiefs are all agreed to dispose . . .', 'signifying His Excellency's approval . . .': Alfred Domett Colonial Secretary, letter to Cooper, 29 November 1852, Enclosure 1, for the Governor, in Item No.12, in Mōkau DLS Box File.

'My Friend Ta Kerei . . .', 'You had better therefore agree . . . worldly prosperity': G.S. Cooper, letter to the Chief Waitara Ta Kerei, Mokau 14 December 1852, in Item No.12, in Mōkau DLS Box File.

p.132 'There is no Reserve whatever . . .': McLean's 1854 'Sale of Lands within the Mōkau Block', in Turton, *Maori Deeds*. The missionary, Cort Schnackenberg, whose name appears as witness to the deed, actually helped the surveyor John Rogan 'draw up the Deed and define boundary, &c.' (letter to Whiteley, April 1854?, Schnackenberg, *Letters*.

'Although the mischief he is doing is very great . . .': Cooper to Civil Secretary, 24 October 1852. Item No.12, in Mōkau DLS Box File.

'at the request of Ta Karei and other chiefs who are anxious to dispose . . .': Donald McLean, letter to Colonial Secretary, 27 March 1850, Item No.12, in Mōkau DLS Box File.

p.133 'the sale of land . . . engrossed their whole attention': Dieffenbach, *Travels*.

Benjamin Franklin and 'Reserves for the Natives': Alexander Mackay, *Memorandum on the origination of the Native Reserves set apart by the New Zealand Company in accordance with their scheme of Colonizing New Zealand*, 1873, WTU qMS: (Mantell), publ. slightly altered in *AJHR* G2B1, 1873. See further re. Franklin repr. in A.D. McKinlay, *Savage's Account of New Zealand in 1805, together with Schemes of 1771 and 1824 for Commerce and Colonization*, L.T. Watkins Ltd., Auckland, 1939, pp.175-180.

McLean's witholding £100 of the £200 purchase price for the 'three places . . . not yet given up': 'Sale of Lands within the Mokau Block' Turton, *Maori Deeds*, p.627.

'Wilderness land it is true is worth nothing to its native owners . . .': cited in Mōkau-Awakino context, in Otorohanga Native Land Court, 19 August 1941, OT MB No.72/342-352; quoted in Alexander Mackay, *AJHR* 1873, G2B, pp.4, 5, 45.

p.134 'on beholding a plain . . . finest place in New Zealand': letter to Whiteley, 24 September 1846, Schnackenberg, *Letters.*

'The Tapu of Mokau'; touched occasionally by nobility', 'the works of the devil': letter to Whiteley, 1844?, Schnackenberg, *Letters.*

'Apply the same rule to the cultivation of your hearts': letter to Whiteley, 1844 ?, Schnackenberg, *Letters.*

p.135 'The natives here are peacable and improving . . . a vessel for 200 pigs': letter to Mr and Mrs Dawsley, Sydney, 23 August 1847, Schnackenberg, *Letters.*

'attended with great respect'; Report to Whiteley, 1846, Schnackenberg, *Letters.*

'war was declared against remaining heathen customs': Schnackenberg, *Letters.*

'An occurrence took place . . . have been made common': letter to Whiteley, 1847?, Schnackenberg, *Letters.*

p.136 'When we got to the place . . .'; 'The religious ceremony . . .': Report, 1846, Schnackenberg, *Letters.*

p.137 'They don't need to be talked about . . .': pers. comm., Graeme Gummer, friend of Mōkau and its people (letter, 29 December 1993).

p.138 Missionaries and tapu: Sinclair, *Origins.*

'those bones of the dead': Best, *Maori Forest Lore*, pp.185-254.

'a tree is selected . . . concealed the remains': Best, *Maori Eschatology*, pp.148-239.

p.139 Cliff Black was interviewed at his home, Mōkau, July, 1986; at a meeting dated 21st April, early 1950s?, his father, Willie Douglas Black, who had lived at Mōkau since 1894, said he had seen bodies at Tauwhare, and although not naming it, cited it as one of several ancient burial grounds at Mōkau: notes from meeting at Mōkau Hall, copied by author, February 1987 from papers in Mōkau DLS Box File.

p.140 'too small to cheer us much . . .': 1857 letter, Schnackenberg, *Letters.*

'If I cut down a Manuka tree . . .'; 'covetousness and ingratitude of New Zealanders'; 'We are in our place': letter to Whiteley, 28 September 1846, Schnackenberg, *Letters.*

'Messrs McLean and Cooper had told me . . .', 'from the bottom of my garden eastward . . .', 'The party who refused to sell . . .': letter to Rev H.H. Turton, 17 August 1854, Schnackenberg, *Letters.*

'The Natives' idolatrous attachments to land': (My Dear Sir), letter to Turton (?), 15 September 1852, Schnackenberg, *Letters.*

'they would sell a tract of land, but they never dream . . .': letter to Whiteley, 1846, Schnackenberg, *Letters.*

'proceed with my improvements . . .': letter to Turton, Schnackenberg, *Letters.*

'Our grand folks tikarohia the most valuable parts . . .': letter to Rev Turton, Messrs Wallis, Smales, Buttle, 1854, Schnackenberg Papers, (Acc.82-174) Series A: Folder 4, WTU.

p.141 'evil adviser' G.S. Cooper, letter to Civil Secretary, Oct 24, 1852, in Item No.12., in Mōkau DLS Box File.

'The sooner the natives part with their land the better . . .': letter to Rev. Turton, 17 Aug, 1854, Schnackenberg, *Letters.*

'all I can to hasten it': Schnackenberg, *Letters.*

Wiremu Kingi's declaration was to Governor Gore Brown, in February 1859: see Sinclair, *Origins.*

John Whiteley's killing, and Tauwhare's concealment of Taianui: Aunty Mary Turner, pers. comm., Waitara, August, 1987.

'only indication of European occupation . . . her distant homeland': Skinner, *Reminiscences, Taranaki*, p.133.

p.142 Thomas Gray and 'the Picturesque', Grevel Lindop, *A Literary Guide to the Lake District, 1993*, Gina Crandell, *Nature Pictorialised: 'The View' in Landscape History*, John Hopkins University Press, Baltimore, 1993.

The Kenyan historian Ali Mazrui is quoted from his television series, *The Africans*, which screened in New Zealand in 1988. See also Ali A. Mazrui and Toby Kleban Levine, *The Africans: A Reader*, Trager, New York, 1986.

p.143 'eye for the picturesque': W. Field, obituary for S. Percy Smith, *The Dominion*, 20 April 1922, p15.

'Land in the Hands of the Natives . . . Extinguished': from legend, *Map of the Middle Island, New Zealand shewing the Land Tenure*, 30 June 1884, in 'Surveys of New Zealand', Report for

1883-84, *AJHR*, 1, C1.

'only when . . . the needs of settlement . . .': SPC, in *AJHR*, 1907, C6, 2 (quoted in M.M. Roche, 'Securing Representative Areas of New Zealand's Environment . . .' *New Zealand Geographer*, 37, 2, 1981, pp.73-77.

'In future . . . attention must be given . . . places of natural beauty . . . hereafter': S.P. Smith, Surveyor-General, memo. (Circular No.267) to all Commissioners and Chief Surveyors, 19 October 1894, NA LS 70/22; 'along the larger rivers . . . travellers': Smith memo (Circular No.368, 21 Feb 1898).

'representative gentlemen . . . the beauties of the Mokau . . .' SPC Minute Book, 22 August 1904, NA LS/70/1.

p.144 'valuable flatlands'; 'in the interests . . . scenic effort of the country': ibid.

'certainly very picturesque': Smith, *Journey from Taranaki*, Taylor, *Early Travellers, NZ*, p.355.

'this most beautiful river': Smith, *History and Traditions*.

James Cowan's 1904 Mōkau visit was to assess its scenic and tourist potential for the Department of Tourist and Health Resorts.

'There are parts of our land that ought to be inviolate . . .', 'on the little Tokomaru flat, we see the remains . . .', 'the river banks close in . . .', 'The timber grows tall . . .': Cowan, *Up the Mokau*.

p.145 Cowan, *Up the Mokau*.

'The beauties were introduced immediately . . .water's edge': 'A Trip up the Mokau River—Some Casual Jottings' (by our own reporter) *Daily News*, 10 December 1900.

'more satisfactory', 'there are in the hands of the Natives . . .': S.P. Smith letter to Sir Joseph Ward, 27 Sept 1904, NA (SPC) LS/70/8.

p.146 'The forest is conservative . . . never again': Best, *Maori Forest Lore*.

'the least nuisance possible': Sir Joseph Ward, letter to Scenery Preservation Commission, 1906, SPC Miscell. Maps and Papers, 1904-1905, NA LS/70/20-21.

'Even where the land is flat enough . . .': map in ibid.

'leaving the culturable flats . . .',' should it turn out . . .', 'bounding the line of vision from the river . . .': Recommendations, SPC minutes, February 1906, NA LS/70/5.

'hard at work cutting and selling the timber . . .': Commissioner of Crown Lands to Chairman, SPC, SPC Miscell Maps and Papers, November 1906, NA LS/70/20-21.

'a great asset for the colony': Taranaki Scenery Preservation Soc., to McNab, Min. of Lands, 23 July 1907, Mōkau Reserves, *HO file*.

p.147 'specially attractive': Kensington, Under-Sec. Lands, letter to E. Phillips Turner, 2 December 1908, Mōkau Reserves, *HO file*.

'There are portions of the land abutting onto the river . . .': Jourdain and Phillips Turner, reported in *Taranaki Herald*, 1909, copy in Mōkau Reserves, *HO file*. Jourdain's 'Report on the Mokau River' was published in Ann. Rept. of SPC, *AJHR*, 1909, Appendix D, C6. It includes extracts of articles by Percy Smith and James Cowan.

Letter from MacKenzie, Min. in charge of Scenery Preservation, to Bedford, Sec. New Plymouth Chamber of Commerce, 4 July, 1911, states that surveyors had already been instructed to survey the areas proposed for scenery preservation, Mōkau Reserves, *HO file*. An earlier letter, from Bedford, on same file reveals the same surveyors, engaged by the Mokau Land Syndicate, had been instructed to survey everything 'only except the Bluffs on the River Bank', and that if this indeed happened the Mōkau's scenic value would be 'quite destroyed'. (19 June 1911).

'the necessary action to secure the land . . .': Kensington, Under-Sec. Lands to Under-Sec Public Works, 1 Sept 1911, Mōkau Reserves, *HO file*.

An Amendment to the Scenery Preservation Act in 1906 specifically excluded it from taking Māori land, but S.P. Smith's urgings rectified this in 1910, enabling the government to use the powers for the purpose under the 1908 Public Works Act: *The New Zealand Gazette*, 10 July 1910.

There are file records of searchs of Māori owners of adjoining river blocks (e.g. Mangiora) proposed for scenery, but not of Tauwhare, Mōkau Reserves, *HO file*.

Despite the apparent lack of record of Tauwhare's native reserve title, survey map, 8567, Awakino Survey District, citing the 1912 *Gazette* notice (p.1030) of its taking for Scenic Reserve, (seen by author in Hamilton office, Dept, Lands and Survey, August 1987) includes the statement 'Produced at N.L. Court Te Kuiti, upon orig. investigation. 4. Feb 1899. H.J. Edger'. Furthermore, the Otorohanga NLC Minutebook records a 15 November 1911 application to partition Tauwhare, NA MLC MB OT/54/77.

The New Zealand Gazette, 16 November 1911, carried the Minister of Public Works' 11 November 1911 Notice of Intention to take Tauwhare 'for scenery-preservation purposes' along with three other areas at Mōkau. It further gave notice that a 'plan of the land so required' was deposited in the post office at Awakino. The Māori version of the Notice was titled 'Whakaaturanga ka tangohia etahi whenua kei roto i Poraka VIII ne X, takiwa Ruri o Awakino North, me etahi whenua kei roto i Poraka I, II, me III, Takiwa Riwi o Awakino'.

p.148 Tauwhare's formal taking under the Public Works Act 1908, by order in Council on 5 March,1912, was notified on p.1030 in *The New Zealand Gazette*, No.24, 14 March 1912, headed 'Native land taken for Scenic Purposes in Awakino Survey District'.

Questioning re. Tauwhare title, 'patupatu land . . . not a gazetted reserve . . .': letter from F.T.O. Neill, for Under-Sec, of Lands to Under-Sec. of Public Works, 26 January 1912, Mōkau Reserves, *HO file*. Continued questioning re. how it became a native reserve: Asst. Under-Sec, Public Works, to Under-Sec. Lands, 16 January 1912, Mōkau Reserves, *HO file*.

Request to NLC re. question of compensation for Tauwhare: Asst. Under-Sec. Public Works, to Registrar, NLC., 27 February 1912, Mōkau Reserves, *HO file*.

Valuations of Tauwhare: Mōkau Reserves, *HO file*.

p.149 Te Ainui Mika ('his mark'), letter re. payment, 4 June 1914, Mōkau Reserves, *HO file*.

'If the interests of the owners . . . due to you': letter to Ngātoki Rikihana from Broderick, Under-Sec. Lands, 27 June 1918, and repeated requests from Ngatoki Rikihana, Mōkau Reserves, *HO file*.

'taking steps to bring the matter on': Earle, Registrar, NLC, letter to Asst. Public Trustee, 23 October 1918. Corres. file, Waikato-Maniapoto District Māori Land Court, Hamilton.

'a beautiful flat which had been cut out for a reserve . . .' Record of Deputation from the Mōkau settlers to the Hon. D.H. Guthrie, DLS, New Plymouth, Mōkau River Trust closed file 13/4, (seen July 1986).

p.150 'I do not know of any flat point . . . now reserved'; CCL, letter to Under-Sec. Lands, 5 March 1921, Mōkau Reserves, *HO file*.

'blasting, winching . . . they were so wet: Don Sutton, pers. comm., New Plymouth, August 1986.

'There are about 60 owners', 'the addresses of the native owners are not stated . . .': District Land Registrar, letter to Under-Sec., Public Works, Mōkau Reserves, *HO file*.

Judge Jones dismissal of the issue of compensation for Tauwhare. Registrar, NLC to Native Trustee, 21 December 1923, Waikato-Maniapoto MLC *corres, file*, Hamilton.

p.151 Newton Taylor's letter to NLC re Ngātoki Rikihana's claim on Tauwhare: 21 May 1931, ibid. This same letter refers to the incident with the farmer, Black, and the visit of the Lands and Survey field inspector.

'It has only now been discovered that Tawari . . .': Registrar, NLC, to Newton Taylor 27 May 1931; 'The question of payment . . .': NLC Registrar to Native Trustee, 17 June, 1931. Waikato-Maniapoto MLC *corres, file*.

'holding moneys due': Native Trustee to NLC Registrar, 17 June 1931; 'insufficient evidence on the Court's records', and evidence of Rikihana/Taylor effort to obtain payment, Waikato-Maniapoto MLC *corres, file*.

p.152 Newton Taylor letter to Native Land Court registrar that he had authority to act for all owners in Tauwhare: 4 August 1931, Waikato-Maniapoto MLC *corres, file*.

Police report on Mōkau Māori threatening to cut reserved forest: Constable Small, Mōkau to Inspector Murray, New Plymouth, 19 May 1922, DLS, New Plymouth, copy in Mōkau Scenic Reserves file, 13/4/1, Vol.1.

Tawhana Kaharoa and Tatana te Awaroa's evidence to Native Land Court re. Rangi-ō-hua land: Waitara hearing, Mōkau–Mohakatino subdivision, 20–22 May 1889 NA MLC 68 (2) Reel No. Micro 2/3710, Waitara MB No.1. Mohakatino—Paraninihi. In the event, the land was awarded to Joshua Jones, who had leased it under the 'free-trade' system since 1878 (NA MA 23/7: Papers relating to Land at Mōkau), a lease later described as 'not the only lease granted under that system that is not beneficial to the Maori owners nor to the people of the colony': 'Native Lands in the Rohe-Potae (King Country) District', *AJHR* 1907, 1. G1B.

Jones' bankruptcy and Royal Commission: 'Case of Mr Joshua Jones' *AJHR* Vol.2, 1888, G4; 'Mokau–Mohakatino Block', A.T. Ngata MP, speech to House of Reps. 27 October 1911, Hansard.

p.153 'The mere fact that these small areas were cultivated . . .': CCL (NP), letter to Under-Sec. Lands, 30 June 1932, file MA 407, Vol.1 DLS, New Plymouth (seen July 1986).

'As long as we have settlements mixed up with scenery . . .': CCL (NP) letter to Under-Sec. of Lands 18 June 1923, DLS, New Plymouth, Mōkau Scenic Reserves file, 13/4/1, Vol.1.

Willows and silting of Mōkau: Mr and Mrs Don Sutton, pers. comm., New Plymouth, August 1986.

p.154 Lands and Survey rangers checking reserve boundaries, stock etc: Public Works gravel quarry; 'In no instance is there a reserve fir for a small farm'; 'Suitable as Scenic Reserve only': James Old letter to CCL (NP) 16 July 1921; DLS, New Plymouth, Mōkau Scenic Reserves file, 13/4/1, Vol.1.

Biological surveys: e.g. B. Clarkson, 'Mokau River Scenic Reserves Biological Survey Draft Report', Dept. Lands and Survey, 1984; specifically, description of Tauwhare, M. Benson (survey team), in DLS, New Plymouth, Mōkau Scenic Reserves file, Vol.5, 1984-1986.

'extremely attractive and unusual sector . . .' J. Carter, Oct 1971, DLS, New Plymouth, Mōkau Scenic Reserves file, 13/4/1.

p.155 Mōkau whitebait: *The Recreational Whitebait Fishery in Taranaki*, Taranaki Catchment Commission, Stratford, November 1981.

Aileen Taimanu: pers. comm., Mōkau; July 1986, August 1987.

p.157 'The idea of a sacred place . . .': Joseph Campbell, *The Masks of God, Creative Mythology*, Penguin, New York, 1976.

p.158 'expressed their interest to hand over the island . . .': James Cowan, letter to Act-Supt., Tourist Dept., 5 May 1904, NA LS/70/11.

'most of the people are willing . . . the island is tapu': Samuel Nicholls, letter, 17 August 1904, NA LS 70/13 (file O4/191).

'You know, in the whole time I was on the river . . . gone back': Robert Wells, pers. comm., New Plymouth, July 1986.

p.159 June Opie's recollection of Tauwhare: pers. comm., from St Ives, Cornwall, England, July 1987.

p.161 'It still has its mana, that place': Aunty Mary Turner, pers. comm., Waitara, August 1987.

Mihi to Tauwhare: courtesy Graeme Gummer, friend of Mōkau and its people.

Chapter 4: The Lake in the Sand Country

p.165 'finest soil in the world': from 1902 auction placard, 'Plan of Town of Levin' McDonald, Wilson and Co., with instructions from Wellington–Manawatu Railway Co. in possession of Lew Prouse, Levin, seen by author, September 1987.

'thought of as a garden . . .harmony with this ideal nature: W.J.T. Mitchell, 'Imperial Landscape', in Mitchell. W.J.T. (ed.), *Landscape and Power*, University of Chicago Press, Chicago, 1994, p.21.

p.166 'one solid forest': Smith, *History and Traditions*.

'distinguished men, foreign as well as English . . .': Wilson, *My First Eighty Years*, p.121.

'The bush scenery was grand . . .': Adkin, *Diary*, 1893.

'sea of standing bush . . .', 'solemn, rapturous beauty': Wilson, *My First Eighty Years*, pp.100-101.

'Few New Zealanders have ever seen . . . virgin rain-forest grown on fertile flats': Wilson, *Land of my Children*, p.2.

p.167 'Shaded with a lofty forest . . .; most picturesque; a pair of papango . . .': W.L. Buller, 'Banded Rail', in Buller, *Birds*, p.168.

'Woe to those who join field to field . . .': *Isiah* Ch.5, v.8, quoted in Wendell Berry, *The Unsettling of America*, Sierra Club Books, San Francisco, 1977.

A long, relentless war between man and the wild things': Wilson, *My First Eighty Years*, pp.101-102.

No more than a place in which to shoot pigeons . . .': McDonald, *Te Hekenga*.

'the most precious part of a state . . .': Thomas Jefferson, 'Letter to Reverend James Madison, Oct 28, 1785', Adrienne Cook and William Peden, *The Life and Selected Writings of Thomas Jefferson*, The Franklin Library, Philadelphia, 1982.

'As far as the features of the country will admit it . . .': The Land Act,1877, in Vogel, *Land*.

p.168 'determined that the bush must be destroyed': James Prouse quoted from tape-recording (undated) in Dreaver, *Horowhenua County*.

'Helen Wilson's green cathedral': Wilson, *My First Eighty Years*, p.127.

'struck by its singular loveliness': Buller, *Supplement*, p.xliii.

p.169 'Sixty miles from Wellington . . . my country home in New Zealand': Buller, *Supplement*.

p.170 'pathos of a great departing race': Buller quoted in *Lyttelton Times*, 9 March 1893, Buller *papers*.

'No doubt whatsover': President's Address, Wellington Philosophical Society, 13 February 1884, *TNZI 16*, 1884, p.444.

'covered to the water's edge with dense bush': Adkin, *Diary*, 1893.

p.171 'nearly all this country is covered with smiling farms . . . ': in *Botaurus poeciloptilus;* Buller, *Supplement.*

'Goths and Vandals': *The Evening Post,* 23 May 1895, scrapbook, Buller *papers.*

'One is glad of course, to see the country thus reclaimed': Buller, *Supplement,* p.157.

'took refuge': ie. 'taken refuge with me . . .': Buller, *Supplement.*

'country seat': Buller, *Supplement,* p. xlviii.

'The perfect place for picnics', 'miserable winding track', We saw the spot . . .': Adkin, *Diary,* 1893.

'The endemic productions of New Zealand . . .': Darwin, *Origin of Species,* p.163.

p.172 'material advancement': Buller, *Notes on Birds,* p.65.

'the leading Native practice in New Zealand': *Horowhenua Commission,* p.242. (Buller was known to Māori as Te Waata Pura.)

'thorough disciple of Darwinism': *Illustrations of Darwinism.*

'The productions of Great Britain . . .': Darwin, *Origin of Species,* p.309.

'one of the most interesting and instructive in the world . . .': Newton quoted from *Encyclopaedia Britannica,* in Buller, *Supplement,* p.xxix.

p.173 'The lake lay clasped . . . and the mountains beyond': McDonald, *Te Hekenga,* p.23.

'how changed everything was . . .': Buller, *Supplement, p.*xxxiii, *op cit.*

p.174 'It is inevitable, of course, that with the progress . . . beautiful land of ours': originally in Buller letter, 20 May 1895, to Wellington Scenery Preservation Soc., and publ. (21-23 May) in *The Evening Post;* Buller *papers,* letterbook.

'the reluctant conservationist': Galbreath, *Buller.*

'erelong . . . exist only in museums . . .': Buller, *Supplement,* p.157.

'dear old Papaitonga': letter to William Mair, 26 December (?) 1902, MS 83/7, Auckland Institute and Museum, quoted in Galbreath, *Buller,* p.257.

'extreme satisfaction . . . cherished': Buller, *Supplement,* p.xxxviii.

'reckless destruction': Buller, *Supplement,* p.xxxv.

'My object . . . endemic forms': Buller, *Supplement,* p.xliii.

p.175 'swept clean in a single season': Buller, *Supplement,* p.xxxv.

'On the slightest alarm . . .'; 'peculiar soaring habit . . .': Buller, *Birds.* See E.G. Turbott (ed.), *Buller's Birds of New Zealand,* Whitcombe & Tombs, Auckland, 1967, p.123.

'Habitat fragmentation . . . the greatest worldwide threat to wildlife': K.V. Rosenberg and M.G. Raphael, 'Effects of forest fragmentation on vertebrates in Douglas-fir forests', in: J. Verner, M.L. Morrison and C.J. Ralph (eds.), *Wildlife 2000: Modelling Habitat Relationships of Terrestrial Vertebrates.* University of Wisconsin Press, Madison, 1986, pp.327-329. See also J.M. Diamond, 'The Island Dilemma: Lessons in Modern Biogeographic Studies for the Design of Natural Reserves', *Biological Conservation* 7, 1975, pp.129-145.

'. . . and the primary cause of species extinction': B.A. Wilcox and D.D. Murphy, 'Conservation strategy: The effects of fragmentation on extinction', *American Naturalist,* 125, 1985, pp.879-887.

'. . . mainly observed in temperate forest landscapes': R.T.T. Forman and M. Godron, *Landscape Ecology,* John Wiley and Sons, New York, 1986. See also Robert L. Burgess and David M. Sharpe, *Forest Island Dynamics in Man-Dominated Landscapes,* Springer-Verlag, New York, 1981.

'endless solitudes . . . a secure and quiet . . .': Buller, *Birds,* p.123.

Seasonal bird counts: D.G. Dawson, P.J. Dilks, P.D. Gaze, J.G.R. McBurney and P.R. Wilson, 'Seasonal Differences in Bird Counts in Forests near Reefton, South Island, New Zealand', *Notornis,* 25, pp.257-278; radio-tracking of kererū: M.N. Clout, B.J. Karl and P.D. Gaze, 'The Dispersal of New Zealand Pigeon from a Forest Reserve', *Notornis 38,* Pt.1, 1991, pp.37-47; design of forest reserves: K.R. Hackwell and D.G. Dawson, 'Designing Forest Reserves', *Forest and Bird,* Vol.13, No.8, 1980, pp.8-16.

'obliterating the old boundary lines . . .': Buller, *Supplement,* p.xlii.

'birds deprived of lowland forest . . .': Sir Robert Falla, 'Wildlife in New Zealand', in *Bulletin of British Ornithology Club* 59, pp.149-151; see also Falla, 'New Zealand bird life past and present', *Cawthron Lecture Series,* 29, pp. 3-14, Nelson.

p.177 'a good deal of flax is cut . . .' etc.: James Cox, Diary 1888-1889, WTU, MS-0621. Cox is the subject of Miles Fairburn, *Nearly out of Heart and Hope: The Puzzle of a Colonial Settler's Diary,* Auckland University Press, Auckland, 1995.

p.178 Horowhenua flax history: see Dreaver, *Horowhenua.*

Mua-upoko traditions relating to Papaitonga, its mauri and Hāpua Kō-rari: interviews with Joseph Tukupua, Kawiu Marae, Levin, April-September 1990.

'persistent', 'a barbaric folk dwelling in a land of forests': Best, *Maori Forest Lore*, pp.185-254.

p.180 The search for Hāpua Kō-rari, the so-called 'lost lake': Chris McLean, *Tararua: the story of a mountain range*, Whitcombe Press, Wellington, 1994, pp.53-72.

'No one owns this landscape . . .', 'everyone owns (or ought to own) . . .': W.J.T. Mitchell, 'Imperial landscape', in W.J.T. Mitchell (ed.), *Landscape and Power*, University of Chicago Press, Chicago, 1994.

p.181 'a round river': Leopold, *Round River*.

'the government's reserve': Urorangi Paki, pers. comm. at fisheries hui, Matau Marae, June 1986.

'when most of the surrounding district has lost much . . .': Adkin, *Horowhenua*, p.287.

'from the dim bush shadows . . .': Wilson, *My First Eighty Years*, p.115.

'intact sequence': in 'Lake Papaitonga Scenic Reserve', in 'Scenic Reserves of the Lower North Island', M.C. Wassilieff, D.J. Clark and I. Gabites, *Biological Survey of Reserves Series*, No.14, DLS, 1986.

p.182 'Do you see . . . water's edge': Buller, 'The Story of Papaitonga', *TNZI 26*, 1895, pp.572-584.

Te hīkioi, 'its resting place was on top of the mountains . . .', 'Te rau ō te Huia . . .': account of a Ngātiapa chief to Sir George Grey, recounted in R.C. Bruce, 'On a Maori waiata', *TNZI 24*, 1893, p.426-428, with translation of waiata. The paper created debate on the actual identity of hokioi.

p.183 'never ending supply of fine specimens', 'what bitterns are left . . .': *Botaurus poeciloptilus*, Buller, *Supplement*.

Whitiki Bush, Mauri Bush and Whare-o-tauira Bush: Adkin, *Horowhenua*.

p.184 'berries grow mostly on the outskirts . . .': P.E. Baldwin, 'Early Native Records of the Manawatu Block', *TNZI 38*, 1905, p.1.

Polynesian shaping of natural ecosystems: see Patrick V. Kirch, *The Evolution of Polynesian Chiefdoms*, Cambridge University Press, London, 1984, pp.123-151; William C. Clarke, 'Learning from the Past: Traditional Knowledge and Sustainable Development', *The Contemporary Pacific*, Vol.2, No.2, University of Hawaii Press, Honolulu, 1990, pp.233-253.

Account of palaeo-ecology of Papaitonga, and pollen analysis of core sample: M.S. McGlone, pers. comm., 1989.

p.185 'treacherously-fluid': Adkin, *Horowhenua*, p.84.

Patu of 'Eastern Polynesian' design: illustrated in M. Orbell, *The Natural World of the Maori*, Collins/Bateman, Auckland, 1985, p.10; design affinity, Roger Neich, ethnologist, Auckland Museum, pers. comm., 1990.

Evidence from earliest known midden: B.G. McFadgen, *Palaeo-environmental Studies in the Manawatu sand Plain with Particular Reference to Foxton*, M.A. Thesis in Anthropology, University of Otago, 1972.

Early inhabitants of Horowhenua crossing Tararua Range: G.N. Park, 'A Maori oven site in the Tararua Range: a palaeoclimatological evaluation', *New Zealand Archaeological Association Newsletter*, 13, 1970, pp.191-197.

Archaeological interpretation of Horowhenua settlement history: Bruce McFadgen, pers. comm., May 1995.

p.186 'In all these patches of bush . . . until the prohibition was removed': McDonald, *Te Hekenga*.

'It is said that virtue . . . wrath of Te Rauparaha': report of church picnic from Shannon, *The Farmer*, 15 July 1895, scrapbook, Buller *papers*,WTU, qMS BUL.

p.187 'the power of his war-parties . . . old residents', 'rifles', 'lent the war a ruthlessness . . .': P.E. Baldwin, 'Early Native Records of the Manawatu Block', *TNZI 38*, 1905, pp.1-3.

'Te Tipi at once swam out . . . the women and children': Waretini Tuainuku's account to Walter Buller, 'The Story of Papaitonga', *TNZI 26*, 1894.

p.188 Musket ball in totara log at sawmill: Buller, *Supplement*, fn, p.xlvi.

p.189 'I have lately seen a flock of two hundred or more . . .' Buller, *Birds*.

p.190 'Statues and trophies, Gardens and groves . . .': John Milton, *Paradise Regained*, quoted in J.D. Hunt and P. Willis (eds.), *The Genius of the Place*, J.M. Dent and Sons, London, 1975, p.206.

'specimens of Maori industry': description of Buller's Māori 'ruins' in Resolution of House of Representatives of acceptance of Buller gift to Dominion Museum, quoted in letter to W. Leo Buller from Speaker of House of Representatives 26 October 1911, MONZ.

'On the island there was a famous obelisk . . .': Buller, *Supplement*, pp.xliv-v.

'Home . . . to represent the Colony . . .': Buller, in evidence to Horowhenua Commission, *AJHR*, 1896, G2, p.242.

'one of the smartest . . .', 'much frequented by boating men . . .': *The Evening Post*, undated, scrapbook, Buller *papers*.

p.191 'Nature has done so much, little was wanting': Capability Brown quoted by Richard Mabey, 'Home Country', in *In a Green Shade: Essays on Landscape, 1970-1983*, Hutchinson, London, 1983, p.25.

Buller's visiting English country estates: Galbreath, *Buller*, p.199.

'In the Hon Walter Rothschild's beautiful collection . . .': Buller, *Notes on Birds*, p.88.

Tring Park and Charles Bridgeman: Hunt, *Garden and Grove*, p.189.

p.192 'Large prolated gardens and Plantations adorn'd . . . statues . . .': Switzer's *Ichnographia Rustica*, Vol.1, xviii-xix, in Hunt, *Garden and Grove*, p.188.

'It seems to me . . . for the student of the future': Buller, 'The Story of Papaitonga; or, A Page of Maori History', *TNZI 26*, pp.572-584.

'ease and pleasure . . . all year around': SPC Report, 23 August 1906. Also in DLS HO file 4/301.

'an unalienable heritage of the Buller family . . .': SPC Minutes, 8 April 1904 (8th sitting), NA LS/70/1.

Ward also requested the Scenery Preservation Commission to visit Papaitonga in 1904: S.P. Smith minutes of SPC, 21st sitting, 3 May 1904, NA LS/70/1, p.22. The Buller family's ownership notwithstanding, government interest in a 'Papaitonga Lake Scenic Reserve' persisted, even to its formal listing: Schedule of Recommendations of the Scenery Preservation Commission, *AJHR*, 1909, 1. C1, p.9.

'rich bush . . . to the water's edge', 'a magnificent large Pataka . . . improves the scenery': SPC Report, *Papaitonga*.

p.193 Walter Buller's grandaughter's visit, 1972: pers. comm., the late Don Murray, Papaitonga, Ohau, May 1987.

Papaitonga was acquired as scenic reserve in 1981. Submissions were called for its management soon after.

Buller and Featherston's 1864 attempt to buy Papaitonga for the Crown: 'Rough Notes of a Meeting at Otaki, on the 24th June, convened to consider questions arising out of the Muhunoa Sale' (annotated by Buller), WP3, 64/530 NA.

'a small whare and eel-fishing weirs': 1850s recollection of Donald Fraser, *Horowhenua Commission*, p.70.

Ngāti Kikopiri pā tuna and Mua Upoko poha: Adkin, *Horowhenua*, p.414.

p.194 'final settlement', 'convey by way of gift', 'there is no permanent water except swamp': *Horowhenua Commission*, p.10 (i.e. 'Then Taueki . . . gave him an eel-weir named Raumatangi, and a piece of land called Mauri; it was a clump of kahikatea bush': T.R. McKee evidence, *Horowhenua Commission*, p 26.)

'beyond question or repudiation', 'since time in memoriam . . .', and concern with names: Ngawini Kuiti, Ngāti Kikopiri Trustees to Commissioner of Crown Lands, Wellington, 19 November 1981, Papaitonga *Reserves files*.

Permission, then refusal for Ngāti Raukawa to gather kie kie: Lake Papaitonga *Reserves files*; 28 April and 25 June 1982, 11 May, 14 June and 12 July 1983; Boardwalk: Papaitonga *Reserves files*, March 1983.

'You know what I think . . .': Ngawini Kuiti, pers. comm., June 1986.

p.195 'which constitutes the kiwi preserve . . . lover of nature': Buller, *Supplement*, p.xliv.

'rites, forms and observances': W.L. Buller, *Observations, Tapu*.

'To prevent any chance of Maori depredations . . .': Buller, *Notes on Birds*, p.87.

'fallen into the error . . .': Buller, *Supplement*, p.xlii.

'Some months ago I received a fine pair from the South . . .', 'island community', 'successfully introduced . . . may be looked upon as being established . . .': Buller, *Notes on Birds*, p.87.

p.196 'the task is a hopeless one': Buller, *Birds*, p.55.

'expiring species always [last] longest on islands . . .': *New Zealand Journal of Science*, Vol.1, 1891, p.235. Also *TNZI 24*, p.713. Almost identical to the statement in Buller's Memo on the Protection of Birds to Onslow, Governor, repr. in *AJHR*, 1892, H6, p.2.

Letter to Buller from Tamati Ranapiri, 'It is very pleasing . . .': in '*Apteryx mantelli*', in Buller, *Supplement*.

'Get any stray Muaupoko to sign . . .', 'Don't say anything to the Muaupoko . . .': letter to Hector McDonald, 13 October 1892, Buller letterbook, MONZ, pp.225-226.

'a perfect necropolis of human bones': Buller, 'The Story of Papaitonga', *TNZI 26*, 1895, p.572. Also Buller, *Supplement*, p.xliii.

'The beaten Muaupoko . . .': Buller, *Observations, Tapu*.

p.197 'the foundation of Maori society . . .', 'so strictly tapu . . .', 'a heavy cranium . . . never been tapu at all': Buller, *Observations, Tapu.*

p.198 O-tomuri Bush as a 'kaka resort': Buller, *Supplement*, p.xlix.

Account of 1895 fire: *New Zealand Times*, 26 March 1895, scrapbook, Buller *papers.*

p.199 'the Goths and Vandals in our midst': *The Evening Post*, 23 May 1895.

'beloved patron and soul-mate': Howe, *Singer, Songless Land.*

W.P. Reeves' poem 'The Passing of the Forest', from his *New Zealand and Other Poems*, Grant Richards, London, 1898.

'perfect in appearance': scrapbook, Buller *papers.*

'excessive individualism': W.P. Reeves, *State Experiments in Australia and New Zealand*, 2 Vols, Grant Richards, London, 1902.

Reeves' poem, 'In Pember Bay', first published in *The New Zealand Graphic*, 19 January 1895, p.64, with accompanying article in support of perserving 'local traditions' of New Zealand's scenery, and Sir Walter Buller's Papaitonga example. It reappeared, altered after Buller's fire, *New Zealand Mail*, 8 February 1895, and in Reeves, *State Experiments.* Buller also published five verses in *Supplement.*

p.201 Buller's quoting of Rudyard Kipling and 'magnificent and silent forests . . .': Buller, *Supplement*, p.xxxiv-v.

'the flinty impassivity . . .', 'dear chief and friend', 'lover of dear Dame Nature', 'charming pieces of forest', 'ruining the hem . . .': Tregear to Reeves, *Letters.*

'up at the State Form last week', 'socialistic experiment . . . hard slogging': Tregear to Reeves, *Letters.*

p.202 'A State Farm is to comprise . . .', 'sunburnt, sinewy men . . .', 'landholder as the master . . .', 'fifty men, eight women . . . be laid out': Edward Tregear, 'Report on the Bureau of Industries', *AJHR* H14, 1892, pp.2-3. Subsequent annual reports dealing with the purchase of land at Horowhenua and its development, e.g. 1893 (H10), 1894 (H6), 1895 (H6), are from the Department of Labour that replaced it.

p.203 'taken the land of the Maori': Tregear to Reeves, *Letters.*

'ought to be in gaol for his dealings . . .': *New Zealand Times*, 26 October 1895, scrapbook, Buller, *papers.*

'country seat': Buller, *Supplement*, p.xliii.

p.204 'strip the woods away', and verse, 'The Passing of the Forest': W.P. Reeves, *New Zealand and Other Poems*, Grant Richards, London, 1898, pp.4-8.

'Since His Excellency, the Earl of Glasgow . . .': Buller, *Supplement*, p.xliii.

'all the new birds are doing well': Buller letter to Mair, 19 April 1894, quoted in Galbreath, *Buller*, p.199.

'quite unsuitable now for a labour depot', Tregear to Reeves, *Letters*, quoted in Howe, *Singer, Songless Land*, p.80.

'awfully put out', 'is simply infatuated . . .', 'beastly State farmers', 'Walter posted a reward . . .': W.G. Mair letter to Gibb (Gilbert Mair), 16 May 1898, WTU, MS papers, 93 folder 15.

p.205 'you can't put 40-50 men on a dairy farm . . .': Tregear to Reeves, *Letters*, 22 November 1896.

'a hard day's tramp . . .': letter from Leo Buller, 2 May 1899, Buller *papers.*

'whose advancing years and domestic . . .': Treager, Annual Report Dept. of Labour, *AJHR*, 1895, H6, p.17.

'forest reserves like the beautiful belt of bush': Buller, *Supplement*, p.xxxix.

'preservation of native bush: 'Places Permanently Reserved under The Land Act, 1892', *The New Zealand Gazette*, 7 January 1901.

p.206 'the tangle of roots on the wet floor; a few remnants in an almost virgin state', 'coastal plain semi-swamp forest': Leonard Cockayne's description in *The Vegetation of New Zealand; Die Vegetation der Erde*, XIV, Leipzig, was not published until 1921.

p.207 G.L. Adkin, 'The Post-tertiary Geological History of the Ohau River and the Adjacent Coastal Plain, Horowhenua County, North Island', *TRSNZ*, Vol.43, 1910.

p.208 A.W.B. Powell, 'The Paraphantidae of New Zealand: their Hypothetical Ancestry, with descriptions of a New Species and and New Genus', *Records of the Auckland Institute and Museum*, Vol.1, 1930.

'Pleistocene plains around Levin; This low country habit . . .': Powell, *Further Species.*

Powell, *The Species Problem.*

p.209 M.T. Te Punga, 'The Paraphantidae and a Cook Strait Land Bridge', *New Zealand Journal of Science and Technology*, 35, 1953, pp.51-63.

'intense localisation . . .; at once apparent . . .' Powell, *The Species Problem.*

p.210 'once-compact snail population . . .': Powell, *The Species Problem.*

Powell's meeting with Adkin, Woodside, Horowhenua, 22 December 1945: G.L. Adkin, Diary, MONZ, courtesy A.J. Dreaver.

Adkin's 'excellent' paper: Powell, *Further Species*, p.117; 'at once apparent', Powell, *The Species Problem*, p.206.

'There have been two prior courses of the Ohau . . . Pleistocene': Powell, *The Species Problem*, p.206.

'It seems evident . . .' Powell, *Further Species.*

'continual dampness': Powell, *Further Species.*

p.211 Buller's awareness of landsnails in the Horowhenua: Buller exhibited 'Manawatu' landsnails at the 28 November 1894 meeting of the Wellington Philosophical Society; three months earlier, its president, W.T.L. Travers, referred to 'Manawatu and Waikanae' snails in 'Notes on the Larger Species of *Paryphanta* in New Zealand, with some Remarks on the Distribution and Dispersal of Land-shells', *TNZI 28*, Art.XIV, 1895, pp.224-228.

'The problem . . . diverge in character as they become modified': Darwin, *Origin of Species.*

'To the old time Maori . . .': P.E. Baldwin, 'Early Native Records of the Manawatu Block', *TNZI 38*, 1905, p.1; 'cuttings from swamp to swamp . . .', 'eel-fisheries . . . as gold-mines are . . .': A.K. Newman, 'on a Stone-carved Ancient Wooden Image of a Maori Eel-god', *TNZI 38*, p.131.

p.212 Eels in Rangitikei-Manawatu: Sir William Fox, quoted by Sir W.L. Buller, in report on 13 July 1892 meeting of Wellington Philosophical Society, *TNZI 24*, 1893, p.526.

p.213 'This seems to be one of the inscrutable laws of Nature . . .', 'must inevitably happen . . .': Buller, Presidential Address to Wellington Philosophical Society, 13 February 1884, *TNZI 16*, p.444.

'It was the lake I was hankering after . . .': *Horowhenua Commission*, p.253.

'kua kite-matou i te tinihanga o taua roia'—i.e. 'we have seen the cheating of that lawyer': quoted in Galbreath, *Buller*, p.198.

Kēpa and the Levin Village Settlement, and reservation of the lakes: in A.J. Dreaver, *Horowhenua*, pp.95-98.

'On my return to the colony . . .': Buller, evidence, *Horowhenua Commission*, p.242.

'the right at all times to erect eelweirs . . .': Memorandum of lease, exhibit AN, ibid, p.319.

p.214 'a reserve two chains wide . . . Right of Way': Buller letterbook, June 1892, MONZ, p.64.

'misconception' and removal of alleged Right of Way: letters to Bell, G.L.R. Scott Esq. and S.P. Smith, Surveyor-General, forwarding declarations from Judge Wilson of Native Land Court, Keepa te Rangihiwinui, and Scott, surveyor, etc., Buller letterbook, June-July 1892, MONZ, pp.58, 59, 64-66, 87.

S.P. Smith's instruction to amend Buller's title: Buller *papers*, WTU, qMS folio 145.

'old primeval grandeur': Buller, *Illustrations of Darwinism.*

'a mile's tramp to no purpose', 'I hope you will be careful . . . tree ferns and nikaus': letter to George Bryers, Muhunoa, 9 June 1892, letter to Bryers, Buller letterbook, MONZ, pp.73-74, 76.

'McLeavey and Hudson have fallen out . . . the bush': Leo Buller to Walter Buller, 2 May 1899, Buller *papers.*

'The Natives have no permission . . .': letter to Henson, Manakau, undated (1892), Buller letterbook, MONZ, pp.231-32.

p.215 'in protest against so insane a policy', 'vermin': Buller, 'On some Curiosities of Bird-life' *TNZI 27*, 1984, quoted in Perrine Moncrieff, 'The Destruction of an Avian Paradise', in *Preservation, Empire*, June 1944.

'Sir Walter Buller on his visit up the Coast . . .': unsourced newspaper cutting, 1892 (?), scrapbook, Buller, *papers.*

'Morris said . . .': Buller to Thistleton-Dyer, 15 October 1893, Royal Botanic Gardens Kew, Archives, English letters, 1866-1900, Vol.81 (148/149); 'the executive of Kew Gardens . . .': *Evening Post*, undated, 1895 (?), scrapbook, Buller *papers.*

'Could you possibly manage . . .': letter to Ayson, 30 August 1892, Buller letter book, MONZ, p.33; 'I shall go up to Papaitonga . . .': Buller to H. MacDonald, 13 October 1892, Buller letterbook, MONZ.

Bert Richards: pers. comm. June 1989, at Papaitonga and his home at Levin.

p.216 Buller's native plant introductions: Buller, *Supplement*, pp.xlviii-xlix.

Buller's 1893 reference to the bird enclosures: *TNZI 27*, 1894.

'hopelessly doomed': Buller, *Supplement*, p.157

Huia's legal protection, including the probability that, despite his role in it, Buller obtained and shot at least ten huia illegally after the protection was gazetted in February 1892. See Galbreath, *Buller*, pp.176-192, 264-268.

'parties of Maories into the woods . . .', his own private collection . . .': letter to Rothschild, 2 March 1892, letterbook, 1877-1892, Buller *papers*.

'Under changed conditions . . .', 'deep shade of its forest home . . .': Buller, *Notes on Birds*, pp.53, 55.

p.217 Buller's 18 January 1893 lecture to Wellington Philosophical Society; 'extreme docility', 'The female bird allowing . . .': Buller, *Notes on Birds*.

'systematically stocking the Island by catching Huias . . .': Buller, letter to [Premier] Ballance, 14 November 1892, letterbook 1892-1894, Buller *papers*; quoted in Galbreath, *Buller*, p.190.

'admirably suited': Buller, *Notes on Birds*, p.87.

'Huia loves the mountain tops . . . in winter to lower forests': Buller, *Supplement*, p.xxxii. Blaming the *combination* of lowland forest clearance, introduced predators and pest poisoning ('at its height in the 1880s') for huia's demise, W.J. Phillips made the point in his 1963 *Book of the Huia*, that 'even such a noted ornithologist as Buller apparently did not know the true distribution of huia' (p.60).

'no love lost': Tregear to Reeves, *Letters*.

p.218 'The beauties of the Country are to be opened . . .': unsourced (newspaper), October 1897 (?), scrapbook, Buller *papers*.

'The Laying Off of Roads . . .', 'Roads taken under Warrant from His Excellency the Governor': SO 7418, *The New Zealand Gazette*, 7 January 1897, pp.33-34. See also Plan of Waiwiri Lake, Horowhenua Block, surveyed for road round lake by Llewellyn Smith, District Surveyor, 24 July 1896, Survey Plan 1399, DOSLI, Wellington.

'specimens of Maori industry': ref. cited in this volume, p.190.

p.219 'The Roera boys came across from Kikopiri . . .': Bert Richards, pers. comm.

Willy Field's lobbying of government to buy Papaitonga: Field to Minister of Tourist and Publicity, 29 May 1911, Papaitonga *Reserves files*.

Telegram 'Buller leaving for England Friday . . .', and other correspondence: 2 November 1911, Papaitonga *Reserves files*.

p.220 'The lake is very shallow . . . dug through the swamp', 'a desirable national undertaking', 'other less costly sanctuaries': P. Dyett to Chief Surveyor, letter with map, Dept. Lands and Survey, October 1911 (sent 23 December 1911), Papaitonga *Reserves files*.

'the lovely lake . . . admirably adapted for regattas . . .': from 1902 auction placard, Plan of Town of Levin, McDonald, Wilson and Co. for Wellington–Manawatu Railway Co., in possession of Lew Prouse, Levin, (seen by author, September 1987).

Department of Conservation's and Wellington Conservation Board's anxiety about Papaitonga lake levels: correspondence with Wellington Regional Council, April 1992; 'Lake Waiwiri (Papaitonga) Water Level Investigations', Ian Cooksley, 24 September 1992, Papaitonga *Reserves files*.

Joseph Tukupua, pers. comm.

p.221 '. . . all the time voices have been calling for care of Papaitonga': e.g. 1896 or 1897 'A well attended and enthusiastic meeting was held last evening at the Town Hall to urge the Government to acquire the lakes in this district . . . Horowhenua, Papaitonga and Waiwera . . . for a pleasure resort . . . (By Telegraph: Our Correspondent, unidentified newspaper, cutting) in Buller *papers*.

'a fountain of energy . . .', 'otherwise have faith in': Leopold, *Round River*.

Leopold, ordinary citizens and members of an ecosystem, 'In short a land ethic changes the role of *Homo sapiens* from conqueror of the land community to plain member and citizen of it': 'The Upshot—The Land Ethic', in *A Sand County Almanac*, p.204.

'religiously preserved', in letter from Humphries (?) 10 September 1908 — 'It is true that, whilst the land . . . remains in the hands of the Buller family, it will be religiously preserved, but a time may come when some persons may acquire it . . . who will sacrifice beauty for utilitarian ends': Notes on Papaitonga Lake, to Scenery Preservation Board, Papaitonga *Reserves files*.

p.222 'hitherto undisturbed . . .', 'has of spreading . . .': 'The Speech of H.R.H The Duke of Gloucester at the Dinner of the Society', *Preservation, Empire*, June 1939.

'archaic birds': anonymous, 1944; 'Protection and Preservation of the Indigenous Land Fauna in New Zealand', *Preservation, Empire*, June 1939, p.76.

'processes by which the land . . .': Leopold, 'The Upshot—Conservation Ethic', in *A Sand County Almanac*, p.173; 'duties to ecosystems': the philosopher, Holmes Rolston III, on Leopold, in Baird Callicott (ed.), *Companion to A Sand County Almanac*, University of Wisconsin Press, Madison, 1987, pp.246-274.

p.223 'a sacred wood': Reeves' poem 'In Pember Bay', this volume, p.200.

Gary Snyder, 'Good, Wild and Sacred', in *The Practice of the Wild,* North Point Press, San Francisco, 1990.

Chapter 5: The Head of the Inlet

p.230 'safe and commodious harbours': Wakefield's *Instructions*, p.4F.

p.233 'the first white man in West Whanganui': Moore, *Early Pioneer Days*, pp.49-113.

'great importance to explore': Wakefield, *British Colonization, NZ*, p.108.

'Good, smooth, landlocked harbour ...': 'best coal found in New Zealand'; 'will one day be deemed ...', 'In the waters of the harbour ...': Moore, *Early Pioneer Days*.

p.234 'God spare the Maoris from such fates ...': Moore, *Early Pioneer Days*.

'a very fine country'; 'very high double land': *Tasman, Discovery*.

p.235 'very desolate'; 'about a mile from the shore ...': *Tasman, Discovery*.

Names of coastal kāinga from 1863: *Plan of Native Reserve at Taitapu* ('as finally arranged by Mr Bell in letter 244, signed James Mackay, Commr Native Reserves'), NA. MA 15/1/26b.

'Many excellent and fertile regions'; 'well-populated districts ...': Tasman's *Instructions*.

Exposed umu at Turimawiwi: Simon Walls, Onekaka, pers. comm., 1992.

'We believed we could see on the coast a vast basin ...': D'Urville, 13 January 1827, *New Zealand*.

p.236 Barry Lopez, *Arctic Dreams*, Picador, London, 1986.

William Spain's 1840s Commission of Inquiry: see Sinclair, *History*, pp.76-78.

'a lofty pine wood ...': Heaphy, *Port Nicholson*.

'When I first saw the Inlet ...': Harry Washbourne, *Further Reminiscences*, p.17-19.

p.237 'long and tedious walk': Heaphy, *Expedition*, p.207.

'Either by cajolery or bullying': Heaphy, *Expedition*.

'made *tapu* for him': F.G. Moore, *Early Pioneer Days*.

'most extortionate natives ...': Heaphy, *Expedition*, p.207.

'along the southern arm to its termination'; 'ascended the hills': Heaphy, *Expedition*, p.209.

'superiority over ... ordinary lands': Wakefield's *Instructions*.

p.238 'The hills nearly all around are too steep ...': Heaphy, *Expedition*, p.206-207.

'The valley of the Wanganui'; 'of a nature that it would render much'; 'It is not worthy of the attention ...': Heaphy, *Expedition*, p.246-247.

'I was particular of my enquiries of Te Rauparaha ...'; 'while he acknowledged the receipt ...': Spain's *Report*, in Mackay, *Compendium*, p.55.

p.239 'the sandy beaches and low hills of the Taitap country'; 'precipitous cliffs': Heaphy, *Expedition*, p.212.

'So the killing went on along that coast ...': Tamihana Te Rauparaha, in Patricia Burns, *Te Rauparaha: a New Perspective*, Reed, Wellington, 1980, p.160.

'dictated to me the native names ...': Wakefield, *Adventure*.

'six single-barrelled guns, five double-barrelled ...': from 'Copy of the New Zealand Company's Second Deed of Purchase, including the Nelson District, dated 9th October, 1839' in Spain, *Report*, pp.64-65.

'Taitap, Wanganui, Onetaua ...': Wakefield, *Adventure*.

p.240 'Taitapa, in Blind Bay, forms the solitary exception ...' Spain, *Report*, p.58.

'ill at ease', 'he asked for some grog ...': Wakefield, *Adventure*.

'visited Te Raupero and Hiko ...': Arthur Wakefield, letter to William Wakefield, from ship *Whitby*, 7 November 1841. NZCo papers MS704, WTU.

'Run no risk of misleading others': Wakefield's *Instructions*, p.11F.

'full and final giving up ...': 'Receipt for £2,000 paid to the Ngatitoa Tribe, being the second and final payment to them of their proportion of the amount agreed on in the deed dated 10th August, 1853', in McLean, *Papers and Documents*; in Mackay, *Compendium*, pp.311-312.

Revered forests like Te Mōtu ... appeared briefly in the earliest sketches': Spain ultimately set aside 16 of the NZCo's sections of The Big Wood, as it was called [see p.3 of 'A Narrative of the Principle Subjects included ...' in Mackay, *Compendium*]. See also Plan of the Native Reserve chosen in the Great Wood of the Motueka District, including the sections required in exchange, 1844, signed Wm. Spain. Le1/1872/200, NA.

p.241 'the pahs and burial places, and grounds actually in cultivation ...': Spain, *Report*, March 31, 1845, No.2, in Mackay, *Compendium*, p.54.

'importance to the Nelson Settlement ...'; 'extinguish the native title ...'; 'More especially, it contains those elements of wealth ...': Richmond, *Massacre Bay letters*, Superintendent of Nelson, letter to Col. Sec., Wellington, 31 May 1852, in Mackay, p.290.

'the more difficult it would be of accomplishment ...' Richmond, *Massacre Bay letters*, p.189.

p.242 'consult with the wishes of the Native Matiaha ..;': John Tinline, letter to Thomas Brunner, 31 August 1852; in Mackay, *Compendium*, p.291.

'grieved to find so many pas deserted . . .'; 'resist the appeal': Richmond, *Massacre Bay letters*, p.189.

'With reference to the native reserves in general . . .': John Tinline, letter, 18 December 1855, MA 13/51, NA.

'profession of reserving lands for the Maories was all gammon, humbug and lies': Frederick Tuckett, Report 11 January 1844, G30/5, pp.365-366. NA.

'subsistence'; 'more a provision for their future wants . . .': McLean, *Papers and Documents*, pp.300-301.

'one place excluded from sale and reserved for our use . . .': 'Deed of Sale by the Ngatirarua and Ngatitama Tribes, ceding claims to land in the Middle Island', 13 November 1855. No.13 in Richmond, *Massacre Bay letters*.

Te Tai Tapu Native Reserve was commonly referred to as West Whanganui Native Reserve. The Enclosure in item No.36 (*Return of Native Reserves . . .*) in Mackay, *Compendium* as 44,000 acres 'excepted from sale in 1855 for the Ngatirarua, Ngatitama and Ngatiawa tribes . . .'

p.243 Paul Colinvaux, *The Fates of Nations: A Biological Theory of History*, Penguin Books, Harmondsworth, 1983, pp.58-65.

'reservation of lands for the benefit of the natives': *Charter of Incorporation of the New Zealand Company*, 1841, in Mackay, *Compendium*. Its origin in 1830s British humanitarianism and colonial reform: see Sinclair, *History*, pp.62-64.

'If the advantage of the Natives alone were consulted . . .': Wakefield's *Instructions*, in Spain, *Report*, in Mackay, *Compendium*, p.51.

p.244 Relative size of Te Tai Tapu Native Reserve: Heaphy, in *Native Reserves, Nelson*.

'having so little intercourse with Europeans . . .': Heaphy, *Expedition*, p.207.

'I was born at Taitapu, West Whanganui . . .': Hoani Tatana, in Nelson Minute Book, Native Land Court, 1883, No.1 folios 3, 43-44, NA.

'about ten Natives living . . .' Alexander Mckay to the Hon. Native Minister, 6 December, 1865 (ref Memo No.876) NA MA-MT/6/19.

'particularly anxious . . .': McLean, *Papers and Documents*.

'ostensibly 120 and five-sixths acres to each Native'; 'lost sight of'; 'remained unutilised'; 'It may not be premature . . .' Heaphy, *Native Reserves, Nelson*, pp.37-38.

p.245 'a few small sheltered areas fit for cultivation . . .'; 'it is chiefly valuable . . .'; 'would subserve equally the native and public interests . . .'; 'judicious expenditure': Heaphy, *Native Reserves, Nelson*.

'many rich mines of precious and other minerals': Tasman's *Instructions*.

'considerable quantities' of gold, 'bad feeling . . . and more serious evils . . .'; 'over which the native title had not been extinguished': Mackay, *Collingwood letters*, p.321-322.

'the peacable pursuit of gold-mining . . .': H. Halse, Acting Native Secretary, to James Mackay, Asst. Native. Sec., Collingwood, 5 March 1862, p.323, and figures on Ngati Rarua goldmining licences, Mackay, *Compendium*, Nos 5, 6.

'their determination not to admit . . .': Mackay, *Collingwood letters*.

Riwai Turangapeke's cart, plough, etc.: his and Rore Pukekohatu's letter to Governor, 29 September 1863; Donald McLean's memo; letter of thanks from Riwai, Nos 7 and 8, in Mackay, *Compendium*.

p.246 'seen some pretty rough and primitive places . . .'; 'in the refreshment line . . .': Harry Washbourne, *Further Reminiscences*.

Weisenhavern, and Pachten, coalmining leases: eg. Otto Wiesenhavern's application for Depasturage Licence, p.128, 22 November 1866, Arnold Pachten's application to register, p.113, 7 September 1867, *N.Z. Government Gazette (Province of Nelson)*.

Oswald Curtis' 26 May 1868 Proclamation bringing land including Te Tai Tapu Native Reserve into the Golden Bay Goldfields under the Goldmines Act: *N.Z. Government Gazette (Province of Nelson)*, 29 May 1868. A resolution of a Select Committee of the Provincial Council on 9 June 1873 reinforced the alienation: V&P, 1873.

Native Land Court, and native reserves, in 1880s: see Hugh Kawharu, *Maori Land Tenure*, Oxford University Press, Oxford, 1977.

Claim of Henare Wiremu et al, to Native Land Court, 27 October 1880, and W.G. Mair's November 1883 Judgement: Nelson NLC *Minute Book*.

p.247 The sketch map, *Te Taetapu, Original Plan of Native Land West Wanganui*: ML931, Nelson Survey Office, 6 December 1880. DOSLI Nelson, is probably Mackay's; i.e. letter to Native Sec., Auckland, 24 September 1862, No.3, in 'Correspondence Respecting the Boundaries of the Native Reserve at West Wanganui', in Mackay, *Compendium*, p.324. Arthur Carkeek's sketch map in the same archive, (MLC3349), is separately annotated as 'sufficient for' and 'used in' the Native

Land Court, by Browning, Chief Surveyor and Mair, Judge, November 1883.

F.G. Moore and A.deB. Brandon's 'The New West Wanganui Coal Company Ltd': 1882 prospectus in MS Papers 36 [Moore Papers] folio 4, WTU.

'locked up and unrenumerative acres': 16 July 1886 Editorial, *Golden Bay Argus.*

Holmes' letter to Alexander Mackay, and subsequent correspondence: Registry book, ML. NA. It is possible that the letters themselves were among the files destroyed in the 1950s Hope Gibbons' fire.

V.S. Naipaul, *A Way in the World,* Heinemann, London, 1994.

'vague description', and Mackay's reference to his sketch map: Mackay, *Compendium*, p.324.

p.248 Alfred D'Bathe Brandon came to NZ in 1840, was a Provincial Council member, Judge of the Supreme Court, Member of the House of Representatives, 1858-1881. His son joined his law firm in 1875, and like his father was President of the Wellington Law Society. His deed of transfer, 28 February 1895: No.4585, Transfer of Sec I Sq 17 situated in Te Taitapu to The Taitapu Gold Estates Ltd, in Register-Book, Vol.9 Folio 175, 29 October 1895. Brandon's Crown Grant, signed Jervois, Governor, and Arthur Carkeek's attached survey map: Nelson Survey Office, Crown Grant, Vol.13, Folio 40. DOSLI Nelson. The establishment of Taitapu Gold Estates Ltd is believed to have been a consequence of Brandon's colleague, William Beetham, taking the geologist Higginson's report to England seeking investors (Joyce Parkinson, daughter of the first white settler, pers. comm., May 1986).

Prospectus of Taitapu Gold Estates Ltd: reference is based on letter from N.L. Buchanan, Manager of Taitapu Gold Estates to Editor, *Golden Bay Argus*, 19 January 1911, correcting statements that 'the Company had brought the Estate from the Maoris at 2/6d per acre and had pocketed large sums over the deal' and was a 'social pest': Joyce Parkinson, pers. comm.

'influential members of both Houses': 16 July Editorial, *Golden Bay Argus.*

Ecologists' discovery of Te Tai Tapu's still-forested estuaries: G.N. Park and G.Y. Walls, *Inventory of Tall Forest Stands on Lowland Plains and Terraces in Nelson and Marlborough Land Districts, New Zealand*, Botany Division, DSIR, September 1978.

p.249 'the Taitap' was sold twice'; 'insider trading, call it what you will': Joyce Parkinson, pers. comm.

'the block was put through the Native Land Court . . .': Harry Moffatt, quoted in Newport, *Collingwood*, pp.230-231.

Opposition of rūnanga to Te Tai Tapu's inclusion in Kahurangi National Park: John Mitchell, pers. comm., June 1993.

Hoani Mahuika, 'I claim Te Whanganui . . .': Nelson NLC *Minute Book.*

p.250 Wiremu Maui, 'I was taken as a slave . . .'; 'The land was taken without a cause . . .'; Meihana Kereopa, 'I claim the whole . . .': Nelson NLC *Minute Book* .

Te Tai Tapu as 'forbidden territory': J.N.W. Newport, *Collingwood*, p.230.

Account of Richards' family finds of obsidian, shell heaps, etc.: Joyce Parkinson, pers. comm., May-June 1986.

p.251 Kati Wae Wae knowledge of karaka on N.W. Nelson coast: Maika Mason, pers. comm., 1989.

Ngāti Rarua, Ngātiawa and Ngāti Tama understanding of Te Tai Tapu's name: John Mitchell, Paul Morgan, pers. comm., 1993.

1846 head count of West Coast Maori, and observation of taro and kumara gardens; 'uninhabited'; 'one long solitude . . .': Heaphy, *Expedition,* in Taylor, *Early Travellers, NZ*, p.241.

Recent archaeological evidence from Bruce Bay: Kevin L. Jones, Ray Hooker, and Atholl Anderson, *Bruce Bay revisited: Archaic Maori occupation and Haast's 'Palaeolithic',*[in press, May 1995].

p.252 Heaphy River site, as a moahunter one: O.R. Wilkes, R.J. Scarlett, and G. Boraman, 'Two moa-hunter sites in north-west Nelson, *N.Z. Archaeological Assoc. Newsletter* 6 (2), 1963, pp.88-93. Wilkes and Scarlett, 'Excavation of a moa-hunter site at the mouth of the Heaphy River, *Records of the Canterbury Museum*, 8 (3), 177-208.

p.253 Archaeological interpretation of early West Coast Maori: Atholl Anderson, 'A Review of Economic Patterns During the Archaic Phase in Southern New Zealand', *N.Z. Journal of Archaeology*, Vol.4, 1982, pp.45-75. Also Anderson's 'West Coast, South Island', in N.J. Prickett, *The First Thousand Years*, N.Z. Archaeol. Assoc. Monograph, Dunmore Press, Palmerston North, 1982, p.103-111.

'to be considered by Tongans as part of the soil itself': Groube, L., 'Tonga, Lapita Pottery and Polynesian Origins', *Journal of the Polynesian Society*, 80, 1971: 278-316.

Poutini or Greenstone Trail: Barry Brailsford, *Greenstone Trails: the Maori search for pounamu*, Wellington, 1984.

'Archaic' and 'Classic' adze forms: Davidson, *Prehistory*.

p.254 'Then comes a tidal inlet . . .': Harry Moffat, quoted in Newport, *Collingwood*.

Archaeological evidence at Whanganui Inlet: Central Index of NZ Archaeological Sites administered by Science and Research Division, Dept of Conservation, Wellington.

Phil Skilton: interviews with author; Nelson, August 1986, Parapara Inlet, November 1986.

p.255 Sue Livingston (née Gooding): interview with author; Atawhai, Nelson, November 1986.

'Working the tide', 'Never once caught by the tide', etc: Jack Nicholls' letters to Joyce Parkinson, Tasman, Nelson; lent to author, May 1986.

p.257 Phil Skilton: interviews with author; Nelson, August 1986, Parapara Inlet, November 1986.

p.258 Ngāti Kuia prohibitions on bird snarers: Elsdon Best, *Maori Forest Lore*.

Dumont D'Urville's description was in Astrolabe Roadstead in today's Abel Tasman National Park: D'Urville, *New Zealand*.

p.259 Ron Walker and friends, tramway and white-pine loading: pers. comm. to Joyce Parkinson, Tasman, Nelson; lent to author, May 1986.

p.260 Don McKay, interview, Parapara, September 1986; Ralph Irons, interview, Collingwood, September 1986.

p.261 Ken MacKenzie, interview, Stoke, Nelson, September 1986.

p.263 'first estuary-based reserve', *Conservation Action; Dept of Conservation Achievements and Plans*, 1993/94, 1994/95; 'the largest unmodified estuary': Minister of Conservation's press statement, *Dept of Conservation Gazette*, 24 January 1995.

Waiata, 'Ka puihi tonu atu ki te tai-uru . . .' quoted in S. Percy Smith, *History and Traditions*, p.73. Also in W.J. Phillips, *The Book of the Huia*, Whitcombe and Tombs, Wellington, 1963, p.60.

Biological survey of the inlet: R.J. Davidson, *A Report on the ecology of Whanganui Inlet, N.W. Nelson*, Dept of Conservation Nelson-Marlborough Conservancy Occasional Publication No.2, 1990.

Chapter 6: The Sandplain Forest

p.267 Smart, *Diary*, 22 February 1863.

p.268 Edward Abbey: 'How it Was' from *Beyond the Wall*, Holt, Rinehart and Winston, 1979.

Michael Smither, *Sand*, privately published, 1987.

p.270 'these sanctuaries from the dim past': from Leonard Cockayne's memorial at Otari Plant Museum, Wilton, Wellington. Cockayne as a member of the 1913 Royal Commission on Forestry: *Report* of the commission, *AJHR* C12, 1913.

p.271 Bird-counting in West Coast forests: I.G. Crook, H.A. Best, M. Harrison, 'A survey of the native bird fauna of forests in the proposed beech project of North Westland', *Proceedings of the N.Z. Ecological Society 24*, 1977, pp.113-126; D.G. Dawson, P.J. Dilks, P.D. Gaze, J.G.R. McBurney, P.R. Wilson, 'Seasonal differences in bird counts in forests near Reefton, New Zealand', *Notornis 25*, 1978, pp.257-278.

New Zealand's 'primitive' birds: Buller, *Birds*.

Research revelations of high winter bird counts near Punakaiki: J.A Bartle, *Preliminary Assessment and Identification of National Park or Reserve Qualities in the Western Paparoa Range; First Report*[to National Parks and Reserves Authority]; G.N. Park and J.A Bartle, 1978; *An Evaluation of the Lowland Forests of the Western Paparoa Ecological District, with a Proposal for a Representative Reserve in the Porarari*, [National Museum and Botany Division, DSIR report to the Scientific Coordinating Committee, NZ Forest Service]. Both reports included Derek Onley's then-to-be-published bird counts. See also J.A. Bartle and G.N. Park, 'The Paparoa Range—a key area for nature conservation', *Forest and Bird 13 (2)*, 1978, pp.3-11.

Buller's 'expiring species always last longer on islands': *NZ Journal of Science* Vol.1, 1891, p.235; see also *TNZI 24*, p.713.

p.272 Robert H. MacArthur and Edward O. Wilson, *The Theory of Island Biogeography*, Princeton University Press, Princeton, 1987.

1970s, crucial time for New Zealand lowland forests: see, for example, Royal Forest and Bird Protection Society's *Policy for New Zealand's Remaining Indigenous Forests*, with *Forest and Bird*, November 1980, No.218. K.R. Hackwell and D.G. Dawson's 'Designing Forest Reserves' appeared in the same issue. C.A. Fleming had earlier introduced the the theory of island biogeography and its application to New Zealand in 'Scientific Planning of Reserves', *Forest and Bird* No.196, 1975, pp.15-18.

'a picture coherent and representative of the original: see Forest and Bird, *Indigenous Forest Policy*.

Scientific ranking of Nīkau Scenic Reserve: *Scenic Reserves of North Westland*, field survey S.R. June, compiled by G. Loh and P. Wardle, Botany Division, DSIR, 1981, *Biological Surveys of Reserves Series No.7*. DLS, Wellington. The reserve's national significance: G.N. Park, NZ Biological Resources Centre, letter to Director, Botany Division, DSIR, 13 November 1985. NZBRC files, NA. DSIR decision not to alter its lower grading: P. Wardle, letter to G.N. Park, 3 December 1985, Botany Division, DSIR, file: B25/9.

Eventual official recognition of reserve's significance: eg. 5 February 1988 note 'Nikau Scenic Reserve—New Perspective', 'hard to understand': Bruce Watson, Regional Manager's, 2 March 1988 letter to G.N. Park, file O181R, Dept of Conservation, Hokitika.

The ecosystem concept is a way of looking at conservation informed by ecology. The basic, underlying ideas are that process is at least as important as pattern, and that most parks and reserves, certainly in the lowlands, are, by themselves, incomplete ecosystems unable to maintain their ecological integrity in the long-term future.

'for reason if its size and isolation': Commissioner of Crown Lands, Hokitika, 16 April 1985 letter to Buller Conservation Group, Westland Reserves *local file*.

p.273 Mining company lawyers meeting with National Parks and Reserves Authority: R.A Fisher of Simpson, Grierson, letter to Director-General of Lands, 11 July 1984. Copy in Westland Reserves *local file*.

Sand-mining technique: Environmental Assessment, Barrytown Mineral Sands, West Coast, New Zealand; Westland Ilmenite Ltd (accompanying mining application).

'substantial advantages', 'could have the effect of preventing . . .': R.A. Fisher letter to Director-General, Lands, re 11 July 1984 meeting, Westland Reserves *local file*.

'I appreciate their concern . . .'; 'generate a lot of heat from the conservation groups': Asst. Commissioner of Crown Lands (ACCL), Minutes of Meeting, 1 August 1984, Westland Reserves *local file*. The same meeting record reveals the DSIR's middling ranking became an influencing factor.

'survivability', 'We are dealing with hard-nosed business men . . .': ACCL, Hokitika, memo to Reserves Ranger, Punakaiki, 9 April 1985, Westland Reserves *local file*.

p.275 *Mining Monitor 67*, 25 May 1985.

'Two biologists who knew the calibre of the reserve': Sandy Bartle, of MONZ, and G.N. Park.

Dep. Director-General of Lands meeting with Ministers of Lands and Environment, 22 May 1985: file note, 'Nīkau Scenic Reserve', Westland Reserves *national file*.

'it would probably be unwise to pursue . . .', The principle is a bad one . . .': I.R.H. Whitwell, for Director-General, Lands, memo to CCL, Hokitika, 3 May 1985, Westland Reserves *national file*.

'This matter is turning into a . . . political hot potato': ACCL, Hokitika to Dep. Director-General, Lands, DLS, memo, 6 June 1985, Westland Reserves *national file*.

'a major industry', 'are questions that cannot be addressed': Minister of Energy to Minister of Lands, 4 July 1995, copy in Westland Reserves *national file*.

'closely looked at the boundaries . . .' and NPRA decision to exclude the sandplain forest from Paparoa National Park: National Parks and Reserves Authority secretary, letter to Koro Wetere, Minister of Lands, 2 August 1985, Westland Reserves *national file*.

p.276 'the only example of successional vegetation . . . country's protected area system': CCL, Hokitika, letter to R.A. Fisher of Simpson and Grierson, Auckland, 13 June 1985, Westland Reserves *national file*.

'sit back . . . and see what develops': Director-General of Lands, memo to CCL, Hokitika, 18 July 1985, Westland Reserves *national file*.

p.277 Māori traditions, Punakaiki: Maika Mason, Kati Wae Wae, September 1988.

Thomas Shepherd's 'a great many beautiful shrubs', and Charles Heaphy's drawing of the flats at the head of Wellington Harbour: see Ch.2, pp.85, 88.

p.278 kererū hunting: Charles Heaphy, quoted by T.H. Smith, in 'On Traditional Maori Implements and Weapons', *TNZI 26*, 1905, p.430.

Observations of kererū: Sandy Bartle, MONZ, pers. comm.

p.279 'isolated', 'an outlyer', 'avoided', 'sufficiently compelling argument to overcome . . . fragmentation': National Parks and Reserves Authority, letter to Minister of Lands, 2 August 1985, Westland Reserves *national file*.

Lindsay Matthias, pers. comm., Barrytown, November 1986.

Victorian bird-watchers hinted . . .: eg. Buller, *Notes on Birds*.

'Birds deprived of lowland forest into which they were accustomed to descend . . .': Robert Falla, 'Wildlife in New Zealand', *Bulletin of British Ornithology Club 59*, 1939, pp.149-151.

'Lowland forest areas were speedily reduced . . .': Falla, 'New Zealand bird life past and present', *Cawthron Lecture Series 29*: pp.3-14, Cawthron Institute, Nelson.

p.280 'in stark contrast to many earlier assumptions about the region . . .': Crook, *Wildlife, North Westland*, p.17.

'at best, irrelevant'; comment on attitude of sawmilling interests, *Future, West Coast Forestry*.

'low altitude, warm forest holds much more species . . .': D.G. Dawson and K.R Hackwell, Ecology Division, DSIR, report on North Westland forest birds, to Scientific Coordinating Committee, NZ Forest Service, 1978.

'Great care must be taken . . . to include these favoured habitats . . .': Derek Onley, 'Bird counts in lowland forest in the Western Paparoas', *Notornis 27*, 1980, pp.335-362.

'it is not going to be easy . . .': *Wildlife Service Newsletter*, Vol.18, No.2 Dept of Internal Affairs, Wellington, September 1977, pp.5-6.

p.281 'complete opposition': Westland County Council letter to Commissioner of Crown Lands, Hokitika, 31 October 1978 re Mananui Bush. DLS Hokitika file, 13/98/4 LG 209.

'merchantable forest would be barely sufficient . . . ornithologists wish to make even further inroads . . . It's as simple as that': Director-General, NZ Forest Service, *Future, West Coast Forestry*. Also quoted in I.G. Crook, *Wildlife, North Westland*, p.15.

Radio-tracking of kererū: M.N. Clout, B.J. Karl and, P.D. Gaze, 'The Dispersal of New Zealand Pigeon from a Forest Reserve', *Notornis 38*, Pt 1, 1991, pp.37-47.

p.282 Tom Robbins, *Jitterbug Perfume*, Bantam, New York, 1984.

Alexander von Humboldt, *Aspects of Nature (Ansichten der Natur)*, trans. by Mrs Sabine, 1st AMS Ed. AMS Press, New York, 1970. Reprint of the 1850 ed.

p.283 Archaeological survey: B.G. McFadgen, 'Report on Barrytown Middens, West Coast', N.Z. Historic Places Trust, 1 June 1978, HP 12/2/0/17. Calibrated radiocardon age(s) on tuatua (*Paphies subtriangulatum*) shells from Site S37/22 sample collected, B.G. McFadgen, 10 November 85; 1500 AD, 450 BP. (Quaternary Isotope Lab, University of Washington).

Kati Wae Wae's mahinga kai claim, whakapapa and perspective on the shell heaps: Maika Mason, pers. comm., Christchurch, 1989.

James Stack, 'Traditional history of the South Island Maoris', *TNZI 10*, 1878, pp.57-59.

p.284 Waitaha traditions: Rangimarie te Maiharoa, pers. comm., December 1994, and his article 'Mana of Waitaha "must not be silenced"', *The Evening Post*, 5 April 1993. Waitaha and Te Punakaiki, *Song of Waitaha—The Histories of a Nation*, Ngatapuwae Trust, Christchurch, 1994.

West Coast kererū preference for older forests: E.B. Spurr, B. Warburton and K.W. Drew, 'Bird abundance in different-aged stands of rimu (*Dacrydium cupressimum*)—Implications for coupe-logging'; B. Warburton, S.J. Kingsford, D.W. Lewitt and E.B. Spurr, 1992, 'Plant species preferences of birds in lowland rimu forest—Implications for selective-logging', *N.Z. Journal of Ecology 16 (2)*, 1992, pp.109-118, pp.119-126.

An atmosphere of secrecy (Pueblo): Carl Jung, *The Pueblo Indians*, (republ. from his collected papers), in *Southwest Stories*, Chronicle Books, San Francisco, 1994.

p.285 T.H. Worthy and R.N. Holdaway, 'Quaternary fossil faunas from caves in the Punakaiki area, West Coast, South Island, New Zealand, *Journal of the Royal Society of New Zealand*, Vol.23, No.2, September 1993, pp.147-254.

p.286 Landscape history from Laughing Owl roosts: Richard Holdaway, pers. comm., 1993 (seminar to Dept. of Conservation scientists), and letter to author, 30 May 1995.

'one of the most remarkable plant-animal communities in the world . . . a largely forested landscape dominated by birds', '67 birds used the coastal and lowland forests . . . 33% of the species were flightless . . .', '40% or more . . . are extinct': I.A E. Atkinson and, P.R. Millener, *An Ornithological Glimpse into New Zealand's Pre-Human Past*, NZ Ornithological Congress Trust Board, Wellington, repr. from ACTA XX Congressus Internationalis Ornithologici, 1991, pp.129-192.

p.287 Barrytown School children and the Westland Black Petrel: Mrs Fischer, pers. comm., Dixon House, Greymouth, November 1986. See also 'The Black Petrel', in Major R.A. Wilson, *Bird Islands of New Zealand*, Whitcombe and Tombs, Wellington, 1959, p.150.

p.288 Petrel netting with fires and mist: Te Rangi Hiroa (Buck), *The Coming of the Maori*, Whitcombe and Tombs, Wellington, 1970, p.99.

p.289 'on the produce of the country', 'for want of proper cultivation', 'December is a glorious month of dietary amongst the natives . . .': Thomas Brunner, *Expedition to the middle of the Middle Island*, in Taylor, *Early Travellers, NZ*, p.293.

'a considerable tract of level land . . .', 'It became especially a matter of interest . . .': Heaphy, *Expedition*, pp.202-203.

'quite useless for agricultural purposes'; 'triangular flat of wood . . . lower portion of the

Hutt Valley': Heaphy, *Expedition*, pp.224-225.

'along the Pakiroa beach, however . . .': Heaphy, *Expedition*, p.235.

p.290 Fred Stewart, pers. comm., at his home, Canoe Creek, Barrytown Flats, November, 1986.

'trees, minerals, rivers, lakes, streams and all appertaining . . . for ever and ever.': Deed of James Mckay's West Coast Purchase, ML 8620, Dept. of Survey and Land Information archives, Hokitika.

'we knew we could get plenty of mussells . . .', '2 huts with some Maori women . . .', etc: Smart, *Diary*.

p.291 'with the right to whole area from sea beach to foot of range . . .': Ryall *papers*.

p.292 'It is known that the district is one of the most promising . . .': Petition to Minister of Mines re Necessity of a Track being Constructed from Barrytown to Brighton, July 1882, Ryall *papers*.

'the bush in its natural state . . .': Road Overseer's Report, 11 July 1882: Ryall *papers*.

'the present extension will afford . . .': List of Works on Goldfields, *AJHR*, 1895, C2, p.2.

'Fairly thick bush, rata, kiekie . . .'; etc., comments on survey maps eg. Plans of Special Claims Nos G177, G178, Applicant Barrytown Gold-dredging Ltd, D.P. Wilson, September-October 1939, F.N. Parnham, December 1940, DOSLI, Hokitika.

p.293 Arthur Sheldon, pers. comm., Dixon House, Greymouth, November 1986.

p.294 Westland Catchment Board's diversion of Hibernia Creek, and reaction to it: Westland Reserves, *local file*.

'investigating the closing of areas . . .'; 'particularly delightful': note for file, Offer of Land in Exchange for Road Reserve, February 1956; Westland Reserves, *local file*.

Legal protection of petrel colony: 'Dr Falla got in touch with the Commissioner of Crown Lands, then Mr Beachman, who arranged to have the area occupied by the black petrel gazetted as a scenic reserve . . .'; R.A. Wilson, *Bird Islands of New Zealand*, Whitcombe and Tombs, Wellington, 1959.

p.295 'The block contains very attractive bush and is worthy . . .': memo, P.H. Whitehead, Field Officer, to CCL, 10 April 1956, Westland Reserves, *local file*.

'The recommendations may be worth investigating': Director-General, Lands' comments (17 April 1956) on Westland Reserves, *local file*.

Minister's approval of land exchange for reserve: Director-General of Lands, letter to CCL, Hokitika, 12 October 1956, Westland Reserves, *local file*.

Discovery of flax-cutting rights: CCL, Hokitika, letter to District Public Trustee, Greymouth, 10 July 1958. Further letters, 18 February 1959 and 22 January 1960, before reply and presentation of the Hill's agreement with Dennehy, Westland Reserves, *local file*.

p.296 'indeed unfortunate . . . damage to the bush.': Director-General, Lands, letter to CCL, Hokitika, 19 February 1960, Westland Reserves, *local file*.

Naming of Nikau Scenic Reserve: CCL, Hokitika, letter to Grey County Council, 26 September 1961. Reply of approval, 19 October 1961, Westland Reserves, *local file*. It was finally gazetted reserve on 9 November 1961. *N.Z. Gazette*, No.71, p.1745.

Hill brothers 'not over keen'; protracted payment to Hill brothers for fencing: DLS, Hokitika, file 13/82; series of memos until telegram of approval of payment, from Head Office, 7 July 1964, Westland Reserves, *local file*.

p.297 'No interference was made with Nikau palms . . .': J.A. Sloane, Secretary, Punakaiki Reserves Board, letter to CCL, Hokitika, re. Carpentaria Exploration Co application 87/68, 8 October 1969, Westland Reserves, *local file*.

p.298 Ministerial decision not to allow mining of Maher Swamp: *Conservation Review 18*, June 1993, Dept of Conservation, Wellington.

'mankind should not change the whole . . . preserved intact': Judge Arnold Turner, 1985, 'The Changing Basis of Decision-making: Is Reason Sufficient?', *New Zealand Engineer*, April 1983, pp.13-23.

Alexis de Tocqueville, *Democracy in America*, trans. and ed. Phillips Bradley, Knopf, New York, 1945.

Kirkpatrick Sale, *Dwellers in the Land: The Bioregional Vision*, New Society Publishers, Philadephia, 1991, p.42.

p.299 Conservation as the life forces of nature and culture allowed to go on expressing themselves: Kevin F. O'Connor, 'The Conservation of Culture and Nature in New Zealand Mountains: Lance McCaskill Memorial Lecture, 1989', *Review 46; Journal of the New Zealand Mountain Lands Institute*, December 1989.

The sandplain forest's distinctive place in Punakaiki's ecology: Robert de Velice, Jean Ward de Velice and G.N. Park, 'Gradient Analysis in Nature Reserve Design—A New Zealand Example, *Conservation Biology 2*, No.2, pp.206-217.

p.300 Bill McKibbin, *The End of Nature*, Penguin, London, 1992.

Conclusion: Necessary Protection

p.301 The title, 'Necessary Protection', is from a series of Colin McCahon paintings about the need for New Zealanders to see beyond the conventional considerations of the landscape, to see that they are living as though in a cultural wilderness in a land they never really known, and whose neglected mysteries have a 'very real need for protection'. See Gordon H. Brown, *Colin McCahon, Artist*, A.H. & A.W. Reed, Wellington, 1984.
p.302 'Arts and letters, ethics and religion . . . place in the sun': Leopold, Foreword to *Great Posessions*, or what became *A Sand County Almanac*, Appendix, in Baird Callicott (ed.), *Companion to A Sand County Almanac*, University of Wisconsin Press, 1987, p.282.
 'Fair earth, we have broken our idols . . .': A.R.D. Fairburn, 'Elements', in *Collected Poems*, Pegasus Press, Christchurch, 1966, p.29.
 'If we are to be properly humble in our use of the world . . .': Wendell Berry, *The Unsettling of America: Culture and Agriculture*, San Francisco, Sierra Club Books, 1977.
p.303 'The savage forests . . .': Charles Brasch, 'The Silent Land', in Allen Curnow (ed.), *The Penguin Book of New Zealand Verse*, Penguin, London, 1966.
 'the uncolonized nothing', 'peaks that plunge their icy heads into space': Charles Brasch, 'The Estate', in Vincent O'Sullivan (ed.), *An Anthology of Twentieth Century New Zealand Poetry*, Oxford University Press, Auckland, 1987.
 'Granary of the New Southern World': *The New Zealand Colonisation Company (1838) to be Incorporated by Charter, or Act of Parliament*. NZCo papers: WTU, q. 325.931. 77039.
 'Planes and Vallies': *Cook Journal I*.
 'Thousands and tens of thousands of acres as level . . .': Wm. Bayley, 29 February 1842. *Letters from Settlers and Labouring Emigrants in the New Zealand Company's Settlements of Wellington, Nelson and New Plymouth from 1842-1843*. Elder and Co., London, 1843.
p.304 'the want of flat land': June 1840 letter of a settler off the New Zealand Company's *Oriental*, in *New Zealand Journal*, London, 1841.
 James MacIntosh Bell, *The Wilds of Maoriland*, McMillan and Co. London, 1914.
 Gabriel de Foigny, *Les Aventures de Jacques Sadeur dans la decouverte de la Terre Australe* (1676) in Marie Louise Berneri, *Journey through Utopia*, Freedom Press, 1982, p.198.
 St. Thomas Aquinas, *De Regimine Principum*, transl. Gerald B. Phelan, New York, quoted in Berneri, *Journey*.
 Sir Thomas More's Utopia, in Henry Morley (ed.), *Ideal Commonwealths*, London, 1885.
 'Every valley shall be made plain . . .': Rev Richard Taylor, *Journal*, Vol.4, Typescript, WTU, p.169.
 The 1913 recommendation that the remaining kahikatea forests of New Zealand's plains should be removed 'forthwith' is from *Report of the Royal Commission on Forestry*. AJHR C12, 1913.
 'yet to be subdued . . .', 'prodigious and alarming' wastage of forests, 'pioneers of Empire': Department of Agriculture's 1914 Annual Report, *AJHR*.
p.305 Charles Darwin's description of the Waimate mission station is from his *Voyage of the Beagle*, Doubleday, Garden City, New York, 1962. The experience of New Zealand had ramifications on his evolutionary theory that he outlined in Darwin, *Origin of Species*.
 Hursthouse, *Zealandia*.
 Vogel, *Land*.
 'to know them never again': Best, *Maori Forest Lore*.
 Quotations from the Land Act 1877: Vogel, *Land*.
p.306 Rev. Phillip Walsh, 'Public Ferneries—A Suggestion', *TNZI*, 1893, pp.619-621.
 W.H. Oliver, 'Belonging to the Land', Michael King (ed.), *Pakeha: the Quest for Identity*, Penguin, Auckland, 1991.
 Peter Hooper, *Our Forests Ourselves*, John McIndoe, Dunedin, 1981, p.43.
 'Full two-thirds . . . a rich alluvial': *The New Zealand Colonisation Company (1838) to be Incorporated by Charter, or Act of Parliament*. NZCo papers, q.325, 931. 77099, WTU.
 'a campaign against nature': Monte Holcroft, *The Shaping of New Zealand*, Paul Hamlyn, Auckland, 1974.
 Vogel, *Land*.
p.307 'What was confiscated was the best of Tuhoe's flat and fertile land': Te Kotahitanga Tait, Te Rere Marae, Opotiki, 18 February 1995; quoted from *Te Puna Wai Kōrero*, National Radio, 4 March 1995.
 Nazi 'Landscape Rules' for Poland: Ralph Neale, 'The Nazi Plant Police', *Landscape Australia*,

3/1994, p.188.

Thomas Berry, 'Creative Energy' in *The Dream of the Earth*, Sierra Club Books, San Francisco, pp.32-34.

E.O. Wilson is quoted from Robert Barbault and Pierre Lasserre 'Biodiversity: Nature in the Balance', *UNESCO Sources* No.60, July-August 1994. E.O. Wilson, Island Press, 1993.

Leopold, 'The Land Ethic', *A Sand County Almanac*.

E.O. Wilson, 'The Conservation Ethic', *Biophilia: The Human Bond with Other Species*. Harvard University Press, Cambridge, Massachusetts, 1984.

'Changing useless swamp . . . ever increasing wealth': *The Weekly News,* Auckland, 31 January 1918, describing settlement progress on the Hauraki Plains.

p.308 The 1940s Member of Parliament quoted is James Thorn. The occasion was the 2 November 1941, opening of the Cook memorial at Te Kopu. NZHPT, *mf.*

The 1935 Labour Party manifesto is quoted from Fairburn, *Ideal Society*, p.263.

Herbert Guthrie-Smith, 1940 Preface to the Third Edition of *Tutira*, A.H. & A.W. Reed, Wellington.

p.309 Moncrieff, *Avian Paradise*. Her phrase 'sylvan Pantheon' is quoted from William Pember Reeves, *The Long White Cloud: Ao tea Roa*, George Allen and Unwin, London, 1898.

'The glorious sight presented by the tall pines . . .': Edwin Stanley Brookes, *Frontier Life, Taranaki, New Zealand*, H. Brett, Auckland, 1892.

p.310 Monte Holcroft, 'The Primeval Shadow', from his 1940 centennial collection *The Deepening Stream*, the first of his trilogy *Discovered Isles* (Caxton Press, Christchurch) on the development of a New Zealand culture. Native forest had barely featured in Holcroft's Canterbury upbringing. The essay was stimulated by first encounter with a West Coast lowland forest when living briefly with his sawmilling brother near Greymouth during the 1930s Depression. (Interview with M.H. Holcroft, Sanson, September 1987).

Janet Frame, *Living in the Maniapoto*, Brasiller, New York, 1978.

A.R.D. Fairburn, 'Conversation in the Bush', in *Collected Poems*, Pegasus Press, Christchurch, 1967.

Hursthouse, *Zealandia*.

D'Urville, *New Zealand*.

Moncrieff: *Avian Paradise*.

p.311 J.B. Priestley, *A Visit to New Zealand*. Heinemann, London, 1967; Auberon Waugh, 'Cloudy Bay Revelation', *Daily Telegraph Weekend Magazine*, London, 1989.

The deep roots of 'the balance of nature' in the western psyche: D.B. Botkin, *Discordant Harmonies: a new ecology for the 21st century*, Oxford University Press, New York, 1990.

p.312 'any New Zealand swamp that preserves . . .': see, for example, M.S. McGlone, 'Polynesian deforestation of New Zealand: a preliminary synthesis', *Archaeology in Oceania*, Vol.18, pp.11-25.

'when you plot all the archeological evidence of pre-19th-century Maori occupancy . . .': based on the accumulated record at 1993 in the Central Index of N.Z. Archaeological Sites, administered by the Science and Research Division, Dept of Conservation.

'The Land with all Wood and Waters': Land Deed No.67; Totara Block, Whangaroa, Mangonui District, 26 December 1839, p.57.

'The ardour with which Maori welcomed European potatoes . . .': Anon. Missionary, *Royal Admiral*.

Kaitoke is quoted from his whaikōrero at Mangungu Mission Station, Hokianga, 12 February 1840: John Caselberg, *Maori is My Name*, John McIndoe, Dunedin, 1975, p.48.

p.313 'I the undersigned, a Chief of New Zealand . . . Mooka on demand': No.1, Maori Agreements, 1815, orig MS, AH47/1-AH47/3, Mitchell Library, Sydney. Simeon Lord, transported to NSW as a convict in 1790, became a hugely successful Sydney trader whose ships, as well as whaling and sealing, traded to New Zealand for flax and spar timber. Lord's *Hunter*, for example, was frequently in the Waihou (Thames) in the late 1790s.

Marion Du Fresne in the Bay of Islands: *Extracts from Journals relating to the visit to New Zealand in May-July 1772 of the French ships* Mascarin *and* Marquis de Castries *under the command of M.-J. Marion du Fresne*, trans. Isabel Oliver, Alexander Turnbull Library Endowment Trust, Wellington, 1985.

Account of the Kawakawa and Waikare river landscape in 1820: Cruise, *Journal*.

p.314 'A stick of first-rate quality': 'Early Timber Trade and Hokianga', *Early History of New Zealand*, Brett's Historical Series, H. Brett, Auckland, 1890, p.242.

Cruise: *Journal*.

'natural man': Spate, *Paradise*.

'We all tried to find the reason . . .': F.E. Manning, quoting an unnamed Ngapuhi, in 1840, in *Old New Zealand, a Tale of the Good Old Times, & The History of the War in the North, by a Pakeha Maori*, Whitcombe and Tombs, Christchurch, 1906, pp.223-225.

Robert Fitz Roy's description comes from evidence he gave to the British House of Lords on 21 May 1838; published in British Parliamentary Papers as *Report from the Select Committee of the House of Lords appointed to inquire into The Present State of The Islands of New Zealand and The Expediency of Regulating the Settlement of British Subjects Therein*; 8 August 1838. Charles Darwin's descriptions from the same visit are in *Voyage of the Beagle*, Doubleday, New York, 1962. His theory, including general observations on the 'imperfect' state of New Zealand fauna and flora and the success of European weeds, is set out in *Origin of Species*.

p.315 'The land is the people, break up the land and you break up the people': Spate, *Paradise*.

The allegory about the surveyors' theodolite is from Ngapuhi oral traditions, recounted by Mei Matiu, Te Aupouri, to Haami Piripi, who related it to the author in May 1993. 'A colony,' according to S.C. Brees, Principal Engineer and Surveyor to the New Zealand Company, 'is commenced by the surveyors opening up the country for settlers. The land is first roughly explored, the hills and rivers traced, upon which numerous alleys, technically termed *lines* are cut straight through the forest . . .': *Pictorial Illustrations of New Zealand*, London, 1847.

Aperahama Taonui, whaikōrero at Mangungu Mission Station, 12 February 1840, in John Caselberg, *Maori is My Name*, John McIndoe, Dunedin, 1975, p.48.

Quote from William Hobson's *Instructions*: Paul Temm, *The Waitangi Tribunal*, Random Century, Auckland, 1990. Events in Sydney in January, 1840: Judith Binney, 'The Maori and the Signing of the Treaty of Waitangi', in A.J. Anderson *et al*, *Towards 2000: seven leading historians examine significant aspects of New Zealand history*, Government Printer, Wellington, 1990, pp.25-26.

'The full, exclusive and undisturbed possession of their Lands . . .', and 'unqualified exercise . . . treasures': Article Two of the Treaty of Waitangi; English version and translation of Maori version respectively, in Kawharu, *Waitangi*.

p.316 'The emergency of the events at Port Nicholson . . .': William Hobson letter to Secretary of State for the Colonies, 25 May 1840, and Hobson's description of the Thames: NZCo, *Doc, 12th Rpt*.

'With much satisfaction . . .': Henry Williams to William Hobson, 11 June 1840, NZCo, *Doc, 12th Rpt*.

'Most valuable sections . . .': Administrator of Port Nicholson Settlers to Hobson, 1 July 1840, NZCo, *Doc, 12th Rpt*.

'The fertility of the soil . . .' Hobson to Secretary of State for the Colonies, 15 October 1840, NZCo, *Doc, 12th Rpt*.

'The breadth of the valley . . .' Martin to Hobson, NZCo, *Doc, 12th Rpt*.

p.317 George Clarke's 1840 trip to the Thames: see Chapter One, pp.42-43.

The 'ecosystems' view of the world, that 'everything is connected to everything else': Barry Commoner, *The Closing Circle: nature, man, and technology*, Alfred A. Knopf, New York, 1971.

The conservation problem for species in small, isolated reserves: Michael Soule (ed.), *Viable Populations for Conservation*, Cambridge University Press, Cambridge, 1987.

The passage on 'progress', 'nature' and 'conservation' in western culture: Jeffrey A. McNeely, *Coping with Change: People, Forests and Biodiversity*, IUCN—The World Conservation Union: Focus Series, Gland, Switzerland, 1994.

The general principles on native peoples' knowledge of nature: Madhav Gadgil, Fikret Berkes and Carl Folke, 'Indigenous Knowledge for Biodiversity Conservation', *Ambio 22*, No.2-3, May 1993, and Peter Knudtson and David Suzuki, *Wisdom of the Elders*, Allen and Unwin, Sydney, 1992.

'many types of ancient forms', 'old primeval grandeur': Buller, *Supplement*, p.xxviii, xxxvi.

p.318 The scenic reserve's origin in the early 1900s in settler picnics and tourism is well expressed in this contemporary account in the *New Zealand Graphic*, 19 January 1895, p.64, of Sir Walter Buller's Lake Papaitonga: 'It will be welcome news to all lovers of New Zealand that the present Government has issued instructions to all Commissioners of Crown Lands throughout the colony to reserve from sale in future all the choicest scenery, the sites of ancient pas and fortifications and other places of public interest. If New Zealand is to be made in every way attractive to the tourist of the future, surely this is sound policy on the part of our rulers, to say nothing of conserving 'local traditions' for the benefit of the future New Zealander . . .' The scenic reserve as a key piece in the local contest at the imperial periphery over symbolic power: David Bunn, 'Our Wattled Cot', in W.J.T. Mitchell (ed.), *Landscape and Power*, University of Chicago Press, Chicago, 1994.

'Evidence of moa butchery-grounds . . . shellfish': Davidson, *Prehistory*.
'He may be a bit primitive but he knows . . .': Best, *Maori Forest Lore*.
Yate, *Account*.
p.319 Material on *mauri*: Maori Marsden, 'God, Man and Universe: A Maori View', in Michael King (ed.), *Te Ao Hurihuri: The World Moves on*, Hicks Smith and Sons, Wellington, 1975; Maori Marsden and other sources in Taiarahia Black, *Submission to the Planning and Development Select Committee on the Supplementary Order Paper, Resource Management Bill*, 31 May 1991; the linguist, Bruce Biggs, pers. comm., May 1992; from Atanraoi Baiteke of Kiribati, July 1992.
Rene Descartes, *Discourse on Method and the Meditations*, trans. F.E. Sutcliffe, Penguin, 1976.
'barbarous and superstitious customs . . .': British House of Commons parliamentary (Select Committee) papers; Papers rel. to New Zealand, Vol.4, 1844.
p.320 'the unseen presence . . .': Best, *Maori Forest Lore*, pp.198-199.
Keri Hulme, *the bone people*, Spiral Collective, Wellington, 1984.
Roman observation of the Anglii (English): Cornelius Tacitus, *Germanie*, Book 40, in H. Mattingly, *On Britain and Germany*, Penguin, Hammondsworth, 1948. See also Jacquetta Hawkes, 'Land and People', in *A Land*, David and Charles, London, 1978.
Albert Schweitzer, *The Teaching of Reverence for Life*, trans. R. Winston & C. Holt. Rinehart and Winston, New York, 1965.
Rene Dubos, *A God Within*, Angus and Robertson, London, 1973, is a good exposition of the elements of a sense of place. Likewise, Yi Fu Tuan, *Topophilia: a study of environmental perception, attitudes, and values*, Prentice-Hall, Englewood Cliffs, 1974.
G.M. Hopkins, *A Hopkins Reader*, ed. John Pick, Oxford University Press, New York, 1953.
'a great reality': D.H. Lawrence, *Phoenix*, William Heinemann, London, 1961; *Studies in Classical American Literature*, Heinemann, London, 1964.
p.321 'Consult the Genius of the Place in all': Alexander Pope, 'Epistle IV, to Richard Boyle, Earl of Burlington, on the Use of Riches', *Works*, ed. W. Elwin and W.J. Courthope, London, 1881, vol.3, p.176.
'uprooted from the native soil': Lawrence, *Phoenix*.
'elemental nature': Foster, *Lawrence in Taos*, pp.136-140.
'those who saw Lawrence write . . .': Foster, *Lawrence in Taos*, p.141.
'For every great locality . . .': D.H. Lawrence: 'The Spirit of Place', in *The Symbolic Meaning*, ed. A. Arnold, Centaur Press, 1962.
Wendell Berry, 'Place and Poetry', *Standing by Words*, North Point Press, San Francisco, 1983, p.145. See also Berry, 'Nature as Measure', *What are People for*, Rider Books, London, 1990, and Sir Albert Howard, *An Agricultural Testament*, London, 1956, pp.1-4.
p.322 Paul Shepard, *Nature and Madness*, Sierra Club, San Francisco, 1982.
Sam Neill, interview, *Sunday Star-Times*, 27 February 1995.
J.C. Beaglehole and the genius loci: *New Zealand, a Short History*, Allen and Unwin, London, 1936, p.159.
'the Pakeha discovery of the precious ecology . . .': J.O.C. Phillips, 'What is Happening to New Zealand Society?', *The Landscape*, Summer 1989, pp.3-7.
Harry Scott, 'Immigrant to Native' *Landfall 1*, 1947.
p.323 'two landscapes': Witi Ihimaera, 'The Maori Landscape', editorial, *The Listener*, 30 July 1977.
'Strikes directly at the preservation basis of our conservation legislation': Hugh Barr, *Federated Mountain Clubs Bulletin* No.118, November 1994, p.3.
'The country was a Paradise': Thomas Arnold, *Passages in a Wandering Life*, Edward Arnold, Bedford St., London, 1900, p. 81. See also Paul Shepard, *English Reaction to the New Zealand Landscape before 1850*, Pacific Viewpoint Monograph No.14, Victoria University of Wellington, 1969.
Mircea Eliade, *The Sacred and the Profane: The Nature of Religion*, Harcourt, Brace & World, New York, 1959.
p.324 'even under the worst auspices . . . most delightful spot on earth': Anon., 'To The People of England!: An Address on the Colonization of New Zealand', *Savage's Account of New Zealand in 1805 . . .*, A.D. McKinlay (ed.), L.A. Watkins Ltd, Wellington, 1939, p.118.
The land is as the Garden of Eden: *The Book of Joel*, Ch.2, v.3.
'primeval solitudes': G.F. Angas, *Savage Life and Scenes in Australia and New Zealand . . .* Vol.1., Smith, Elder and Co, Cornhill, London.
'English pleasure grounds': Nicholas, *Narrative*, p.250.
'beau ideal of a new country': Thomas Cholmondeley, *Ultima Thule; or Thoughts suggested by a*

residence in New Zealand, John Chapman, London, 1854, p.133.

'Picture to yourself this scenery': E.J. Wakefield, quoted in Heaphy, *Narrative,* p.93.

'Instead of the breadfruit tree . . .', the complaining New Zealand Company settlers: Fairburn, *Ideal Society.*

The Trinity College cleric's piece, using Shakespeare's *The Winter's Tale,* on New Zealand as a garden: 'an anonymous writer, MA Trinity College, Cambridge', *New Zealand Journal,* 7 March 1840, WTU.

p.325 'Great, creating nature' and other lines from Shakespeare, and the suggestion of Michel de Montaigne's influence on him: J.H.P. Pafford (ed.), *The Winter's Tale, The Arden Shakespeare,* Methuen, London, 1966.

P.J. O'Rourke: *All the Trouble in the World,* Picador, London, 1994.

Michel de Montaigne: 'Of the Cannibales', *Montaigne's Essays,* I, trans. John Florio (1603), Saintsbury, 1892.

p.326 Wakefield's and Mein Smith's *Instructions*: NZCo papers q325.931 53748, WTU.

p.328 Colin McCahon, 'Beginnings', *Landfall 80,* Vol.20 No.4, December 1966, pp.360-364.

John Fowles, quoted in *Coastlines, Britain's Threatened Heritage,* Greenpeace, Kingfisher Books, London, 1987, p.153.

'Where the Tall forest and the Plains . . .': prefatory poem, Savage, *Account.*

p.329 Wendell Berry, 'Nature as Measure', *What are People For?,* Rider Books, London, 1990.

'over half the country being farmed unsustainably': Owen Jennings (1992 President of NZ Federated Farmers, in discussion of his address 'Sustainable Land Management: a User's Perspective' [regarding Jennings' point that 'degradation of the natural resource is being faced up to' by NZ's farmers but that it 'has not always been that way']), P. Henriques (ed.), *Proceedings of the International Conference on Sustainable Land Management,* Napier, 1992, Hawkes Bay Regional Council.

p.330 'A culture is no better than its woods': W.H. Auden, 'Woods', *W.H. Auden, The Penguin Poets,* Penguin, London, 1958.

'here and there . . . to make the countryside . . . a source of pleasure': Harry Ell, MP, letter to Minister of Lands, quoted in Circular from J.W.A. Marchant, Surveyor-General, 7 March 1903, to North Island Commissioners of Crown Land, at time of formation of Scenery Preservation Commission, NA LS/70/22.

The phases of colonial land description, ecological insight and moral, spiritual and emotional connection: Brian Elliott, *The Landscape of Australian Poetry,* F.W. Cheshire, Melbourne, 1967.

p.331 The *genius loci* as 'a token of lost Eden . . .': Helen Armstrong, 'Australian Cities and their Past—The Landscape of Symbols of a Lost Eden', *Landscape Australia,* 2/90, pp.143-148.

p.332 'An Intimate New Zealand': Gary Catalano, *An Intimate Australia,* Hale and Iremonger, Sydney, 1985.

Missionary destruction of musical instruments like koauau and puririhua: Richard Nunns, pers. comm., Nelson, December 1994.

Gary Snyder, 'Good, Wild and Sacred', *The Practice of the Wild,* North Point Press, San Francisco, 1990.

Our destiny as a country is to be continually revisiting the past: Shane Jones, quoted by Finlay McDonald, 'Waitangi Daze', *NZ Listener,* 11 March 1995.

Tim Flannery, *The Future Eaters: An Ecological History of the Australasian Lands and People,* Reed, Sydney, 1994.